OXFORD STUDIES IN EUROPEAN LAW

Series Editors

PAUL CRAIG
Professor of English Law at St John's College, Oxford

GRÁINNE DE BÚRCA
Professor of Law at New York University School of Law

Europe's Passive Virtues

OXFORD STUDIES IN EUROPEAN LAW

Series Editors:
Paul Craig, Professor of English Law at St John's College, Oxford and
Gráinne de Búrca, Professor of Law at New York University School of Law

The aim of this series is to publish important and original research on EU law. The focus is on scholarly monographs, with a particular emphasis on those which are interdisciplinary in nature. Edited collections of essays will also be included where they are appropriate. The series is wide in scope and aims to cover studies of particular areas of substantive and of institutional law, historical works, theoretical studies, and analyses of current debates, as well as questions of perennial interest such as the relationship between national and EU law and the novel forms of governance emerging in and beyond Europe. The fact that many of the works are interdisciplinary will make the series of interest to all those concerned with the governance and operation of the EU.

OTHER TITLES IN THIS SERIES

Official Secrets and Oversight in the EU
Law and Practices of Classified Information
Vigjilenca Abazi

Risk Regulation in the Internal Market
Lessons from Agricultural Biotechnology
Maria Weimer

EU Health Law & Policy
The Expansion of EU Power in Public Health and Health Care
Anniek de Ruijter

The Horizontal Effect of Fundamental Rights in the European Union
A Constitutional Analysis
Eleni Frantziou

EU Powers Under External Pressure
How the EU's External Actions Alter its Internal Structures
Christina Eckes

Frontex and Human Rights
Responsibility in 'Multi-Actor Situations' under the ECHR and EU Public Liability Law
Melanie Fink

EU Equality Law
The First Fundamental Rights Policy of the EU
Elise Muir

Subnational Authorities in EU Law
Michèle Finck

Accessing Asylum in Europe
Violeta Moreno-Lax

National Parliaments after the Lisbon Treaty & the Euro Crisis
Davor Janĉiĉ

Environmental Integration in Competition and Free-Movement Laws
Julian Nowag

EU Agencies
Legal and Political Limits to the Transformation of the EU Administration
Merijn Chamon

Coherence in EU Competition law
Wolf Sauter

Foreign Policy Objectives in European Constitutional Law
Joris Larik

Economic Governance in Europe
Comparative Paradoxes and Constitutional Challenges
Federico Fabbrini

Europe's Passive Virtues

Deference to National Authorities in EU Free Movement Law

JAN ZGLINSKI

OXFORD
UNIVERSITY PRESS

OXFORD
UNIVERSITY PRESS

Great Clarendon Street, Oxford, OX2 6DP,
United Kingdom

Oxford University Press is a department of the University of Oxford.
It furthers the University's objective of excellence in research, scholarship,
and education by publishing worldwide. Oxford is a registered trade mark of
Oxford University Press in the UK and in certain other countries

First Edition published in 2020
Impression: 1

Published in the United States of America by Oxford University Press
198 Madison Avenue, New York, NY 10016, United States of America

British Library Cataloguing in Publication Data
Data available

Library of Congress Control Number: 2019957831

ISBN 978–0–19–884479–2

Printed and bound by
CPI Group (UK) Ltd, Croydon, CR0 4YY

Pamięci Jadwigi Orłowskiej—z wdzięcznością za jej miłość, mądrość i kartacze

Series Editor's Preface

In this book Jan Zglinski writes about the 'passive virtues' of the European Court of Justice in the field of freedom of movement, and specifically about the Court's deference to national decision-making in the context of cases which come before it. Given the rich existing EU law scholarship on the 'activism' of the Court of Justice, this book is an interesting and welcome exploration of an alternative seam of CJEU decision-making.

The book examines CJEU deference in two distinct contexts: first, deference by the Luxembourg Court to the regulatory decision-making of national legislatures and executives in the form of a lighter scrutiny of these decisions; and second, 'decentralized judicial review' in the form of the delegation of responsibility for the judicial review of free movement restrictions to national courts. The book contains a rich empirical survey of all of the case law of the Court of Justice in the field of free movement, tracing the extent to which the level of scrutiny exercised by the court over national decisions has changed over time towards greater deference, and tracing the degree of delegation by the CJEU to national courts in this field. These chapters are highly valuable, providing a degree of solid empirical support for the claims made by the author as to the gradual shift by the Court of Justice towards greater deference to national decision-making.

To some, the active or even 'activist' approach of the CJEU in many of its cases is a vice, while to others it can be seen as a virtue. Zglinski's title reflects the latter perspective, suggesting that the passive approach of the Court—its deference to domestic decision-making—is indeed a virtue, something to be welcomed.

This perspective on the CJEU's deference contrasts with many of the critiques of the 'margin of appreciation' doctrine used by the European Court of Human Rights to explain its deference to state choices. While a number of commentators in recent years have begun to commend the ECtHR for its deference in the light of states' resistance to its rulings, the majority of scholars have long been critical of the Strasbourg Court's use of the 'margin of appreciation' given that essential human rights are generally at stake in its decisions. The case law of the European Court of Justice on free movement, on the other hand, sometimes implicates human rights issues, but more often concerns balancing commercial freedom with other national or local values and interests.

In Chapter 6, the author presents his normative case in further detail, arguing that the move by the Court of Justice that he has identified in this book towards a more deferential approach in the free movement field is to be defended and applauded. Drawing on the two values of representation and expertise,

Zglinski argues that deferring to national institutions is indeed, at times, the best option for the CJEU.

This is a rich and carefully argued book which should be of interest to all of those who study, practice or research in the field of EU law, including in the areas of free movement and of judicial decision-making more generally.

Paul Craig
Gráinne de Búrca

Acknowledgements

This book started as a doctoral thesis at the European University Institute and has, since, travelled with me to Oxford and London. I have been fortunate to have outstanding working environments in each of these places. They provided me with the necessary institutional support for my research but, perhaps more importantly, enabled me to cross paths with the many people who helped bring the project to fruition. Although not all can be named, a few I would like to mention.

I owe a debt of gratitude to Joseph HH Weiler for supervising my doctorate. Critical and encouraging in equal measure, he was instrumental in shaping the arguments put forward here. Our early morning conversations, or 'contestations', will remain among the fondest memories of my time in Florence. Miguel Poiares Maduro oversaw the first phase of my doctoral research and helped with setting its general direction, for which I am immensely grateful. His intellectual influence on this book will no doubt be apparent to the reader. I am deeply indebted to Hans Micklitz for his personal and academic generosity during my time at the EUI and since. Loïc Azoulai has been a constant source of insight and support. Neil Komesar has, through his work, seminars, and many long conversations, had an impact on this project and my understanding of law far beyond what citations can express.

The book has profited from the intellectual input of a number of friends and colleagues. I received stimulating comments on earlier versions of the manuscript from Joshua Andresen, Marcin Barański, Maciej Borowicz, Gráinne de Búrca, Marta Cartabia, Janneke van Casteren, Johanna Croon-Gestefeld, Gareth Davies, Barend van Leeuwen, Sabine Mair, Kai Möller, Gordon Silverstein, Lawrence Solum, Boško Tripković, Steve Weatherill, Mike Wilkinson, and Floris de Witte. Special thanks go to Filip and Mikołaj Barczentewicz, Gijs van Dijk, Daniel Gerber, Juan Antonio Mayoral, and Felix Pflücke for their patient advice on statistical matters. The usual disclaimer applies with more than usual force.

Two research stays were important for developing the ideas presented here. Yale Law School hosted me as a visiting researcher, providing me with the time and space to discover the great masters of American constitutional theory. The cabinet of Pedro Cruz Villalón granted me a glimpse into the inner workings of the European Court of Justice. I would like to express my gratitude to Yves Bot, Koen Lenaerts, Sacha Prechal, Allan Rosas, and Eleanor Sharpston who, during this period, kindly agreed to share their thoughts on judicial deference and European constitutional adjudication with me.

I am grateful to Paul Craig and Gráinne de Búrca for including the book in the Oxford Studies in European Law series and to the team at Oxford University Press for their editorial support throughout the publication process. Parts of the argument have previously appeared as 'The Rise of Deference: The Margin of Appreciation and Decentralized Judicial Review in EU Free Movement Law' (2018) Common Market Law Review 1341 and are reproduced with the permission of the publisher.

Three people require special mentioning. My parents have supported me all along the way, celebrating every little success and providing comfort whenever there were setbacks. Words cannot begin to capture what I owe them. Alexandra Ortolja-Baird has been by my side from the first ideas to the final proofs. Only her encouragement and help have made this endeavour possible, her love has given it meaning.

Table of Contents

List of Figures

List of Tables

Table of Cases

EUROPEAN COURT OF JUSTICE

EUROPEAN COURT OF HUMAN RIGHTS

US SUPREME COURT

OTHER JURISDICTIONS

Introduction

Judicial deference is legally disputed and politically contested. Some demonize it as an 'abdication of the judicial role' and a facilitator of moral relativism.[1] Others praise it as an armour for national values and a remedy for the problems resulting from legal pluralism.[2] That deference stirs up such controversy, in the EU and elsewhere, is unsurprising in light of the intricate constitutional problems which it raises. How far can judges intervene in the work of legislators? To what extent can European institutions interfere with the decision-making powers of the Member States? How much of the responsibility for judicial review belongs with the European Court of Justice (ECJ), and how much with national courts? Embodied in these questions are all the grand dilemmas of EU constitutionalism: judicial review *versus* democratic governance, centralization *versus* decentralization, unity *versus* diversity.

Although deference to national authorities is not a product of our times, it reflects them neatly. The phrase 'it is for the Member States to decide . . .' has become a political demand, threat, and reality in the Union of formerly 28, now 27 nations. It has also begun to appear with growing regularity in the jurisprudence of the ECJ. A dispute regarding an environmental protest on the Brenner highway inspired the Court to grant the competent national authorities a 'wide margin of appreciation' as to how to protect freedom of expression.[3] When reviewing the legality of a ban on laser tag in Germany, the Court declared that Member States were free to adhere to their own understanding of human dignity, even if it was not universally shared across Europe.[4] Similarly, in a number of cases concerning national laws on casinos, sports betting, and online gambling, it underlined the decision-making leeway of the Member States and entrusted domestic judges with policing the boundaries.[5]

[1] TRS Allan, 'Human Rights and Judicial Review: A Critique of "Due Deference"' (2006) 65 Cambridge Law Journal 671; Ignacio de la Rasilla del Moral, 'The Increasingly Marginal Appreciation of the Margin-of-Appreciation Doctrine' (2006) 7 German Law Journal 611; James A Sweeney, 'Margins of Appreciation: Cultural Relativity and the European Court of Human Rights in the Post-Cold War Era' (2005) 54 International and Comparative Law Quarterly 459; Eyal Benvenisti, 'Margin of Appreciation, Consensus, and Universal Standards' (1999) 31 International Law and Politics 843.

[2] Janneke Gerards, 'Pluralism, Deference and the Margin of Appreciation Doctrine' (2011) 17 European Law Journal 80; Niamh Nic Shuibhne, 'Margins of Appreciation: National Values, Fundamental Rights and EC Free Movement Law' (2009) 34 European Law Review 230.

[3] Case C-112/00 *Schmidberger* [2003] ECLI:EU:C:2003:333.

[4] Case C-36/02 *Omega Spielhallen* [2004] ECLI:EU:C:2004:614.

[5] Case C-243/01 *Gambelli* [2003] ECLI:EU:C:2003:597; Cases C-338/04, 359/04 and 360/04 *Placanica* [2007] ECLI:EU:C:2007:133; Case C-409/06 *Winner Wetten* [2010] ECLI:EU:C:2010:503;

Europe's Passive Virtues. Jan Zglinski, Oxford University Press (2020). © Oxford University Press.
DOI: 10.1093/oso/9780198844792.001.0001

These rulings attracted much attention because they exhibit some unfamiliar traits of EU law and adjudication. They are marked by judicial self-restraint, accentuate national regulatory autonomy, the limits of the 'ever closer Union', and the non-economic dimension of the European project. In this way, they seem to signal an evolution: of the ECJ, free movement law, and the Union as a whole.

This book investigates the phenomenon of deference to Member State authorities in cases on free movement rights. This focus is the function of three considerations. First, free movement has always been a central area of the European law and constitutes the source of some of its most significant legal innovations. Although secondary legislation has consumed a sizeable portion of the case law that used to be decided under the four freedoms, judgments in this area remain a numerically and doctrinally important part of the ECJ's activity. Second, free movement disputes have been the main and, at the same time, most controversial application field of judicial deference in EU law. Although deference doctrines are, in variations, employed by the Court in other areas too,[6] they appear most frequently in decisions on Member State restrictions on free movement. Finally, free movement jurisprudence, like few other domains, allows us to study the development of the Court of Justice. Litigation on free movement rights has been a staple of the Court's docket since the late 1960s, and remains so today. It therefore provides a formidable opportunity for examining how the ECJ's relationship with and behaviour towards national institutions has evolved over time.

I. The European Court and the 'Passive Virtues'

The central argument of this book is that the ECJ has, over the past four decades, gradually lowered its level of scrutiny over Member State action. This goes against the standard narrative that the Court of Justice—and with it, EU law—is taking every opportunity to expand its influence and authority over domestic affairs. From near the beginning of its existence, the Court has been criticized for engaging in judicial activism, unduly restricting national regulatory autonomy, and taking away the powers of Member State institutions. Its case law on free movement rights is a key piece of evidence for such allegations, commonly considered to symbolize the expansive interpretation of the Treaty rules at the cost of Member State power. This book will try to show that the ECJ is, in fact, scaling down its involvement in free movement matters by increasingly deferring to national authorities.

Case C-212/08 *Zeturf* [2011] ECLI:EU:C:2011:437; Cases C-186/11 and 209/11 *Stanleybet International* [2013] ECLI:EU:C:2013:33.

[6] This notably concerns judicial review of EU action, see Case 29/77 *Roquette Frères* [1977] ECLI:EU:C:1977:164; Case 265/87 *Schräder* [1989] ECLI:EU:C:1989:303; Case C-491/01 *British American Tobacco* [2002] ECLI:EU:C:2002:741.

I use the idea of the 'passive virtues' as a *leitmotif* here, loosely borrowing from Alexander Bickel and his analysis of the US Supreme Court.[7] Bickel was an advocate for judicial restraint, arguing that, at times, less can be more when it comes to constitutional review of legislative and executive action. This is, partly, due to the fact that courts are well-equipped to take certain types of decisions, not others. More profoundly, it relates to questions of legitimacy. The constitutional order has given the judiciary a particular—and limited—role to play. It is designed to complement, not to absorb the functions of other institutions.[8]

This book explores whether and how these considerations apply to the EU constitutional setting. It examines to what extent the ECJ can be said to practise passive virtues by means of judicial deference or otherwise. It enquires into the circumstances and reasons for which the Court defers to national authorities. Finally, it addresses the question as to whether such deference should, indeed, be viewed as a virtue. Bickel's analysis was not a plea for judicial inertia, but rather for selective judicial involvement.[9] Where the Court of Justice should step in and where it is better-advised to let the domestic political or judicial branches decide—or, in other words, how to draw the line between its passive and active virtues—will be investigated.

Underneath this overarching theme, two subplots unfold. The first concerns change. Forty years have passed since the *Cassis de Dijon* ruling.[10] The judgment is widely recognized as 'groundbreaking', a 'milestone', and a 'revolution'.[11] Some have even called its key passage 'a thing of beauty, a judicial work of art'.[12] *Cassis* has both broadened and deepened the reach of EU free movement law and, thus, contributed to expanding the power of the ECJ. It is among the Court's most cited and, indubitably, most influential rulings. This book provides an analysis of what

[7] Alexander M Bickel, *The Least Dangerous Branch: The Supreme Court at the Bar of Politics* (Bobbs-Merrill 1962).

[8] In Bickel's words: 'The search must be for a function which might (indeed, must) involve the making of policy, yet which differs from the legislative and executive functions; which is peculiarly suited to the capabilities of the courts; which will not likely to be performed elsewhere if the courts do not assume it ... which will be effective when needed; and whose discharge by the courts will not lower the quality of the other departments' performance by denuding them of the dignity and burden of their own responsibility' (ibid 24).

[9] Gerald Gunther famously summarized Bickel's thesis by saying that it entailed the Supreme Court doing 100 per cent but only 20 per cent of the time; see 'The Subtle Vices of the "Passive Virtues"—A Comment on Principle and Expediency in Judicial Review' (1964) 64 Columbia Law Review 1, 3.

[10] Case 120/78 *Rewe-Zentral AG v Bundesmonopolverwaltung für Branntwein ('Cassis de Dijon')* [1979] ECLI:EU:C:1979:42.

[11] Kalypso Nicolaïdis, 'Kir Forever? The Journey of a Political Scientist in the Landscape of Mutual Recognition' in Miguel Poiares Maduro and Loïc Azoulai (eds), *The Past and Future of EU Law* (Hart 2010) 447; Stefan Enchelmaier, 'Restrictions on the Use of Goods and Services' in Mads Andenas, Tarjei Bekkedal, and Luca Pantaleo (eds), *The Reach of Free Movement* (Springer 2017) 86; Robert Schütze, *From International to Federal Market: The Changing Structure of European Law* (Oxford University Press 2017) 186. But see the more critical appraisals in Karen J Alter, *The European Court's Political Power* (Oxford University Press 2009) 139 and Jukka Snell, '*Cassis* at 40' (2019) 44 European Law Review 445.

[12] Stephen Weatherill, 'The Beauty and the Beast: Is EU Internal Market Law "Over-Constitutionalised"?' (forthcoming).

free movement law looks like four decades after *Cassis*—and how it got there. It will be shown that, although the free movement rules in the Treaties have remained largely the same since the decision was rendered, the field has changed considerably. This has to do with the evolution of the Court of Justice's approach to free movement adjudication but, in equal measure, with developments in its broader operating context. The result of these is the gradual demise of the *Cassis* model.

The second theme is choice. Free movement and the internal market are open-textured concepts. Although the European Treaties provide some guidance as to what these notions entail, different interpretations can and have been advanced.[13] The Court of Justice, in its role as chief interpreter of EU law, holds a privileged position in this respect. It has the power to determine the extent to which European rules intervene in national law, set the balance between regulation and deregulation, and decide how the relevant rights, interests, and policy concerns are reconciled. In this way, the Court imbues the idea of the internal market with meaning. Deference is one important tool in this endeavour.

Choice and deference interact in a further way. Deference is a judge-made tool. Unlike concepts such as liberty, equality, fundamental rights, and proportionality, it is not an external idea that was, at a certain point, adopted by judges. Deference doctrines like the margin of appreciation were created by judges.[14] Therefore, their patterns of application give us a privileged insight into the workings of the judiciary. They indicate which matters courts prioritize, in which cases they feel confident to decide, and what, in their view, ought to be settled by other institutions. In this way, they help understand judicial behaviour or, in other words, 'what judges do and why do they do it'.[15]

II. Measuring Judicial Deference

This book addresses a variety of questions—conceptual, doctrinal, comparative, normative—but at its heart lies an empirical study of ECJ jurisprudence. The aim was to understand the extent to which deference marks the Court's activity and the scenarios in which it appears. The study is based on an original data set of every complete fifth year of free movement case law between 1974 and 2013.[16] The year 1974 was chosen as the starting point as it is the year in which the ECJ first deferred to a Member State institution in a free movement case.[17] It is, at the same time,

[13] See Miguel Poiares Maduro, *We the Court* (Hart 1998) ch 4.

[14] In the ECHR context, see Dean Spielmann, 'Allowing the Right Margin: The European Court of Human Rights and the National Margin of Appreciation Doctrine: Waiver or Subsidiarity of European Review?' (2011–2012) 14 Cambridge Yearbook of European Legal Studies 381.

[15] Jeffrey A Segal, 'Judicial Behavior' in Gregory A Caldeira, R Daniel Kelemen, and Keith E Whittington (eds), *The Oxford Handbook of Law and Politics* (Oxford University Press 2008) 19.

[16] The full data set is available at <global.oup.com/academic/product/europes-passive-virtues-9780198844792>.

[17] Case 41/74 *Van Duyn* [1974] ECLI:EU:C:1974:133.

when the landmark *Dassonville* ruling was rendered, thus providing an appropriate vantage spot for exploring the evolution of free movement law.[18] The year 2013 was the last full year available at the time of the research (taken instead of 2014).

The limitation to one fifth of the case law constitutes a trade-off between having a data set which is sufficiently large yet manageable. The decision was made to go 'deep' rather than 'broad', that is, code the judgments for a series of potential explanatory variables as well as some ancillary phenomena, such as developments relating to the scope of free movement law and the principle of proportionality. The analysis proceeds systematically in five-year steps instead of examining every fifth case to enable a comparison of annual deference rates and, thus, identify possible changes in judicial behaviour over time.[19]

The cases were collected through the Curia database.[20] For the years studied, all ECJ judgments on alleged Member State violations of free movement rights were included, focusing on preliminary references and infringement actions, the two types of proceedings in which the Court can defer to national authorities. (They are also a suitable choice for a longitudinal analysis as they form the numerically most important procedural routes in EU law, with preliminary references ranking first, by a great margin, and infringement actions second.[21]) This yielded a total sample of 247 judgments. Although still modest in size, it represents around 20 per cent of all free movement cases ever decided, which is enough to draw conclusions about the Court's activity in this field.

The data set was compiled so as to allow for two types of analyses. Where the objective was to identify broader developments and changes over time (as in Chapters 2 and 5), each ECJ judgment was counted as one case. Where the objective was to grasp the exact circumstances in which the Court of Justice defers to national authorities (as in Chapters 3 and 4), a more granular approach was taken: in proceedings in which multiple Member State acts were reviewed, each was treated as a separate case, bringing the total number up to 294.[22] This method

[18] Case 8/74 *Dassonville* [1974] ECLI:EU:C:1974:82.

[19] The choice of years should not yield distorted findings. There is no reason to believe that the Court's behaviour in 1974, 1979, and 1984 differed substantially from that in, say, 1975, 1980, and 1985 or 1976, 1981, and 1986.

[20] The cases were found in a two-step procedure. First, all judgments referring to free movement rights (Arts 34, 45, 49, or 63 TFEU as well as their predecessors in older Treaty versions) in their operative part or grounds of decision were gathered. From these, the decisions that concerned judicial review of EU action or were, in substance, about other areas of EU law (eg secondary law, acts of accession, or association agreements) were removed.

[21] This relates to the whole of the Court of Justice's activity. Note that, in recent years, the number of appeals against decisions of the General Court has overtaken that of infringement proceedings; see the ECJ's Annual Report of Judicial Activity 2018.

[22] Take, by way of illustration, Case C-171/02 *Commission v Portugal (Security Services)* [2004] ECLI:EU:C:2004:270. Portugal had required that foreign undertakings wishing to pursue surveillance activities in the private security sector must: (i) have their head office or an establishment in Portugal; (ii) be constituted as a legal person; (iii) have a specific share capital; (iv) not rely on evidence and guarantees already presented in their Member State of establishment; (v) employ guards who hold a professional certificate issued by the Portuguese authorities. Each of these measures was treated as a separate case.

was chosen to allow a more accurate detection of the differences in how the Court behaves in certain scenarios, depending on the characteristics of the dispute.[23]

The study's main objects of interest—or dependent variables—are the Court's deference doctrines: the margin of appreciation and decentralized judicial review. The analysis examines whether or not the ECJ applies them in the cases in the sample. In addition, the judgments have been coded for a number of factors that could potentially influence whether national authorities are granted deference. Twelve such independent variables were examined, ranging from the policy field at stake, to the applicable free movement right, to the level of harmonization and the year in which a ruling was rendered. The results are discussed in Chapters 3 and 4.

Some readers may ask: why all the numbers, tables, and graphs? The reason is twofold. Scholars working on free movement law often claim to be observing 'trends', 'tendencies', and 'evolutions'. They make statements about the 'factors' that affect the ECJ's decisions and 'patterns' in how particular issues are handled. Such claims are empirical in language. Yet, most of the time, they are made based on a small number of hand-picked rulings only. This poses the problem of robustness and selection bias. Are these decisions, in fact, representative of the developments in the case law? To what extent do they reflect the Court of Justice's behaviour? To produce a reliable picture, a broader systematic investigation is needed. This book aims to provide such an analysis.

There is a second, perhaps less immediately evident reason to empirically study the Court's jurisprudence. It has to do with conceptual discipline. As the social sciences teach us, the value of measuring a phenomenon need not only lie in gathering data about its prevalence or patterns, but having a definition of it. Ambiguities as to the exact meaning of a doctrine or concept will not become apparent when one works from three, five, or ten judgments. They will, however, inevitably come to the fore when the numbers are in the hundreds. What exactly makes a case a deference case? How can we distinguish between low and high levels of EU harmonization? What constitutes a serious and what a light restriction on free movement? Analysing large numbers of decisions forces us to be precise about what it is that we are looking for. It, thereby, indirectly benefits the conceptual work.

III. The Structure of the Book

The structure of the book follows somewhat naturally from the subject matter. Chapter 1 begins by asking what defines judicial deference in free movement law. EU law scholarship on deference has, so far, not attached much weight to

[23] For a similar approach, see Clifford J Carrubba, Matthew Gabel, and Charles Hankla, 'Judicial Behavior under Political Constraints: Evidence from the European Court of Justice' (2008) 102 American Political Science Review 435.

conceptual matters.[24] The result is a lack of understanding of how the ECJ's deference doctrines operate, what consequences they carry for judicial review, and which institutions they affect. The chapter will explain that the Court of Justice has created two distinct deference techniques in its free movement case law. While structurally similar in giving domestic actors the freedom to make certain assessments autonomously, they concern different types of institutions and have, as a result, different consequences for judicial review. The margin of appreciation doctrine is employed to pass certain regulatory decisions over to national legislatures and executives and, thus, to lower the intensity of scrutiny. Decentralized judicial review is used to delegate responsibilities connected with free movement review to national courts.

Chapter 2 examines the empirical magnitude of deference in free movement law: how often does the ECJ defer to national authorities? Has the intensity with which it reviews Member State action evolved over time? The analysis here draws on the case law survey. The results reveal that the Court of Justice's behaviour in free movement disputes has changed since the 1970s, a development which challenges some common presumptions about the ECJ and free movement law. The chapter will look into possible reasons for the evolution, arguing that they are connected to broader legal, political, and institutional changes in the EU.

Chapters 3 and 4 complement this macroanalysis with an investigation into how deference operates at the micro level: in which cases does the ECJ grant Member States a margin of appreciation? Which decisions does it decentralize to national courts? The examination here consists of two parts. In a first step, the legal parameters concerning when Member State authorities are meant to be deferred to are identified. In a second step, this vision is put to the test. A statistical analysis of the data from the case law survey will reveal to what extent practice follows theory, in which areas the Court chooses to be more and less deferential, and the role which national authorities occupy in free movement law.

Chapter 5 zooms in on one element of judicial review which is particularly affected by deference: proportionality analysis. Proportionality has been the object of extensive research at the national and international level. Intrigued by the principle's swift spread across the globe, scholars have studied its nature and effects. The common conclusion is that proportionality is an attractive tool for judges. Against this background, the reality that the Court of Justice decides, through its deference doctrines, to not engage in full proportionality review so frequently is a riddle. The chapter examines the reasons for the Court's behaviour. It will show that the fact that the European judges often refrain from engaging in a comprehensive

24 This is a broader phenomenon in the literature on deference and the margin of appreciation, see Andrew Legg, *The Margin of Appreciation in International Human Rights Law* (Oxford University Press 2012) 4 ('startlingly little has been written examining how the margin of appreciation operates conceptually in international human rights law or offering a justification for it').

assessment of the proportionality of Member State action is understandable in light of the obligations which this imposes on them. Existing scholarship has overly focused on the benefits of proportionality analysis for judges. Yet, the test equally creates a series of duties which can easily become a burden, a burden which courts will try to reduce by resorting to deference techniques.

Chapter 6 provides a normative evaluation of the developments that have taken place in free movement law. It pursues the question as to whether the Court of Justice's increasing refusal to exercise substantive scrutiny over national laws is a welcome or worrying trend. This issue touches upon some fundamental questions of EU constitutional law. The Union has, over the past two and a half decades, embraced a number of conflicting constitutional goals. They concern the place of democratic governance, the question of federalism, and the uniformity of European law. The margin of appreciation and decentralized judicial review stand in the crossfire of these developments, which makes delineating an appropriate scope for the two doctrines challenging. The chapter proposes a solution based on the ideas of representation and expertise, which reconciles the fundamental constitutional commitments of the EU with insights from comparative institutional analysis.

1

The New Free Movement Architecture

Over the past decades, we have become accustomed to the European Court of Justice (ECJ) deciding some of the most challenging questions the 'peoples of Europe' grapple with: who is entitled to social benefits? What are the limits of industrial action? How much health care can society afford? Which are the most effective ways to combat alcoholism? The tool through which the Court established its power to shape this broad range of topics goes by the name of the 'four freedoms'. That these, at first glance, inconspicuous economic rights allowed for such far-reaching judicial activity has to do with a series of bold interpretive choices. They enabled the Court to exercise detailed scrutiny over wide parts of national law, a function it keenly assumed. Its active attitude towards judicial review of domestic policies became a fixed point in and a hallmark of EU law. It turned the Court of Justice into a driving force of the integration project and, as such, the object of scholarly and, with some delay, political interest.

Recently, a different wind is blowing in Luxembourg. Bold decisions that reverse national legislative choices or administrative practices have not disappeared from free movement jurisprudence. Yet, they have been complemented by another class of rulings, those marked by caution. Increasingly, one finds the Court of Justice refraining from making certain legal and regulatory assessments, thus according Member State institutions greater decision-making autonomy. Doctrines of judicial deference are among the most visible manifestations, and key drivers, of this phenomenon. They have been employed to grant national authorities a 'margin of appreciation' to balance free movement with free speech,[1] to articulate their understanding of human dignity,[2] and to choose whether to prohibit the carrying of nobility titles.[3] They surfaced when Member State courts were allowed to decide whether national press laws,[4] gambling regulations,[5] and rules imposing age restrictions on videos[6] were compatible with the free movement provisions.

That Member State authorities receive discretionary powers of this sort raises a number of questions: how common is deference in free movement adjudication?

[1] Case C-112/00 *Schmidberger* [2003] ECLI:EU:C:2003:333.

[2] Case C-36/02 *Omega Spielhallen* [2004] ECLI:EU:C:2004:614.

[3] Case C-208/09 *Sayn-Wittgenstein* [2010] ECLI:EU:C:2010:806.

[4] Case C-368/95 *Familiapress* [1997] ECLI:EU:C:1997:325.

[5] Case C-243/01 *Gambelli* [2003] ECLI:EU:C:2003:597; Cases C-338/04, 359/04 and 360/04 *Placanica* [2007] ECLI:EU:C:2007:133; Case C-409/06 *Winner Wetten* [2010] ECLI:EU:C:2010:503; Case C-212/08 *Zeturf* [2011] ECLI:EU:C:2011:437.

[6] Case C-244/06 *Dynamic Medien* [2008] ECLI:EU:C:2008:85.

Europe's Passive Virtues. Jan Zglinski, Oxford University Press (2020). © Oxford University Press.
DOI: 10.1093/oso/9780198844792.001.0001

Which types of decisions does the ECJ defer to the national level? What motivates its practice? And is this a desirable or a troubling phenomenon? All of these issues will be tackled in the course of this book. The present chapter, however, will start with a prior question: how exactly does the European Court defer to national institutions? What conceptually defines deference in EU free movement law?

Although much ink has been spilled on deference techniques such as the margin of appreciation, conceptual problems have, with few exceptions, been neglected.[7] The focus is usually on the scenarios in and conditions under which the Court defers to national authorities. This disregard for matters conceptual is unfortunate. For one thing, it prevents us from understanding the precise nature of deference. It remains unclear how doctrines like the margin of appreciation operate, in what way they change judicial review, and which institutions they affect. Perhaps more importantly, it prevents us from realizing the significant impact they have on free movement law and the EU constitutional landscape more generally.

This chapter will begin by explaining why the question of deference has become relevant in free movement adjudication, a development which has to do with a structural shift towards justification and proportionality. It will be shown that the ECJ has developed different approaches for judicial review of Member State action. The searching model adopted in the *Cassis de Dijon* ruling will be contrasted with two deferential forms of scrutiny: the margin of appreciation approach and decentralized judicial review. Despite being structurally similar, both represent distinct types of deference and concern different domestic institutions. The chapter will conclude by shedding light on their implications for free movement law and adjudication.

I. A Shifted Centre of Gravity: From Scope of Rights to Justification and Proportionality

From early on, the Court of Justice has dealt with cases on free movement rights in what can, in essence, be described as a two-step process.[8] When a Member State act (or, more rarely, an EU act) is alleged to violate the free movement rules, the Court will, first, examine whether the measure constitutes a barrier to the free circulation of goods, persons, services, or capital. This is usually called the 'restriction' or 'scope of application' stage. If the national law passes—or rather fails—this hurdle, the second part of the inquiry begins: the justification stage. Here, the ECJ will investigate whether the Member State had legitimate and sufficiently weighty

[7] For two notable exceptions from the literature on international human rights law, see Andrew Legg, *The Margin of Appreciation in International Human Rights Law* (Oxford University Press 2012) and George Letsas, *A Theory of Interpretation of the European Convention of Human Rights* (OUP 2007) 80.

[8] This structure is becoming increasingly common in constitutional adjudication across the globe, see Kai Möller, *The Global Model of Constitutional Rights* (Oxford University Press 2012).

reasons to limit free movement, an analysis frequently done by means of proportionality review.

From almost as soon as this two-part structure emerged, thinking and writing about free movement law has been marked by an asymmetry. While taking note of the jurisprudential developments concerning questions of justification, academic observers devoted much of their attention to how the European Court interpreted the scope of the free movement provisions. New rulings would be scrutinized carefully as to their potential implications for the reach of the four freedoms, particularly with regard to Article 34 TFEU,[9] with an enthusiasm which one author has likened to a 'fetish'.[10]

This fascination should not surprise—it is the result of the ECJ's innovative and often daring case law in this area. Starting in the mid-1970s, the Court expanded the material reach of the free movement provisions, taking them far beyond what was common in free trade agreements and understandings prevalent among the nascent class of internal market lawyers at the time. The free movement of goods was the first to be affected by this development. In *Dassonville*, the Court of Justice departed from traditional, anti-protectionist readings of Article 34 TFEU and ruled that the provision caught 'all trading rules enacted by Member States which were capable of hindering, directly or indirectly, actually or potentially, intra-[Union] trade'.[11] Shortly after, in *Cassis de Dijon*, it extended this interpretation to indistinctly applicable technical standards, giving birth to what the European Commission would coin the principle of mutual recognition.[12] Goods lawfully produced in one Member State could, in the absence of countervailing policy reasons, henceforth be sold anywhere in Europe.

In the 1990s, this broad vision of freedom of movement was transposed step-by-step to the remaining Treaty rights. In a series of decisions, the *Dassonville* formula was—partly verbatim, partly in spirit—adopted for the free movement of persons, services, and capital. In *Säger*, the Court established that Article 56 TFEU prohibited not only discrimination against non-nationals but also required the abolition of any restriction which is 'liable to prohibit or otherwise impede the activities of

[9] For a small selection, see Derrick Wyatt, 'Article 30 EEC and Non-Discriminatory Trade Restrictions' (1981) European Law Review 185; René Barents, 'New Developments in Measures Having Equivalent Effect' (1981) 18 Common Market Law Review 271; Guliano Marenco, 'Pour une Interprétation Traditionnelle de la Notion de Mésure d'Effet Equivalent à une Restriction Quantitative' (1984) 20 Cahiers de Droit Européen 291; Eric L White, 'In Search of the Limits of Article 30 of the EEC Treaty' (1989) 26 Common Market Law Review 235; Laurence W Gormley, '"Actually or Potentially, Directly or Indirectly"?: Obstacles to the Free Movement of Goods' (1989) 9 Yearbook of European Law 197; Anthony Arnull, 'What Shall We Do on Sunday?' (1991) 16 European Law Review 112; Josephine Steiner, 'Drawing the Line: Uses and Abuses of Article 30 EEC' (1992) 29 Common Market Law Review 749; Miguel Poiares Maduro, '*Keck*: The End? The Beginning of the End? Or Just the End of the Beginning?' (1994) 1 Irish Journal of European Law 30.

[10] Michael Dougan, 'Legal Developments' (2010) 48 Journal of Common Market Studies 163, 165.

[11] Case 8/74 *Dassonville* [1974] ECLI:EU:C:1974:82, para 5.

[12] Case 120/78 *Rewe-Zentral AG v Bundesmonopolverwaltung für Branntwein ('Cassis de Dijon')* [1979] ECLI:EU:C:1979:42.

a provider of services established in another Member State'.[13] *Kraus* introduced a similar *ratio* into the case law on workers, prohibiting national measures that are 'liable to hamper or to render less attractive ... the exercise of the fundamental freedoms'.[14] The same line of reasoning appeared in the context of establishment in *Gebhard*[15] and, some years later, in the jurisprudence on capital movement.[16] Although the Court would continue to resort to different tests in the following,[17] market access gradually emerged as the central idea in the case law. It stipulates that national measures which 'impede' or 'directly affect' the access of economic actors to the domestic market constitute obstacles to free movement.[18]

In the same period, the Court of Justice, in an almost contrapuntal motion, recalibrated its position on the free movement of goods. Traders were, based on the wide interpretation established in *Dassonville*, challenging a growing number of national laws restricting economic freedom, many of them with no more than tenuous links to trade.[19] In *Keck and Mithouard*, the ECJ chose to halt this trend.[20] It announced that non-discriminatory 'selling arrangements' would no longer fall within the scope of Article 34 TFEU.[21] The effects of this manoeuvre were, in the late 2000s, if not entirely undone, then significantly muffled. In *Commission v Italy (Italian Trailers)* and *Mickelsson and Roos*, two cases on regulatory restrictions on the use of goods, the ECJ decided to broaden the reach of the free movement

[13] Case C-76/90 *Säger* [1991] ECLI:EU:C:1991:331, para 12.

[14] Case C-19/92 *Kraus* [1993] ECLI:EU:C:1993:125, para 32. Similarly, in Case C-415/93 *Bosman* [1995] ECLI:EU:C:1995:463 the Court ruled that all national measures that 'preclude or deter' EU citizens from making use of their right to free movement constitute an obstacle to Art 45 TFEU (para 96).

[15] Case C-55/94 *Gebhard* [1995] ECLI:EU:C:1995:411, para 37 ('national measures liable to hinder or make less attractive the exercise of fundamental freedoms').

[16] Case C-367/98 *Commission v Portugal (Golden Shares)* [2002] ECLI:EU:C:2002:326, para 45 (measures 'liable to impede the acquisition of shares ... and to dissuade investors in other Member States from investing').

[17] Even in some recent judgments, the ECJ will, for instance, rely on more traditional discrimination tests, see Cases C-544 and 545/03 *Mobistar* [2005] ECLI:EU:C:2005:518, para 32 and Case C-134/03 *Viacom Outdoor* [2005] ECLI:EU:C:2005:94, para 37.

[18] Case C-384/93 *Alpine Investments* [1995] ECLI:EU:C:1995:126, para 38; *Bosman* (n 14), para 103; Case C-190/98 *Graf* [2000] ECLI:EU:C:2000:49, para 28; Case C-405/98 *Gourmet International* [2001] ECLI:EU:C:2001:135, para 21.

[19] Among the more memorable ones are: Case 155/80 *Oebel* [1981] ECLI:EU:C:1981:177 (prohibition of night-time work in bakeries); Case 286/81 *Oosthoek* [1982] ECLI:EU:C:1982:438 (prohibition of offering gifts to incentivize the purchase of encyclopaedias); Cases 60 and 61/84 *Cinéthèque* [1985] ECLI:EU:C:1985:329 (two-year time limit for the commercial exploitation of films after their cinematic release); Case C-145/88 *Torfaen Borough Council* [1989] ECLI:EU:C:1989:593 (Sunday trading ban).

[20] Case C-267/91 *Keck and Mithouard* [1993] ECLI:EU:C:1993:905.

[21] The transplantation of the *Keck* exception into the remaining free movement rights has frequently been discussed but never realized by the Court: see *Bosman* (n 14), para 102; *Alpine Investments* (n 18), para 36; Case C-98/01 *Commission v UK (BAA)* [2003] ECLI:EU:C:2003:273, para 45. For the academic debate, see Stephen Weatherill, 'After *Keck*: Some Thoughts on how to Clarify the Clarification' (1996) 33 Common Market Law Review 885; Wulf-Henning Roth, 'The European Court of Justice's Case Law on Freedom to Provide Services: Is *Keck* Relevant?' in Mads Andenas and Wulf-Henning Roth (eds), *Services and Free Movement in EU Law* (Oxford University Press 2002) 1; Catherine Barnard, 'Fitting the Remaining Pieces into the Goods and Persons Jigsaw?'(2001) 26 European Law Review 35.

of goods provisions once again.[22] A market access test was introduced as a self-standing category into the case law on Article 34 TFEU,[23] and placed alongside the established principles of non-discrimination and mutual recognition, thus capturing national laws that stand in the way of the marketing of a product by exerting 'considerable influence on the behaviour of consumers'.[24]

The story so told describes—in broad brush strokes, omitting some secondary themes[25]—the developments which have taken place in the Court of Justice's case law relating to the scope of EU free movement law since the mid-1970s. They leave us in a place where the reach of the free movement rights is wider than it has ever been. This could be said of each individual freedom; the only potential exception being the free movement of goods which, post-*Keck*, went through a period of consolidation but has recently been expanding in radius again.[26] It is certainly the case if we look at all freedoms collectively. The move from unequally to equally applicable measures, or discrimination to restrictions and obstacles to free movement more broadly, coupled with a growing emphasis of the idea of market access, have dramatically widened the range of situations in which the free movement rules apply. This has led some authors to conclude that free movement law has established a 'general right to pursue an economic activity in a cross-border context',[27] others to warn that the four freedoms have become 'unbounded'.[28]

This expansion of the reach of EU free movement law has a series of consequences. Perhaps most immediately, it means that a growing number of Member State acts can potentially fall into the web of the free movement rules and, thus, be subjected to judicial scrutiny. At the same time, it has another, somewhat paradoxical side effect: it diminishes the relevance of questions relating to the scope of the four freedoms. In a world where national measures constitute restrictions on free movement with increasing ease, the centre of gravity shifts towards justification

[22] Case C-110/05 *Commission v Italy (Italian Trailers)* [2009] ECLI:EU:C:2009:66; Case C-142/05 *Mickelsson and Roos* [2009] ECLI:EU:C:2009:336.

[23] Although *Keck* had already employed the terminology of 'market access', the concept played—contrary to, for instance, the case law on the free movement of services—only a peripheral role in the jurisprudence on Art 34 TFEU before and was not used as a separate test by the ECJ.

[24] This was met with wide criticism in the literature: see Jukka Snell, 'The Notion of Market Access: A Concept or a Slogan?' (2010) 47 Common Market Law Review 437; Gareth Davies, 'Understanding Market Access: Exploring the Economic Rationality of Different Conceptions of Free Movement Law' (2010) 11 German Law Journal 671.

[25] Including the application of free movement rights to purely internal situations; the question of reverse discrimination; *de minimis* thresholds; the recognition of positive obligations; and horizontal effect.

[26] There has been some debate as to whether *Keck* continues to apply after *Italian Trailers*; Case C-198/14 *Visnapuu* [2015] ECLI:EU:C:2015:751, para 104 and Case C-148/15 *Deutsche Parkinson* [2016] ECLI:EU:C:2016:394, Opinion of AG Szpunar, paras 20 et seq suggest that the answer is in the positive.

[27] Alina Tryfonidou, 'Further Steps on the Road to Convergence Among the Market Freedoms' (2010) 35 European Law Review 36, 55. Similarly Eleanor Spaventa, 'From *Gebhard* to *Carpenter*: Toward a (Non-)Economic European Constitution' (2004) 41 Common Market Law Review 743.

[28] Lars Klenk, *Die Grenzen der Grundfreiheiten* (Mohr Siebeck 2019) 421 ('entgrenzt').

and proportionality.[29] As will be shown in greater detail in Chapter 5, the ECJ has, over the past four decades, found that national laws restrict free movement in more than 7 out of 8 cases; in recent years, the number has gone up to almost 90 per cent. This leads to a situation where, as Snell observes, the 'real scrutiny' in free movement disputes increasingly takes place at the justification stage or, more precisely, at the level of proportionality where 'the case is normally won or lost'.[30] The central problem has ceased to be: do national laws fall into the scope of the free movement rules? It has become: can these laws be justified and, most importantly, are they proportionate? By the same token, the focus moves from the question of *whether* the Court of Justice will exercise judicial review to *how* it will exercise judicial review. This brings the issue of intensity of scrutiny into the limelight.

Justification and proportionality absorb many of the questions that have always been the bread and butter of free movement jurisprudence: how much market regulation is warranted; to what extent EU law should intervene in national regulatory autonomy; and in what circumstances it is legitimate for the ECJ to interfere with democratic decision-making. Yet, they do more than that. The shift towards justification and proportionality review changes the types of problems which the ECJ has to deal with. It brings a variety of difficult empirical and normative questions to the fore that the European judges would otherwise not have to face, or not with such regularity. These range from inquiries into national policy aims, to analyses of the socio-economic effects of regulatory measures, to conflicts between competing, often politically sensitive rights and interests. Do the activities of a religious sect harm society? What kind of pornography offends public mores? How can road safety be effectively guaranteed? To what extent should children be protected from disturbing videos? It is in relation to these kinds of questions that the ECJ needs its deference doctrines.

II. The *Cassis de Dijon* Model: European Judicial Oversight

To understand how the Court of Justice defers to national authorities, it is easiest to start with the opposite scenario: how it acts when granting them no deference.

[29] Barend van Leeuwen, 'Rethinking the Structure of Free Movement Law: The Centralisation of Proportionality in the Internal Market' (2017) 10 European Journal of Legal Studies 235; Gareth Davies, 'Abstractness and Concreteness in the Preliminary Reference Procedure' in Niamh Nic Shuibhne (ed), *Regulating the Internal Market* (Edward Elgar 2006) 218; Niamh Nic Shuibhne, *The Coherence of EU Free Movement Law* (Oxford University Press 2013) 70 (who observes that 'the justification framework has evolved over time to become the prime space within which public interest arguments are aired' and 'where the multifaceted construction of the internal market … is explored and contested', even if concentrating exclusively on the scope of the free movement provisions in her analysis).

[30] Jukka Snell, 'General Principles in Free Movement Law: Applicability and Application' in Katja Ziegler, Päivi Neuvonen, and Violeta Moreno-Lax (eds), *Research Handbook on General Principles of EU Law* (Edward Elgar forthcoming).

Almost 40 years on, the paradigm case in this regard remains *Cassis de Dijon*.[31] It was already mentioned that the ruling innovated free movement law in one important way, by widening the reach of Article 34 TFEU to include equally applicable technical standards. Yet, it is another aspect of *Cassis* which has, over time, proven perhaps even more significant. It introduced a highly influential type of judicial review into free movement adjudication.

The facts of *Cassis* are well-rehearsed. Germany prohibited the importation and marketing of liqueurs with an alcohol content below 25 per cent, a requirement that made it impossible to sell products such as the French *crème de cassis*, which contains between 15 and 20 per cent alcohol by volume. According to the German government, the regulation was notably intended to protect consumers by saving them from the risk of purchasing weaker and, thus, 'inferior' alcoholic beverages.[32]

The Court of Justice found the German law to obstruct the free movement of goods but went on to examine whether it could be justified on grounds of 'mandatory requirements' in the public interest. The crucial question became whether a measure as drastic as a prohibition was required for consumer protection, indeed, or whether putting labels on beverages would be equally effective. Whereas the German legislature said yes (consumers would be misled all too easily), the Court famously said no. Labelling, so the European judges opined, would be a perfectly adequate, less intrusive alternative. This conclusion has been endlessly disputed on empirical grounds.[33] Yet, for our purposes, it is not the outcome of the decision that matters but how it was reached. Faced with the question as to what was necessary to protect consumers, the ECJ made its own assessment and substituted its view for that of the domestic legislature.

Although it was always contentious given its restrictive effects on national regulatory autonomy, the *Cassis* approach is one to which we have grown deeply accustomed. It has been used by the Court of Justice time and again, across different policy fields and free movement rights, yielding many of the best-known rulings in free movement law. It came to the fore in *Centros* when the Court, asked about whether letting companies register in Member States with low minimum capital requirements put creditors at risk, held that business partners and customers could inform themselves on the financial status of the company abroad or require

[31] *Cassis de Dijon* (n 12).

[32] A second defence rested on considerations of public health: weak liqueurs would 'more easily induce a tolerance towards alcohol than more highly alcoholic beverages' (see paras 10–11).

[33] For a recent experimental study testing the assumption of the 'reasonably circumspect' consumer, see Kai P Purnhagen and Erica Herpen, 'Can Bonus Packs Mislead Consumers? A Demonstration of How Behavioural Consumer Research Can Inform Unfair Commercial Practices Law on the Example of the ECJ's *Mars* Judgement' (2017) 40 Journal of Consumer Policy 217. Even the EU legislature seems to believe that labelling alone is insufficient to protect consumers and must be complemented with rules on ingredients and production methods, as evidenced by Regulation 110/2008; see Stephen Weatherill, 'Did *Cassis de Dijon* Make a Difference?' in Catherine Barnard, Albertina Albors-Llorens, and Brigitte Leucht (eds), *Cassis de Dijon: 40 Years On* (Bloomsbury forthcoming 2020).

guarantees;[34] in *Säger* when, examining whether special professional qualifications were required for monitoring patents, it ruled that these were superfluous as the task was simple and the risk for consumers limited;[35] and in *Bosman*, when confronted with the problem as to whether transfer fees promoted a competitive balance between football clubs, it concluded that the richest teams would be able to buy the best players anyway.[36]

The essence of the *Cassis* model is as simple as it is consequential: the ECJ fully assesses all questions related to the justification and proportionality of a Member State act. It examines in detail which policy objectives are legitimate grounds for regulation, which means are suitable to achieve them, and which measures are necessary to do so. This approach has been called 'substantive' review by some scholars as it entails the Court of Justice evaluating the regulatory substance of national legislation.[37] Others have referred to it as 'full' or 'strict' scrutiny because it imposes the highest requirements on Member State acts and thus makes it the hardest to pass free movement muster.[38]

Exercising *Cassis*-style judicial review turned the ECJ into a motor of the internal market project. It provided the Court with the power to determine the balance between regulation and deregulation, European integration and national autonomy, and free movement and social policy concerns. (Likewise, it permitted the Luxembourg judges to expose the need for positive integration: where national restrictions on free movement were found to be justified, EU harmonization would be required.) This was particularly useful in the early stages of economic integration, in which the prime concern was market building.[39] National institutions and economic operators had to get used to stop thinking in the narrow terms of the domestic market place and embrace the idea of a broader pan-European economic community. The active reliance on free movement rights enabled the ECJ to eliminate obstacles to free movement one case at a time. By the same token, it served as a tool for 'judicial harmonization'. In a period marked by legislative stagnation at the European level, the Court set out EU rules on matters relating to intellectual property, consumer protection, public health, professional qualifications, and co-determined the technical standards for a variety of goods.

[34] Case C-212/97 *Centros* [1999] ECLI:EU:C:1999:126.

[35] *Säger* (n 13).

[36] *Bosman* (n 14).

[37] Floris de Witte, 'Sex, Drugs & EU Law: The Recognition of Moral and Ethical Diversity in EU Law' (2013) 50 Common Market Law Review 1545, 1566; Jotte Mulder, *Social Legitimacy in the Internal Market* (Hart 2018) 84.

[38] Alec Stone Sweet, *The Judicial Construction of Europe* (Oxford University Press 2004) 127; Ioannis Lianos, 'Efficient Restrictions of Trade in the EU Law of the Internal Market: Trust, Distrust and the Nature of Economic Integration' CLES Research Paper 1/2010; Malcolm A Jarvis, *The Application of EC Law by National Courts: The Free Movement of Goods* (Clarendon Press 1998) ('extremely rigorous').

[39] Miguel Poiares Maduro, *We the Court* (Hart 1998) 88. This is not to say that the ECJ no longer uses the *Cassis* approach, see Chapter 2 I.

Yet, although famous, the *Cassis* model was never the Court of Justice's sole *modus operandi*. In some free movement cases, a more lenient attitude towards domestic policy choices transpired, frequently coupled with references to the 'margin of appreciation' of the Member States. What defines this approach?

III. The Margin of Appreciation: Deference to National Legislatures and Executives

The margin of appreciation is a notoriously elusive doctrine.[40] A creation of the European Court of Human Rights (ECtHR),[41] it has, in the past decades, become a cornerstone of a number of national and international legal orders, appearing in human rights cases, international trade disputes as well as, more recently, investment arbitration proceedings.[42] The doctrine's ubiquity stands in marked contrast to its conceptual clarity. Scholars have struggled with defining its nature and effects, drawing attention to incoherencies and inflationary tendencies in the way in which the concept of the margin of appreciation is used.[43]

In EU free movement law, *Van Duyn* is the inevitable starting point for enquiries into the doctrine. Usually discussed for its contribution to the direct effect of directives, it is the first ruling to refer to the margin of appreciation of the Member States.[44] A Dutch national seeking to work for the Church of Scientology was denied entry to the United Kingdom. What was a clear obstacle to the free movement of workers was argued to be an indispensable measure for reasons of public policy. The activities of Scientology, so the British government claimed, were socially harmful. Accepting public policy as a justification for derogating from the free movement of workers, the Court of Justice granted the national authorities an

[40] In what follows I will be referring to the margin of appreciation as a 'doctrine'; for a discussion about whether this title is deserved: see Legg (n 7) 13–14.

[41] The 1976 ruling in Handyside v UK (1976) 1 EHRR 737 is commonly considered the starting point, but predecessors can be traced back to the early 1970s and 1960s: see De Wilde, Ooms and Versyp v Belgium (1971) 1 EHRR 373, para 93 and Case 'Relating to Certain Aspects of the Laws on the Use of Languages in Education in Belgium' v Belgium (1968) 1 EHRR 252. Before the Strasbourg Court, the (now dissolved) European Commission of Human Rights already applied the margin of appreciation doctrine in cases like Lawless v Ireland (1961) 1 EHRR 15 and the 1958 decision *Greece v United Kingdom* (1997) 18 Human Rights Law Journal 348. For a historical account of the doctrine in the ECHR, see Howard Charles Yourow, *The Margin of Appreciation in the Dynamics of European Human Rights Jurisprudence* (Kluwer 1996) 15 et seq.

[42] Legg (n 7); Donald H Regan, 'The Meaning of "Necessary" in GATT Article XX and GATS Article XIV: The Myth of Cost–Benefit Balancing' (2007) 6 World Trade Review 347; Julian Arato, 'The Margin of Appreciation in International Investment Law' (2014) 53 Virginia Journal of International Law 545.

[43] Letsas (n 7); Jan Kratochvíl, 'The Inflation of the Margin of Appreciation by the European Court of Human Rights' (2011) 29 Netherlands Quarterly of Human Rights 324; Ignacio de la Rasilla del Moral, 'The Increasingly Marginal Appreciation of the Margin-of-Appreciation Doctrine' (2006) 7 German Law Journal 611.

[44] Case 41/74 *Van Duyn* [1974] ECLI:EU:C:1974:133.

'area of discretion'—or, in French, a *pouvoir d'appréciation*—as to 'the particular circumstances justifying recourse' to it.[45]

A few years later, the ECJ was confronted with national obscenity laws in *Henn and Darby*.[46] Two Brits were caught violating the United Kingdom's importation ban on hard pornography, and their purchases were seized. As in *Van Duyn*, the restriction on free movement (*in casu*, of goods) was evident, but the British government claimed that the measure was necessary for protecting public morality. Examining whether the ban was justified, the Court took notice of the fact that the confiscated material was legal in other parts of the EU. Nonetheless, it upheld the measure, underlining that 'it is for each Member State to determine in accordance with its own scale of values and in the form selected by it the requirements of public morality in its territory'.[47]

Subsequent decades brought a proliferation of rulings alluding to the domestic margin of appreciation and gradually fine-tuned the doctrine's place in free movement law. In *Schindler*, looking at the necessity of a national lottery ban, the Court of Justice gave Member States a 'degree of latitude' to decide on how to regulate games of chance.[48] In *Omega*, when assessing whether the decision to shut down a laser tag game was proportionate, it granted a local city council a 'margin of discretion' to define the meaning of human dignity.[49] In *Commission v Italy (Italian Trailers)*, examining the proportionality of a prohibition on motorcycles towing trailers, it explained that the 'margin of appreciation' of the Member States extended to questions of road safety.[50]

These statements look simple at first. They seem to suggest that the margin of appreciation has to do with the justification and proportionality of Member State action[51] and that it gives national authorities the freedom to make certain

[45] ibid, para 18.
[46] Case 34/79 *Henn and Darby* [1979] ECLI:EU:C:1979:295.
[47] ibid, para 15.
[48] Case C-275/92 *Schindler* [1994] ECLI:EU:C:1994:119, para 61.
[49] *Omega Spielhallen* (n 2), para 31.
[50] *Commission v Italy (Italian Trailers)* (n 22), para 65.
[51] The ECJ's use of the margin of appreciation doctrine is limited to questions relating to justification and proportionality. It does not concern the scope of application of free movement law; cf Niamh Nic Shuibhne, 'Margins of Appreciation: National Values, Fundamental Rights and EC Free Movement Law' (2009) 34 European Law Review 230; James A Sweeney, 'A "Margin of Appreciation" in the Internal Market: Lessons from the European Court of Human Rights' (2007) 34 Legal Issues of Economic Integration 27, 39. A comparison of the Court's judgment with the Opinion of AG Van Gerven in Case C-159/90 *Society for the Protection of Unborn Children v Grogan* [1991] ECLI:EU:C:1991:378 is instructive in this context. The Court held that the Irish abortion ban did not fall into the scope of free movement law (or, at least, not in the case at stake). The ruling gives Ireland an essentially unlimited regulatory freedom in this area but manages without a single reference to the margin of appreciation. Van Gerven, by contrary, concluded that the Irish law restricted free movement and, therefore, examined its proportionality. Here, we see repeated references to the 'fairly considerable margin of discretion' and 'margin of appreciation' of the Member States in relation to questions connected with the proportionality of the abortion ban. For another example see *Keck and Mithouard* (n 20) and the ECJ's subsequent case law in this field which, similarly, lacks any mention of the margin of appreciation, despite significantly expanding national regulatory autonomy.

assessments: what is required to protect a policy objective; how to define the meaning of values; which regulatory solutions are effective; how to reconcile free movement and competing policy interests. Yet, upon closer inspection, difficult questions arise. What does it mean for national authorities to be 'free' to decide upon such matters? Does this affect judicial review and, if so, how? What, in other words, do Member States have in virtue of the margin of appreciation?

A. A Doctrine in Search of Meaning

When trying to make conceptual sense of the margin of appreciation in free movement law, a first stumbling block is terminology. Although the ECJ uses the notion of the 'margin of appreciation' in some rulings, we equally find a number of other expressions and phrases in its case law. For the same type of leeway, the Court will speak interchangeably of the 'degree of latitude', 'power of assessment', 'area of discretion', or simply 'discretion' of national authorities. Alternatively, it will say that 'it is for the Member States to determine', 'assess' or 'decide' a certain matter. The learned observer of the Court may suspect translation to be the culprit—it is not. While the terminology is slightly more coherent in French, the ECJ's working language, the diversity remains.[52]

The true difficulties, however, lie beyond the realm of semantics: the margin of appreciation creates a tension. When resorting to the doctrine, the Court of Justice sends out two conflicting messages. It signals that it will exercise *and* not exercise judicial control, that it will subject the Member State act to full scrutiny *and* accord the national authorities some special decision-making freedom. Take the previously cited passage from *Van Duyn*, this time in its entirety:

> [T]he concept of public policy in the context of the [Union] and where, in particular, it is used as a justification for derogating from the fundamental principle of freedom of movement for workers, must be interpreted strictly, so that its scope cannot be determined unilaterally by each Member State without being subject to control by the institutions of the [Union].
>
> Nevertheless, the particular circumstances justifying recourse to the concept of public policy may vary from one country to another and from one period to another, and it is therefore necessary in this matter to allow the competent national authorities an area of discretion within the limits imposed by the Treaty.[53]

[52] Terms like 'discretion', 'margin of discretion', 'area of discretion', and 'degree of latitude' are usually translated as either 'pouvoir' or 'marge d'appréciation'. Yet, on occasion, the French-language versions of the ECJ's rulings also use terms such as 'marge de manoeuvre' and 'étendue/niveau de protection' or state that 'il appartient aux autorités nationales de choisir' or 'déterminer' a certain issue. This is an important difference with the ECtHR, which is much more consistent and speaks of the domestic 'margin of appreciation' in the vast majority of cases.

[53] *Van Duyn* (n 44), para 18.

The Court starts by declaring that the notion of public policy must be 'interpreted strictly', cannot be 'defined unilaterally', and will be subjected to 'control by the institutions of the [Union]'. Member States, so it appears, are constrained by the free movement rules and are consequently not free to act as they wish. Their judgment on what public policy means will be reviewed—rigorously—by the ECJ. As the judgment continues, the direction of the argument changes. We find out that public policy 'may vary from one country to another', something which gives national authorities an 'area of discretion'. This seems to suggest that Member States have the liberty to decide what public policy means, under which circumstances it needs to be protected, and how this protection is to be achieved. On the same point, the Court seems to insist on full judicial control and an exemption from, or limitation of, such control.

In later margin of appreciation rulings, where the doctrine appears in the context of proportionality analysis, this tension becomes even more visible. In *Läärä*, one of the early gambling cases, the Court of Justice had to rule on the question whether Finland's state monopoly on slot machines was compatible with free movement law.[54] The Finnish government argued that the system, although restrictive, could be justified on grounds of consumer protection and as a means to fight gambling addiction. The Court replied that:

> [T]hose objectives are amongst those which may be regarded as overriding reasons relating to the public interest. However, it is still necessary ... that measures based on such grounds guarantee the achievement of the intended aims and do not go beyond that which is necessary in order to achieve them.[55]

This vantage point is familiar terrain. A national law restricting free movement must not go beyond what is necessary to achieve its goals. The Court of Justice will examine whether other, less intrusive measures would be as effective in attaining the policy objectives pursued by the Member State. What follows is more unusual:

> However, the power to determine the extent of the protection to be afforded by a Member State on its territory with regard to lotteries and other forms of gambling forms part of the national authorities' power of assessment ... It is for those authorities to assess whether it is necessary, in the context of the aim pursued, totally or partially to prohibit activities of that kind or merely to restrict them and, to that end, to establish control mechanisms, which may be more or less strict.[56]

[54] Case C-124/97 *Läärä* [1999] ECLI:EU:C:1999:435.
[55] ibid, para 33.
[56] ibid, para 35.

The Court identifies, as one would expect it to do when assessing the necessity of Member State action, the regulatory alternatives to a state monopoly: a total prohibition of slot machines, a partial prohibition, or a liberalization of the market accompanied by administrative checks. Yet, it also states that it is for the Finnish authorities to determine which of these regulatory options are 'necessary'. This leads to a curious consequence. What is necessary for consumer protection and preventing gambling addiction becomes a judgment to be made by both the ECJ (*qua* proportionality) and the Member State (*qua* its margin of appreciation). Again, control meets no control, this time in what seems to be a perfect overlap.

Human rights lawyers might be reminded of a sentence that has become common in the jurisprudence of the ECtHR: the 'margin of appreciation and European supervision *go hand in hand*'.[57] The matter is unfortunately not that simple. If the margin of appreciation and judicial review are to coexist, their relationship needs further explanation.

The ECJ resolves this problem by giving the doctrine a trait one could call 'modesty'. Member States enjoy a margin of appreciation only 'within the limits imposed by the Treaty',[58] meaning that every national measure must fully respect the requirements of free movement law. This, most importantly, includes proportionality. The Court of Justice does not tire of reiterating that in exercising their margin of appreciation Member States 'must comply with the principle of proportionality'.[59] The doctrine, on this account, does not restrict the scope of free movement scrutiny. Nor does it lower the standards by which national authorities have to abide. Therein lies its modesty: it does not alter the normal review routine in free movement cases.

Although this solution fixes the tension described above, it does some collateral damage conceptually: it renders the margin of appreciation obsolete.[60] If the doctrine expresses the idea that Member States have the freedom to regulate as long as they do not violate the principle of proportionality, is unclear why we need it in the first place. Measures that are justified and proportionate fall into the national margin of appreciation, whereas measures that are not fall outside of it. The margin of appreciation simply becomes, to paraphrase an image popularized by Yutaka Arai-Takahashi, 'the other side of proportionality'.[61] This,

57 *Handyside v UK* (n 41), para 49.

58 *Omega Spielhallen* (n 2), para 31; Case C-95/01 *Greenham and Abel* [2004] ECLI:EU:C:2004:71, para 37.

59 Case C-41/02 *Commission v Netherlands (Food Additives)* [2004] ECLI:EU:C:2004:762, para 46; Cases C-316/07 et al *Markus Stoß* [2010] ECLI:EU:C:2010:504, paras 76–77.

60 For a similar criticism in the ECHR context, see Letsas (n 7) 84 et seq on the 'substantive concept' of the margin of appreciation.

61 Arai-Takahashi described proportionality 'as the other side of the margin of appreciation', by which he means that '[i]f a reasonable or fair balance is found, the national authorities are considered to remain within the bounds of appreciation'; see *The Margin of Appreciation Doctrine and the Principle of Proportionality in the Jurisprudence of the ECHR* (Intersentia 2002) 14.

however, only restates how judicial review works; some acts pass judicial scrutiny, others do not. The margin of appreciation does not do any distinct doctrinal work in this picture.

B. The Level of Protection

Some consider the principle whereby Member States have the freedom to choose their level of protection, which is often invoked by the ECJ in relation to the domestic margin of appreciation, to provide a way out of this conundrum.[62] A typical formulation reads as follows:

> [I]t is for the Member States to determine the level of protection which they wish to afford to public health and the way in which that level is to be achieved.[63]

Two types of discretion follow from this: call them 'aims' and 'means discretion'. First, Member States have the freedom to decide to what degree they want to pursue a given policy objective (*aims discretion*). They can choose to try to accomplish it fully, further it substantially, or contribute towards it to a minimal extent. Second, they are free to determine how this objective is to be achieved, that is, which measures promise to attain the policy aim at the level of protection chosen (*means discretion*).

The central idea behind the 'level of protection' principle lies in customizing judicial review. Member States, not the Court of Justice, set the reference point for free movement scrutiny. National measures are only judged by what they seek to achieve, the degree to which they want to achieve it, and by which means. As every Member State is free to make a choice in this respect, different policy aims can be pursued to different extents. What is more, even for the same aim pursued to the same extent, different 'systems of protection' are allowed:

[62] Note that the relationship between the 'level of protection' principle and the national margin of appreciation is not entirely clear. On the basis of the ECJ's case law, at least three readings seem possible: the two could be completely separate (see *Commission v Italy (Italian Trailers)* (n 22), para 65: 'in the field of road safety a Member State may determine the degree of protection which it wishes to apply ... Since that degree of protection may vary from one Member State to the other, Member States must be allowed a margin of appreciation'); fully identical (compare *Placanica* (n 5), para 47 and Case C-169/07 *Hartlauer* [2009] ECLI:EU:C:2009:141, para 30, where both terms appear to be used to express the same idea); or the former an element of the latter (Case C-67/98 *Zenatti* [1999] ECLI:EU:C:1999:514, para 33: 'determination of the scope of the protection which a Member State intends providing in its territory in relation to lotteries and other forms of gambling falls within the margin of appreciation').

[63] Cases C-171 and 172/07 *Apothekerkammer des Saarlandes* [2009] ECLI:EU:C:2009:316, para 19. See also Case C-108/09 *Ker-Optika* [2010] ECLI:EU:C:2010:725, para 58; Cases C-570 and 571/07 *Blanco Pérez* [2010] ECLI:EU:C:2010:300, para 44; Case C-159/12 *Venturini* [2013] ECLI:EU:C:2013:791, para 59; Case C-148/15 *Deutsche Parkinson* [2016] ECLI:EU:C:2016:776, para 30.

> The mere fact that a Member State has opted for a system of protection which differs from that adopted by another Member State cannot affect the assessment of the need for, and proportionality of, the provisions enacted ... Those provisions must be assessed solely by reference to the objectives pursued by the competent authorities of the Member State concerned and the degree of protection which they seek to ensure.[64]

Is the 'level of protection' principle the key to a meaningful account of the margin of appreciation? Let us take a look at means discretion first. The case law provides few clues as to what it actually means for Member States to be able to determine the way in which a certain level of protection is achieved (in addition to choosing the level of protection itself), except for the general statement that a higher level of protection justifies more restrictive measures.[65] What is made plain, though, is that every choice of means must still comply with the free movement rules and the principle of proportionality. Take, for example, *Commission v Germany* on the prohibition of high-dosage vitamin supplements.[66] After explaining that, in the area of public health, Member States have the freedom to choose the level of protection and the means that will achieve it, the Court of Justice states that:

> in exercising their discretion relating to the protection of public health, the Member States must comply with the principle of proportionality. The means which they choose must therefore be confined to what is actually necessary to ensure the safeguarding of public health; they must be proportional to the objective thus pursued, which could not have been attained by measures which are less restrictive of intra-[Union] trade.[67]

We seem to find ourselves in the same quandary as earlier. *Qua* means discretion, the choice as to which measure is necessary to achieve a certain level of protection belongs to the Member State. At the same time, *qua* proportionality, this question is subjected to judicial review. The way the Court of Justice seems to make sense of this is that Member States can freely choose how to achieve a policy goal as long as this choice is not disproportionate. If this is true, though, the added value of means discretion is not evident. It creates the following series of events: first, Member States will make a primary assessment as to how to regulate; then, the Court will make a secondary assessment as to the proportionality of this decision, judged in light of what the latter sought to achieve. This, however, quite simply describes

[64] Case C-42/07 *Liga Portuguesa* [2009] ECLI:EU:C:2009:519, para 58.

[65] *Zeturf* (n 5), para 41.

[66] Case C-387/99 *Commission v Germany (Vitamins)* [2004] ECLI:EU:C:2004:235.

[67] ibid, para 71. See also *Placanica* (n 5), para 48 and Case 104/75 *De Peijper* [1976] ECLI:EU:C:1976:67, paras 15–16.

what always happens during proportionality analysis. Means discretion is redundant in this picture.[68]

Things are slightly more complicated when it comes to aims discretion. Despite the frequent allusions to the 'level of protection' principle in the ECJ's case law, judgments in which the actual level of protection is scrutinized are practically nonexistent.[69] Does aims discretion give Member States genuine leeway to decide on the intensity with which to pursue a policy goal? Cases such as *Pharmaceutical Importers* indicate that even this choice has its boundaries:

> [I]t is for the Member States, *within the limits laid down in Article 36 [TFEU]*, to decide on the degree to which they wish to protect human health and life and how that degree of protection is to be achieved.[70]

This passage suggests that not every level of protection will be accepted, and free movement case law provides plenty of evidence that these are not just empty words. Consider the Court's labelling jurisprudence and decisions like *Walter Rau*.[71] Belgium required margarine to be sold in cube shape to protect consumers from the risk of confusion. Belgians had grown accustomed to butter being sold in cones; if the two products did not come in different shapes, they could make the mistake of buying (cheaper) margarine when what they really wanted was butter. Was this regulation necessary to protect consumers? The Court took the view that consumers could be protected just as effectively by appropriate labelling.[72] The underlying controversy was not about whether labelling requirements were less restrictive than packaging rules—they certainly were. It concerned the vision of the average consumer.[73] Whereas the Member State advocated the model of a vulnerable consumer (ie one who is easily misled), the Court put forward the model of a 'reasonably circumspect' consumer (ie one who reads and understands labels). The dispute thus turned on different ideas about the

[68] Donald Regan has, commenting on the jurisprudence of the World Trade Organization Appellate Body, gone even further and called the simultaneous insistence on the level of protection doctrine and proportionality 'logically contradictory', see Regan (n 42) 348.

[69] *Zeturf* (n 5) on the French horse-betting monopoly is a rare exception, and even there the reader is essentially forced to read between the lines in order to infer that the ECJ considers the measure to pursue a high level of protection (para 41).

[70] Cases 266 and 267/87 *Pharmaceutical Importers* [1989] ECLI:EU:C:1989:205, para 21 (emphasis added). For a similar passage, see Case 274/87 *Commission v Germany (Meat Products)* [1989] ECLI:EU:C:1989:51, para 6.

[71] Case 261/81 *Rau* [1982] ECLI:EU:C:1982:382. For further examples see: *Cassis de Dijon* (n 12); Case 178/84 *Commission v Germany (Beer Purity)* [1987] ECLI:EU:C:1987:126; Case 407/85 *3 Glocken* [1988] ECLI:EU:C:1988:401; Case C-470/93 *Mars* [1995] ECLI:EU:C:1995:224.

[72] *Rau* (n 71), para 17.

[73] Stephen Weatherill, 'Who Is the "Average Consumer"?' in Stephen Weatherill and Ulf Bernitz (eds), *The Regulation of Unfair Commercial Practices under EC Directive 2005/29* (Hart 2007) 115, at 126.

appropriate level of protection. Belgium had opted for a high level, the Court of Justice did not accept this choice.[74]

Thus, aims discretion appears to give national authorities the freedom to determine the level of protection but, once again, only as long as they do not violate the requirements of free movement law and proportionality. Member States decide how intensely they want to regulate, but the Court of Justice will control whether they have acted in compliance with these requirements. This, however, is what happens without aims discretion as well. National authorities set a level of protection which is then subjected to judicial review. In sum, nothing appears to be won for the Member States. What it all eventually boils down to is regular free movement review.

C. Partial and Full Margins

The Court of Justice's explanations of the nature of the margin of appreciation make it difficult to understand the doctrine's precise effect on judicial review. This, however, is not to say that it lacks an effect. When we move our focus away from how the Court describes and conceptualizes the margin of appreciation to its actual behaviour in margin of appreciation cases, that is, how it exercises judicial scrutiny, it becomes clear that the doctrine introduces a distinct type of scrutiny into free movement law. I want to illustrate this with the aid of *Schindler*, one of the most widely cited margin of appreciation rulings.

In *Schindler*, two agents selling tickets for a German lottery challenged the British lottery ban.[75] The prohibition constituted a restriction on the free movement of services, so the ECJ examined whether it could be justified on public interest grounds and, in particular, if it was proportionate. The question arose as to whether the prohibition was necessary to protect consumers and prevent organized crime or whether less restrictive measures would be just as effective. In the judgment, the Court explained, similarly to *Läärä*, that there were three basic ways to regulate games of chance: a total prohibition, a partial prohibition, and a liberalization of the market coupled with administrative control. Given that these vary in terms of how seriously they restrict free movement and that the UK had chosen the most restrictive option, deciding on the necessity of the lottery ban would, in principle, require analysing to what extent each of these were effective in accomplishing

[74] Gareth Davies observes, similarly, that '[w]hen the Court says that an interest can be protected in a more proportionate way it is in substance often insisting that a state accept a slightly lower level of protection because of the free movement benefits that this would bring . . .'; see 'Free Movement, the Quality of Life and the Myth that the Court Balances Interests' in Panos Koutrakos, Niamh Nic Shuibhne, and Phil Syrpis (eds), *Exceptions from EU Free Movement Law: Derogation, Justification and Proportionality* (Hart 2016) 233.

[75] *Schindler* (n 48).

the envisaged policy objectives. Yet, in *Schindler*, the ECJ ruled that Member States were free to choose either of the three options. It did so without inquiring into the effectiveness of the different types of gambling regulation, neither across the EU nor in the UK.

The *Schindler* decision was centrally driven by the idea that deciding how to regulate gambling is a politically sensitive and culturally complex issue.[76] The Court of Justice mentioned the 'peculiar nature' and 'moral, religious or cultural aspects' of lotteries. It acknowledged the 'general tendency' across Europe to restrict games of chance. It pointed to the 'specific social and cultural features' of each country when it came to gambling. Based on these considerations, the Court concluded that it should not settle the matter of how to regulate the provision of services in this area itself. Instead, it granted the Member States a 'sufficient degree of latitude' (*pouvoir d'appréciation*) to 'assess not only whether it [was] necessary to restrict the activities of lotteries but also whether they should be prohibited'.

The difference with *Cassis de Dijon* is striking. Instead of defining what is required for consumer protection, as in *Cassis*, in *Schindler* the Court left this judgment in the hands of the national law-makers. The margin of appreciation doctrine is responsible for this shift. On a doctrinal level, it enabled the Court to make the sweeping statement that all three regulatory options were, in principle, proportionate in all Member States (no matter what the factual circumstances). On an institutional level, it allowed the Court to defer the decision on a delicate political and socio-economic problem to the national authorities.

We can see this type of behaviour in many of the aforementioned margin of appreciation cases. In *Van Duyn*, the Court of Justice refrained from assessing whether the activities of Scientology constituted a risk for public policy; the decision was handed over to the British government. In *Omega*, it avoided defining the meaning of human dignity; the local city council was given the freedom to interpret this notion. In *Italian Trailers*, it chose not to engage in an analysis of how to effectively protect road safety; the domestic authorities were allowed to determine the issue. All of these cases constitute a departure from the *Cassis* approach. The Court of Justice does not pronounce itself on which way of regulating is effective, which value judgments are acceptable, or how to strike a balance between the competing policy interests. It defers these decisions to the national authorities instead. The Court may cling onto the rhetoric of full judicial scrutiny—and the 'modesty' of the margin of appreciation—in these judgments. In reality, however, the doctrine leads to a lowering of the intensity of justification and proportionality review.

The difference between (strict) *Cassis* and (deferential) *Schindler*-style scrutiny can be made sense of as one between exercising and not exercising substantive review. The Court can comprehensively analyse the justification and proportionality

[76] ibid, paras 60–61.

Table 1.1 The Concept of the Margin of Appreciation

Type of MoA	Case	Review Exercised
No	*Cassis de Dijon*	ECJ makes justification/proportionality assessment itself
Partial	*Commission v Denmark (Food Additives)*	ECJ defers justification/proportionality assessment to national legislature or executive but stipulates how it is to be made
Full	*Schindler*	ECJ defers justification/proportionality assessment completely to national legislature or executive

of the Member State act, engage with the substance of the subject matter and decide, as it did in *Cassis, Centros*, and *Säger*, what is legitimate, suitable, and necessary. Member States have no margin of appreciation here. This is not to say that they lose the competence to regulate the field at hand, or that their decisions will always be unjustified and disproportionate. Yet, these will be subjected to detailed scrutiny by the ECJ. The Court can, however, also abstain from fully reviewing the assessments connected with the justification and proportionality of the national measure. This can concern specific points (is the law suitable to achieve a given aim? Is it effective? What is the right balance between the competing policy concerns?) or the whole investigation (is the law justified and proportionate?). In this scenario, the Court does not take a position on the substance of the regulatory problem at stake and defers the decision to the Member State. This is what defines the margin of appreciation approach.

There are two ways in which the Court of Justice can defer to Member State authorities or, if you will, two types of margins of appreciation—one more far-reaching than the other (see Table 1.1). The first is the *full margin of appreciation*. Here, the ECJ grants the national authorities complete deference on a particular matter. One finds this approach in cases like *Van Duyn, Henn and Darby, Schindler*, and *Omega*.[77] Member States are given the freedom to define what constitutes a threat to public policy, which acts offend public morality, what is necessary to protect consumers, and what human dignity means. This freedom comes with 'no strings attached'; the Court does not constrain the national assessment in any way. For the Member States, this scenario brings the widest leeway. Not only can they take the policy decision they want, they can also choose how to make that decision. For the ECJ, it entails the biggest loss of control. Judicial scrutiny of the national measure remains minimal, as does the Court's opportunity to shape the relevant subject matter.

[77] *Van Duyn* (n 44); *Henn and Darby* (n 46); *Schindler* (n 48); *Omega Spielhallen* (n 2).

The second variant, the *partial margin of appreciation*, is of a more limited nature. One finds it, for instance, in the case law on national restrictions on food additives, such as *Commission v Denmark*.[78] The ECJ states that it is for the national authorities to decide which vitamins, minerals, and substances pose health dangers and at which level of consumption. At the same time, however, it demands that their decision be based on a detailed risk assessment, which is done on a case-by-case basis and considers international scientific studies, without exclusively relying on local consumption habits.[79] This approach resembles the full margin of appreciation in one respect: ultimately, it is the Member States, not the Court, that determine which substances are dangerous. Yet, there is a crucial difference. Although national authorities are left to decide, the Court lays down *how* their decision ought to be made. It specifies the procedure to be followed, the questions to be taken account, and the evidence to be considered. The outcome of the regulatory assessment thus, again, lies in the hands of the Member States; the Court will not intervene.[80] The decision-making process, however, is controlled by the ECJ, which is why this form of review could be called 'procedural'.[81]

Identifying whether the Court of Justice grants national authorities a margin of appreciation so understood can be difficult at times. This goes especially for judgments in which the Court declares that national authorities are free to make a decision but, in spite of this, reviews their action to some degree.[82] Nonetheless, I want to avoid two potential misunderstandings. First, the margin of appreciation is not simply about Member States 'winning' a case. It is, in other words, a form of judicial review, not an outcome. The mere fact that a national measure is upheld does not mean that the ECJ has engaged in deferential scrutiny. *UTECA* illustrates this.[83] Spanish law required television operators to allocate 5 per cent of their revenue to the production of European films and 60 per cent of that sum for films shot in one of the official languages of Spain. The obligation was challenged under the

[78] Case C-192/01 *Commission v Denmark (Food Additives)* [2003] ECLI:EU:C:2003:492.

[79] ibid, para 43.

[80] Perhaps nowhere is this as evident as in *Commission v Germany (Vitamins)* (n 66). Germany had prohibited food supplements containing three times the recommended daily amount of vitamins and minerals. The ECJ held that the measure was in breach of the free movement rules as the national authorities had failed to make a detailed risk assessment for each substance. At the same time, it made clear that this did not affect the outcome of future regulation in this area. The German legislature could set the exact same limits as the ones that were quashed *in casu*, that is, the tripe amount rule, as long as it fulfilled the procedural requirements set out by the Court (see para 82).

[81] This is to be distinguished from what some authors have called 'procedural proportionality', meaning the procedural safeguards imposed on national legal orders through free movement law; see Sacha Prechal, 'Free Movement and Procedural Requirements: Proportionality Reconsidered' (2008) 35 Legal Issues of Economic Integration 201. However, note the conceptual proximity with the 'procedural' version of proportionality review proposed in de Witte, 'Sex, Drugs & EU Law' (n 37) (Court restricts itself to examining the coherence and consistency of national laws).

[82] See, for example, Case 159/78 *Commission v Italy (Customs Agents)* [1979] ECLI:EU:C:1979:243; Case 274/87 *Commission v Germany (Meat Products)* [1989] ECLI:EU:C:1989:51; Case 249/86 *Commission v Germany (Housing Conditions for Migrants)* [1989] ECLI:EU:C:1989:204.

[83] Case C-222/07 *Unión de Televisiones Comerciales Asociadas (UTECA)* [2009] ECLI:EU:C:2009:124.

free movement provisions. The crux of the matter lay in the question as to whether an appropriate balance had been struck between the aim of promoting local languages and the interests of television operators. The Court eventually ruled that the legislation was proportionate. Despite that, it would be inaccurate to say that it retreated from exercising full judicial scrutiny and deferred the decision to the national authorities. The Court engaged in a detailed balancing exercise, took all relevant facts into consideration, and weighed them against each other.[84] Even though ultimately agreeing with the domestic legislature, it took a position on whether the balance which had been struck was acceptable. This is not a 'you decide, national authorities' as in *Schindler*—it is a 'well done, Member State'.

Second, the margin of appreciation approach is about more than words: it concerns what the ECJ does, not what it says. Not every time the Court employs terms such as 'margin of appreciation', 'discretion', or 'level of protection' does it actually lower the intensity of scrutiny. Take *Schmidberger*.[85] A decision to authorize an environmental protest blocking the Brenner motorway was alleged to violate the free movement of goods. The Court of Justice held that the situation constituted a restriction on Article 34 TFEU but accepted free speech to be a legitimate justification as long as an acceptable balance with free movement was struck, and granted the Austrian authorities a 'wide margin of appreciation' in this regard.[86] What followed, however, was a long balancing assessment addressing every relevant aspect of the case: the filing of a request for the protest; the limited damage done to free movement; the expression of an opinion that was important to society; the measures taken to limit the disruption of road traffic; and so forth. Based on these considerations, the Court concluded that allowing the protest was proportionate. Is it justified to think of this as deferential review? Although the Court alluded to the domestic margin of appreciation, the type of scrutiny it exercised was, in fact, comprehensive. It enquired in great detail into the balance between free speech and free movement. There is no reason to classify this approach as anything other than standard proportionality review.

Note that, at times, the opposite can occur as well. The lack of references to the 'margin of appreciation' need not mean that the Court of Justice exercises full judicial scrutiny. *ARD* is an example for this.[87] Germany had restricted television advertising times for reasons of cultural policy and consumer protection. The Court's examination of the legislation's proportionality looked as follows:

> As regards the proportionality of the restriction at issue, it is settled case-law that requirements imposed on the providers of services must be appropriate

[84] ibid, paras 30 et seq.
[85] *Schmidberger* (n 1).
[86] ibid, paras 82 et seq.
[87] Case C-6/98 *ARD* [1999] ECLI:EU:C:1999:532.

> to ensure achievement of the intended aim and must not go beyond what is necessary in order to achieve that aim. There is nothing in the case-file to warrant the conclusion that those conditions are not satisfied in the case before the national court.[88]

The Court of Justice went directly from stipulating that the German law must be proportionate to accepting that it was, without any veritable scrutiny in between. Most importantly, it refrained from addressing the main regulatory question that gave rise to the dispute: how much advertising time is too much? Although there is no mention of the margin of appreciation doctrine, the approach is essentially the same. The Court accepts the factual and normative assessment made by the Member State without questioning it. The review exercised is not any stricter than in *Schindler*.

IV. Decentralized Judicial Review: Deference to National Courts

A. The Distinct Role of National Courts

Until now, I have spoken, with convenient ambiguity, about 'Member States' and 'national authorities' as beneficiaries of the margin of appreciation. This leaves one important question unresolved: how far do these notions stretch? Can all national institutions receive a margin of appreciation, or is the doctrine more limited in scope?

Before delving into the specificities of EU free movement law, it is worthwhile taking a look at the ECtHR first. In *Handyside*, the judgment in which the margin of appreciation doctrine was established, the ECtHR explicitly addressed its institutional breadth:

> Article 10 para. 2 [ECHR] leaves to the Contracting States a margin of appreciation. This margin is given both to the domestic legislator ('prescribed by the law') and to the bodies judicial amongst others, that are called upon to interpret and apply the laws in force.[89]

The conception of the doctrine put forward by the Strasbourg Court is wide. The national judiciary and executive, who interpret and apply the law, can be granted a margin of appreciation just as the national legislature, who creates it. This reflects the classical understanding of the state in public international law. Every

[88] ibid, paras 51–52.
[89] *Handyside v UK* (n 41), para 48.

authority equipped with public powers, regardless of the branch of government it belongs to, counts as an element of the state. In the same way, every national institution—no matter if legislative, executive, or judicial—can enjoy a margin of appreciation.[90]

The ECJ's vision of the doctrine is narrower. Think of any of the margin of appreciation rulings that were discussed in the previous section: *Schindler* and *Läärä* turn on national gambling legislation; *Omega* involves the interpretation of a constitutional provision by a city council; *Van Duyn* concerns the executive's freedom to define public policy; *Henn and Darby* is about domestic obscenity laws; *Italian Trailers* deals with road traffic regulation. When applying the margin of appreciation doctrine, the Court of Justice appears to primarily defer to national legislative and, on occasion, executive bodies.

One institutional actor is conspicuously absent on this list: the national judiciary. That Member State courts are not given a margin of appreciation might seem odd given the important role they are known to play in free movement adjudication, especially when it comes to examining the justification and proportionality of national laws. We might recall the Sunday trading saga, in which the ECJ (at first) chose not to settle whether domestic trading bans struck an acceptable balance between free movement and social policy and entrusted the national judiciary with that decision.[91] Similarly, in *Gourmet International*, the Court left the examination of the proportionality of the Swedish alcohol ban in the hands of the referring judges.[92] In *Viking Line*, it passed the final decision on the justification of the strike organized by the Finnish Seamen's Union over to the national court.[93] Thus, the ECJ does defer to Member State courts. In fact, the way in which it defers to them strongly resembles the way in which it defers to national legislatures and executives.[94] Despite that, national courts do not seem to form part of the idea of the margin of appreciation.

[90] This does not mean that there are no differences in how the ECtHR treats the domestic political and adjudicative branches in substance, see Jan Zglinski, 'Doing Too Little or Too Much? Private Law Before the European Court of Human Rights' (2018) 37 Yearbook of European Law 98, 107 et seq. For an argument in favour of a narrower reading of the margin of appreciation doctrine which is restricted to national courts, see Dean Spielmann, 'Allowing the Right Margin: The European Court of Human Rights and the National Margin of Appreciation Doctrine: Waiver or Subsidiarity of European Review?' (2011–2012) 14 Cambridge Yearbook of European Legal Studies 381.

[91] *Torfaen Borough Council* (n 19). This deferential position was later given up, see Case C-332/89 *Marchandise* [1991] ECLI:EU:C:1991:94; Case C-312/89 *Conforama* [1991] ECLI:EU:C:1991:93; Case C-169/91 *Stoke-on-Trent* [1992] ECLI:EU:C:1992:519.

[92] *Gourmet International* (n 18).

[93] Case C-438/05 *Viking Line* [2007] ECLI:EU:C:2007:772.

[94] This similarity is the reason why scholars often mention deference to national courts in the same breath as, or even consider it to belong to, the Member States' margin of appreciation: see Gráinne de Búrca, 'The Principle of Proportionality and Its Application in EU Law' (1994) 14 Yearbook of European Law 105; Daniel Sarmiento, 'Half a Case at a Time: Dealing with Judicial Minimalism at the European Court of Justice' in Monica Claes and others (eds), *Constitutional Conversations in Europe* (Intersentia 2013) 21.

Is this conceptual confusion on the part of the ECJ? The omission of Member State courts in the margin of appreciation case law is no accident. It is the result of a deliberate distinction between what one could call political and judicial deference. Differentiating between, on the one hand, deference to national legislatures or executives and, on the other, deference to national courts is warranted, even crucial, in EU law due to the radically different consequences that flow from the two options. When the ECJ grants a national legislature deference in the context of justification and proportionality review, it limits judicial control over the subject matter. The Member State is given the freedom to choose how to regulate with restricted or minimal scrutiny. When the ECJ, in contrast, defers the decision on justification and proportionality to a national court, judicial review of the Member State act is not curtailed—it is merely 'relocated'. The relevant measure is put under full free movement scrutiny, just with the national judge acting *in lieu* of the Court of Justice.

The difference is most evident in judgments in which both types of deference appear. *Dynamic Medien* is one example.[95] An importer of Japanese *anime* films challenged the German age classification system for videos, which was designed to protect children from disturbing content. The Court of Justice quickly identified the two main issues to be, first, whether the (more lenient) safeguards adopted by other Member States in this area sufficed in ensuring the well-being of children and, second, whether adequate procedural remedies to challenge classification decisions were available. As to the former, the Court explained that the regulatory differences across Europe justified a 'margin of discretion' for the German legislature as to the level of protection of children's rights.[96] As to the latter, it held that 'it [was] for the national court' to 'ascertain' whether appropriate procedural mechanisms existed for producers and importers of videos.[97] The difference is fundamental. With regard to assessing what is harmful for children, the Court's ruling gives Member States full regulatory autonomy. Free movement law will not interfere in their choice, no matter how strict or lenient it may be. On the matter of adequate procedural remedies, there is no comparable discretion. Member States must ensure that their laws entail sufficient safeguards that comply with the standards of EU free movement law. However, it will not be the ECJ who checks this, but rather the national courts.

That the Member State judiciary is not among the addressees of the margin of appreciation does not mean that it is a less important institution. Quite the opposite. National courts are accorded decision-making powers which, in terms of significance, are similar to those granted to national political bodies. They too are sometimes left to determine whether legislative measures work,[98] how effective

[95] *Dynamic Medien* (n 6).
[96] ibid, para 45.
[97] ibid, para 51.
[98] Case C-350/07 *Kattner Stahlbau* [2009] ECLI:EU:C:2009:127, para 91.

alternative regulatory solutions would be,[99] and in which way free movement and competing concerns would be best reconciled.[100] The point is that such deference to Member State courts constitutes a distinct doctrinal and institutional option, one which differs in nature and effect from deference to the national legislative and executive branches. Therefore, in the following, I shall refer to it as 'decentralized judicial review'.

A note on this terminological choice is warranted. Decentralized judicial review is an expression sometimes used to describe legal systems in which lower courts are permitted to engage in constitutional review.[101] This form of review does, of course, exist in EU law. National courts examine—they are encouraged, even obliged to do so[102]—the compatibility of Member State acts with EU law. The here-proposed concept denotes a different phenomenon. It is not about national courts inquiring into the justification and proportionality of national laws *ex proprio motu*. It is about the Court of Justice handing down or, in other words, *decentralizing* review responsibilities to national judges which it could, in principle, exercise itself.

B. Degrees of Freedom

As much as their effects differ, the way in which the margin of appreciation doctrine and decentralized judicial review are used remarkably resemble each other. Just as national legislatures and executives can be granted wider or narrower discretionary powers, the ECJ can delegate the task of judicial review to national courts to different extents (see Table 1.2).[103]

To begin with, just as there can be no margin of appreciation, there can be no decentralization of judicial review. The ECJ can choose not to involve the referring judge in the review process and assess the justification and proportionality of the Member State act all by itself, that is, decide in a centralized manner. This, once again, is the *Cassis de Dijon* scenario. The question as to what is necessary to protect consumers is single-handedly determined by the Court of Justice. As was explained, the national legislature enjoys no deference in this scenario (hence, no margin of appreciation). Neither does the national court. The ECJ makes a

[99] Case C-33/97 *Colim* [1999] ECLI:EU:C:1999:274, para 41.

[100] Cases C-482/01 and 493/01 *Orfanopoulos* [2004] ECLI:EU:C:2004:262, paras 95 et seq.

[101] Mauro Cappelletti, 'Judicial Review in Comparative Perspective' (1970) 58 California Law Review 1017, 1033 et seq.

[102] Case 106/77 *Simmenthal II* [1978] ECLI:EU:C:1978:49.

[103] See Takis Tridimas, 'Constitutional Review of Member State Action: The Virtues and Vices of an Incomplete Jurisdiction' (2011) 9 International Journal of Constitutional Law 737, who distinguishes between outcome, guidance, and deference cases. 'Outcome cases' correspond to what will be called centralized judicial review in the following; 'guidance' cases to the guidelines approach; and 'deference' cases to fully decentralized judicial review.

Table 1.2 The Concept of Decentralized Judicial Review

Type of Decentralization	Case	Review Exercised
None	*Cassis de Dijon*	ECJ makes justification/proportionality assessment itself (= centralized judicial review)
w/ Tendency	*Dynamic Medien*	ECJ defers justification/proportionality assessment to national court but gives prima facie appraisal
w/ Guidelines	*Familiapress*	ECJ defers justification/proportionality assessment to national court but stipulates how it is to be made
Adoption	*Placanica*	ECJ takes justification/proportionality assessment over from national court
Full	*Libert*	ECJ defers justification/proportionality assessment completely to national court

conclusive assessment of the necessity and effectiveness of the regulation itself. This leaves the national judge without any decision-making power; they simply have to implement the solution crafted by the Court.

At the other end of the spectrum we find *full decentralization*. The ECJ can give the national judge complete autonomy when deciding on the justification and proportionality of the Member State act at stake. *Libert* illustrates this approach.[104] Reviewing a Belgian regulation imposing an obligation on developers to provide social housing, the Court of Justice states that the measure:

> may be justified by requirements relating to social housing policy in a Member State as an overriding reason in the public interest. It is however for the referring court to assess, in the light of the circumstances of the case before it, whether such an obligation satisfies the principle of proportionality, that is, whether it is necessary and appropriate to attain the objective pursued.[105]

The ECJ hands down the task of exercising proportionality review to the referring court without any guidance. The national court has complete discretion as to both the outcome and the process of the inquiry: it is not only free to decide whether the Belgian measure is proportionate, it can also choose which considerations to take into account, which questions to address, and which evidence to base its decision on.

[104] Cases C-197/11 and 203/11 *Libert* [2013] ECLI:EU:C:2013:288.
[105] ibid, paras 67–68.

The same degree of decentralization occurs in the *adoption* scenario. The ECJ can, where they have been submitted in the order for reference, take over the justification and proportionality assessments already made by the national judiciary. *Placanica* on the Italian gambling monopoly illustrates this.[106] Examining whether Italy pursued the objective of curbing gambling addiction in a consistent and systematic manner, the Court relies on the analysis of the *Corte suprema di cassazione*, which previously held that the Italian legislature was pursuing a policy of expanding activity in this sector which was incoherent and, consequently, unjustified.[107] The ECJ simply appropriates this finding in its judgment, without reviewing the matter anew. *Because* the national court attested that the Italian system lacked consistency in combatting gambling addiction, the European judges concludes that it is inconsistent. Note the parallels with the full decentralization scenario: it is the referring court who decides on the proportionality of the Member State act (or aspects of it). The difference is one of time. Instead of making the national judge decide after the preliminary reference ruling, the Court incorporates an earlier assessment into its judgment.

The options presented thus far mark the two extremes: the ECJ determines everything or (practically) nothing regarding the justification and proportionality of a Member State act. However, as with deference to national legislatures, the Court has created intermediate approaches in relation to decentralized judicial review. It can pass review tasks onto the referring court but constrain or direct the latter's decision.

One way in which this can be done is through *guidelines*. Here, the ECJ hands the decision on the proportionality of the given measure down to the national court but instructs it as to how to make this decision. These instructions can concern a variety of issues: which considerations to take into account, which questions to address, or which types of measures to strike down. *Familiapress* is a well-known example of this approach.[108] The Court of Justice states that, in order to comply with free movement rules, the Austrian prohibition of prize competitions in print publications must be proportionate. This, as the judgment clarifies, is 'for the national court to determine'. Nonetheless, the ECJ specifies the two decisive questions in this respect: first, 'whether newspapers which offer the chance of winning a prize ... are in competition with ... small press publishers' on the Austrian market; second, 'whether such a prospect of winning constitutes an incentive to purchase capable of bringing about a shift in demand'.[109] The parallels with the partial margin of appreciation are unmistakable. While the outcome of the decision (ie

[106] *Placanica* (n 5).
[107] ibid, para 54.
[108] *Familiapress* (n 4).
[109] ibid, paras 28–29.

whether the legislation is proportionate) is left with the national court, the process (ie how to determine this question) is set out by the Court of Justice.

Conceptually distinct, although often overlapping in practice,[110] is the *tendency* approach. The ECJ lets the referring court decide but gives a *prima facie* assessment of the justification and proportionality of the Member State act. *Dynamic Medien* relies on this technique.[111] It was mentioned earlier that, in the judgment, the Court of Justice held that the proportionality of the German law depended on the existence of appropriate procedural safeguards and left the task of examining whether this is the case with the national judge. What was not mentioned was that the Court, in addition, remarked that 'it appear[ed] from the observations [that the German law] fulfil[ed] the conditions' laid down in the ruling.[112] Again, the final judgment on the proportionality of the measure was left with the national court. However, the ECJ influenced the latter's decision by sharing its 'gut feeling' on the matter.

The ECJ can thus interact with national courts in a variety of ways when it comes to reviewing Member State acts. It can choose not to involve the national court at all and decide on the justification and proportionality of the relevant act itself (centralized judicial review). Alternatively, it can defer this decision to national courts by giving them minimal review responsibilities (tendency), substantial decision-making tasks (guidelines), or even complete freedom of judgment (full decentralization/adoption). Note that these forms of judicial deference are independent of the deference granted through the margin of appreciation. The ECJ can defer to national courts without deferring to national legislatures, and *vice versa*. However, where necessary, the two can be combined. The Court may, to come back to the example of food additives, choose to leave the final decision regarding which substances damage human health with a national parliament or agency, but require it to be based on a detailed risk assessment relying on international research—while placing the responsibility of supervising whether these conditions are fulfilled with the referring court.[113]

V. The New Free Movement Law: Doctrine and Institutions

Free movement law has undergone a series of changes over the past four decades. The Court of Justice has significantly widened the scope of the free movement rules, thereby prompting a shift towards justification and proportionality analysis. At the same time, it has created two deference doctrines: the margin of appreciation

[110] See Chapter 4 II A.
[111] *Dynamic Medien* (n 6).
[112] ibid, para 51.
[113] *Greenham and Abel* (n 58). For further examples, see *Orfanopoulos* (n 100) (immigration law) or Case C-575/11 *Nasiopoulos* [2013] ECLI:EU:C:2013:430 (professional qualifications).

and decentralized judicial review. Both represent a departure from the substantive review approach made famous by the *Cassis de Dijon* ruling. The margin of appreciation entails deference to national legislatures and executives, whereas decentralized judicial review results in deference to national courts. Both techniques can be used to different degrees, with domestic actors being granted a narrower or wider decision-making leeway. Yet, each carries different consequences for free movement review. While the margin of appreciation leads to a lowering of the intensity with which national laws are examined, a decentralization of judicial review only affects where this scrutiny will take place.

The conceptual story so told forms the analytical backbone of this book. It will serve as the basis for the doctrinal, empirical, and normative enquiries that are undertaken in the following chapters. At the same time, it exposes two fundamental features of contemporary free movement adjudication: doctrinal and institutional variety.

A. Doctrinal Variation

I want to return to *Cassis de Dijon* one final time. As was explained, the model adopted in *Cassis* has been an influential approach in free movement adjudication. It entails that the ECJ subjects a Member State act, once it is found to restrict freedom of movement, to substantive justification and proportionality review. Doctrines such as the margin of appreciation and decentralized judicial review constitute a departure from this model. They create alternative approaches which the Court of Justice can employ when reviewing national laws. Although *Cassis*-style scrutiny remains an option, it has become only one out of many. The result is a 'sliding scale' of judicial review, ranging from the highly deferential, to the more searching, to the strict and intrusive.

This scale is best illustrated by a small thought experiment: a comparison of how *Cassis* was decided with how it could have been decided. It was mentioned that the critical part of the case was whether prohibiting liqueur with low alcohol content was necessary to protect consumers. In the actual ruling, the ECJ chose to determine this issue itself and found the prohibition to be excessive in light of the possibility of labelling. This is the no margin of appreciation or centralized judicial review approach: the Court of Justice subjects a national measure to substantive proportionality scrutiny.

What may feel like the natural, only imaginable approach turns out to be just one option. The Court could have taken a number of different paths. It could have held that the question as to how to effectively protect consumers was factually complex and therefore called for an answer by the national legislature (*full margin of appreciation*). It could have granted Member States the freedom to decide what adequately protects purchasers of alcoholic beverages, but required that the decision be made on the basis of empirical studies on consumer behaviour (*partial margin of appreciation*). Alternatively, it could have passed the issue onto the referring judge, who may have better knowledge of local consumption habits (*fully decentralized judicial review*). Had the national court submitted an assessment on the necessity of the legislation, the ECJ could have taken over the latter's position (*adoption*). Likewise, it could have let the national judge assess the measure's necessity but set out which points to address (*guidelines*): how often do consumers read labels? How frequently are they misled by product designations? How great is the potential financial damage? Yet another possibility would have been to let the referring court decide, but provide a prima facie assessment of the matter, by stating that for reasons X, Y, and Z the national law appears or does not appear to be proportionate (*tendency*). Finally, a combination of some of these approaches would have been possible. The ECJ could have allowed the national legislature to choose how to protect consumers while requiring it to consider international research on the topic (*partial margin of appreciation*), but made the referring court supervise whether this condition had been complied with (*guidelines*).

What sounds like legal fiction are, as this chapter shows, actual ways in which the Court of Justice has come to behave in its case law. When a Member State measure is challenged under the four freedoms, it is, in principle, possible that the Court will adopt any of the above approaches. This demonstrates the significant doctrinal impact which deference has on free movement law. The field has become varied, complex, one may even say messy. By the same token, it forces us to reconsider one ambition which has marked wide parts of scholarship in this area: finding coherence.[114] All too often academic commentators have worked from the premise that the ECJ's free movement jurisprudence is a long body of cases that can be made seen as following one overarching idea, if one only looks hard enough. From this perspective, there is—or, at least, there should be—no selectivity, no heterogeneity, and no ruptures in the way in which the Court exercises judicial review.

Thinking in terms of coherence is at odds with present-day free movement law. Allan Rosas has, writing in a personal capacity, recently acknowledged this by saying that the ECJ's treatment of Member State derogations from free movement rights 'does not easily lend itself to clear-cut or well-structured answers'.[115] Different fields require different approaches and review standards must be adjusted to the relevant context. (Similarly, different times may call for different solutions.) But is this actually a problem? Free movement law has come to encompass a variety of subject matters, ranging from the technical to the simple, from the mundane to the politically delicate. There is no reason to think that a dispute on

[114] For a recent endeavour in this direction, see Nic Shuibhne, *The Coherence of EU Free Movement Law* (n 29).

[115] Allan Rosas, 'Foreword' in Panos Koutrakos, Niamh Nic Shuibhne, and Phil Syrpis (eds), *Exceptions from EU Free Movement Law: Derogation, Justification and Proportionality* (Hart 2016) v.

architects' fees should be approached in the same way as one on trade union rights, or a case on technical standards for pasteurized milk as one on the recognition of same-sex marriages.[116] The doctrinal diversity introduced through the margin of appreciation and decentralized judicial review can, against this background, be put to good use.

B. Institutional Choice

Legal rules hardly ever have purely legal consequences. They affect the institutions that apply them as well as the institutions they are applied to.[117] It will have become clear by now that this adage holds particularly true for the margin of appreciation and decentralized judicial review. Institutional aspects are not mere corollaries of these doctrines, they are at the very heart of them. Every time the Court of Justice decides between a *Cassis, Schindler*, or *Familiapress* type of scrutiny, it decides who will decide an issue and to what extent. From doctrinal diversity follows institutional choice.

Under the *Cassis* model, free movement law is, to an important degree, ECJ-centred. The Court assumes the ultimate authority to settle the legal and regulatory questions brought before it. Deference changes this institutional one-sidedness. It creates a free movement law which is defined by the presence of, and interaction between, different actors: the ECJ, national law-makers, and national courts. The power to make a certain decision can primarily rest with a single institution. This is the case when Member States are granted a full margin of appreciation or an assessment is completely decentralized to the national judiciary. Likewise, however, it can be divided between two or even all three actors. When the ECJ defers a decision to a national institution but makes stipulations as to how this decision is to be made, the matter is co-determined by both actors. When the Court, as hypothesized at the end of the *Cassis* variations, passes a judgment over to the national parliament, defines the conditions it has to abide by, and puts the monitoring of these in the hands of the national judiciary, all three actors partake in the decision-making process.

Selecting between substantive or centralized judicial review, the margin of appreciation, and decentralized judicial review is, consequently, no minor issue. The choice affects which actor will decide a matter and, by the same token, how

[116] In a similar vein, see Floris de Witte, 'The Constitutional Quality of the Free Movement Provisions: Looking for Context in the Case Law on Article 56 TFEU' (2017) 42 European Law Review 313, 321.

[117] Neil Komesar, *Imperfect Alternatives* (University of Chicago Press 1997); Neil Komesar, *Law's Limits* (Cambridge University Press 2001). The relevance of Komesar's work for the question of deference is explored in greater detail in Chapter 6, but its fundamental insight—that law has an essentially institutional dimension—informs the analysis throughout this book.

satisfied we will be with that decision. Some institutions will be more competent in certain areas and less so in others. They will possess detailed knowledge on medical products, consumer behaviour, and road safety, but lack an understanding of the socio-economic effects which a legislative measure has on foreigners. Likewise, some institutions will have greater legitimacy to deal with a given issue than others. Is the ECJ the appropriate body to decide on abortion or should we entrust the matter to a democratically elected parliament? Should Member States be free to set environmental standards or should we control their laws at the European level? Are we better off leaving social policy to legislatures or should courts have a say in it? Nothing less is at stake when we choose between the different types of free movement review.

2

The Rise of Deference

For most of its existence, the European Court of Justice (ECJ) has been criticized for infringing upon national decision-making autonomy. The oft-invoked 'motor of integration' from a European perspective, its decisions have frequently been perceived as undue limitations of Member State competences and obstacles to the pursuit of domestic policies. Already in the 1970s, critiques of 'compulsive megalomania' were raised in light of the Court's 'insufficient deference to the sovereign rights and interests' of the Member States.[1] In recent years, the pressure seems to have increased. National politicians have—motivated by the desire to 'take back control'—called for the liberation of their legal orders from the yoke of its jurisdiction, depicting the Court of Justice as 'rogue'.[2] Domestic high courts have revolted against some ECJ rulings, or threatened to do so.[3] Even among EU legal scholars criticisms are growing, with claims surfacing that the Court is making it exceedingly difficult for Member States to defend their policies against the exigencies of European law.[4]

The question of how much—or how little—deference the ECJ accords Member State authorities acquires a particular constitutional and political weight in this setting. It has a bearing on whether worries that the Court of Justice is becoming growingly activist and intrudes into domestic affairs are well-founded. Likewise, it is an indicator of how tight the grip of EU law over national legal orders has become and to what degree Member State autonomy is restricted.

This chapter will provide a macro-level analysis of the phenomenon of deference, focusing on two questions: how frequently does the ECJ defer to national authorities? Has its intensity of review of Member State action changed over time? These matters will be investigated with the aid of a systematic study of free movement jurisprudence (1974–2013). The findings will expose that deference has become an increasingly prominent feature of the ECJ's case law during the past four

[1] G Federico Mancini, 'The Making of a Constitution for Europe' (1989) 26 Common Market Law Review 595. This remark goes back to Michel Debré, former prime minister of France, who in front of the *Assemblée Nationale* accused the ECJ of 'mégalomanie maladive', an expression translated in a later version of Mancini's article as 'morbid megalomania', but better rendered as 'compulsive' or 'pathological'.

[2] See the manifesto of 'Vote Leave' ahead of the 2016 Brexit referendum: <voteleavetakecontrol.org/a_framework_for_taking_back_control_and_establishing_a_new_uk_eu_deal_after_23_june.html>.

[3] See n 111.

[4] Catherine Barnard, 'Derogations, Justifications and the Four Freedoms: Is State Interest Really Protected?' in Catherine Barnard and Okeoghene Odudu (eds), *The Outer Limits of European Union Law* (Hart 2009) 273.

Europe's Passive Virtues. Jan Zglinski, Oxford University Press (2020). © Oxford University Press.
DOI: 10.1093/oso/9780198844792.001.0001

decades. This suggests there has been a change in the Court's approach towards and relationship with national authorities. The chapter will close by looking into possible reasons for this development. It will become apparent that not just the Court has evolved, but also the context in which it operates.

I. Deference Over Time

In the previous chapter, we came across some famous instances of deference to Member State authorities in free movement law. Judgments like *Omega*, *Schmidberger*, and *Familiapress* attracted considerable attention among the ECJ's observers as they appeared to signal a more lenient attitude towards (certain) domestic regulatory and adjudicative decisions. Yet, the question arises as to how representative they are. Is deference an exceptional occurrence, a doctrinal tool taken out from the drawer for particularly controversial or complex cases? Or is it a more stable part of free movement adjudication, which genuinely defines the Court of Justice's interaction with national institutions?

A systematic study of free movement jurisprudence will help answer these questions. The study covers every fifth year of ECJ rulings in preliminary reference and infringement proceedings on alleged Member State violations of the four freedoms for the period between 1974 and 2013.[5] In this chapter, we shall focus on cases in which the scope of at least one free movement right was affirmed (216 decisions).[6] The results shed light on the empirical magnitude of deference by showing how often the ECJ defers to national authorities. They also provide a longitudinal perspective on how the intensity of free movement review has changed over the years. We will look into the margin of appreciation doctrine and decentralized judicial review separately at first, before examining the phenomenon of deference as a whole.

A. Margin of Appreciation

The ECJ grants Member State authorities a margin of appreciation in 47 cases in the sample (21.76 per cent). In line with the conceptual account presented in Chapter 1, this figure does not represent the number of rulings in which the Court

[5] For a more detailed description of the research design, see Introduction.

[6] The reason is simple: given that the margin of appreciation and decentralized judicial review were defined as the practice of deferring questions from justification and proportionality to national authorities, the doctrines can only be applied in cases that make it (or could make it) to the justification stage. I include judgments in which the ECJ expressly affirms that a case falls into the scope of free movement law or lets the referring court decide whether the conditions for this are fulfilled. In any event, the difference is small: in only 31 free movement cases in the sample (12.15 per cent) are Member State acts found not to restrict at least one free movement right; see Chapter 5 IV B 1.

of Justice simply uses terms such as the 'margin of appreciation', 'discretion', 'power of assessment', or similar expressions.[7] It only includes cases in which the Court actually refrains from subjecting Member State acts to full justification and proportionality review and defers certain regulatory decisions, partly or entirely, to national authorities. This distinction—what the Court *does* as opposed to what it *says*—is important for two reasons. Sometimes, the Court will state that it is applying the margin of appreciation without in fact doing so ('saying without doing'). Despite expressly making reference to the doctrine, it will exercise strict justification and proportionality review.[8] Other times, it will lower the intensity of review without expressly signalling this ('doing without saying').[9] Needless to say, both phenomena are problematic as they make it difficult to tell which type of scrutiny the ECJ will ultimately exercise based on the way it presents the applicable standard of review.

The Court of Justice can, as was explained, grant national authorities two types of margins of appreciation: full and partial. While the former gives Member States deference in relation to both the decision-making process and outcome, the latter is narrower and entails that the ECJ monitors how national authorities make their decision. The search shows that the full margin of appreciation is the more common option. It is applied in 29 judgments, in areas ranging from road safety,[10] to gambling,[11] to pharmacy regulation.[12] A partial margin of appreciation is applied less frequently, on 18 occasions. It is a more recent phenomenon, with most of the cases dating from the 1990s onwards. Also, its reach is narrower. Although appearing sporadically in disputes on public policy[13] and consumer law,[14] its application is essentially limited to the field of public health.[15]

[7] For studies relying on keyword searches, see Mikael Rask Madsen, 'Rebalancing European Human Rights: Has the Brighton Declaration Engendered a New Deal on Human Rights in Europe?' (2018) 9 Journal of International Dispute Settlement 199 (analysis of 'margin of appreciation' usage by the European Court of Human Rights); Adam Winkler, 'Fatal in Theory and Strict in Fact: An Empirical Analysis of Strict Scrutiny in the Federal Courts' (2006) 59 Vanderbilt Law Review 793, 810 (analysis of 'strict scrutiny' cases in US federal judiciary).

[8] See, for example, Case C-131/93 *Commission v Germany (Crayfish)* [1994] ECLI:EU:C:1994:290; Case 107/83 *Klopp* [1984] ECLI:EU:C:1984:270; Case 249/86 *Commission v Germany (Housing Conditions for Migrants)* [1989] ECLI:EU:C:1989:204; Case C-496/01 *Commission v France (Bio-Medical Laboratories)* [2004] ECLI:EU:C:2004:137; Case C-212/11 *Jyske Bank Gibraltar* [2013] ECLI:EU:C:2013:270.

[9] See, for example, Case C-55/93 *Van Schaik* [1994] ECLI:EU:C:1994:363; Case C-6/98 *ARD* [1999] ECLI:EU:C:1999:532; Case C-265/12 *Citroën Belux* [2013] ECLI:EU:C:2013:498.

[10] *Van Schaik* (n 9); Case C-110/05 *Commission v Italy (Italian Trailers)* [2009] ECLI:EU:C:2009:66.

[11] Case C-275/92 *Schindler* [1994] ECLI:EU:C:1994:119; Case C-124/97 *Läärä* [1999] ECLI:EU:C:1999:435; Case C-243/01 *Gambelli* [2003] ECLI:EU:C:2003:597.

[12] Cases C-171 and 172/07 *Apothekerkammer des Saarlandes* [2009] ECLI:EU:C:2009:316; Case C-531/06 *Commission v Italy (Pharmacies)* [2009] ECLI:EU:C:2009:315.

[13] Case C-348/96 *Calfa* [1999] ECLI:EU:C:1999:6.

[14] Case C-239/02 *Douwe Egberts* [2004] ECLI:EU:C:2004:445.

[15] See Case C-17/93 *Van der Veldt* [1994] ECLI:EU:C:1994:299; Case C-95/01 *Greenham and Abel* [2004] ECLI:EU:C:2004:71; Case C-112/02 *Kohlpharma* [2004] ECLI:EU:C:2004:208; Case C-88/07 *Commission v Spain (Herbal Products)* [2009] ECLI:EU:C:2009:123.

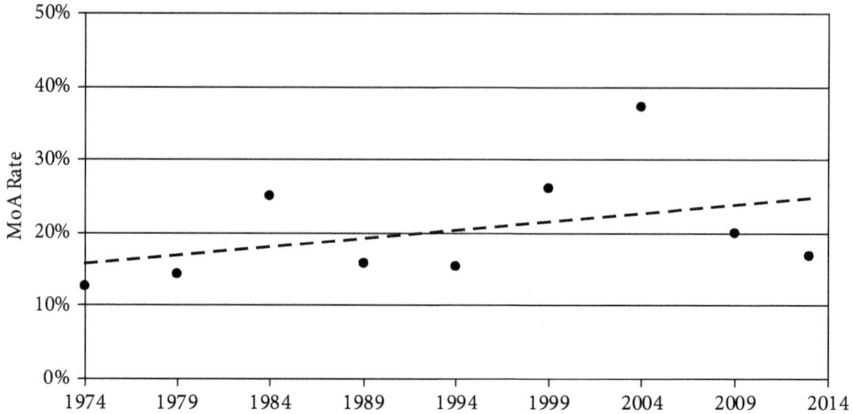

Figure 2.1 Margin of Appreciation in Free Movement Cases, 1974–2013

Notes: Percentage of margin of appreciation cases in all cases in which a national measure falls within the scope of at least one free movement right (infringement proceedings and preliminary references). Trendline serves interpretative purposes only and does not make predictive claims about in-between years.

When granting a partial margin of appreciation, the extent to which the Court intervenes in national decision-making varies. Sometimes, its stipulations remain general and limited. National authorities are, for example, just asked to take fundamental rights into account when deciding on the expulsion of migrants.[16] Other times, the list of requirements can be long and specific, as in the case law on food additives.[17]

The findings suggest that the margin of appreciation doctrine is a selective but relevant feature of free movement adjudication, appearing in over a fifth of the Court of Justice's decisions. What is more, its role has grown over time. This is visible in absolute figures. Making only a single appearance in 1974, the doctrine was applied 4 times in 1984, 7 times in 1999, and 13 times in 2004. It is also noticeable in relative terms (Figure 2.1). The number of free movement cases has consistently increased over the past decades, from 8 cases in 1974 to over 40 in 2013.[18] Even taking this development into account, the frequency with which the ECJ defers to national political actors has grown. Whereas the 1970s show application rates of less than 15 per cent, we find rates of 20 per cent or more for 1984, 1999, 2004, and

[16] Cases C-482/01 and 493/01 *Orfanopoulos* [2004] ECLI:EU:C:2004:262, paras 95–99.

[17] Case C-387/99 *Commission v Germany (Vitamins)* [2004] ECLI:EU:C:2004:235, paras 79–84; Case C-24/00 *Commission v France (Food Additives)* [2004] ECLI:EU:C:2004:70, paras 49 et seq; Case C-150/00 *Commission v Austria (Food Additives)* [2004] ECLI:EU:C:2004:237, paras 85 et seq; Case C-41/02 *Commission v Netherlands (Food Additives)* [2004] ECLI:EU:C:2004:762, para 41 et seq.

[18] Thirty-six cases in which the national measure fell into the scope of application of at least one free movement right.

2009. The year 2004 marks the highest point with 37.13 per cent,[19] an almost three-fold increase compared with 1974.

The results cast doubt on claims, widely spread in the literature on free movement law, that the Court of Justice's scrutiny of national measures has become ever more strict over time. In a pioneering, albeit small-scale study of free movement jurisprudence, Catherine Barnard argued that the Court has steadily intensified its control over Member State action.[20] Her analysis found that while being marked by 'considerable deference to Member States' regulatory freedom' in the mid-1980s, the Court's approach became increasingly uncompromising during the subsequent two decades.[21] Other authors have put forward similar claims, arguing that judicial review of national measures has become 'more intensive' and 'pervasive', notably due to the increasingly strict application of proportionality analysis.[22] The upshot appears to be that Member State interests are no longer sufficiently protected and that, ever more frequently, concerns of market integration trump national regulatory autonomy.

The present findings tell a different story. The intensity with which the Court of Justice exercises free movement review has not become stricter over the years. In fact, there has been a development in the opposite direction. When examining the legality of Member State action, the ECJ opts for lenient forms of control in a growing number of cases.[23] This does not mean that strict review approaches have disappeared from free movement adjudication; they continue to mark an important part of the Court's case law.[24] However, overall, the national margin of appreciation appears to be expanding. For Member States, protecting their interests has become easier rather than harder.

B. Decentralized Judicial Review

A similar trend can be observed in relation to national courts. The sample shows 43 cases in which judicial review is decentralized. This includes any of the four types: full decentralization, adoption, guidelines, or tendency. Looking at all

[19] Without being a statistical outlier.

[20] Barnard (n 4) (36 ECJ rulings between 1984 and 2004).

[21] ibid 296. This finding may be due to the survey's exclusive focus on ECJ rulings in which Member State acts were found to be in breach of EU free movement law (which tend to involve stricter forms of scrutiny), not all free movement cases for the given years.

[22] Paul Craig and Gráinne de Búrca, *EU Law* (6th edn, Oxford University Press 2015) 554; Dorte Sindbjerg Martinsen, 'Judicial Policy-Making and Europeanization: The Proportionality of National Control and Administrative Discretion' (2011) 18 Journal of European Public Policy 944, 948–49; Jotte Mulder, *Social Legitimacy in the Internal Market* (Hart 2018) 66.

[23] For a more critical assessment, see Lars Klenk, *Die Grenzen der Grundfreiheiten* (Mohr Siebeck 2019) 382.

[24] See, for instance, Case C-531/07 *Fachverband der Buch- und Medienwirtschaft* [2009] ECLI:EU:C:2009:276 and Case C-202/11 *Las* [2013] ECLI:EU:C:2013:239.

preliminary references on free movement rights (160)—national courts play no role in infringement proceedings—this yields a mean decentralization rate of 26.88 per cent. Compared with the margin of appreciation, the ratio of complete as opposed to partial deference is inversed. The ECJ fully decentralizes judicial review to the national judiciary only 6 times, while passing down review tasks alongside guidelines and/or a tendency on 34 occasions.

In comparison with the margin of appreciation, the case law is more consistent in terms of language. The ECJ usually makes explicit not only if it hands review tasks over to the national court—by stating that 'it is for the national court to determine', 'ascertain', 'decide', or 'assess' a certain issue—but also which ones.[25] For the referring judge, this has the consequence that they will, on the basis of the preliminary ruling, know fairly precisely *whether* they have to determine parts of the justification and proportionality assessment autonomously and, if so, *what* it is that they have to assess. (This is not to say that they will always find it easy to perform this task.[26])

Looking at the development over time, we see a fairly constant and steep increase (Figure 2.2). In 1974, national courts were not asked once to assess, or help assess, the justification or proportionality of Member State action. Between 1979 and 1989 the rate of decentralized judicial review hovered around 20 per cent, with 2 to 3 cases per year delegated to national judges. By the late 1990s, it was already approaching 30 per cent (7 cases in 1999 and 2004). In 2013, the ECJ deferred to Member State courts in two out of five free movement disputes (14 cases).

The figures indicate that national courts have come to play an important role in free movement adjudication. Increasingly, they are made to review Member State acts autonomously, or semi-autonomously, fulfilling a role which the ECJ used to occupy. The Court of Justice continues to exercise centralized judicial review in a substantial number of cases. This phenomenon is unlikely to ever disappear completely given the need to ensure the predictability and uniformity of EU law,

[25] There is one exception to this. At times, the ECJ will set out requirements for a Member State act but will leave it open whether these are met, without explicitly asking the referring court to assess the matter. One could call this 'decentralizing through vagueness': the lack of a conclusive outcome in the Court of Justice's ruling forces the national judge to autonomously review the measure. Numerically speaking, this phenomenon is limited, though, affecting only five cases in the entire sample: see, for example, Cases 110 and 111/78 *Van Wesemael* [1979] ECLI:EU:C:1979:8 and Case C-379/87 *Groener* [1989] ECLI:EU:C:1989:599.

[26] The Sunday trading saga is a famous illustration of difficulties in this respect. The reference of the House of Lords in Case C-169/91 *Stoke-on-Trent* [1992] ECLI:EU:C:1992:519 laid bare that the instructions the ECJ had given in the earlier Case C-145/88 *Torfaen Borough Council* [1989] ECLI:EU:C:1989:593 confused the British courts: they were asked to examine whether the 'restrictive effect' of the Sunday trading ban on the free movement of goods exceeded 'the effects intrinsic to trade rules'. '[O]n what criteria and by reference to what, if any, factual or other evidence' were national judges to determine this, wondered the House of Lords? For more recent examples, see Case C-478/07 *Budějovický Budvar* [2009] ECLI:EU:C:2011:605 and Case C-333/14 *Scotch Whisky Association* [2015] ECLI:EU:C:2015:845.

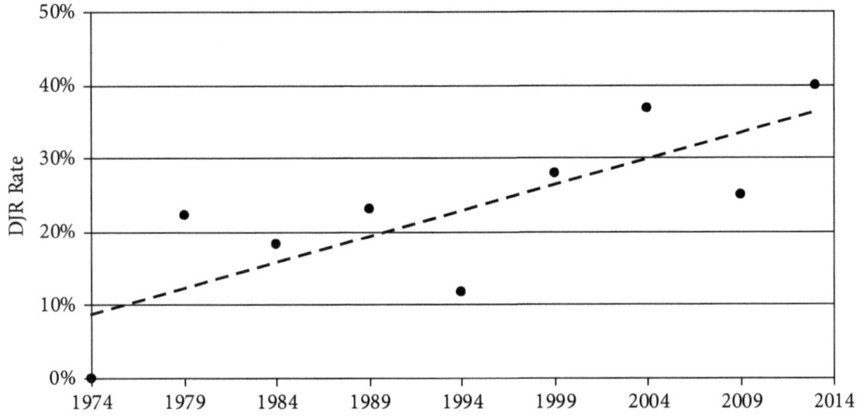

Figure 2.2 Decentralized Judicial Review in Free Movement Cases, 1974–2013
Notes: Percentage of cases with decentralized judicial review in all cases in which a national measure falls within the scope of at least one free movement right (preliminary references only). Trendline serves interpretative purposes only and does not make predictive claims about in-between years.

which will make it necessary for the Court to render centralized decisions on certain legal and regulatory questions arising in the internal market. Yet, its urge to determine the legality of every Member State act and, thus, every aspect of free movement law appears to have decreased. Free movement adjudication has become considerably more decentralized.

Interestingly, Member State courts are, among national institutions, the true 'winners' in terms of decision-making power. The likelihood of the ECJ decentralizing judicial review in free movement cases is higher than that of it granting a margin of appreciation. Also, deference to national courts has grown more steeply over time than deference to national political actors. Note, however, that this victory might not be as sweet as it sounds—for national judges, it also comes with an increasing number of responsibilities. The shift from centralized to decentralized judicial review means that Member State courts are no longer given a fully-fledged analysis of the legality of the national measure. Instead, they have to, partly or completely, perform that analysis themselves. Studies have shown that national judges desire as detailed guidance as possible from the ECJ.[27] This is understandable: the basic premise of the preliminary reference mechanism is that they can reach out to the Court of Justice, the 'expert contact' for problems relating to EU law, if they need help. The decentralization of review tasks pushes forward the idea

[27] Juan A Mayoral, 'In the CJEU Judges Trust: A New Approach in the Judicial Construction of Europe' (2017) 55 Journal of Common Market Studies 551; Jasper Krommendijk, 'The Highest Dutch Courts and the Preliminary Ruling Procedure: Critically Obedient Interlocutors of the Court of Justice' (2019) 25 European Law Journal 1.

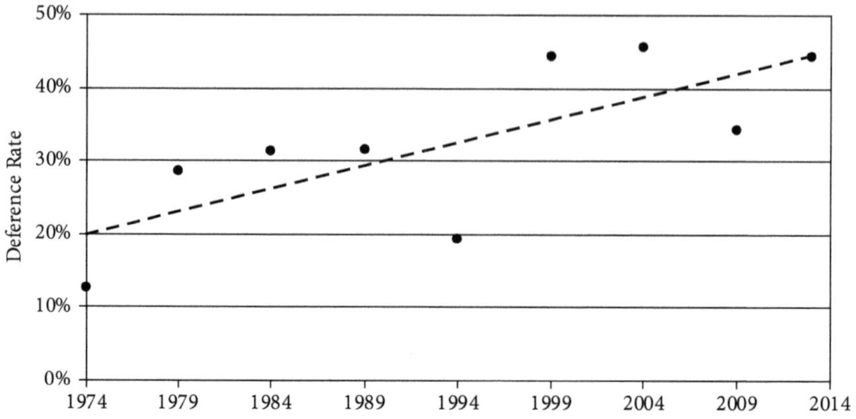

Figure 2.3 Deference in Free Movement Cases, 1974–2013

Notes: Percentage of cases in which the ECJ grants Member State authorities a margin of appreciation and/or decentralizes judicial review in all cases in which a national measure falls within the scope of at least one free movement right (infringement proceedings and preliminary references). Trendline serves interpretative purposes only and does not make predictive claims about in-between years.

of co-operation, often invoked in relation to Article 267 TFEU.[28] Judicial review of Member State acts becomes a joint endeavour, with national courts being forced to partake more actively.

C. The Turn Towards Deference

The true significance of deference in free movement adjudication only becomes apparent when we combine both parts of the analysis, that is, look at all cases in which the ECJ defers to national authorities by means of the margin of appreciation and/or decentralized judicial review. The data show a steep increase over time (Figure 2.3). In 1974, 12.50 per cent of free movement cases (1 out of 8) involved deference to national authorities of any sort. With the exception of one dip in 1994, this figure continuously rose during the subsequent three decades, surpassing 30 per cent in 1984 (5 out of 16) and 40 per cent in 1999 (12 out of 27). In 2004, the deference rate reached 45.71 per cent and was at 44.44 per cent in 2013 (16 out of 36).

[28] Case C-244/80 *Foglia (No 2)* [1981] ECLI:EU:C:1981:302, para 14; Case C-83/91 *Meilicke* [1992] ECLI:EU:C:1992:332, para 25; Case C-412/93 *Leclerc-Siplec* [1995] ECLI:EU:C:1995:26, para 12; Case C-415/93 *Bosman* [1995] ECLI:EU:C:1995:463, para 60.

The results suggest that free movement adjudication has undergone a change. While only one out of eight ECJ judgments used to be marked by deference 40 years ago, now almost every other one is. In other words: it has become nearly as likely to find rulings of the *Schindler* or *Familiapress* variety as those of the *Cassis de Dijon* type in the (electronic) European Court Reports. Deferential review, once a marginal phenomenon in the Court of Justice's free movement case law, has practically turned into the new standard form of scrutiny.

The relationship between deference and the passage of time appears to go even deeper. If we run a regression analysis with the year in which a case was decided as the independent variable and deference as the dependent variable, we find a statistically significant positive effect of the latter on the former.[29] This suggests that time has an impact on review behaviour: *when* a case was decided affects *if* the Court of Justice deferred to national authorities. The older free movement law grows, the higher the likelihood of judgments on free movement rights entailing some form of deference.

The findings demonstrate the importance of looking not just at the scope of the EU free movement rules but at the way in which free movement review is conducted. As was explained in Chapter 1, the four freedoms have been given an increasingly wide reading over time, leading to a broadening of the range of scenarios in which national laws are subjected to judicial review. This, quite plausibly, led to fears that the Court of Justice would absorb the decision-making powers of national institutions. The data show that although more Member State action falls into the scope of free movement law, this does not mean that the Court is doing more in substance. Whether the ECJ exercises free movement review is one thing; how it exercises this review is another.

II. A Changed Court

The turn towards deference means that the Court of Justice has gradually lowered the intensity with which it conducts judicial review of Member State action. This makes it easier for domestic legislation to pass free movement muster and results in national courts being involved more heavily in the review process. But the developments we see in the case law also have broader implications. They signal a transformation of the European Court and free movement law, which forces us to revisit some old assumptions concerning judicial activism, centralization, and the uniformity of EU law.

[29] A univariate logistic analysis between the year in which a case was decided and deference (coded as 0 = not granted, 1 = granted) indicates a positive (0.026) and statistically significant effect ($p < 0.05$). See, in addition, the effects of time on the margin of appreciation and decentralized judicial review individually described in Chapter 3 II B and Chapter 4 II F.

A. Judicial Restraint

It has become conventional wisdom that the ECJ has constantly 'seized the opportunities presented to it to enlarge its jurisdictional authority and power'.[30] This is the narrative of activism, and we have become accustomed to it since the beginning of the European integration project. Few, if any, observations on EU law have produced such an overwhelming consensus among academic and non-academic commentators, beyond the traditional frontiers of eurosceptics and euro-enthusiasts.[31] Nic Shuibhne has called this one of the two 'basic presumptions' about the ECJ: it is an 'activist court'.[32]

The now decades-long activism debate, resurfacing with astonishing regularity, has failed to provide robust answers as to what counts as activist. Is it creating legal rules (as opposed to interpreting them)? Is it engaging in politics (as opposed to law)? Is it relying on *effet utile* (as opposed to traditional methods of interpretation)? Or is it rendering judgments supported by society (as opposed to those which are not)?[33] What is clear, though, is that the label amounts to a charge, a charge of doing too much. When accused of being activist, the ECJ is criticized for overstepping the boundary of what is considered to be legitimate for a court, however this boundary may be drawn.

With all the activism talk, a parallel phenomenon has entered EU law largely unnoticed: restraint.[34] Although restraint can be just as challenging to pin down conceptually as activism,[35] it is, at a basic level, present when a court does little or less than it could. Doing little, or 'not doing',[36] has never been thought of as a defining feature of the ECJ's behaviour. Yet, over the past two and a half decades, growing symptoms of such self-limitation have come to light, in free movement law and beyond. The narrowing down of the scope of Article 34 TFEU in *Keck and Mithouard*

[30] Karen J Alter, *Establishing the Supremacy of European Law* (Oxford University Press 2001) 37.

[31] See Jürgen Basedow, 'The Judge's Role in European Integration' in Hans Micklitz and Bruno de Witte (eds), *The European Court of Justice and the Autonomy of the Member States* (Intersentia 2012) 65; R Daniel Keleman, 'Judicialisation, Democracy and European Integration' (2013) 49 Representation 295, 297–98.

[32] Niamh Nic Shuibhne, *The Coherence of EU Free Movement Law* (Oxford University Press 2013) 1.

[33] To name but a few proposals: see Hjalte Rasmussen, *On Law and Policy in the European Court of Justice* (Nijhoff 1986) 93; Takis Tridimas, 'The Court of Justice and Judicial Activism' (1996) 21 European Law Review 199; Andreas Grimmel, 'Judicial Interpretation or Judicial Activism? The Legacy of Rationalism in the Studies of the European Court of Justice' (2012) 18 European Law Journal 518; Anthony Arnull, 'Judicial Activism and the Court of Justice: How Should Academics Respond?' Maastricht Faculty of Law Working Paper 2012/3; Fabien Terpan and Sabine Saurugger, 'Assessing Judicial Activism of the CJEU the Case of the Court's Defence Procurement Rulings' (2018) 20 Journal of European Integration 1.

[34] An important exception is Renaud Dehousse, *The European Court of Justice: The Politics of Judicial Integration* (Macmillan 1998) 148.

[35] Richard Posner has, commenting on the American debate, called the notion of judicial self-restraint a 'chameleon'; see 'The Rise and Fall of Judicial Self-Restraint' (2012) 100 California Law Review 519, 520.

[36] In reference to Louis Brandeis who is reported to have said about his work at the US Supreme Court: 'The most important thing we do is not doing.'

is perhaps the best-known example.[37] But it is not the only one. The Court has introduced *de minimis* rules into its free movement jurisprudence, excluding national measures with 'too indirect and uncertain' effects on trade and economic activity from judicial scrutiny.[38] It has adopted a more cautious interpretation of EU citizens' rights regarding access to social benefits.[39] It has started to render minimalist rulings whose effects are narrowly tailored to the dispute at hand.[40] It shows greater willingness to declare preliminary references from national courts inadmissible.[41]

The margin of appreciation and decentralized judicial review are not just further expressions of this new-found restraint, they have become its most effective weapons. (This has to do with the limited success of the other activity-controlling techniques, an issue which will be examined in greater detail in Chapter 5.) The doctrines permit the ECJ to hand legal and regulatory decisions over to national institutions and, thus, to reduce its involvement in certain areas. The choice for deference represents a choice for exercising more limited control over Member State action. Just as it would be wrong to claim that this deferential posture has become the Court of Justice's sole *modus operandi*—we continue to find stricter, more 'hands-on' forms of review in a good many free movement cases—, it would be erroneous to ignore the profound changes which have taken place. Deferential review, which used to be no more than an exceptional occurrence, has come to form the basis for almost half of all free movement rulings. From a perspective of activism, this is unexpected. Not only does the ECJ not 'enlarge its power', it seems to shrink it of its own volition.

B. Decentralization

Intimately connected with the topic of activism is centralization. The integration process has led to a shift of decision-making powers from the national to the EU level. This increasing Europeanization is, for one thing, a simple matter of fact. More and more aspects of national law are determined by the EU. At the

[37] Case C-267/91 *Keck and Mithouard* [1993] ECLI:EU:C:1993:905.

[38] Case C-379/92 *Peralta* [1994] ECLI:EU:C:1994:296; Case C-418/93 *Semeraro Casa Uno* [1996] ECLI:EU:C:1996:242; Case C-190/98 *Graf* [2000] ECLI:EU:C:2000:49; Case C-256/06 *Jäger* [2008] ECLI:EU:C:2008:20.

[39] Case C-333/13 *Dano* [2014] ECLI:EU:C:2014:2358; Case C-67/14 *Alimanovic* [2015] ECLI:EU:C:2015:597.

[40] Daniel Sarmiento, 'Half a Case at a Time: Dealing with Judicial Minimalism at the European Court of Justice' in Monica Claes and others (eds), *Constitutional Conversations in Europe* (Intersentia 2013) 21.

[41] Tommaso Pavone and R Daniel Kelemen, 'The Evolving Judicial Politics of European Integration: The European Court of Justice and National Courts Revisited' (2019) 25 European Law Journal 1, 18; Nils Wahl and Luca Prete, 'The Gatekeepers of Article 267 TFEU: On Jurisdiction and Admissibility of References for Preliminary Rulings' (2018) 55 Common Market Law Review 511.

same time, it is perceived to be a matter of concern. The Union in general ('competence creep'[42]) and the ECJ in particular ('Stop the European Court of Justice'[43]) have been criticized for excessively taking decision-making powers away from the Member States. In free movement law, this argument has a long pedigree. Member States have bemoaned that the Court overstepped the legitimate boundaries of its role already around the time of *Cassis*.[44] More recently, the problem has become acute again with the application of the four freedoms to politically sensitive areas such as social security, higher education, and public health, which triggered painful conflicts with national legal orders.[45]

The margin of appreciation and decentralized judicial review demonstrate that constant centralization is not an inevitable consequence of the internal market project. Nor is it the sole direction it moves in. Both doctrines enable the ECJ to pass certain decisions down to Member State institutions, a possibility it is willingly making use of. The result is a decentralizing pull. What form of regulation is appropriate, which policy measures are effective, and how to reconcile economic freedom with social policy concerns are questions that are frequently not settled in Luxembourg anymore, but in Antwerp, Palermo, or Wrocław. The periphery decides instead of the centre.

The inevitable consequence of this decentralization is that the internal market and free movement law become, to a greater degree, 'infused' with national and, at times, even local practices and values.[46] Deference creates the normative space required for this.[47] The British government will be able to define, based on domestic moral attitudes, which types of pornography count as decent and which ones as obscene. A city council in North Rhine-Westphalia will determine, based on the sensitivities of its citizens, whether 'playing at killing' offends human dignity. And a first-instance criminal court in Luleå will end up, based on its view and understanding of the matter, striking the appropriate

[42] See Stephen Weatherill, 'Competence Creep and Competence Control' (2004) 23 Yearbook of European Law 1.

[43] Roman Herzog and Lüder Gerken, 'Stoppt den Europäischen Gerichtshof' *Frankfurter Allgemeine Zeitung* (8 September 2008).

[44] See, in addition to Michel Debré's critique (n 1), the submission of the German government in Case 120/78 *Rewe-Zentral AG v Bundesmonopolverwaltung für Branntwein ('Cassis de Dijon')* [1979] ECLI:EU:C:1979:42.

[45] Peter Hilpold, 'Hochschulzugang und Unionsbürgerschaft: Das Urteil des EuGH vom 7. 7. 2005 in der Rechtssache C-147/03, Kommission gegen Österreich' (2005) 16 Europäische Zeitschrift für Wirtschaftsrecht 647; Gareth Davies, 'The Price of Letting Courts Value Solidarity: The Judicial Role in Liberalizing Welfare' in Malcolm Ross and Yuri Borgmann-Prebil (eds), *Promoting Solidarity in the European Union* (OUP 2010) 106; Floris de Witte, 'Sex, Drugs & EU Law: The Recognition of Moral and Ethical Diversity in EU Law' (2013) 50 Common Market Law Review 1545. For a broader political critique of the ECJ's case law on free movement rights, see David Cameron, 'Free Movement Needs to be Less Free' *Financial Times* (London, 26 November 2013).

[46] Michèle Finck, *Subnational Authorities in EU Law* (Oxford University Press 2017) 110.

[47] Boško Tripković and Jan Zglinski, 'Contestation and Accommodation: Constitutional and Private Law Pluralism(s) in the EU' in Lucila de Almeida and others (eds), *The Transformation of Economic Law: Essays in Honour of Hans-W Micklitz* (Hart 2019) 297.

balance between environmental protection and free trade when it comes to restricting the use of jet skis.

C. Diversity

A direct result of decentralization is diversity. What is and what is not compatible with free movement law ceases to receive a single answer, valid for the whole of the internal market. It is determined at the national level for the specific national setting. As a result, it is possible that the very same issue will be approached in different ways across the continent (potentially even within a single Member State), depending on the views prevailing in a given parliament, agency, or courtroom.

At a regulatory level, this means that the likelihood of Member States adopting different laws and solutions increases.[48] When national legislatures are given the freedom to decide whether and how to pursue certain policies, outcomes will almost inevitably vary. Note that this holds not only true for decisions involving thick normative judgments, such as the regulation of gambling, obscenity, or abortion, where divergences will result from persisting religious, moral, and political differences across Europe. It can also concern supposedly less contentious, technical matters. Regulatory decisions on product safety features, the prohibition of potentially dangerous food supplements, and the legality of cultivating genetically modified crops will, in addition to hard factual data (impact assessments, expert opinions, etc), also be the function of a polity's trust in the market and its willingness to expose citizens to risks. For economic actors, this translates into higher regulatory burdens as they have to adjust their production processes and marketing strategies to each domestic setting.

At an adjudicative level, decentralization has the consequence that the free movement rules can potentially end up meaning different things in different places. Consider the first phase of the Sunday trading saga, where the ECJ deferred the decision on whether the social benefits of trading bans outweighed the economic costs on trade to the British and French judiciary. Judges in both countries came to opposite conclusions; even within United Kingdom, contradictory rulings emerged.[49] The result was that restrictions on shop opening hours were compatible with EU free movement law in some places and not in others. These divergences

[48] Even under the strict *Cassis*-style review approach regulatory differences can arise as the ECJ will sometimes find the justifications that national governments put forward for restricting freedom of movement convincing; only full EU harmonization can entirely eliminate this possibility. Nonetheless, a lower intensity of judicial scrutiny has a direct impact on survival rates of Member State laws, making it easier for them to pass free movement review. For a similar connection in the US constitutional context compare the findings in Winkler (n 7) and Robert C Farrell, 'Successful Rational Basis Claims in the Supreme Court from the 1971 Term through *Romer v. Evans*' (1999) 32 Indiana Law Review 357.

[49] Malcolm A Jarvis, *The Application of EC Law by National Courts: The Free Movement of Goods* (Clarendon Press 1998) 175 et seq. For a more recent example, see the diverging positions of English and Scottish courts on the proportionality of the UK prohibition of tobacco sales from vending machines, see Malcolm A Jarvis, 'The Proportionality Test: Constructive Dialogue between the English

are the natural consequence of letting different courts decide on questions as open-textured as the proportionality of legislation.

This is no minor deal for a legal order centrally premised on the uniform application of its rules. The ECJ has emphasized on many occasions that EU rules must be 'applied uniformly by national courts'.[50] As Mancini and Keeling observe:

> And no one should be mistaken about the need for such uniformity. It is not just a question of achieving an aesthetic symmetry that is pleasing to the eye; uniformity of interpretation and application is vital for the continued existence of the European Community. Suppose, for example, that [Article 267 TFEU] did not exist and that the German courts held that [Article 157 TFEU], laying down the principle of equal pay for men and women workers, had direct effect, but that the courts in the other Member States came to the opposite conclusion; the result would be a crippling, competitive disadvantage for German manufacturers. Or suppose that in relation to the free movement of goods the French and Italian courts held that restrictive measures applicable without distinction to domestic and imported goods were caught by [Article 34 TFEU], but that the British and German courts took the view that only discriminatory measures were prohibited; the resulting distortions in competition would shake the very foundations of the Community.[51]

Mancini and Keeling's observations stem from a different time, one before the shift towards justification and proportionality review in free movement law had become apparent. But it is easy to restate their point in a more contemporary form: as it becomes the responsibility of national courts to decide whether particular measures are justified and proportionate, they ultimately determine the content of the free movement rules. Different courts will strike the balance between regulation and deregulation, or free movement and social policy concerns, differently. As a consequence, the meaning of free movement law will also vary. The only way out of this is if the ECJ, as it did in the Sunday trading cases, eventually renders a centralized decision on the given problem, that is, states that a certain type of legislation is or is not proportionate.[52] Otherwise, the turn to deference means just that: a partial departure from the uniform application of EU law.

and Scottish Courts' in Panos Koutrakos, Niamh Nic Shuibhne, and Phil Syrpis (eds), *Exceptions from EU Free Movement Law: Derogation, Justification and Proportionality* (Hart 2016) 265.

[50] Case 314/85 *Foto-Frost* [1987] ECLI:EU:C:1987:452, para 15; Cases C-143/88 and 92/89 *Zuckerfabrik Süderdithmarschen* [1991] ECLI:EU:C:1991:65, paras 25–26; Opinion 2/13 *Accession of the EU to the ECHR* [2014] EU:C:2014:2454, para 174; Case C-284/16 *Achmea* [2018] ECLI:EU:C:2018:158, para 35.

[51] Federico Mancini and David Keeling, 'From *CILFIT* to *ERT*: the Constitutional Challenge facing the European Court' (1991) 11 Yearbook of European Law 1, 2.

[52] *Stoke-on-Trent* (n 26).

III. A Changed Context

In light of these far-reaching consequences, the question arises as to why the Court of Justice has come to act in a more deferential manner. What has caused its gradual retreat from control over Member State action? What explains its turn towards deference in free movement law? This is a complex matter, requiring a certain degree of speculation. Yet, it is clear that it would be insufficient to look for reasons only within the ECJ itself. It is not just the Court that has changed, but the context in which it operates. Four decades separate cases such as *Dassonville* and *Cassis de Dijon*, which were decided in the 1970s, from the last free movement rulings captured in the study, rendered in the mid-2010s. During this period, many developments—legal, political, and institutional—have taken place in the EU. They are likely to have contributed to the changes that we can observe in the case law.

A. Maturing of European Legal Order

The body of EU law has substantially grown over the past decades. Not only is there a greater number of European rules (both legislative and judge-made), there is also a greater understanding of what they entail. In light of this maturing of the European legal order, the Court may be inclined to engage in deferential forms of review, especially in areas with a well-developed jurisprudential heritage such as free movement law. Where the central questions are settled and the big legal battles are fought, it may, in the eyes of the ECJ, appear safe to give Member States more autonomy.

The free movement of goods is a case in point. From early on, the scope of Article 34 TFEU was given a broad reading, leading to a high caseload which enabled the Court of Justice to lay down the basic dos and don'ts. Many of these principles have meanwhile settled and been internalized by national institutions and economic actors.[53] (This does not mean that they are always complied with.) Forty years have passed since *Dassonville* and *Cassis de Dijon*; even subsequent innovations like *Keck* are, by now, in their mid-20s. Fundamental doctrinal problems have not ceased to arise in the case law—the last one perhaps being how to deal with restrictions on the use of goods[54]—but they have become rarer. No one, to come back to

[53] As perhaps most clearly evidenced by the fact that openly protectionist rules, once a common occurrence, have practically disappeared; see notably the dramatic decrease in directly discriminatory national laws discussed in Chapter 3 (n 96). This has gone along with a change in the types of cases which the ECJ receives, which tend to involve more plausible justifications than some of the earlier disputes decided under the free movement provisions; see Stephen Weatherill, 'The Beauty and the Beast: Is EU Internal Market Law "Over-Constitutionalised"?' (forthcoming).

[54] *Commission v Italy (Italian Trailers)* (n 10); Case C-142/05 *Mickelsson and Roos* [2009] ECLI:EU:C:2009:336.

Mancini and Keeling's example, fights over the question as to whether Article 34 TFEU has direct effect anymore; whether equally applicable technical standards are caught by the provision; or, to add to this list, whether national restrictions can be justified on grounds going beyond those listed in Article 36 TFEU and need to comply with the principle of proportionality.

As this maturing process advances, the incentive for the European Court to take a hands-on approach in relation to new questions concerning free movement law declines. This is the idea of marginal benefits: the added value of analysing in depth every increasingly more specific problem about the scope and limits of the four freedoms ceases to outweigh the costs for the Court in terms of time and resources spent.[55] This is not to say that a decision on the proportionality of each new national betting law, product ban, or advertising restriction is not politically significant. Legally, however, these have become questions of detail, shaping the content of the free movement provisions at its fringes only.

The maturing of free movement law is likely to affect the ECJ's behaviour particularly in relation to national courts.[56] It is common in well-established legal orders that high courts will not settle every problem themselves. They will feel confident—and, due to their workload, forced—to share the task of interpreting and applying the law with the lower judiciary, intervening only punctually to provide guidance on the most important issues. The rise in decentralized judicial review suggests that the Court of Justice believes that it can increasingly afford to do that: having clarified the central Member State obligations in sufficient detail, it can outsource some of the more specific and context-dependent questions relating to the application of the four freedoms to national courts. Note that the risks connected with this strategy are relatively small. The decision of the referring court on whether a specific piece of legislation is proportionate is, regardless of the outcome, unlikely to 'shake the foundations' of free movement law. Also, Member State courts have proven, as will be discussed below, to be diligent enforcers of EU rules and ECJ rulings. At the same time, the benefits can be substantial. National judges will often have a better understanding of the domestic legal and socio-economic setting, which will lead to a more accurate assessment of the questions connected with the justification and proportionality of the Member State law under scrutiny.

[55] See Alec Stone Sweet, *The Judicial Construction of Europe* (Oxford University Press 2004) 140. For a similar argument voiced from within the Court in a different area of EU law, see Case C-338/95 *Wiener* [1997] ECLI:EU:C:1997:552, Opinion of AG Jacobs, paras 8 et seq.

[56] See Koen Lenaerts, 'The Court's Outer and Inner Selves: Exploring the External and Internal Legitimacy of the European Court of Justice' in Maurice Adams and others (eds), *Judging Europe's Judges* (Hart 2013) 42. For a similar observation, couched in terms of 'familiarity', see Gareth Davies, 'Abstractness and Concreteness in the Preliminary Reference Procedure' in Niamh Nic Shuibhne (ed), *Regulating the Internal Market* (Edward Elgar 2006) 217.

B. Positive Integration

A second reason for the ECJ's restraint is likely to lie in the growth of EU harmonization. The internal market was always designed as a two-engine project. The four freedoms were inserted into the Treaties as 'negative' safeguards, created to prevent Member States from maintaining or enacting new protectionist legislation that obstructed cross-border economic activity. The real regulatory rapprochement was, however, meant to be accomplished by other means: through the gradual adoption of common European rules, or 'positive integration', which would do away with the diverging laws and regulatory practices at the national level.

A common explanation—and justification—for the ECJ's activist stance in the 1960s and 1970s is that the European political process had stalled.[57] Member States made no visible effort to remove barriers to freedom of movement and the Community legislature did not provide an effective counterweight.[58] Work in the Council of Ministers had been rendered difficult due to the 'empty chair' crisis provoked by de Gaulle, which resulted in the 1966 Luxembourg Compromise, an agreement to deviate from the initially envisaged mode of qualified majority voting and stick to unanimity on all questions deemed sensitive by at least one Member State. The Commission endeavoured to be a constructive force in this situation but only succeeded to a limited extent.[59] With the engine of positive integration seriously underperforming, the Court of Justice's bold interpretation of the four freedoms, especially the free movement of goods, was crucial to pushing forward the internal market programme.[60]

Things changed with the adoption of the Single European Act in 1986. In what was the first major revision of the Treaties, the Member States decided to create a new competence norm for harmonization (now, Article 114 TFEU), move from consensus to qualified majority voting, and set 1992 as the deadline for completing the internal market. In parallel, a 'new approach' to technical harmonization was announced.[61] Even if the time frame ultimately turned out to be unrealistic, the Single European Act proved inspirational: the amendments unblocked the European legislative process, prompting a veritable wave of harmonization.

[57] Joseph HH Weiler, 'The Transformation of Europe' (1991) 100 Yale Law Journal 2403.

[58] Stone Sweet (n 55) 109.

[59] On free movement, see notably Directive 70/50 on the abolition of measures which have an effect equivalent to quantitative restrictions on imports [1970] OJ L13/29.

[60] The Court itself hints at the connection between legislative inertia and judicial activism in the *Cassis* ruling, where it emphasizes 'the absence of common rules relating to the production and marketing of alcohol' and points out that 'a proposal for a regulation submitted to the Council by the Commission on 7 December 1976' had, over two years later, not yet 'received the Council's approval' (para 8).

[61] Resolution on a new approach to technical harmonization and standards [1985] OJ C136/1. For a discussion, see Jacques Pelkmans, 'The New Approach to Technical Harmonization and Standardization' (1987) 25 Journal of Common Market Studies 249.

Internal market legislation did not only grow in numbers, but in scope and depth.[62] The Community's activities expanded to fields such as consumer law, environmental protection, and public health. The standards adopted at the European level were often higher than those in many Member States.

Subsequent decades solidified this development. Despite periodical changes in policy priorities and regulatory approaches, the Commission has actively pursued the internal market agenda,[63] assisted by the ECJ's generous reading of Article 114 TFEU[64] and the constitutional adjustments of the thresholds for qualified majority voting in the Council.[65] The result has been a steady increase in EU harmonization as well as the adoption of a variety of flanking measures, including prior notification obligations of new technical standards,[66] the designation of specialized contact points in each Member State,[67] and the introduction of a non-judicial dispute resolution mechanism for traders ('SOLVIT').[68]

This advancement of positive integration has two consequences. Institutionally, it means that the EU legislature takes the driver's seat when it comes to internal market governance. The ECJ is less essential for protecting European interests. This does not mean that it is out of the picture: the Court will be involved in the interpreting of the harmonizing measures. However, its strict control over Member State laws by means of the free movement rights stops being vital for the functioning of the internal market.[69] Doctrinally, EU secondary legislation removes disputes in sectors which have been fully harmonized from the Court's free movement docket. Cases on geographical indications of spirits,[70] restrictions on

[62] Dehousse (n 34) 155.

[63] To name but a few initiatives: 'Action Plan for the Single Market' SEC (1997) 1 final; 'An Internal Market Strategy for Services' COM (2000) 888 final; 'Single Market Act: Twelve Levers to Boost Growth and Strengthen Confidence' COM (2011) 206 final; 'Upgrading the Single Market: More Opportunities for People and Business' COM (2015) 550 final.

[64] Stephen Weatherill, 'The Limits of Legislative Harmonization Ten Years after *Tobacco Advertising*: How the Court's Case Law has Become a Drafting Guide' (2011) 12 German Law Journal 827.

[65] The current rules are laid down in Art 16(4)–(5) TEU and Art 238(3) TFEU.

[66] Directive 2015/1535 laying down a procedure for the provision of information in the field of technical regulations and of rules on Information Society services [2015] OJ L241/1. There are plans to extent the notification obligations to the area of services: see Proposal for a Directive on the enforcement of the Directive 2006/123/EC on services in the internal market COM(2016) 821 final.

[67] Decision 3052/95 establishing a procedure for the exchange of information on national measures derogating from the principle of the free movement of goods within the Community [1995] OJ L321/1; Regulation 764/2008 laying down procedures relating to the application of certain national technical rules to products lawfully marketed in another Member State [2008] OJ L218/21; replaced by Regulation 2019/515 on the mutual recognition of goods lawfully marketed in another Member State [2019] OJ L91/1. See also the 'points of single contact' for service providers established in Directive 2006/123/EC (n 66).

[68] Commission Recommendation on principles for using 'SOLVIT': The Internal Market Problem Solving Network [2001] OJ L331/79; now Commission Recommendation on the principles governing SOLVIT [2013] OJ L249/10.

[69] Miguel Poiares Maduro, *We the Court* (Hart 1998) ch 4; Joseph HH Weiler, 'The Constitution of the Common Market Place: Text and Context in the Evolution of the Free Movement of Goods' in Paul Craig and Gráinne de Búrca (eds), *The Evolution of EU Law* (1st edn, Oxford University Press 1999) 371.

[70] Case C-44/17 *Klotz* [2018] ECLI:EU:C:2018:415.

genetically modified organisms,[71] and bans of menthol cigarettes[72]—which would have been decided on the basis of the four freedoms some decades ago—are now all governed by EU regulatory instruments which set out, in relative detail, the rights and obligations of producers and traders. This, tellingly, includes *Cassis de Dijon* which would, were the same facts brought before the Court today, be decided based on Regulation 110/2008, not Article 34 TFEU.[73] Even in fields which have been only partly harmonized, judicial review tools like proportionality analysis and the margin of appreciation become less important.[74] Where detailed written rules are available, the ECJ can rely on more traditional adjudicative methods to solve disputes, such as interpreting the wording of the provision or analysing the legislature's intent behind a rule.[75]

C. Workload

Further, there is the issue of workload. As is well-known, the Court of Justice's caseload is high.[76] Long gone are the days when, so legend has it, you would hear champagne bottles popping in the hallways of the Court as the first preliminary references arrived. Over the years, the number of cases brought before the ECJ has skyrocketed, a development driven in particular by the growing reliance on the Article 267 TFEU mechanism by national courts and the enlargement of the European Union.[77] While being in the double digits throughout the 1960s and only marginally higher during most of the 1970s, it surpassed 300 in 1981 and 400 already four years later.[78] By the turn of the millennium, the 600 mark was reached.

[71] Case C-165/08 *Commission v Poland (Genetically Modified Organisms)* [2009] ECLI:EU:C:2009:473.

[72] Case C-358/14 *Poland v Parliament and Council (Menthol Cigarettes)* [2016] ECLI:EU:C:2016:323.

[73] Stephen Weatherill, 'Did *Cassis de Dijon* Make a Difference?' in Catherine Barnard, Albertina Albors-Llorens, and Brigitte Leucht (eds), *Cassis de Dijon: 40 Years On* (Bloomsbury forthcoming).

[74] Bradley W Miller, 'Proportionality's Blind Spot: "Neutrality" and Political Philosophy' in Grant Huscroft, Bradley W Miller, and Grégoire CN Webber (eds), *Proportionality and the Rule of Law: Rights, Justification, Reasoning* (Cambridge University Press 2014) 179; Mattias Kumm, 'The Idea of Socratic Contestation and the Right to Justification: The Point of Rights-Based Proportionality Review' (2010) 4 Law and Ethics of Human Rights 140, 150.

[75] This point is explored in greater detail in Chapter 5 II A 2.

[76] Scholars have proposed a variety of solutions over the years, ranging from creating regional EU courts to removing the possibility to submit preliminary references for lower-instance Member State courts: see Jean P Jacqué and Joseph HH Weiler, 'On the Road to European Union—A New Judicial Architecture: An Agenda for the Intergovernmental Conference' (1990) 27 Common Market Law Review 185; Hjalte Rasmussen, 'Remedying the Crumbling EC Judicial System' (2000) 37 Common Market Law Review 1071; Jan Komárek, 'In the Court(s) we Trust? On the Need for Hierarchy and Differentiation in the Preliminary Ruling Procedure' (2007) 32 European Law Review 467.

[77] Thomas de la Mare and Catherine Donnelly, 'Preliminary References and EU Legal Integration: Evolution and Stasis' in Paul Craig and Gráinne de Búrca (eds), *The Evolution of EU Law* (Oxford University Press 2011) 363.

[78] See the analysis in Dehousse (n 34) 163, who compiles the data from the ECJ's Annual Reports of Judicial Activity.

Recent years brought a further increase, with the latest figures approaching 850 incoming cases *per annum*.[79]

Courts are, as Neil Komesar has so forcefully argued, institutions with limited resources, especially when it comes to time and people.[80] Consequently, increases in workload pose serious challenges, more than in other branches of government. At the ECJ, this became particularly visible during the late 1980s and early 1990s, when the average time for the delivery of rulings in preliminary reference proceedings reached two years. Institutional reforms of the European judiciary provided some relief. In 1989, the General Court—or, then, Court of First Instance—was created to help process direct actions against EU measures; its number of judges has recently been doubled in light of the growth of litigation in areas such as state aid, competition law, and intellectual property.[81] Some years later, the Civil Service Tribunal was established to handle EU staff matters (and has, in the meantime, been dissolved again[82]). In addition, there have been some internal refurbishments at the ECJ itself, notably in relation to its rules of procedure.[83] The establishing of, and increasing reliance on, the chamber system has enabled the Court to dispose of run-of-the-mill cases in smaller bodies of five or three judges.[84] Moreover, the possibility of disposing of cases by reasoned order[85] or without opinions of Advocates General[86] was introduced.

Despite these changes, it is evident that the ECJ continues to operate at maximum capacity or, more likely, beyond it. It has become normal to read in each new Annual Report of Judicial Activity that yet another record number of incoming cases has been reached, often coupled with concerned remarks about the

[79] Court of Justice of the European Union, Annual Report 2018, available at < curia.europa.eu/jcms/upload/docs/application/pdf/2019-04/ra_pan_2018_en.pdf >.

[80] Neil Komesar, *Law's Limits* (Cambridge University Press 2001) 35. See also, with a focus on the US Supreme Court, Andrew Coan's *Rationing the Constitution: How Judicial Capacity Shapes Supreme Court Decision-Making* (Harvard University Press 2019).

[81] The reform is the result of a lobbying campaign of the Court of Justice, which in 2014 warned that the situation in relation to the General Court's workload was becoming increasingly 'serious', with the number of cases pending approaching 1,600 (it currently stands at around 1,300) and claims for damages being brought as a result of the General Court's failure to adjudicate within a reasonable time; see the observations of V Skouris, then-President of the ECJ, submitted to the Chairman of COREPER (Committee of the Permanent Representatives of the Governments of the Member States to the European Union), available at < data.consilium.europa.eu/doc/document/ST-14448-2014-REV-1/en/pdf >.

[82] Its responsibilities were reallocated to the General Court.

[83] The last major change was the 2012 recasting of the Court's Rules of Procedure which was made 'primarily', as Press Release No 122/12 explains, 'to adapt to the changes in its caseload'; available at <curia.europa.eu/jcms/upload/docs/application/pdf/2012-10/cp120122en.pdf>.

[84] Only cases which are of particular 'difficulty or importance' are assigned to the Grand Chamber (Art 60(1) Rules of Procedure) or those in which a Member State or an EU institution is party to the proceedings and requests so (Art 16(3) Statute).

[85] Art 99 Rules of Procedure (for situations 'where a question referred to the Court for a preliminary ruling is identical to a question on which the Court has already ruled, where the reply to such a question may be clearly deduced from existing case law or where the answer to the question referred for a preliminary ruling admits of no reasonable doubt').

[86] Art 20(5) Statute (where case 'raises no new point of law').

functioning of the Union's *fabrique du droit*.[87] Indeed, not much imagination is required to picture the significant impact which the change from having 7 judges decide around 50 cases per year to 28 judges dealing with almost 850 would have on the operation of the Court.

This oversized docket is likely to contribute to the rise of deference in free movement adjudication. As explained, the number of cases on the four freedoms has, in line with a general trend in EU law, significantly increased over the past decades.[88] This is, in large part, due to the extension of the scope of free movement rights, which incentivizes legal challenges against unwanted regulation. It could, as some have argued, equally be the result of a more general change in mentality towards litigation in Europe.[89] In addition, the types of questions the ECJ is confronted with have become more complex. Due to the spread of adjudicative techniques like proportionality analysis, free movement disputes nowadays often involve difficult factual and normative problems. This quantitative and qualitative expansion of responsibilities puts pressure on the European judges. The Court, quite simply, may have reached the limits of what it can do. Being increasingly unable to examine every Member State act in depth, it is forced to choose which issues to focus on. It needs to distinguish between matters that require its full attention (and will, consequently, be subjected to substantive review) and those which can be managed in a more hands-off manner.

D. Compliance and Trust

Given that EU law lacks the enforcement machinery available to domestic legal orders, its effectiveness crucially depends on implementation by national authorities. This has not always been a given, certainly not at the time of *Dassonville* and *Cassis de Dijon*. Unforgotten are the open refusals of some Member States to comply with European rules, or the clashes between the ECJ and national high courts about the doctrines of supremacy and direct effect which lasted from the 1960s until, in some cases, the late-1980s.[90] Karen Alter sums up the situation in the early days of the European project as follows:

> The Treaty of Rome envisioned that the Common Market would be complete by 1970. Instead by 1970 the process of European integration was at

[87] The Annual Report 2014 recognizes the EU judiciary's 'good performance' but warns against 'the risk of the system becoming clogged up in the future'; the 'constant workload' may 'compromise [the EU courts'] effectiveness'. Similarly, the Annual Report 2018 highlights the 'record number' of cases brought and closed, but emphasizes 'the need for measures to relieve the Court of Justice'.

[88] Even if there is significant variation between the freedoms: while, for instance, the number of cases on the free movement of workers and services has increased over the years, disputes on Art 34 TFEU have practically vanished from the ECJ's docket.

[89] R Daniel Keleman, *Eurolegalism: The Transformation of Law and Regulation in the European Union* (Harvard University Press 2011).

[90] Alter (n 30).

> a virtual standstill, and national barriers to trade were rampant. It was clear to all that states were not being held accountable to their obligations under European law.[91]

Compliance is a complex topic which has received greater attention in EU literature only in recent years.[92] One central problem is that it is hard to identify.[93] There is only little readily available information on the compliance record of national institutions.[94] Even where data is accessible, it frequently only constitutes one part—not necessarily the most important—of the story: official accounts, typically focusing on the adoption, withdrawal, or notification of domestic legislation, frequently fail to adequately represent 'street-level' compliance, that is, whether European law is accurately applied in day-to-day operations.[95] Despite these obstacles, by now a considerable number of investigations have been conducted on different aspects of Member State compliance. As a consequence, the question of how EU law operates at the national level is, even if some (important) gaps in our understanding remain, no longer a 'black hole'.

As regards national legislatures, much research has focused on the transposition of directives. It has shown that compliance rates in this area are high: they average over 90 per cent and have in some years reached 98 per cent, with internal market directives having a particularly good chance of being transposed.[96] Studies on infringement proceedings have yielded similar results. It has been revealed that Member States often abide by the Commission's reasoned opinions in the pre-litigation stage and, once found to be in breach of EU law by the Court of Justice, tend to implement the ruling, even if with a delay. The share of infringement proceedings resulting in the imposition of penalties for non-compliance with ECJ rulings, an option introduced in the Treaty of Maastricht,

[91] ibid 212.

[92] For a small selection of the burgeoning literature: see Tanja Börzel, 'Non-Compliance in the European Union: Pathology or Statistical Artefact?' (2001) 8 Journal of European Public Policy 803; Lisa Conant, *Justice Contained: Law and Politics in the European Union* (Cornell University Press 2002); Diana Panke, 'The European Court of Justice as an Agent of Europeanization? Restoring Compliance with EU law' (2007) 14 Journal of European Public Policy 847; Gerda Falkner and Oliver Treib, 'Three Worlds of Compliance or Four: The EU-15 Compared to New Member States ' (2008) 46 Journal of Common Market Studies 293.

[93] Another challenge is that it is hard to explain: see Lisa Conant, 'Compliance and What EU Member States Make of It' in Marise Cremona (ed), *Compliance and the Enforcement of EU Law* (Oxford University Press 2012) 3.

[94] Two useful resources are the Commission's scoreboards on Member State compliance with EU law (for Internal Market Affairs, see < ec.europa.eu/internal_market/scoreboard >) and the National Decisions Database of the Association of the Councils of State and Supreme Administrative Jurisdictions of the European Union, which contains around 30,000 national court decisions on EU law matters (available at < aca-europe.eu/index.php/en/dec-nat-en >).

[95] Esther Versluis, 'Even Rules, Uneven Practices: Opening the "Black Box" of EU Law in Action' (2007) 30 West European Politics 50.

[96] Conant (n 93) 15–16 (providing an overview of existing studies).

has been in the single digits, which translates into a 'respectable' compliance rate of 90 per cent.[97]

A second strand of research has looked into national judicial compliance with EU law. Although studies here are usually limited to a particular jurisdiction and modest time frame, the available evidence suggests that Member State courts, by and large, execute their role as EU courts diligently. Compliance is especially high where a national judge makes use of the preliminary reference mechanism. Stacy Nyikos found that the implementation rate of ECJ rulings in the top three domestic legal systems with the highest reference rates was at a staggering 96 per cent.[98] Similar findings were made in country-specific studies for Germany (92 percent)[99] and the Netherlands (90 per cent).[100] Outside the preliminary reference context, the picture is more opaque, with systematic analyses hindered by the fact that national court decisions on EU law are often not reported.[101] Yet, even here, the limited available data warrants cautious optimism. Ramos Romeu found that Spanish courts, when citing ECJ rulings, comply with them in 81 per cent of cases.[102] Studies in other jurisdictions, though less systematic, have come to comparable conclusions in relation to the application of EU law more broadly, the general tone being that private litigants actively invoke European rules and national judges apply them conscientiously.[103] This includes new Member States such as Poland.[104]

[97] Andreas Hofmann, 'Resistance against the Court of Justice of the European Union' (2018) 14 International Journal of Law in Context 258, 263 (data for 1997–2016). Note that Hofmann is sceptical as to whether this actually is a good result and whether the numbers 'compare favourably with those of national supreme courts with which the CJEU is often equated', especially in light of the fact that implementation of ECJ rulings is delayed in around half of cases.

[98] Stacy A Nyikos, 'The Preliminary Reference Process: National Court Implementation, Changing Opportunity Structures and Litigant Desistment' (2003) 4 European Union Politics 397.

[99] Jürgen Schwarze, *Die Befolgung von Vorabentscheidungen des Europäischen Gerichtshofs durch deutsche Gerichte: Ergebnisse einer rechtstatsächlichen Bestandsaufnahme* (Nomos 1988).

[100] Joest Korte (ed), *Primus Inter Pares: The European Court and National Courts. The Follow-up by National Courts of Preliminary Rulings ex Art. 177 of the Treaty of Rome: A Report on the Situation in the Netherlands* (Nomos 1991).

[101] The National Decisions Database created by the Association of Councils of States and Supreme Administrative Jurisdictions of the European Union is likely to change that and facilitate empirical research: see Denise Carolin Hübner, 'The "National Decisions" Database (Dec.Nat): Introducing a Database on National Courts' Interactions with European Law' (2016) 17 European Union Politics 324; Juan A Mayoral, 'Judicial Empowerment Expanded: Political Determinants of National Courts' Cooperation with the CJEU' (2017) 25 European Law Journal 374.

[102] Francisco Ramos Romeu, 'Law and Politics in the Application of EC Law: Spanish Courts and the ECJ 1986–2000' (2006) 43 Common Market Law Review 395.

[103] Adelina Adinolfi, 'The Judicial Application of Community Law in Italy (1981–1997)' (1998) 35 Common Market Law Review 1313; Niilo Jääskinen, 'The Application of Community Law in Finland: 1995–1998' (1999) 36 Common Market Law Review 407; Damian Chalmers, 'The Application of Community Law in the United Kingdom, 1994–1998' (2000) 37 Common Market Law Review 83; Ulf Bernitz, 'Sweden and the European Union: On Sweden's Implementation and Application of European Law' (2001) 38 Common Market Law Review 903; Jarvis (n 49) 451.

[104] Adam Łazowski, 'Half Full and Half Empty Glass: The Application of EU Law in Poland' (2011) 48 Common Market Law Review 503.

Taken as a whole, these findings suggest that over the past decades a 'habit of obedience'[105] has been established: Member States have learned to live with and by EU law. In the words of Lisa Conant:

> Today most political scientists would agree that the EU legal system boasts a compliance record that is extraordinary by standards used to evaluate international law and probably more comparable to the compliance situation of domestic legal systems.[106]

This is not to say that problems, some of them serious, do not continue to arise.[107] Member States have, for instance, been found to contain the effects of ECJ rulings in politically sensitive areas by narrowly tailoring their legislative responses.[108] Instances of open defiance of EU law have recently re-emerged in relation to the Union's refugee allocation policy.[109] Domestic courts have been shown to avoid referring questions to the ECJ through a broad interpretation of the *acte clair* doctrine.[110] Perhaps most gravely, a handful of high courts has threatened to disapply European law (the German Constitutional Court in *OMT* and the Italian Constitutional Court in *Taricco*) or held ECJ rulings to be *ultra vires* (the Czech Constitutional Court in *Landtová* and the Danish Supreme Court in *Ajos*).[111]

Indisputably significant, these instances should not detract from the fact that the EU has made great strides in terms of compliance since the 1960s and 1970s. This is likely to generate a heightened trust of the European judges in national institutions. In a climate where internal market legislation is transposed at remarkably high rates and national legislation is amended if found to be in violation of

[105] Weiler (n 57), 2421.

[106] Conant, 'Compliance and What EU Member States Make of It' (n 93) 1.

[107] For a good overview of the various forms of backlash and pushback against the ECJ, see Hofmann (n 97).

[108] Conant, *Justice Contained: Law and Politics in the European Union* (n 92).

[109] See Cases C-715, 718 and 719/17 *Commission v Poland, Hungary, and the Czech Republic* [2019] ECLI:EU:C:2019:917, Opinion of AG Sharpston.

[110] A practice which has prompted successful lawsuits for violations of Art 267(3) TFEU in Case C-160/14 *Da Silva e Brito* [2015] ECLI:EU:C:2015:565 (Portuguese Supreme Court) and C-416/17 *Commission v France (Duty to Refer)* [2018] ECLI:EU:C:2018:811 (Conseil d'État). Similar problems have been reported in Sweden, Denmark, and the UK.

[111] Pl. ÚS 5/12 *Landtová* (Czech Constitutional Court); BVerfGE 134, 366 *OMT* (German Federal Constitutional Court); Case 15/2014 *Dansk Industri Acting for A/S v The Estate Left by A* (Danish Supreme Court); *Order 24/2017 Taricco (Italian Constitutional Court)*. For a discussion of the implications of these rulings for the interaction between national high courts and the ECJ, see Daniel Sarmiento, 'An Instruction Manual to Stop a Judicial Rebellion (Before It Is Too Late, of Course)' *Verfassungsblog* (2 February 2017); Mikael Rask Madsen, Henrik Palmer Olsen, and Urška Šadl, 'Competing Supremacies and Clashing Institutional Rationalities: the Danish Supreme Court's Decision in the *Ajos* Case and the National Limits of Judicial Cooperation' (2017) 23 European Law Review 140; Franz Mayer, 'Rebels Without a Cause? A Critical Analysis of the German Constitutional Court's *OMT* Reference' (2014) 15 German Law Journal 111; Davide Paris, 'Carrot and Stick: The Italian Constitutional Court's Preliminary Reference in the Case Taricco' (2017) 37 Questions of International Law 5; Jan Komárek, 'Playing With Matches: The Czech Constitutional Court Declares a Judgment of the Court of Justice of the EU *Ultra Vires*' (2012) 8 European Constitutional Law Review 323.

EU law, it will appear justified to grant Member States some autonomy in relation to free movement matters. In a setting where national judges duly implement ECJ rulings in the vast majority of cases, especially those resorting to the preliminary reference procedure, the Court will be more willing to defer parts of proportionality analysis to the referring court. Greater national compliance may, thus, lead to greater European deference.

E. Constitutional Changes

The turn towards more restraint at the ECJ is, finally, also a reflection of the constitutional changes that have taken place in the EU during the past two and a half decades. This evolution will be examined in greater detail in Chapter 6, as will its consequences for the role of the ECJ and free movement law. A couple of observations shall, however, be made at this point already.

Since Maastricht, Treaty revisions have, on the one hand, gradually broadened the legislative competences of the EU and enriched its mission. The Union can now act in areas ranging from consumer rights, to environmental protection, to education and energy. It has evolved from a predominantly economic enterprise to a political endeavour which is committed to values such as democracy, justice, pluralism, and solidarity. On the other hand, the amendments have introduced centrifugal forces into EU constitutional law. The principles of conferral, subsidiarity, and proportionality, which are enshrined in Article 5 TEU, all underline in different ways that law making is, in principle, the prerogative of the national and not the European level. In addition, a number of red lines have been inserted into the competence norms in the TFEU, preventing EU action in certain areas, such as social policy and public health, thus reserving strategic regulatory decisions for national legislatures.

Connected with this, there is an evergrowing emphasis in EU constitutional law on local values and cultural differences. Article 4(2) TEU protects the national identities of Member States. Thought to be a lofty declaration of intent when adopted, the clause has gained increasing clout in recent years.[112] Article 167(1) TFEU contains a similar, if legally softer obligation in the context of the EU's supporting competence on cultural policy. It charges the Union with contributing to the 'flowering of the cultures of the Member States' and demands that 'national and regional diversity' be respected.

The ECJ may respond to these changes in its free movement case law. It is increasingly mindful of national decision-making powers, acting in line with the

[112] Case C-208/09 *Sayn-Wittgenstein* [2010] ECLI:EU:C:2010:806; Case C-391/09 *Runevič-Vardyn and Wardyn* [2011] ECLI:EU:C:2011:291; *Las* (n 24); Case C-156/13 *Digibet* [2014] ECLI:EU:C:2014:1756; Case C-673/16 *Coman* [2018] ECLI:EU:C:2018:385.

overall constitutional evolution of the EU. Consider, further, that critical attitudes towards the EU have been growing over the past 15 years and that the ECJ—no longer 'blessed by benign neglect'—is under greater scrutiny from politicians, national judges, and the media,[113] and it becomes clear that this is not the most fertile environment for interventionism.

IV. Conclusion: The Growing Role of National Authorities

This chapter has provided a general overview of deference, shedding light on its prevalence and evolution in the Court of Justice's case law. It has emerged that free movement adjudication has experienced a turn towards deferential scrutiny. The ECJ is granting Member State authorities a growing degree of decision-making autonomy, a trend which is particularly pronounced in relation to national courts. This challenges some conventional wisdoms about the ECJ and free movement law. No longer is the Court an exclusively activist institution, promoting centralization and uniformity of EU law. It has scaled down its intensity of scrutiny of Member States action, allowing for greater regulatory diversity at the national level, and increasingly decentralizes decisions relating to justification and proportionality. That the European judges are behaving differently in the 2010s than in the 1970s is no surprise. As was shown, the world surrounding them has changed, thus affecting the legal, political, and institutional parameters in which the Court operates. When does the Court of Justice reach for its deference doctrines? In which types of cases does it defer to national institutions? These issues will be explored next. Chapter 3 will examine the application of the margin of appreciation. Chapter 4 will focus on decentralized judicial review.

[113] See Michael Blauberger and others, 'ECJ Judges Read the Morning Papers: Explaining the Turnaround of European Citizenship Jurisprudence' (2018) 25 Journal of European Public Policy 1422.

3

The Margin of Appreciation

Theory and Practice

When granting Member States a margin of appreciation, the European Court of Justice (ECJ) limits its control over a given subject matter and entrusts the decision, to different degrees, to the domestic legislature or executive. How widely the doctrine is employed, therefore, indicates how much decision-making power Member States retain under free movement law. Where it is used points us to the place of this freedom. Similarly, the doctrine gives us an intimate look into the Court of Justice's *Seelenleben*, exposing which concerns it prioritizes, which questions it struggles with, and which assessments it considers safe to delegate. For the Court, the decision as to whether or not to grant a margin of appreciation amounts to the choice between determining a matter itself and leaving it in the hands of national institutions. The doctrine's patterns of application disclose which problems do not require, or permit, a 'personal' engagement in the eyes of the European judges.

This chapter will investigate the use of the margin of appreciation in free movement law, proceeding in two steps. The first section will examine the doctrine's legal scope and limits, based on a classical doctrinal analysis. It will shed light on the scenarios in which the Member States should, in theory, enjoy a margin of appreciation. The second section will put this legal model to the test. A statistical analysis of free movement case law will reveal in which cases the ECJ actually defers to national legislatures and executives.

I. Theory

The Court of Justice has—given its style of reasoning, perhaps unsurprisingly—never laid down a grand theory of the margin of appreciation. Despite the substantial body of case law which has developed around the doctrine, we find no ruling that would constitutionally justify its adoption, explain its rationale, or synthesize its rules of use. Nonetheless, over the years, the Court has rendered a number of judgments that touch on different aspects of the doctrine, issuing *dicta* about its scope and limits in the process. In this way, step-by-step, a veritable law of the margin of appreciation has emerged.

The building blocks of this law are specific scenarios in which Member States are and are not supposed to have a margin of appreciation. Collecting them is a challenge

Europe's Passive Virtues. Jan Zglinski, Oxford University Press (2020). © Oxford University Press.
DOI: 10.1093/oso/9780198844792.001.0001

as they are scattered throughout the case law and, in addition, do not form a closed class, meaning that the list of grounds justifying a domestic margin of appreciation expands over time.[1] This is the result of the piecemeal fashion in which the Court of Justice has chosen to deal with the doctrine: explanations about its application are given on a case-by-case basis, for the particular setting of the dispute. Moreover, it can, at times, be unclear why Member States are granted a margin of appreciation. The Court will defer to national authorities but will not articulate the reasons for doing so.[2]

Despite these difficulties, we find remarkably detailed 'operating instructions' for the margin of appreciation in the case law. The Court has created a catalogue consisting of over 50 different factors which have a bearing on the application of the doctrine. These can be clustered into a dozen broader categories which, in turn, fall into two groups: scenarios in which Member States have a margin of appreciation and scenarios in which they have none (see Table 3.1).

In relation to the former, the Court of Justice concentrates on two main factors. The first is the policy field of the dispute. Certain areas are said to automatically generate a national margin of appreciation. Sometimes, the relevant domain can be very wide, spanning whole regulatory fields. For instance, the ECJ has stated that Member States would be granted a margin of appreciation for all measures relating to public health,[3] consumer protection,[4] and road safety.[5] Other times, it can be fairly narrow and specific. The Court has suggested that it

[1] An approach which can be compared to the 'mandatory' or 'imperative requirements'-jurisprudence initiated in *Cassis de Dijon*. The ECJ clarifies on a case-by-case basis which national policy objectives count as mandatory requirements, with new developments occurring even decades later: see, for instance, Case C-384/93 *Alpine Investments* [1995] ECLI:EU:C:1995:126 (good reputation of national financial sector); Case C-368/95 *Familiapress* [1997] ECLI:EU:C:1997:325 (press diversity); Case C-438/05 *Viking Line* [2007] ECLI:EU:C:2007:772 (right to strike); Case C-212/11 *Jyske Bank Gibraltar* [2013] ECLI:EU:C:2013:270 (prevention of money laundering).

[2] Case C-394/97 *Heinonen* [1999] ECLI:EU:C:1999:308, on the Finnish alcohol import restrictions, illustrates the problem. The ECJ states that: 'Member States, which retain exclusive competence as regards the maintenance of public order and the safeguarding of internal security, enjoy a margin of discretion in determining, according to particular social circumstances and to the importance attached by those States to a legitimate objective under [Union] law . . . the measures which are likely to achieve concrete results.' Although the Court makes clear that the dispute falls into an area in which Member States have exclusive competence, that it touches on public policy, and that, finally, the national authorities have a margin of appreciation, the relation between these three elements remains ambiguous. Does the fact that the law concerns public policy and/or falls into the exclusive competence of the Member States result in the application of the doctrine? We can only assume, somewhat benevolently, this to be the case.

[3] Case C-95/01 *Greenham and Abel* [2004] ECLI:EU:C:2004:71, para 39; Case C-24/00 *Commission v France (Food Additives)* [2004] ECLI:EU:C:2004:70, para 50; Cases C-171 and 172/07 *Apothekerkammer des Saarlandes* [2009] ECLI:EU:C:2009:316, para 19; Case C-169/07 *Hartlauer* [2009] ECLI:EU:C:2009:141, para 30.

[4] Cases C-186/11 and 209/11 *Stanleybet International* [2013] ECLI:EU:C:2013:33, para 44; Cases C-660/11 and 8/12 *Biasci* [2013] ECLI:EU:C:2013:550, para 40.

[5] Case 50/83 *Commission v Italy (Roadworthiness Test)* [1984] ECLI:EU:C:1984:128, para 12; Case C-110/05 *Commission v Italy (Italian Trailers)* [2009] ECLI:EU:C:2009:66, para 61.

Table 3.1 The Law of the Margin of Appreciation

Member States Have Margin of Appreciation	Member States Have No Margin of Appreciation
Policy Field	**Discrimination**
public policy; public morality; public order; public security; public health; animal health; organization of social security systems; extent of sickness cover; consumer protection; road safety; criminal law; games of chance; advertising; protection of literary and artistic property; regulation of foodstuffs/food additives; organization of health care; planning of pharmacies/opticians shops; professional qualifications; access to/exercise of liberal professions; allocation of powers of taxation; double taxation; risk of confusion between trademarks	
EU Harmonization	**Disproportionality**
absence of EU harmonization; absence of 'adequate' or 'full' harmonization; 'state of EU law'; exclusive competence or 'jurisdiction' of Member States	
Free Movement Rights	
all objectives protected by Arts 36, 52, and 65 TFEU (and 'overriding reasons in the public interest')	
Political Sensitivity/Local Particularities	
'national or regional socio-cultural characteristics'; political and economic choices; moral, religious, or cultural relevance	
Consensus	
'general tendency among Member States'	
No Consensus	
'significant moral, religious and cultural differences between the Member States'; differences between Member States and periods; variations between national levels of protection	
Protected Interest	
importance of protected interest; significant risks/serious consequences for protected interest; 'significant contribution' to public interest	
'Peculiar' Nature of Activity	
Fundamental Rights	
Scientific Uncertainties	

Note: Expressions and passages in quotation marks are citations from the ECJ's case law.

will defer to national authorities when it comes to questions of double taxation,[6] determining risks of confusion between trademarks,[7] and the extent of sickness cover in national health insurance schemes.[8]

The second factor that is meant to be central to the application of the margin of appreciation is the extent to which a given area has been harmonized by secondary law. According to the Court, Member States have a margin of appreciation when there is no EU harmonization. This includes cases in which there is a complete absence of harmonization, that is, in which no secondary legislation exists at all.[9] However, as some rulings clarify, even the lack of 'adequate'[10] or 'full'[11] harmonization suffices and will result in deference to national authorities.

Other factors are referred to more rarely in the Court of Justice's case law but are no less important. Member States have a margin of appreciation in relation to how they protect the interests set out in the derogation clauses of certain freedoms of movement as well as the concomitant unwritten 'mandatory requirements' in the public interest. This has been explicitly established for the free movement of goods (Article 36 TFEU),[12] the right to establishment (Article 52 TFEU),[13] the free movement of services (Articles 62 and 52 TFEU),[14] and the free movement of capital (Article 65 TFEU).[15] The political sensitivity of a subject matter[16] and the existence of 'national or regional socio-cultural particularities'[17] are equally meant to prompt a national margin of appreciation. The same goes for regulatory consensus among Member States, even if the Court's pronouncements on this point are somewhat contradictory. In some judgments, the existence of consensus is presented as a reason for deferring to national authorities;[18] in others, the lack of consensus is said to have the same effect.[19] Finally, Member States will be given a margin of appreciation in the case of

[6] Case C-307/97 *Saint-Gobain* [1999] ECLI:EU:C:1999:438, paras 55 and 57.

[7] Case C-9/93 *IHT Internationale Heiztechnik* [1994] ECLI:EU:C:1994:261, para 18.

[8] Case C-8/02 *Leichtle* [2004] ECLI:EU:C:2004:161, para 48.

[9] Case 341/87 *EMI Electrola* [1989] ECLI:EU:C:1989:30, para 11; Case C-317/92 *Commission v Germany (Expiry Dates)* [1994] ECLI:EU:C:1994:212, para 14; Case C-496/01 *Commission v France (Bio-Medical Laboratories)* [2004] ECLI:EU:C:2004:137, para 55; Case C-88/07 *Commission v Spain (Herbal Products)* [2009] ECLI:EU:C:2009:123, para 86.

[10] Case 247/81 *Commission v Germany (Pharmaceutical Products)* [1984] ECLI:EU:C:1984:79, para 7.

[11] Case 125/88 *Nijman* [1989] ECLI:EU:C:1989:401, para 14.

[12] *Heinonen* (n 2), para 36.

[13] Case C-299/02 *Commission v Netherlands (Ship Flagging)* [2004] ECLI:EU:C:2004:620, para 18.

[14] Case C-255/04 *Commission v France (Artists' Agencies)* [2006] ECLI:EU:C:2006:401, paras 43–44.

[15] Case C-326/07 *Commission v Italy (Golden Shares)* [2009] ECLI:EU:C:2009:193, paras 41–42.

[16] Case C-275/92 *Schindler* [1994] ECLI:EU:C:1994:119, para 61; Case C-124/97 *Läärä* [1999] ECLI:EU:C:1999:435, para 13.

[17] Case C-145/88 *Torfaen Borough Council* [1989] ECLI:EU:C:1989:593, para 14; similarly, also Case C-518/06 *Commission v Italy (Motor Insurance)* [2009] ECLI:EU:C:2009:270, para 84.

[18] *Schindler* (n 16), para 60.

[19] Case 41/74 *Van Duyn* [1974] ECLI:EU:C:1974:133, para 18; Case C-42/07 *Liga Portuguesa* [2009] ECLI:EU:C:2009:519, para 57; Case C-36/02 *Omega Spielhallen* [2004] ECLI:EU:C:2004:614, para 31.

scientific uncertainties[20] as well as in relation to decisions involving fundamental rights.[21]

There is a series of further ancillary factors that appear occasionally in the case law as grounds of deference. Member States are, for instance, meant to be given a margin of appreciation if they pursue important policy interests—that is, interests that 'rank foremost among the assets and interests protected by the Treaty' (something which has so far been accepted only for human life and health[22])—or when there is a serious risk for the policy objective at stake.[23] Likewise, national authorities are supposed to be subjected to deferential scrutiny when their measures 'significantly' contribute to a policy aim.[24] Finally, the regulation of 'peculiar' or 'particular' goods and services involves a national margin of appreciation, even if the meaning of these notions remains vague; only games of chance[25] and medicinal products[26] are mentioned as examples in the case law.

When we turn to the factors precluding or narrowing the national margin of appreciation, the list is considerably shorter. The Court of Justice has laid down only two scenarios. First, Member States act outside their margin of appreciation if they discriminate against non-nationals.[27] Second, they do not enjoy a margin of appreciation for measures which violate the principle of proportionality.[28]

Why is there such an asymmetry between both sides of the table? The answer has to do with the way in which the ECJ exercises judicial review or, more precisely, the review techniques upon which it relies. Standard justification and proportionality scrutiny knows no margin of appreciation; it is based on the idea of full review.[29] The Court of Justice's default modus operandi is to examine Member State acts comprehensively. When the ECJ intends to exercise full justification and proportionality analysis, there is, consequently, no need to expressly 'disapply' the margin of appreciation—whenever the doctrine is not invoked, full review is warranted. When the Court, in contrast, wants to deviate from comprehensive

[20] Case 174/82 *Sandoz* [1983] ECLI:EU:C:1983:213, para 16; Case C-387/99 *Commission v Germany (Vitamins)* [2004] ECLI:EU:C:2004:235, para 69; Case C-150/00 *Commission v Austria (Food Additives)* [2004] ECLI:EU:C:2004:237, para 86; Case C-41/02 *Commission v Netherlands (Food Additives)* [2004] ECLI:EU:C:2004:762, paras 43 and 51.

[21] Case C-112/00 *Schmidberger* [2003] ECLI:EU:C:2003:333, para 82; Case C-71/02 *Karner* [2004] ECLI:EU:C:2004:181, para 51.

[22] Case 215/87 *Schumacher* [1989] ECLI:EU:C:1989:111, para 11; Case C-320/93 *Ortscheit* [1994] ECLI:EU:C:1994:379, para 16; *Apothekerkammer des Saarlandes* (n 3), para 19.

[23] *Läärä* (n 16), para 13; Case C-67/98 *Zenatti* [1999] ECLI:EU:C:1999:514, para 14.

[24] *Schindler* (n 16), para 60. Paradoxically, the same seems to be the case where measures have a negligible effect on the policy objective: see *Karner* (n 21), para 51.

[25] *Schindler* (n 16), para 59.

[26] *Apothekerkammer des Saarlandes* (n 3), para 31; Case C-531/06 *Commission v Italy (Pharmacies)* [2009] ECLI:EU:C:2009:315, para 55.

[27] *Schindler* (n 16), para 61; *Läärä* (n 16), para 14; *Zenatti* (n 23), para 15.

[28] *Greenham and Abel* (n 3), para 39; Case C-112/02 *Kohlpharma* [2004] ECLI:EU:C:2004:208, para 14; Case C-262/02 *Commission v France (Loi Evin)* [2004] ECLI:EU:C:2004:431, para 24; Case C-443/02 *Schreiber* [2004] ECLI:EU:C:2004:453, para 43.

[29] This issue is examined in greater detail in Chapter 5.

scrutiny, it has to make this explicit. This is why we find more information on when Member States are granted a margin of appreciation than when they are not.

This, in short, is the law of the margin of appreciation. Although it is not without ambiguities (what are 'peculiar' economic activities or important policy interests?) or frictions (how can both the existence and the lack of regulatory consensus among Member States prompt a margin of appreciation?), it gives us a relatively precise understanding of the role the ECJ intends for the doctrine. The margin of appreciation is presented as an instrument of broad scope. It does not only apply in numerous policy fields and across free movement rights, but also in all areas that have not been harmonized at the European level. At the same time, the doctrine is meant to be context-sensitive. An intricate web of factors affects whether and where it applies, ranging from the political sensitivity of the dispute, to the existence of scientific uncertainties, to the discriminatory nature of the Member State action. How well do these factors capture the Court of Justice's adjudicative practice?

II. Practice

The Court of Justice's pronouncements on the margin of appreciation paint the 'official' portrait of the doctrine, informing us about how it is meant to be applied in free movement law. A different question is how it is used in practice. Does the Court actually subject national laws to deferential scrutiny whenever fundamental rights are at stake or there is no pan-European regulatory consensus? Does its intensity of scrutiny depend on the given policy field or the level of EU harmonization?

The case law study that already formed the basis for the analysis in Chapter 2 will help answer these questions. The same set of free movement rulings will be used here, but instead of taking each ECJ judgment as one unit of measurement, the data will be split into the different Member State acts that are at stake in every dispute (257 in total[30]). This more granular analysis is warranted because in some free movement cases multiple national laws are challenged, each raising different legal issues and leading to different outcomes. While parts of a case will concern areas that have been harmonized, others will be in fields in which there is no secondary legislation yet; certain aspects of the disputed regulation may restrict the right to establishment, others the freedom to provide services; and so on. Focusing on how these individual measures are treated allows us to more accurately trace how the ECJ responds to certain characteristics of a case.[31]

All the factors presented in the previous section will be examined, with two exceptions. The analysis will omit factors that are insufficiently clear, namely the

[30] The total sample size is 294 cases but, for reasons explained in Chapter 2, the analysis is limited to decisions in which at least one free movement right was found to be restricted.

[31] For a similar approach, see Clifford J Carrubba, Matthew Gabel, and Charles Hankla, 'Judicial Behavior under Political Constraints: Evidence from the European Court of Justice' (2008) 102 American Political Science Review 435. Note the differences with the results reported in Jan Zglinski,

'peculiar' nature of an economic activity (a term which the Court of Justice never defined) and the high importance of a policy interest (which appears to be limited to human health). Also, it will not examine whether Member States enjoy a margin of appreciation as long as they do not violate the principle of proportionality. As explained in Chapter 1, the margin of appreciation and proportionality are not separate tests; the former affects how intensely the latter is exercised. Therefore, measuring the outcome of proportionality review to determine whether the ECJ has granted national authorities a margin of appreciation would make little sense.

The analysis will proceed in two steps. It will start with some descriptive statistics about how frequently the ECJ grants national authorities a margin of appreciation in cases marked by a certain factor. This is important as many of the statements the Court of Justice makes about the doctrine are categorical. Member States, for instance, are *never* meant to be given a margin of appreciation if they discriminate against non-nationals. They are, in contrast, *always* supposed to be granted a margin when a policy area has not been harmonized. In a second step, the relationship between these factors and the ECJ's behaviour will be investigated by means of a logistic regression. The results will show which aspects of a case actually have an influence on whether the ECJ does or does not grant a margin of appreciation.

A. Patterns of Deference

1. Policy Fields and Political Sensitivity

According to the ECJ, Member States enjoy a margin of appreciation in two main scenarios. The first one is related to the policy field of the dispute. Certain regulatory areas are said to automatically come with a national margin of appreciation.[32] As was shown, the Court's list is vast, comprising more than two dozen domains. Among the most important ones we find: public health; public policy, order, and morality; national security; consumer protection; games of chance; road safety; the regulation of liberal professions and professional qualifications; intellectual property; and

'The Rise of Deference: The Margin of Appreciation and Decentralized Judicial Review in EU Free Movement Law' (2018) 55 Common Market Law Review 1341.

[32] A claim echoed in the literature, albeit with variations as to which areas matter. Paul Craig argues that Member States have a margin of appreciation when it comes to public health: see *EU Administrative Law* (3rd edn, Oxford University Press 2018) 684. Loïc Azoulai mentions public health, gambling, and higher education: see 'The European Court of Justice and the Duty to Respect Sensitive National Interests' in Mark Dawson, Bruno de Witte, and Elise Muir (eds), *Judicial Activism at the European Court of Justice* (Edward Elgar 2013) 185. Sybe de Vries argues that, in addition, national authorities have some discretion in relation to consumer protection: see 'Balancing Fundamental Rights with Economic Freedoms According to the European Court of Justice' (2013) 9 Utrecht Law Review 169, 173–74. According to Gráinne de Búrca, the ECJ defers to the Member States on matters relating to national security and health care: see 'The Principle of Proportionality and Its Application in EU Law' (1994) 14 Yearbook of European Law 105, 133, and 137. Janneke Gerards lists public health, transport, road safety, animal welfare, and public policy as margin of appreciation areas: see 'Pluralism, Deference and the Margin of Appreciation Doctrine' (2011) 17 European Law Journal 80, 93–94.

questions relating to social policy and tax law. This long catalogue suggests, firstly, that the margin of appreciation is a doctrine of wide usage, to be found in a large number of areas. Secondly, one would expect it to be evenly spread throughout these fields.

Against this background, the Court of Justice's case law is surprising (Table 3.2). There are only a few areas in which we find a noteworthy usage of the margin of appreciation at all. In just five domains is the doctrine applied more than once: public and animal health (26), games of chance (6), public policy/morality and security (6), consumer protection, and road safety (each 3). Even within this group, we find a strong concentration on one field: 26 out of 51 cases in which the doctrine is used concern public health. This makes every other margin of appreciation case a health-related dispute.

In addition to this concentration in absolute terms, there are considerable differences as to how frequently the doctrine is applied in each of the policy fields. In four domains, the chances that the ECJ will defer to national authorities are very high, with a margin of appreciation being accorded in around half of all cases or more: games of chance (75 per cent), road safety (60 per cent), public policy/

Table 3.2 Margin of Appreciation Across Policy Fields

Policy Field	MoA Cases (Full/Partial)	All Cases	MoA Rate
Public and Animal Health	26 (12/14)	53	49.06%
Games of Chance	6 (6/0)	8	75.00%
Public Policy/Morality and Security	6 (3/3)	11	54.55%
Road Safety	3 (3/3)	5	60.00%
Consumer Protection	3 (3/0)	16	18.75%
Liberal Professions/Professional Qualifications	1 (0/1)	24	4.17%
Social Policy	1 (0/1)	22	4.55%
Intellectual Property	1 (1/0)	10	10.00%
Tax Law	0 (0/0)	37	0.00%
Other	4 (2/2)	71	5.63%

Note: For cases touching on multiple policy fields the one most central to the decision is indicated.

morality/security (54.55 per cent), and public health (49.06 per cent). Outside of these areas, only consumer protection shows a meaningful deference rate, close to the average across the whole of free movement law (18.75 per cent).[33] In the remaining fields, the margin of appreciation is virtually absent. Intellectual property (10 per cent), social policy (4.55 per cent), and professional qualifications (4.17 per cent)—although part of the margin of appreciation catalogue—are areas in which the ECJ employs the doctrine only rarely. This is the most extreme for tax law: in the 35 cases from the sample it is applied not once.[34]

The findings indicate that the policy field of a dispute may, indeed, matter for the application of the margin of appreciation, but in a different way than anticipated. The reach of the doctrine is much narrower than suggested by the Court of Justice. The margin of appreciation is applied neither too widely nor particularly evenly across the manifold areas in which free movement adjudication takes place. It is a targeted tool, predominantly used in four domains.

For Member States, this means that legislation in these areas is likely to be subjected to deferential review and, therefore, stands higher chances of being upheld. Note, however, that even within this group, there are differences as to the level of scrutiny. In cases on road safety (3 out of 3) and games of chance (6 out of 6), the ECJ tends to grant national authorities a full margin of appreciation. Member States enjoy the furthest-reaching regulatory autonomy here. By contrast, in cases on public health and public policy/morality/security, it opts for a partial margin of appreciation in around half of the cases (14 out of 26 and 3 out of 6 respectively). The discretion national institutions have is, as a consequence, more limited.

The results also help to shed light on the impact of a further factor on the ECJ's behaviour. The Court has, on occasion, held that politically sensitive matters, such as decisions involving 'political and economic choices' or in areas marked by 'moral, cultural, and religious differences', belong with the Member States.[35] Many of the best-known margin of appreciation cases like *Van Duyn, Henn and Darby*, and *Omega* turn on such issues. One might, therefore, expect to find a connection between the national margin of appreciation and sensitivity, with national authorities being subjected to more deferential scrutiny in cases involving controversial or salient topics.[36] Although the

[33] This contradicts claims that the ECJ exercises particularly strict scrutiny in cases on consumer protection, cf Catherine Barnard, 'The Worker Protection Justification: Lessons From Consumer Law' in Panos Koutrakos, Niamh Nic Shuibhne, and Phil Syrpis (eds), *Exceptions from EU Free Movement Law: Derogation, Justification and Proportionality* (Hart 2016) 109.

[34] Cases on tax law tend to follow a different logic than many other areas of free movement jurisprudence, with the ECJ relying much more on EU harmonization and less on techniques such as proportionality analysis and the margin of appreciation when reviewing national measures.

[35] *Torfaen Borough Council* (n 17), para 14; *Schindler* (n 16), para 61.

[36] The literature certainly does: see de Vries (n 32) 173; Gerards (n 32) 95; Niamh Nic Shuibhne, 'Margins of Appreciation: National Values, Fundamental Rights and EC Free Movement Law' (2009)

notion of sensitivity is, by nature, somewhat imprecise, we can loosely define it as comprising disputes that have a heightened political, cultural, or moral relevance and are therefore likely to attract attention beyond the courtroom.[37] Policy fields can serve us as a (very rough[38]) proxy in this regard, the assumption being that litigation in certain areas tends to raise sensitive questions more frequently than in others. When we look at the list of the policy fields in which free movement disputes arise, some can be classified as sensitive rather easily: cases on games of chance, public policy/morality, social security, and taxes involve, with some regularity, questions on the right way to live, on what behaviour to tolerate in our society, and what is just to give or to take. In contrast, those on road safety, consumer protection, intellectual property, professional qualifications, and public health (at least looking at the issues commonly dealt with by the ECJ: food supplements, plant protection, regulation of pharmacies, etc) are of a more limited interest to the general public and can be counted as non-sensitive.

If we compare the respective margin of appreciation rates, the differences are limited. While two of the sensitive areas show a frequent use of the doctrine (games of chance and public policy/morality), the other two have very low rates (social security and tax law). If we add up the numbers, we get a deference rate of 16.67 per cent. This is not just below the mean overall margin of appreciation rate but also below the rate in non-sensitive areas (31.48 per cent). Political sensitivity does, in sum, not appear to lead to more deferential scrutiny in free movement law.

2. EU Harmonization

According to the Court of Justice, the absence of EU harmonization in a given area, or the lack of 'full' or 'adequate' harmonization, means that Member States

34 European Law Review 230; Stephen Weatherill, 'Justification, Proportionality and Consumer Protection' in Panos Koutrakos, Niamh Nic Shuibhne, and Phil Syrpis (eds), *Exceptions from EU Free Movement Law: Derogation, Justification and Proportionality* (Hart 2016) 256.

[37] See Heather K Gerken and Ari Holtzblatt, 'The Political Safeguards of Horizontal Federalism' (2014) 113 Michigan Law Review 57, 83.

[38] Relying on policy fields as indicators for political sensitivity is, of course, a crude simplification which will not always yield accurate results. Take, for instance, an area like social policy, commonly thought of as politically sensitive. Whereas many disputes in this field will turn on high salience issues indeed—decisions on minimum wage, student aid, or retirement pensions—the possible increase of a separation allowance for civil servants by the equivalent of €1.25 will not (Case 152/73 *Sotgiu* [1974] ECLI:EU:C:1974:13). For alternative ways of measuring sensitivity, see Clifford J Carrubba and Matthew J Gabel, *International Courts and the Performance of International Agreements: A General Theory with Evidence from the European Union* (Cambridge University Press 2015) 125 (number of third-party interventions submitted to the ECJ) or Lee Epstein and Jeffrey A Segal, 'Measuring Issue Salience' (2000) 44 American Journal of Political Science 66 (analysis of which court rulings make it to the front pages of newspapers).

enjoy a margin of appreciation.[39] Scholars concur with this proposition, though they present the impact of harmonization in a more nuanced way. The argument is usually couched in terms of levels or degrees of harmonization. A high level of harmonization is said to render the Court's scrutiny more searching, a low level more deferential.[40]

Terms such as 'level' or 'degree' of harmonization sound simple and straightforward. Only when trying to measure them systematically do we realize how elusive they are. Despite its doctrinal and political significance, our understanding of the interplay between EU harmonization and free movement rights remains rudimentary. Scholarship typically only distinguishes between non-harmonized and harmonized fields and, within the latter, between minimum and maximum harmonization (also referred to as 'full', 'complete' or 'exhaustive').[41] Reality, however, is more complex than this. A dispute can be governed by harmonizing measures in different ways and to different extents, with distinct consequences for the applicable free movement right. Three broader categories can be distinguished.

No harmonization depicts the situation where a dispute is not governed by EU secondary legislation at all and is decided entirely under the free movement rules. This can be due to an actual absence of harmonization, that is, when a field has not been regulated at the European level, or where a harmonizing measure exists but is inapplicable to the case (*rationae temporis* or *materiae*[42]) or its application to the concrete factual circumstances is explicitly excluded.[43] A greater—*medium*—degree of harmonization can be found in scenarios where secondary legislation determines some aspects of the dispute but not others (partial harmonization)[44]

[39] *Liga Portuguesa* (n 19), para 57; *Greenham and Abel* (n 3), para 37; Case C-293/93 *Houtwipper* [1994] ECLI:EU:C:1994:330, para 22; *Nijman* (n 11), para 14; *Commission v Italy (Italian Trailers)* (n 5), para 61; *Commission v Germany (Pharmaceutical Products)* (n 10), para 7.

[40] de Búrca (n 32) 127 et seq; Jan H Jans, 'Proportionality Revisited' (2000) 27 Legal Issues of Economic Integration 239, 253; similarly, see Koen Lenaerts, 'The Court's Outer and Inner Selves: Exploring the External and Internal Legitimacy of the European Court of Justice' in Maurice Adams and others (eds), *Judging Europe's Judges* (Hart 2013) 29 and 37.

[41] Stephen Weatherill, 'Maximum versus Minimum Harmonization: Choosing between Unity and Diversity in the Search for the Soul of the Internal Market' in Niamh Nic Shuibhne and Laurence W Gormley (eds), *From Single Market to Economic Union: Essays in Memory of John A Usher* (Oxford University Press 2012). But see Catherine Barnard, *The Substantive Law of the EU: The Four Freedoms* (5th edn, Oxford University Press 2016) 580.

[42] Case 136/78 *Auer* [1979] ECLI:EU:C:1979:34, para 30; *IHT Internationale Heiztechnik* (n 7), para 18; Case C-379/97 *Upjohn* [1999] ECLI:EU:C:1999:494, para 29; Case C-442/02 *CaixaBank France* [2004] ECLI:EU:C:2004:586, para 7.

[43] Case C-539/11 *Ottica New Line* [2013] ECLI:EU:C:2013:591, paras 18–22; Case C-388/12 *Comune di Ancona* [2013] ECLI:EU:C:2013:734, para 45.

[44] Take, by means of example, the case law on tax deductions for non-residents: Case C-1/93 *Halliburton Services* [1994] ECLI:EU:C:1994:127; Case C-55/98 *Vestergaard* [1999] ECLI:EU:C:1999:533; Cases C-155/08 and 157/08 *X and Passenheim-Van Schoot* [2009] ECLI:EU:C:2009:368. National laws prohibiting such deductions are in principle subjected to normal free movement review: the ECJ will examine whether they restrict the applicable free movement right and, if so, whether they can be justified as a means to combat tax evasion. However, when it comes to the necessity test, the Court refers to the system of mutual assistance between tax authorities put in place by Directive 77/799, which is held to be a less restrictive alternative. In this way, the Directive governs one particular aspect of the dispute, but not the rest.

Table 3.3 Margin of Appreciation and EU Harmonization

Level of Harmonization	MoA Cases	All Cases	MoA Rate
No	29	131	22.14%
Medium	19	80	23.75%
High	1	41	2.44%

Note: Cases with missing values ($n = 5$) were excluded from the analysis. Where a case involves multiple pieces of EU legislation representing different levels of harmonization, the highest level is indicated.

or sets the base standard of protection (minimum harmonization).[45] Here, EU harmonization governs the dispute to some extent but remains outside the spotlight, with the legality of the Member State act still being mainly assessed on the basis of the freedoms of movement. When there is a *high level of harmonization*, this role allocation is turned upside down: secondary legislation becomes as important as, or even more important than, free movement rights for the resolution of the case. This happens when EU harmonizing measures are applied in parallel to a free movement right (as joint yardsticks of legality);[46] when secondary legislation is 'interpreted in the light of' a freedom of movement;[47] or when an area has been fully harmonized.[48]

How does EU harmonization affect the Member States' margin of appreciation? The data from the case law survey point towards differences between the three levels of harmonization (Table 3.3). Judgments in non-harmonized sectors show an application rate of 22.14 per cent. The figure for disputes in areas marked by a medium degree of harmonization is similar (23.75 per cent). In contrast, the doctrine appears in only 2.44 per cent of cases when there is a high level of harmonization.

At the same time, the results demonstrate that the Court of Justice overstates the role of harmonization for the national margin of appreciation. That Member States enjoy a margin of appreciation whenever there is an 'absence of harmonization', as the Court frequently says, is inaccurate. Even if the margin of appreciation rate

[45] A common regulatory approach in the field of consumer protection: see Case 382/87 *Buet* [1989] ECLI:EU:C:1989:198, para 16; Case C-315/92 *Verband Sozialer Wettbewerb* [1994] ECLI:EU:C:1994:34, para 10.

[46] Cases C-197/11 and 203/11 *Libert* [2013] ECLI:EU:C:2013:288; Case C-514/12 *Zentralbetriebsrat der Gemeinnützigen Salzburger Landeskliniken* [2013] ECLI:EU:C:2013:799; Case C-314/93 *Rouffeteau* [1994] ECLI:EU:C:1994:284.

[47] Case 249/86 *Commission v Germany (Housing Conditions for Migrants)* [1989] ECLI:EU:C:1989:204, para 8; Case 141/88 *Jordan* [1989] ECLI:EU:C:1989:311, para 15.

[48] Disputes in fully harmonized areas are, in principle, entirely governed by EU secondary law; free movement rights are meant to play no role here. Yet, the ECJ does not adhere to this rule too strictly and will, at times, examine whether Member State acts comply with the four freedoms despite the existence of complete harmonization: see Case C-249/92 *Commission v Italy (Plant Protection)* [1994] ECLI:EU:C:1994:335, paras 27–28; Case C-323/93 *Centre d'Insémination de la Crespelle* [1994] ECLI:EU:C:1994:368, para 33; Case C-165/08 *Commission v Poland (Genetically Modified Organisms)* [2009] ECLI:EU:C:2009:473.

in non-harmonized fields is slightly higher than the mean application rate, the results reveal that the ECJ does not apply the doctrine in over three out of four cases in which there is no secondary legislation. The ratio skews further if we limit our focus to cases without 'full' harmonization in which Member States are, likewise, always supposed to enjoy a margin of appreciation. More than four out of five decisions do not apply the doctrine here.

Interestingly, the main gap in deference rates lies not between harmonized and non-harmonized fields, but between a high level of harmonization on the one side and no/a medium level of harmonization on the other. What could explain this? Some authors have speculated that a greater degree of EU harmonization makes the Court of Justice feel 'more confident' when reviewing national measures.[49] Although the argument carries great intuitive plausibility, a look at the case law suggests that things might be more complicated. While the application of the margin of appreciation doctrine certainly indicates some form of restraint—the Court decides not to exercise full judicial review—, its lack of application need not imply confidence. ECJ rulings on secondary law can be cautious even without any reference to the national margin of appreciation by endorsing narrow, Member-State-friendly interpretations of EU rules. Recent case law on access to social benefits illustrates this neatly.[50]

A different reason may account for the ECJ's behaviour, one of a legal-technical nature. Judges create tools like proportionality analysis and the margin of appreciation in areas with few formal constraints, typically constitutional rights or equivalents; the four freedoms are paradigm examples in this respect.[51] These doctrines provide structure where there is not much else to be relied on: an ambiguous wording, an unclear scope, and no knowledge about the drafters' intent. The higher the degree of harmonization, the more these problems disappear. When a field is covered by detailed secondary legislation, the harmonizing measure will determine many of the issues that are relevant for deciding a dispute. The existence, scope, and limits of rights will be set out (sometimes with more, other times with less clarity), the attached recitals may disclose the policy aims behind the act and its legislative history. Consequently, the ECJ will be able to resort to more traditional interpretive techniques, such as examining a provision's wording, putting it into the wider regulatory context, and investigating the purpose of the rule. This decreases the need to use structuring doctrines such as the margin of appreciation.

[49] de Búrca (n 32) 127; similarly Daniel Thym, 'The Constitutional Dimension of Public Policy Justifications' in Panos Koutrakos, Niamh Nic Shuibhne, and Phil Syrpis (eds), *Exceptions from EU Free Movement Law: Derogation, Justification and Proportionality* (Hart 2016) 184.

[50] Despite the substantial level of EU harmonization, at least for workers, the Court of Justice at times decides in a fairly conservative manner: see Case C-138/02 *Collins* [2004] ECLI:EU:C:2013:860; Case C-166/12 *Časta* [2013] ECLI:EU:C:2013:792; Case C-443/11 *Jeltes* [2013] ECLI:EU:C:2013:224. See also the jurisprudence on welfare benefits under the Citizenship Directive, notably Case C-333/13 *Dano* [2014] ECLI:EU:C:2014:2358 and Case C-67/14 *Alimanovic* [2015] ECLI:EU:C:2015:597.

[51] See Chapter 5 II A.

3. Free Movement Rights

The Court of Justice has held that Member States, when restricting free movement rights in order to pursue the policy objectives listed in the derogation clauses of the Treaty, or those in the general interest, have a margin of appreciation to decide at what level and how they wish to protect these objectives. This has been accepted explicitly for four rights—goods,[52] establishment,[53] services,[54] and capital[55]—but there is no reason to believe that the Court, given the chance, would find differently regarding the free movement of workers. One would, against this backdrop, expect a consistent pattern of margin of appreciation cases across all freedoms of movement.[56]

An analysis of the case law reveals a different picture (Table 3.4). There is considerable variation among the individual rights. The free movement of workers and capital are at the bottom of the list, displaying margin of appreciation rates of around 10 per cent, followed by the right to establishment which has an only minimally better score (12.50 per cent).[57] The figures are higher for the free movement of services, coming close to the mean application rate for the whole sample (20.45 per cent). The free movement of goods ranks at the top, with almost one in three cases applying the margin of appreciation (30.68 per cent).

The results are remarkable for several reasons. To begin with, they demonstrate that national authorities, contrary to the ECJ's assurances, are not given a margin of appreciation each time they restrict free movement for reasons laid down in the derogation clauses (or other 'mandatory requirements'). More importantly,

Table 3.4 Margin of Appreciation Across Free Movement Rights

Free Movement Right(s)	MoA Cases	All Cases	MoA Rate
Goods	27	88	30.68%
Workers	4	40	10.00%
Establishment	4	32	12.50%
Services	9	44	20.45%
Capital	2	19	10.53%
Multiple	5	34	14.71%

52 *Heinonen* (n 2), para 36.
53 *Commission v Netherlands (Ship Flagging)* (n 13), para 18.
54 *Commission v France (Artists' Agencies)* (n 14), paras 43–44.
55 *Commission v Italy (Golden Shares)* (n 15), paras 41–42.
56 Note that the literature considers free movement rights to be 'central' EU interests which consistently trigger the 'strictest level of review': see Gerards (n 32) 91.
57 In judgments in which one free movement right was held to be 'entirely secondary' to another, the former was not counted; see, for example, *Omega Spielhallen* (n 19), para 25.

they suggest that there might be meaningful differences between the four freedoms when it comes to standard of review. Deference rates for the free movement of goods are three times higher compared with those for the free movement of workers and capital. This is a curious finding as there is nothing in the Court's case law to suggest that Member State acts will be subjected to stricter or more deferential scrutiny depending on the applicable free movement right.[58] That free movement of goods cases show the highest margin of appreciation rate is, in itself, noteworthy. The ECJ's jurisprudence on Article 34 TFEU is usually thought of as the area of its boldest activism. Yet, it is here that the European judges are most willing to defer to national authorities.

What may account for these variations? They could, in parts, be the result of what was called maturity in the previous chapter. The Court will be more inclined to engage in deferential forms of review in areas that are well developed jurisprudentially, that is, whose core principles have been fleshed out to a sufficient extent. This would explain why the free movement of goods shows the highest margin of appreciation rate. It was the first freedom of movement to be interpreted broadly by the ECJ, thus triggering a substantial amount of litigation from as early as the 1970s which, in turn, gave the Court the opportunity to pronounce itself on many fundamental issues surrounding Articles 34 and 36 TFEU.[59] Other free movement rights had, in comparison, a more delayed development. The widening of the scope of the free movement of persons and services to non-discriminatory measures, and the increase in litigation that resulted from it, only occurred in the 1990s.[60] The free movement of capital could not even be directly invoked by private litigants before the entering into force of the Maastricht Treaty in 1994.[61] The result has been a belated doctrinal development which may lead to a more hands-on approach on the part of the Court.

Another reason could have to do with EU harmonization. As was explained, the existence of secondary legislation can render doctrines like the margin of appreciation less important as judges are able to rely on other interpretive tools to solve a dispute. In this way, higher levels of harmonization may translate into lower margin of appreciation rates. Important parts of the free movement of workers, which shows the lowest margin of appreciation usage, have been covered by secondary legislation already in the late 1960s (notably through Regulations

[58] It is also somewhat at odds with the claim that the four freedoms are 'indivisible', a position which the EU has adopted in the Brexit negotiations: see Michel Barnier's speech from 5 May 2017 at the 'State of the Union' conference in Florence, available at <europa.eu/rapid/press-release_SPEECH-17-1236_en.htm>.

[59] Case 8/74 *Dassonville* [1974] ECLI:EU:C:1974:82; Case 120/78 *Rewe-Zentral AG v Bundesmonopolverwaltung für Branntwein ('Cassis de Dijon')* [1979] ECLI:EU:C:1979:42.

[60] Case C-76/90 *Säger* [1991] ECLI:EU:C:1991:331; Case C-415/93 *Bosman* [1995] ECLI:EU:C:1995:463; Case C-55/94 *Gebhard* [1995] ECLI:EU:C:1995:411.

[61] As a result of the ECJ's ruling in Case 203/80 *Casati* [1981] ECLI:EU:C:1981:261.

1612/68 and 1408/71[62]), whereas broader harmonizing measures on goods and services came to light only later. Similarly, the free movement of capital was codified in EU directives long before becoming an invocable Treaty right.[63] This may have contributed to the ECJ's less frequent reliance on the margin of appreciation doctrine.

4. Consensus

Consensus is a further factor said to affect the national margin of appreciation. It is, unlike what the term itself might suggest, commonly understood not as true unanimity, but agreement of a majority of Member States on a subject matter.[64] As already mentioned, the Court of Justice, somewhat paradoxically, says that both the existence and the lack of consensus result in a margin of appreciation for the national authorities. In this light, two opposing patterns could be expected in the case law: a high deference rate in disputes on topics on which there is pan-European consensus and a high rate in areas in which there is none.

Given the methodological choices of the study, the data on consensus is more limited than for other variables. On the basis of the information provided in the Court of Justice's judgments, it was only possibly to establish for 43 cases if there was a majority position on the subject matter of the dispute. This has, for one thing, to do with how rarely the European judges resort to the 'comparative method'.[65] The days in which ECJ rulings included detailed analyses of the laws of all or even most Member States are long gone,[66] a development caused in equal shares by the increase in workload (which means there is less time for comparative investigations) and the enlargement of the EU (which increases the number of countries to analyse). For another, there is a considerable number of cases in which one, based on the Court's decision, simply cannot determine with certainty whether Member States align or diverge on a given issue.[67] This warrants a degree of caution as to the validity of the findings.

[62] Regulation 1612/68 on freedom of movement for workers within the Community [1968] OJ L257/2; Regulation 1408/71 on the application of social security schemes to employed persons and their families moving within the Community [1971] OJ L149/2.

[63] First Directive for the implementation of Article 67 EEC [1960] OJ L43/921; Directive 63/474 liberalising transfers in respect of invisible transactions not connected with the movement of goods, services, capital or persons [1963] OJ L125/2240; Directive 88/361 for the implementation of Article 67 EEC [1988] OJ L178/5; Directive 86/566 amending the First Directive for the implementation of Article 67 EEC [1986] OJ L332/22. A good historical account is provided in John A Usher, 'The Evolution of the Free Movement of Capital' (2008) 31 Fordham Journal of International Law 1533.

[64] See Bilyana Petkova, 'The Notion of Consensus as a Route to Democratic Adjudication?' (2011–2012) 14 Cambridge Yearbook of European Legal Studies 663.

[65] For a famous example, see Case 44/79 *Hauer* [1979] ECLI:EU:C:1979:290, paras 20–22.

[66] Robert Schütze, 'Judicial Majoritarianism Revisited: "We, the Other Court"?' (2018) 43 European Law Review 269, 271–72.

[67] Frequently the Court will explain that there is a difference between two or three Member States but not provide information about the rest of the EU: see *EMI Electrola* (n 9); Case C-9/02 *De Lasteyrie du Saillant* [2004] ECLI:EU:C:2004:138; Case C-67/08 *Block* [2009] ECLI:EU:C:2009:92.

Table 3.5 Margin of Appreciation and Consensus

	MoA Cases	All Cases	MoA Rate
Consensus			
Pro-Member State	3	3	100.00%
Anti-Member State	0	8	0.00%
Total	3	11	27.27%
No Consensus	16	32	50.00%

Note: Cases with missing values ($n = 214$) were excluded from the analysis.

What will immediately strike those acquainted with the case law of the European Court of Human Rights (ECtHR) is how little the ECJ refers to consensus in relation to the margin of appreciation. For the Strasbourg Court, consensus is one of the main factors determining the application of the doctrine.[68] Contracting States have a narrow margin of appreciation only, or none at all, in domains in which a pan-European approach has crystallized, and a wide(r) margin where one is lacking.[69] In the ECJ's jurisprudence, a direct link between the doctrine and consensus has just been established in the cases on games of chance, and even there, it is somewhat nebulous. On the one hand, the Court holds the 'general tendency of the Member States' to limit access to gambling services to justify a margin of appreciation.[70] On the other, it states that the 'moral, cultural and religious differences' across Europe have the same effect.[71]

In the sample, we find 11 cases that address issues on which there is Member State consensus (Table 3.5).[72] The margin of appreciation doctrine is applied in three of them, a rate above the mean application rate (27.27 per cent). Looking at all instances of consensus would, however, be too crude. Consensus can affect Member States in two radically different ways: the national position can be in line with the European trend (*pro-Member State consensus*) or run against it (*anti-Member State consensus*). Three cases are of the former kind, with the domestic

[68] George Letsas, *A Theory of Interpretation of the European Convention of Human Rights* (OUP 2007) 92.

[69] See *Sunday Times v United Kingdom* (1979) 2 EHRR 245, para 59; *Goodwin v United Kingdom* (2002) 35 EHRR 18, paras 84–85; *Dickson v United Kingdom* (2007) 41 EHRR 21, para 78; *Lautsi v Italy* (2012) 54 EHRR 3, para 70.

[70] *Schindler* (n 16), para 60.

[71] ibid; *Liga Portuguesa* (n 19), para 57. A similar, if less direct connection can be found in cases in which the ECJ states that the mere existence of 'different systems of protection' among the Member States does not automatically render a national measure disproportionate: see *Omega Spielhallen* (n 19), para 38; *Stanleybet International* (n 4), para 28; Case C-575/11 *Nasiopoulos* [2013] ECLI:EU:C:2013:430, para 27.

[72] See, for instance, Case 51/83 *Commission v Italy (Gelatin)* [1984] ECLI:EU:C:1984:261; *Commission v Austria (Food Additives)* (n 20); Case C-350/97 *Monsees* [1999] ECLI:EU:C:1999:242.

legislation being in harmony with the developments in the rest of the EU; in all of them, the ECJ grants national authorities a margin of appreciation. By contrast, among the eight cases involving anti-Member State consensus, one finds the doctrine not once. This lends some support to the 'majoritarian activism' thesis according to which the Court of Justice, when reviewing national laws under the free movement rules, tends to enforce the dominant position across Europe (even if, at the same time, exposing how few free movement rulings can in fact be explained on this basis).[73]

When we turn to the lack of consensus, the number of observations grows slightly. In 32 cases from the sample we can detect regulatory discrepancies across Europe. The Court of Justice gives Member State institutions a margin of appreciation in 16 of them (50 per cent). That, again, is a rate (substantially) above the mean application rate.

One may feel puzzled by these findings. Both of our starting hypotheses have been confirmed. The data seem to suggest that the Court is, compared with the average use of the margin of appreciation in all free movement cases, more likely to defer to national authorities on topics on which there is a majority position, at least as long as the national law under scrutiny aligns with this position. The same appears to be true where divergences exist. Although both observations make sense on their own, they are paradoxical if read together. Consensus is a binary phenomenon: either there is a majority among the Member States or there is none. This makes it impossible that both the existence and lack of consensus increase the likelihood of a national margin of appreciation. One can only speculate about the reasons for the outcome. It is safe to assume that most free movement disputes concern areas in which legislative differences persist. This is the natural consequence of having 28 Member States regulate large parts of economic activity. Despite that, the Court addresses these differences in selected judgments only, in which it considers the issue to be relevant for one reason or another (and has knowledge of it in the first place). This could mean that the lack of consensus is not decisive in itself and that it becomes significant just in combination with other factors, such as the policy field of the dispute or the complexity of the questions raised. The data may, in that case, under-represent the real number of cases in which regulatory divergences exist.

5. Fundamental Rights

In *Schmidberger*, the ECJ famously declared that Member States enjoy a 'wide margin of discretion' to balance fundamental rights with free movement concerns, a principle reiterated elsewhere.[74] How the Court of Justice handles fundamental

[73] Miguel Poiares Maduro, *We the Court* (Hart 1998) 72–76. For a more critical reading of the results, see Lars Klenk, *Die Grenzen der Grundfreiheiten* (Mohr Siebeck 2019) 329.

[74] *Schmidberger* (n 21), para 82; *Karner* (n 21), para 51. Some read the *Omega* ruling in this way, too: see de Vries (n 32.

rights questions is, of course, an issue of broader constitutional significance. In the literature, there is an optimistic and a less optimistic view on this. Some scholars believe that fundamental rights are a central concern of EU law, with the Court carefully watching over possible violations.[75] Others are more critical of its record, arguing that it does too little rather than too much.[76]

Analysing the data, a first curious finding is how rarely fundamental rights actually appear in the case law. Only 9 cases mention fundamental rights of any type—from the European Convention on Human Rights, the EU Charter of Fundamental Rights, or general principles—a meagre 3.5 per cent. In two out of these the Court of Justice denies an examination of the relevant fundamental right straightaway.[77] Although the focus of the study is on free movement law, this number is still remarkably low. Implementation of secondary legislation aside, restrictions on the four freedoms are considered to be a key area in which EU fundamental rights apply to Member State action.[78] In spite of this, they are, numerically speaking, an almost negligible phenomenon in free movement jurisprudence.

In the seven judgments in which fundamental rights form part of the merits, the ECJ grants a margin of appreciation in three cases and, in addition, decentralizes review tasks to the referring court in two of them. Consequently, we find only four cases in which the Court does not directly refuse to examine the alleged fundamental rights violation or defers the issue to Member State authorities. Yet, even here, the fundamental rights scrutiny is mostly monosyllabic. In *Commission v Germany (Housing Conditions for Migrants)*, the Court just states that Regulation 1612/89 must be 'interpreted in light of' the respect for family life; the right is not mentioned again in the remainder of the judgment.[79] In *TV10* (freedom of expression) and *Las* (linguistic diversity), fundamental rights are only cited to affirm the legitimacy of the national policy aim; beyond that they are irrelevant for the decision. Only one case—that is, one out of 257—displays what one would think of as a normal fundamental rights inquiry: an analysis which spans more than one sentence, has an actual bearing on the legality of the Member State act, and is fully exercised by the ECJ.[80]

How to interpret these findings? Two readings seem possible. Sympathetic voices might take the results as a sign of the Court of Justice taking fundamental

[75] Tor-Inge Harbo, 'The Function of the Proportionality Principle in EU Law' (2010) 16 European Law Journal 158, 173 et seq; Gerards (n 32) 100; de Búrca (n 32) 146.

[76] Jason Coppel and Adam O'Neill, 'The European Court of Justice: Taking Rights Seriously?' (1992) 29 Common Market Law Review 669; Mattias Kumm, '*Internationale Handelsgesellschaft, Nold* and the New Human Rights Paradigm' in Miguel Poiares Maduro and Loïc Azoulai (eds), *The Past and Future of EU Law* (Hart 2010) 1717.

[77] Case C-523/12 *Dirextra Alta Formazione* [2013] ECLI:EU:C:2013:831, para 19 (insufficient information to decide); Case C-233/12 *Gardella* [2013] ECLI:EU:C:2013:449, para 39 (fundamental rights review obsolete in light of application of Art 45 TFEU).

[78] Case C-260/89 *ERT* [1991] ECLI:EU:C:1991:254; *Familiapress* (n 1).

[79] *Commission v Germany (Housing Conditions for Migrants)* (n 47), para 10.

[80] Case C-418/11 *Texdata Software* [2013] ECLI:EU:C:2013:588.

rights seriously. Although the numbers are small, Member States are granted a margin of appreciation in three out of seven cases involving fundamental rights, over double the frequency with which the doctrine is used on average (42.86 per cent). This could indicate that the Court, indeed, understands their special significance and allows national authorities to prioritize them over free movement concerns. Yet, a more critical interpretation seems equally plausible. The data show that fundamental rights are not only addressed extremely rarely in the case law, but that the Court of Justice does not show great interest in protecting them 'personally'. When potential problems are brought to its attention, the Court is likely to either not engage in an in-depth analysis or to defer to the relevant Member State authorities. This may suggest that fundamental rights are not a concern which is particularly dear to the ECJ, at least not in the free movement context.[81]

6. Scientific Uncertainties

The Court of Justice has repeatedly stated that national authorities should be given a margin of appreciation to the extent that, in relation to a particular problem, 'uncertainties continue to exist in the current state of scientific research'.[82] Providing a systematic analysis of this variable is difficult. If we want to go beyond the blind acceptance of the formulaic statements made in the case law, even identifying whether scientific uncertainties exist poses a challenge. Although research data is cited in some cases by the parties or the Commission, it is impossible to verify, without an inquiry into the state of the relevant field (human medicine, organic chemistry, behavioural economics, etc), whether actual gaps or uncertainties persist.[83] Therefore, the following observations remain somewhat impressionistic.

Only two types of scientific uncertainties come up in the Court of Justice's free movement case law, both of which relate to public health. The first concerns the question as to whether certain products or substances pose dangers for human or, occasionally, animal health.[84] The second concerns planning decisions, such as

[81] Things might be different in other areas. In recent years, for instance, the ECJ appears willing to subject EU action to more searching scrutiny in some fundamental rights cases (in marked contrast to its traditional, highly deferential approach): see Eirik Bjorge and Jan Zglinski, 'The Principle of Proportionality in EU Law and Its Domestic Application: *Ni tout à fait le même, ni tout à fait un autre*' in Katja Ziegler, Päivi Neuvonen, and Violeta Moreno-Lax (eds), *Research Handbook on General Principles of EU Law* (Edward Elgar forthcoming).

[82] *Sandoz* (n 20), para 16; *Commission v Austria (Food Additives)* (n 20), para 86; *Commission v Netherlands (Food Additives)* (n 20), para 43.

[83] See, for instance, Case 274/87 *Commission v Germany (Meat Products)* [1989] ECLI:EU:C:1989:51; Case 40/82 *Commission v United Kingdom (Newcastle Disease)* [1984] ECLI:EU:C:1984:33; Case 74/82 *Commission v Ireland (Newcastle Disease)* [1984] ECLI:EU:C:1984:34.

[84] Case 97/83 *CMC Melkunie* [1984] ECLI:EU:C:1984:212, paras 17–18; *Commission v Germany (Vitamins)* (n 20), paras 79–84; *Commission v France (Food Additives)* (n 3), paras 49 et seq; *Greenham and Abel* (n 3), paras 37 et seq; *Commission v Austria (Food Additives)* (n 20), paras 85 et seq; *Commission v Spain (Herbal Products)* (n 9), paras 54 et seq.

how to ensure an equal distribution of doctor's offices or pharmacies in a Member State.[85] In the sample, the Court of Justice mentions such uncertainties in 10 cases. With one exception, it grants a margin of appreciation in all of them. This seems to suggest that the Court is indeed willing to defer to national authorities where uncertainties or knowledge gaps exist. Note, however, that the degree to which the ECJ actually engages with the relevant problem varies. Some judgments show a detailed assessment of the empirical questions at stake. The Court will cite reports of scientific committees, examine their scope and meaning, and form a conclusion as to the risks of the given product.[86] In other cases, it does not delve into the substance of the matter at all.[87] References to scientific uncertainties seem to be a mere rhetorical device here, enabling the European judges to evade exercising substantive judicial review.

Overall, scientific questions and empirical research more broadly have occupied a modest place in the ECJ's free movement jurisprudence so far. Cases in which research-related arguments are invoked are few and far between. Also, they are limited to the domain of public health. The importance which empirical data have acquired in proceedings before other national and international courts,[88] as well as in some other fields of EU law,[89] has not yet been matched. Only in recent years have scientific studies become a more prominent part of free movement litigation, with a growing number of actors supporting their claims by reference to research data. In this way, free movement law might, if slowly, experience an evidence-based turn. Should this development become more pronounced, it will significantly affect the Court's work. The European judges will be forced to inquire into questions they traditionally did not have to deal with, through methods they may, at least currently, be not familiar with.[90]

[85] *Apothekerkammer des Saarlandes* (n 3), paras 30 et seq; *Commission v Italy (Pharmacies)* (n 26), paras 54 et seq.

[86] *Commission v Netherlands (Food Additives)* (n 20); *Commission v France (Food Additives)* (n 3); *Commission v Germany (Vitamins)* (n 20).

[87] *Apothekerkammer des Saarlandes* (n 3); *Commission v Italy (Pharmacies)* (n 26).

[88] The US Supreme Court, for instance, regularly relies on empirical evidence in areas such as discrimination, sexual harassment, and capital punishment: see Rosemary J Erickson and Rita J Simon, *The Use of Social Science Data in Supreme Court Decisions* (University of Illinois Press 1998); David L Faigman, '"Normative Constitutional Fact-Finding": Exploring the Empirical Component of Constitutional Interpretation' (1991) 139 University of Pennsylvania Law Review 541; Paul S Appelbaum, 'The Empirical Jurisprudence of the United States Supreme Court' (1987) 13 American Journal of Law & Medicine 335.

[89] See Alberto Alemanno and Amandine Garde, 'The Emergence of EU Lifestyle Risk Regulation: New Trends in Evidence, Proportionality and Judicial Review' in Hans-W Micklitz and Takis Tridimas (eds), *Risk and EU Law* (Edward Elgar 2015) 134; Eric Barbier de la Serre and Anne-Lise Sibony, 'Expert Evidence Before the EC Courts' (2008) 45 Common Market Law Review 941.

[90] The ECJ will notably have to act as a 'gatekeeper' and screen out unreliable expert evidence: see Scott Brewer, 'Scientific Expert Testimony and Intellectual Due Process' (1998) 107 Yale Law Journal 1535.

7. Discrimination and Economic Freedom

The ECJ is concise regarding when Member States enjoy no margin of appreciation. The most important factor is discrimination. According to the Court, national authorities will not be granted a margin of appreciation if they adopt discriminatory measures, in the sense of disadvantaging nationals from other Member States. Scholars affirm this link between the interference with free movement and the intensity of review but speak, more generally, of measures constituting 'serious restrictions'[91] or having a 'severe impact' in this context.[92]

Does discrimination affect the national margin of appreciation? According to a distinction common in free movement case law and scholarship, there are three types of Member State acts: directly discriminatory, indirectly discriminatory, and non-discriminatory. *Direct discrimination* (or 'in law') represents the strongest form of discrimination. It occurs when national legislation puts foreigners at a disadvantage by explicitly differentiating on the basis of nationality, or in the case of goods, origin.[93] *Indirect discrimination* (or 'in fact') is a milder, or less explicit, form of discrimination. It transpires when domestic laws apply to everyone but burden foreign goods or economic actors more heavily in substance, for instance by imposing requirements which are easier for locals to fulfil.[94] Member State acts, finally, display *no discrimination* if they affect equally all goods and economic operators, no matter if local or foreign.

If we look at the usage of the margin of appreciation throughout these categories, we see, to begin with, that the doctrine is applied to all three types of measures (Table 3.6). Importantly, this includes discriminatory laws. The ECJ grants Member

Table 3.6 Margin of Appreciation and Discrimination

Form of Discrimination	MoA Cases	All Cases	MoA Rate
No	41	113	36.28%
Indirect	6	93	6.45%
Direct	4	36	11.11%

Note: Cases with missing values ($n = 15$) were excluded from the analysis.

[91] Gerards (n 32) 92; similarly, see Allan Rosas, 'Foreword' in Panos Koutrakos, Niamh Nic Shuibhne, and Phil Syrpis (eds), *Exceptions from EU Free Movement Law: Derogation, Justification and Proportionality* (Hart 2016) v ('gravity of the restriction on free movement').

[92] de Búrca (n 32) 126.

[93] This concerns, for instance, laws excluding non-nationals from being tourist guides (Case C-375/92 *Commission v Spain (Tourist Guides)* [1994] ECLI:EU:C:1994:109), punishing them more severely than locals for drug possession (Case C-348/96 *Calfa* [1999] ECLI:EU:C:1999:6), or granting banks which have their seat abroad less favourable tax rates (Case C-311/97 *Royal Bank of Scotland* [1999] ECLI:EU:C:1999:216).

[94] Classic examples include residence, knowledge of the local language, and the acquiring of professional qualifications or working experience in the given Member State.

States a margin of appreciation in situations where non-nationals are treated worse than nationals, sometimes even where they are directly discriminated against. This runs against the Court's insistence on discrimination being the doctrine's non-negotiable boundary. The oft-repeated mantra that Member States forfeit their margin of appreciation if they discriminate does not reflect adjudicative practice. Almost a fifth of all margin of appreciation cases concern directly or indirectly discriminatory national measures. This, perhaps ironically, includes the very first margin of appreciation ruling, *Van Duyn*, in which the UK ban on working for Scientology could, for domestic constitutional reasons, not be extended to British nationals.[95]

Nonetheless, there are considerable differences between the categories. Cases brought against non-discriminatory acts show the highest margin of appreciation rate, of 36.28 per cent. The figures for the other two types of measures are significantly lower (indirect discrimination: 6.45 per cent; direct discrimination: 11.11 per cent). The correlation between the degree of discrimination and the margin of appreciation may not be entirely perfect; direct discrimination shows a slightly higher deference rate than indirect discrimination. There is, however, a vast gap between Member State acts that discriminate, be it directly or indirectly, and those that do not.[96]

It is interesting to compare these results with how the Court of Justice responds to national restrictions on economic freedom. Internal market lawyers have long debated the ultimate purpose of the EU free movement rules. While some have argued that it is to 'liberalize' cross-border economic activity, that is, remove market barriers that unduly disadvantage foreign actors (*anti-discrimination rationale*),[97] others have claimed that it lies in encouraging 'unhindered pursuit of commerce', that is, protecting non-nationals from any regulatory obstacle (*economic freedom rationale*).[98] After several decades of free movement jurisprudence, one may have

[95] *Van Duyn* (n 19).

[96] Interestingly, the share of directly discriminatory Member State acts has gone down from over 30 per cent of all free movement cases in the 1970s to just 5 per cent in 2013, while that of indirectly discriminatory measures has increased from around 20 per cent to over 50 per cent over the same period. This suggests that Member States have, as was argued in Chapter 2, internalized the fundamentals of EU free movement law (and/or have learned how to restrict free movement more effectively, given that indirect discrimination is harder to detect than direct discrimination).

[97] Paraphrasing the famous opening paragraph of Case C-292/92 *Hünermund* [1993] ECLI:EU:C:1993:863, Opinion of AG Tesauro. In his opinion, Tesauro advocated an anti-discrimination reading of the free movement rules, a view shared by many other Advocates General: see Cases C-158 and 159/04 *Alfa Vita* [2006] ECLI:EU:C:2006:212, Opinion of AG Maduro; Case C-442/02 *CaixaBank France* [2004] ECLI:EU:C:2004:187, Opinion of AG Tizzano; Case C-142/05 *Mickelsson and Roos* [2006] ECLI:EU:C:2006:782, Opinion of AG Kokott.

[98] The most famous proponent of this position is AG Jacobs who, in the direct aftermath of *Keck and Mithouard*, criticized the new path taken by the ECJ and lobbied for an interpretation of the free movement rules resting on the idea of economic freedom: see Case C-412/93 *Leclerc-Siplec* [1995] ECLI:EU:C:1994:393, Opinion of AG Jacobs (arguing that '[i]f an obstacle to inter-State trade exists, it cannot cease to exist simply because an identical obstacle affects domestic trade').

expected the issue to have been settled. Yet, nothing is further from the truth.[99] To this day, neither of the two visions—anti-discrimination or economic freedom—is able to account for the whole body of free movement jurisprudence.[100] Nonetheless, scholars like Eleanor Spaventa have put forward the argument that the Court of Justice has, over time, altered its focus. Instead of being concerned with fighting discrimination as it was in the beginning, it is said to have started, roughly since the mid-1990s, to concentrate on protecting economic freedom, thus turning the four freedoms into 'individual right[s] to exercise an economic activity free of disproportionate regulation'[101] or, in short, an instrument of 'economic due process'.[102] Do the data provide evidence for this shift?

Contrary to discrimination, there is no well-established classification scheme for restrictions on economic freedom. But one can divide national measures into three categories here as well: those which constitute *serious interferences* with economic activity, that is, prevent it completely or almost completely (product bans, monopolies, expulsions, etc); *medium interferences* which do not prohibit the activity but make it conditional upon economic operators fulfilling certain requirements (authorization, residence, licence, professional qualifications); *light interferences* which impose minor limitations on the exercise of the activity or reduce sales to a small extent only (limitations of shop opening hours, prior declaration requirements for imports, or similar).

As with discrimination, one would expect that light interferences show the highest and serious ones the lowest margin of appreciation rates. Yet, the exact opposite is true (Table 3.7). The doctrine is applied least frequently in relation to measures that restrict economic freedom mildly (13.33 per cent), followed by those of medium (15.58 per cent) and serious intensity (31.94 per cent). The picture from above is practically turned upside down. Member States are more likely to be given a margin of appreciation in relation to measures as restrictive as

[99] It bears underlining that the principle of market access, which is increasingly invoked in free movement cases, does not provide a 'third way' or 'middle ground' between anti-discrimination and economic freedom; see Jukka Snell, 'The Notion of Market Access: A Concept or a Slogan?' (2010) 47 Common Market Law Review 437, 470–471.

[100] The anti-discrimination rationale cannot explain the application of EU free movement law to product bans and rules on the use of goods, which have been held to fall into the scope of the four freedoms in spite of affecting nationals and non-nationals alike. Also, it fails to make sense of the ECJ's occasional reliance on *de minimis* rules, which exclude Member State acts from judicial review that hinder economic activity only marginally. The economic freedom rationale cannot account for developments such as *Keck*, where unequal treatment constitutes a criterion for assessing the legality of selling arrangements. Nor can it explain the continuous appearance of discrimination tests more generally, even in some recent free movement cases.

[101] Eleanor Spaventa, 'From *Gebhard* to *Carpenter*: Toward a (Non-)Economic European Constitution' (2004) 41 Common Market Law Review 743, 772; Eleanor Spaventa, 'The Outer Limits of the Treaty Free Movement Provisions: Some Reflections on the Significance of *Keck*, Remoteness and *Deliège*' in Catherine Barnard and Okeoghene Odudu (eds), *The Outer Limits of European Union Law* (Hart 2009). Similarly, Alina Tryfonidou, 'Further Steps on the Road to Convergence Among the Market Freedoms' (2010) 35 European Law Review 36.

[102] Alexander Somek, 'The Argument from Transnational Effects I: Representing Outsiders Through Freedom of Movement' (2010) 16 European Law Journal 315, 344.

Table 3.7 Margin of Appreciation and Economic Freedom

Interference with Economic Freedom	MoA Cases	All Cases	MoA Rate
Light	4	30	13.33%
Medium	24	154	15.58%
Serious	23	72	31.94%

Note: Cases with missing values ($n = 1$) were excluded from the analysis.

monopolies[103] and product bans[104] than in relation to minimal-impact regulation such as museum admission policies[105] or rules on tax deductions for professional training courses.[106] Note that the figures do not change if we narrow down the search to cases decided after the mid-1990s, which is when the change of focus towards economic freedom is meant to have taken place. Between 1994 and 2013, the ECJ is even more willing to grant national authorities deference in relation to severe economic restrictions than before.[107] The results contradict claims that the protection of economic freedom has become—or ever was—the guiding principle behind free movement law. Fighting unequal treatment of non-nationals remains the prime concern of the Court of Justice. This supports an anti-discrimination reading of the free movement rules.

In light of these clear results, one may wonder what has misled scholars in the first place. What made them think that the Court of Justice's priorities had changed? The answer, in a nutshell, is: they have been looking in the wrong place. The literature continues to be fixated on questions relating to the scope of the free movement rules. When the four freedoms apply and when not remains at the centre of academic interest, just like in classical free movement scholarship in the 1980s and 1990s. Yet, free movement law has changed. As was explained in Chapter 1 (and will be further explored from an empirical perspective in Chapter 5), the scope of application stage has largely lost its relevance. Most important aspects of free movement law are nowadays settled through justification and proportionality analysis. To take the Court of Justice's back-and-forths regarding the scope of free movement rights as an indication of its priorities is, therefore, a misunderstanding.

Mickelsson and Roos and *Italian Trailers*, the two decisions that sparked the most recent debate on the purpose of free movement law, illustrate this

[103] *Schindler* (n 16); *Läärä* (n 16); *Heinonen* (n 2).

[104] *Commission v Italy (Roadworthiness Test)* (n 5); *Commission v Germany (Meat Products)* (n 83); *Schumacher* (n 22); Cases 266 and 267/87 *Pharmaceutical Importers* [1989] ECLI:EU:C:1989:205.

[105] Case C-45/93 *Commission v Spain (Free Museums)* [1994] ECLI:EU:C:1994:101.

[106] *Vestergaard* (n 44).

[107] The respective margin of appreciation rates are: 11.11 per cent for light infringements; 15.67 per cent for medium infringements; 40.82 per cent for serious infringements.

well.[108] Introducing a novel 'market access' test, the ECJ held that rules restricting the use of goods fell into the scope of Article 34 TFEU. Scholars saw in this evidence of a reinvigorated judicial activism and the final step towards economic freedom becoming the overarching theme of free movement law. What went largely unnoticed in the discussion is that, in both cases, the actual review of the proportionality of the national law was neither activist nor driven by a concern for economic freedom. Although the measures were severe obstacles to the marketing of motorboats and trailers—do not let the soft-sounding notion of 'restrictions on use' misguide you: they effectively amounted to total product bans[109]—the Court of Justice opted for a hands-off approach in relation to the central regulatory problems in both cases. In *Trailers*, it granted Italy a margin of appreciation to decide whether moped trailers constituted a risk for road safety and how to best deal with this risk.[110] In *Mickelsson and Roos*, it let the Swedish authorities define what was necessary to protect the environment and, in addition, put the task of controlling this decision in the hands of the national judiciary.[111] What the Court appeared to signal at the scope of application stage (its increased concern for economic freedom), it undid during proportionality analysis by granting Member States broad discretion.

B. Effects on Deference

The results suggest that there are differences in how frequently the ECJ grants national authorities a margin of appreciation in cases displaying certain attributes. But do these attributes have an actual effect on the Court of Justice's behaviour? In other words: can we, based on the data, conclude that factors such as the relevant policy field, the existence of EU harmonization, or the application of fundamental rights influence—positively or negatively—the likelihood of Member States being granted a margin of appreciation? To verify the relationship between these factors and the application of the doctrine, a logistic regression analysis was conducted. For this purpose, the distinction between the partial and full margin of appreciation was dropped and the variable coded in a binary way (0 = margin not granted, 1 = granted).[112] All previously analysed factors were included as independent variables, with the exception of consensus, which was excluded due to the high number of missing values. The type of proceeding (0 = preliminary reference,

[108] Eleanor Spaventa, 'Leaving Keck Behind? The Free Movement of Goods after the Rulings in Commission v Italy and Mickelsson and Roos' (2009) 34 European Law Review 914; Gareth Davies, 'Understanding Market Access: Exploring the Economic Rationality of Different Conceptions of Free Movement Law' (2010) 11 German Law Journal 671; Snell (n 99).

[109] Davies, 'Understanding Market Access' (n 108) 696.

[110] *Commission v Italy (Italian Trailers)* (n 5), paras 63–64 and 67.

[111] Case C-142/05 *Mickelsson and Roos* [2009] ECLI:EU:C:2009:336, paras 37–39.

[112] Otherwise the number of observations would have been too low for some variables, rendering the regression analysis difficult.

1 = infringement proceeding) and the year of the ruling were added as control variables. Table 3.8 reports the results of the regression.

Four policy fields show a strong positive and statistically significant effect on the margin of appreciation: public health; games of chance; public policy/morality and security; and road safety. This means that the ECJ is considerably more likely to apply the doctrine when a dispute falls into these areas. The outcome makes sense in light of the descriptive findings in the previous section, which indicated high margin of appreciation rates in these domains. All remaining policy fields are not significant. The fact that a dispute touches on issues of consumer protection, the regulation of professional qualifications, social policy, intellectual property, or tax law has no tangible effect on the application of the doctrine. The standard errors are quite large here (as they are for the other variables), denoting a high level of statistical uncertainty, which is due to the limited number of observations in the sample.[113]

The main counterweighing factor, diminishing the likelihood of a national margin of appreciation, is discrimination. A negative and statistically significant effect can be observed for indirect discrimination, indicating that the Court of Justice is less likely to defer to Member State authorities if a national measure disadvantages foreigners. Direct discrimination is also negatively correlated with the margin of appreciation (if only significant at the 10 per cent level).[114]

EU harmonization equally has an impact on the application of the doctrine. A high level of harmonization strongly decreases the likelihood of the Court of Justice granting Member State authorities a margin of appreciation, showing a negative and statistically significant effect. By contrast, the fact that a dispute falls into an area that is marked by a medium level of harmonization displays no tangible effect on the Court's behaviour. This is in line with the descriptive findings which indicated that the main fault line runs not between the existence and lack of EU harmonization, but between highly harmonized areas and others.

Interestingly, the year in which a case was decided by the ECJ shows to have a positive and statistically significant effect on the margin of appreciation. In other words, the more time passes, the more likely the Court of Justice is to defer to national authorities. This lends further support to the argument advanced in Chapter 2: the European judges are gradually scaling down their control of Member State acts and behave in an increasingly deferential manner in free movement law.

The final variable with significant results is the applicable free movement right. The analysis indicates that the fact that a dispute turns on the free movement of workers makes it more likely for the Court of Justice to defer to national authorities. This is a curious outcome in light of the earlier findings which showed that the case law on workers has the lowest margin of appreciation rate of all freedoms of movement. How is this possible? A closer look at the Article 45 TFEU cases reveals

113 They are particularly large for two policy fields (liberal professions and tax law), a result of the lack of positive outcomes of the dependent variable in both cases.

114 The commonly accepted threshold for statistical significance is 0.05.

Table 3.8 Logistic Regression: Effects of Variables on Margin of Appreciation

Independent Variable	Coefficient (Standard Error)
Policy Field	
Public Health	2.424***
	(0.731)
Games of Chance	3.703**
	(1.326)
Public Policy and Morality	4.568**
	(1.525)
Road Safety	4.279**
	(1.433)
Consumer Protection	0.421
	(0.993)
Professional Qualifications	-18.768
	(7,044)
Social Policy	-1.282
	(1.583)
Intellectual Property	-0.384
	(1.339)
Tax Law	-18.603
	(5,915)
Level of EU Harmonization	
Medium	-0.829
	(0.618)
High	-2.582*
	(1.289)
Free Movement Right	
Goods	1.796
	(1.169)
Workers	3.385*
	(1.652)
Establishment	-0.744
	(1.301)
Services	1.001
	(1.144)
Capital	1.896
	(1.572)
Fundamental Rights	-1.186
	(1.725)
Discrimination	
Indirect	-1.679*
	(0.741)

Table 3.8 *Continued*

Independent Variable	Coefficient (Standard Error)
Direct	−2.040†
	(1.234)
Economic Freedom	
Medium	−0.847
	(0.879)
Serious	−0.506
	(0.872)
Type of Proceeding	−0.501
	(0.556)
Year	0.350*
	(0.149)
Constant	−4.144*
	(1.838)
Chi-Square	114.789
R^2	0.599
N	238

*** p < 0.001, ** p < 0.01, * p < 0.05, † p < 0.1

Notes:

1. Dependent variable is the margin of appreciation doctrine (0 = not applied, 1 = applied).
2. Base categories are: others (policy fields); no harmonization (EU harmonization); multiple (free movement rights); not applied (fundamental rights); no discrimination (discrimination); light interference (economic freedom); preliminary reference (type of proceeding).
3. Cases with missing values (*n* = 19) were excluded from the analysis.

that they are strongly correlated with cases in sectors that have been harmonized to a high degree as well as with those involving discriminatory Member State acts (indirectly and directly). This means that the effect we observe is not actually driven by that fact that a dispute turns on the free movement of workers, but by the variables of harmonization and discrimination.[115]

As important as the statistically significant variables are the not significant ones. This, perhaps surprisingly, includes fundamental rights cases which have, despite their high margin of appreciation rate, no measurable impact on the application of the doctrine. The same goes for the degree to which a Member State act restricts economic freedom, supporting earlier conclusions according to which this factor does not play the role in free movement adjudication as has been suggested in parts of the literature. Finally, the type of proceeding, that is,

[115] A univariate analysis between the applicable free movement right and the margin of appreciation yields a negative (−0.433)—and statistically insignificant (p = 0.545)—effect for the free movement of workers.

whether a dispute is decided under the preliminary reference procedure or as an infringement action, has no effect on the application of the margin of appreciation either.

The results stand in marked contrast to the ECJ's long and complex list of margin of appreciation factors. They indicate that, in reality, a relatively small group of variables drive the application of the doctrine. In a simplified way, the regression analysis warrants the following conclusion: the likelihood of the Court of Justice granting national authorities a margin of appreciation increases if a dispute falls into the four aforementioned policy fields; it decreases if the area has been densely harmonized at the European level or when a Member State discriminates against non-nationals. In addition, the European judges are, overall, becoming more deferential over time.

This provides some insights into the operation of margin of appreciation and the ECJ's behaviour more broadly. Free movement jurisprudence is largely marked by a 'precedential' approach or, as one could equally put it, path dependence: once the Court of Justice decides to grant national authorities a margin of appreciation in a given area, it sticks to this choice. For Member States and litigants, this makes it fairly easy to predict which types of legislation will be subjected to deferential and which ones to stricter judicial review. The Court will only depart from this default position when it detects discriminatory behaviour—an indication of its continued commitment to protecting non-nationals—or when there is (significant) progress in terms of EU harmonization.

III. Conclusion

What started off as a sporadic phenomenon, has become a doctrine increasingly cherished by the ECJ. The margin of appreciation has turned into an important element of free movement adjudication. Not exercising full justification and proportionality review appears to be, in some circumstances, an attractive option for the European judges. This chapter examined when exactly they find this possibility appealing. It took the Court of Justice's statements as to when national authorities are meant to enjoy a margin of appreciation and put them to the test. The results show that adjudicative practice is not as black-and-white as theory. None of the factors supposed to always trigger or prevent a national margin of appreciation actually do so. What is more, they fail to predict the Court's behaviour to an important degree. The margin of appreciation is not spread over a wide range of policy fields. Its use is essentially limited to four areas, the most important of which is public health. Neither the degree to which Member States restrict economic freedom nor the fact that a dispute touches on fundamental rights issues has an impact on its use. By contrast, EU harmonization and discrimination play an important role.

Understanding these patterns of use is not a mere probability calculus which informs us about the likelihood of the margin of appreciation being applied in specific scenarios. It also teaches us a great deal about national regulatory autonomy. Member States have the widest decision-making freedom in relation to games of chance and road safety, a more confined one concerning public health and public policy/morality, and the narrowest one in fields such as consumer protection, intellectual property, and professional qualifications. They are free to regulate market activity, even if the result is a serious interference with economic and commercial freedom, but will lose their margin of appreciation when discriminating against non-nationals.

At the same time, the analysis sheds light on the Court of Justice's behaviour: its aims, priorities, and the challenges which it faces. The ECJ's intensity of control over Member State legislation and free movement matters has gradually decreased over time. The Court feels uneasy deciding in areas marked by technical complexity, such as public health, but does not shy away from engaging in politically delicate subject matters. It remains committed to fighting discrimination and will step in where non-nationals are disadvantaged. Likewise, it proves responsive to legislative activity at the European level and will modify its review approach where comprehensive secondary legislation is adopted.

4

Decentralized Judicial Review

Theory and Practice

The EU is a composite legal order: two sets of courts—European and national—share the task of adjudication. The relationship between the European Court of Justice (ECJ) and Member State judges is often depicted as one of co-operation, with each level meant to play their part in putting Union law into effect. It is also built on the idea of judicial dialogue, the main platform for which is the preliminary reference procedure, through which national courts can obtain advice from the Court of Justice on the interpretation and validity of EU law.

Much academic effort has been devoted to the national side of this interaction. Scholars have enquired into how many references national judges submit, which factors drive their decisions, and what explains the variation between different Member States and types of courts. In the process, we have learned that participating in the European dialogue comes with benefits for (some) national courts, notably by empowering them vis-à-vis other domestic institutions;[1] that structural factors such as a country's population size, litigation rates, and the level of cross-border economic activity influence the number of references submitted;[2] and that softer variables like trust in the EU judiciary, support for European integration, and cultural differences as to the appropriate role of judges also matter.[3]

Curiously, less attention has been paid to the European perspective. What are the ECJ's strategic interests when interacting with Member State courts? On some level, the answer, of course, is plain. National courts are indispensable when it comes to 'supply' and 'enforcement'. To be able to exercise meaningful judicial activity, the Court of Justice is dependent on them submitting references and, once it has rendered judgment, implementing the ruling. But the phenomenon of

[1] Joseph HH Weiler, 'A Quiet Revolution: The European Court of Justice and its Interlocutors' (1994) 26 Comparative Political Studies 510; Karen J Alter, *Establishing the Supremacy of European Law* (Oxford University Press 2001).

[2] Morten Broberg and Niels Fenger, 'Variations in Member States' Preliminary References to the Court of Justice: Are Structural Factors (Part of) the Explanation?' (2013) 19 European Law Journal 488; Alec Stone Sweet and Thomas L Brunell, 'The European Court and the National Courts: a Statistical Analysis of Preliminary References, 1961–95' (1998) 5 Journal of European Public Policy 66.

[3] Juan A Mayoral, 'In the CJEU Judges Trust: A New Approach in the Judicial Construction of Europe' (2017) 55 Journal of Common Market Studies 551; Clifford J Carrubba and Lacey Murrah, 'Legal Integration and Use of the Preliminary Ruling Process in the European Union' (2005) 59 International Organization 399; Marlene Wind, 'The Nordics, the EU and the Reluctance Towards Supranational Judicial Review' (2010) 48 Journal of Common Market Studies 1039.

Europe's Passive Virtues. Jan Zglinski, Oxford University Press (2020). © Oxford University Press.
DOI: 10.1093/oso/9780198844792.001.0001

decentralized judicial review suggests that the relationship may be beneficial in a further, more substantial way. Chapter 2 revealed that the ECJ increasingly decentralizes assessments relating to the justification and proportionality of Member State action, a crucial part of free movement adjudication. It is here that domestic policy decisions are scrutinized, regulatory choices are struck down, and the content of free movement law is shaped.

This chapter will examine when and which decisions the Court of Justice defers to national judges. As in the case of the margin of appreciation, the analysis will proceed in two steps. The first section will identify the legal parameters. It will examine what division of responsibilities EU law envisages for the ECJ and Member State courts when it comes to justification and proportionality. The second section will test this legal model, drawing on the data from the case law study. It will investigate the actual role allocation between the two judiciaries, exposing the scenarios in which national courts decide and those in which the ECJ retains control.

I. Theory

For its part, the Court of Justice has always considered the division of judicial functions in the EU to be 'clear'.[4] The respective tasks of the European and national judiciary are largely determined based on two conceptual pairs: law/fact and interpretation/application (see Table 4.1). Whereas interpreting the law is the task of the ECJ, applying it to the facts of the case is for national courts.

Table 4.1 The Division of Functions between the ECJ and National Courts

National Courts Decide/Determine	**Court of Justice Decides/Provides**
Facts	**Law**
including proportionality analysis; interpretation of national law; effects of national measures; domestic policy objectives	
Application	**Interpretation**
ECJ has Insufficient Information	'All the Guidance Necessary'
National Court is 'Better Placed'	

[4] This statement goes back to Case 6/64 *Costa v ENEL* [1964] ECLI:EU:C:1964:66, 593: 'Article 177 is based upon a clear separation of functions between national courts and the Court of Justice'. It has been repeated many times since, see Case C-341/05 *Laval* [2007] ECLI:EU:C:2007:809, para 45; Case C-42/07 *Liga Portuguesa* [2009] ECLI:EU:C:2009:519, para 37; Cases C-316/07 et al *Markus Stoß* [2010] ECLI:EU:C:2010:504, para 46.

Both distinctions have a firm standing in European law. The Treaties acknowledge the Court of Justice's responsibility to ensure that 'the law is observed'.[5] The Court itself articulated the importance of distinguishing between law and fact as early as in *Costa/ENEL*[6] In an attempt to soothe the intervening Member States which disputed its jurisdiction, the ECJ pledged that it would only interpret 'the law' (meaning EU law). The preliminary reference procedure did not empower it to 'investigate the facts of the case'; this competence resided with the referring tribunal.[7] Ever since, it has been undisputed that the European judges deal with questions of law and national judges with questions of fact. Subsequent case law clarified that fact-finding comprises the duty to interpret national law (a 'fact' from the perspective of EU law),[8] to identify the policy objectives pursued by the national legislature,[9] and to assess the socio-economic effects of Member State regulation.[10] Most importantly, however, it entails the task of exercising proportionality analysis.[11]

The distinction between interpretation and application can also be found in the EU's constitutional materials. Article 267 TFEU, a provision which was hotly debated during the negotiations of the Treaty of Rome,[12] states that the ECJ has 'jurisdiction to give preliminary rulings concerning … the interpretation of the Treaties'. As with law and fact, the Court of Justice underlined the difference between interpretation and application from the beginning. Already in *Van Gend & Loos*, the Court delineated the functions of the European and national judiciary by explaining that the 'application' of EU law came 'within the jurisdiction of the national court'.[13] The ECJ, by contrast, was only competent to rule on the interpretation of EU rules.[14]

For a long time, the allocation of powers between EU and Member State courts was exclusively governed by these two distinctions. The Court of Justice would provide the interpretation of European law (or, at least, was meant to do so), while national courts would apply it to the facts of the case. Recently, this picture has

5 Art 19(1) TEU.

6 *Costa v ENEL* (n 4).

7 ibid, 593.

8 See Case C-302/97 *Konle* [1999] ECLI:EU:C:1999:271, paras 27 and 30; Case C-539/11 *Ottica New Line* [2013] ECLI:EU:C:2013:591, para 48.

9 Cases C-186/11 and 209/11 *Stanleybet International* [2013] ECLI:EU:C:2013:33, para 26.

10 Case C-145/88 *Torfaen Borough Council* [1989] ECLI:EU:C:1989:593, para 16.

11 ibid; Case C-169/91 *Stoke-on-Trent* [1992] ECLI:EU:C:1992:519, para 12.

12 Under an initial proposal, the ECJ was meant to have exclusive jurisdiction every time that a provision of European law was involved in a dispute, including cases before national courts; see Anne Boerger-De Smedt, 'Negotiating the Foundations of European Law, 1950–1957: The Legal History of the Treaties of Paris and Rome' (2012) 21 Contemporary European History 339, 351–52.

13 Case 26/62 *Van Gend & Loos* [1963] ECLI:EU:C:1963:1, 11.

14 See also Case C-235/95 *Dumon and Froment* [1998] ECLI:EU:C:1998:365, para 25; Case C-279/06 *CEPSA* [2008] ECLI:EU:C:2008:485, para 28; Case C-259/18 *Sociedad Estatal Correos y Telégrafos* [2019] ECLI:EU:C:2019:346, para 17. Sometimes, the ECJ is adamant about the limitations of its role, see Case C-162/06 *International Mail Spain* [2007] ECLI:EU:C:2007:681, para 24 and Case C-14/09 *Genc* [2010] ECLI:EU:C:2010:57, para 31.

become a little more complex. The Court has sporadically started to refer to three further factors that influence the distribution of functions in EU law.

The first factor is *insufficient information*. Whether the ECJ has sufficient knowledge about a dispute can traditionally only become relevant as an inadmissibility ground. The Court has reserved the right to dismiss preliminary references if the referring court fails to specify the factual and legislative context to a minimal degree of clarity.[15] In recent case law, information appears to have acquired a broader role. Even in references that comply with the foregoing minimum threshold (and are admissible), the ECJ seems inclined to hand over review tasks to the national judge if it lacks the necessary knowledge to decide. *A-Punkt Schmuckhandels* hints at this possibility.[16] Confronted with the question as to whether a domestic prohibition of door-to-door jewellery sales affected the marketing of products from other Member States more seriously than local ones, the Court stated that the available information did not allow it to ascertain the issue 'beyond doubt'. 'In such circumstances', the judgment continued, 'it [was] therefore for the national court to determine whether that condition [was] met'.[17] The lack of sufficient information was presented as a reason to refrain from exercising judicial review.

Closely related to this is the *'better placed'-principle*. The Court of Justice has indicated it will defer review tasks to national courts if they are better suited to assess the relevant factual circumstances. The origins of this principle lie in *Gourmet International*, a case on the Swedish prohibition of alcohol advertising.[18] The ECJ passed the decision on the proportionality of the advertising ban onto the referring judge as this required 'an analysis of the circumstances of law and of fact which [characterized] the situation in the Member State concerned, which the national court [was] in a better position than the Court of Justice to carry out'.[19] It was not simply the factual nature of proportionality analysis which made the ECJ defer to the referring judge here; it was the latter's greater knowledge of the national setting. The *Gourmet* formula has appeared in a number of judgments since, in free movement law and beyond.[20] It creates, if taken seriously, the possibility to allocate functions between the EU and Member State courts on a comparative basis.

[15] Cases C-320/90, 321/90 and 322/90 *Telemarsicabruzzo* [1993] ECLI:EU:C:1993:26, para 6.

[16] Case C-441/04 *A-Punkt Schmuckhandels* [2006] ECLI:EU:C:2006:141.

[17] ibid, para 25.

[18] Case C-405/98 *Gourmet International* [2001] ECLI:EU:C:2001:135. But, in a similar vein, already Case C-9/93 *IHT Internationale Heiztechnik* [1994] ECLI:EU:C:1994:261, para 20: 'it is for the court hearing the main proceedings to assess the similarity of the products in question. Since that is a question involving determination of the facts of which *only the national court can have direct knowledge* and so, to that extent is outside the Court's jurisdiction under [Art 267 TFEU] ...'

[19] *Gourmet International* (n 18), para 33.

[20] See Case C-434/04 *Ahokainen* [2006] ECLI:EU:C:2006:609, para 38 (free movement of goods); Case C-261/00 *Lohmann* [2002] ECLI:EU:C:2002:637, para 26 (customs union); Case C-438/14 *Bogendorff von Wolffersdorff* [2016] ECLI:EU:C:2016:401, para 78 (EU citizenship); similarly, also in Case C-201/15 *AGET Iraklis* [2016] ECLI:EU:C:2016:972, para 43 (Collective Redundancies Directive).

Whenever national judges are more competent to determine a particular question, they should decide.

These two factors—insufficient information and the 'better placed'-principle—pull towards national courts, establishing scenarios in which they can receive review responsibilities in addition to, or independently of, fact-finding and applying the law. A third factor pulls in the opposite direction, towards the ECJ: the *'all the necessary guidance'-doctrine*. Originally created in the Court's case law on fundamental rights, the doctrine has since made its way into free movement law.[21] It was used, for instance, in *Mickelsson and Roos*.[22] When reviewing the Swedish laws on the use of jet skis, the ECJ emphasized that it was, in principle, for the domestic judiciary to decide whether the measures were proportionate, given that 'any assessment of the facts' was 'a matter for the national court'. Yet, it also stated that 'in order to give the national court a useful answer, the Court may, in a spirit of co-operation with national courts, provide it with all the guidance that it deems necessary'.[23] What followed were fairly detailed remarks on how to evaluate the measure's proportionality. The Court found that Swedish law obliged the national authorities to designate some waterways as freely navigable, that they had to fulfil this obligation, and that they had to do so within a reasonable period of time. The function of the 'all the necessary guidance'-formula is clear: it creates flexibility, by enabling the ECJ to go beyond just interpreting the law and to address some of the factual aspects of a dispute.

Although the adding of these three factors is, as shall be argued later, convincing in substance, it inserts a degree of tension and unpredictability into the ECJ's relationship with Member State courts. The tension results from the insufficient information and 'better placed'-principles. If fact-finding is the exclusive domain of the national judge, it is puzzling how the Court of Justice's inadequate knowledge of the factual setting can matter—factual questions belong with the national judge, anyway (even if the Court has sufficient information). Likewise, it is unclear how the referring court's better position to determine the factual context of the dispute can become relevant—again, factual questions always belong with the national judge (even the poorly informed one). The unpredictability is caused by the 'all the necessary guidance'-doctrine. The ECJ uses it to justify more intense engagement in justification and proportionality review, a responsibility meant to rest with the national judiciary. Although this overstepping will often be exactly what Member State judges will have hoped for,[24] it comes, from a legal

[21] Case C-260/89 *Elliniki Radiophonia Tiléorassi (ERT)* [1991] ECLI:EU:C:1991:254, para 42; Case C-617/10 *Åkerberg Fransson* [2013] ECLI:EU:C:2013:105, para 19. As well as into other areas of EU law, see Case C-144/04 *Mangold* [2005] ECLI:EU:C:2005:709, para 74; Case C-224/11 *BGŻ Leasing* [2013] ECLI:EU:C:2013:15, para 33; Case C-157/15 *Achbita* [2017] ECLI:EU:C:2017:203, para 33.

[22] Case C-142/05 *Mickelsson and Roos* [2009] ECLI:EU:C:2009:336.

[23] ibid, para 41.

[24] See Chapter 2 I B.

perspective, at a cost by creating uncertainty as to the division of judicial competences. The Court of Justice may encroach upon the powers of national courts to the degree which it deems 'necessary', an assessment which appears to essentially lie in its discretion.

The more serious problem with this framework, however, lies elsewhere. It concerns its very foundations: the distinctions between law/fact and interpretation/application. Created to provide a basic allocation of responsibilities in proceedings under Article 267 TFEU, they have been directly transposed to free movement adjudication. This solution may seem consequential, even elegant. Yet, it is in equal measure problematic as it fails to provide a clear division of tasks regarding justification and proportionality review. We will now take a close look at the reasons for this failure.

A. Law and Fact

The distinction between law and fact appears in many legal orders with an appellate structure.[25] It typically entails the following division of responsibilities: lower-instance courts are in charge of fact-finding (as well as applying the relevant legal rules), higher-instance courts of determining the meaning of the law at stake.

Drawing the line between law and fact can be challenging *in casu* as courts tend to apply the law to concrete facts and examine facts in the light of particular laws.[26] However, at a basic level, the difference between the two can be made sense of as one concerning the type of information which is required to make a decision. Questions of law are based on legal information. They involve evidence such as the constitution, laws, regulations, and precedents.[27] Questions of fact require information from outside the legal universe—findings about 'who, when, what, and where'.[28] Facts can be determined by observing the real world. They are law-free, so to say; even a layperson without any legal training should be able to make these observations.[29] Law, to the contrary, is fact-free. It is a 'statement of a general principle or rule, made in advance of a case, awaiting application to the particular facts that

25 This, inter alia, includes the US (where the Constitution already alludes to the difference between law and facts), Germany, England, and France.

26 David Edward, 'The Exceptions to the Four Freedoms: The Historical Context' in Panos Koutrakos, Niamh Nic Shuibhne, and Phil Syrpis (eds), *Exceptions from EU Free Movement Law: Derogation, Justification and Proportionality* (Hart 2016) 9.

27 Ronald J Allen and Michael S Pardo, 'The Myth of the Law-Fact Distinction' (2003) 97 Northwestern University Law Review 1769, 1793.

28 Kevin Casey, Jade Camara, and Nancy Wright, 'Standards of Appellate Review in the Federal Circuit: Substance and Semantics' (2002) 11 Federal Circuit Bar Journal 279; see also Allen and Pardo (n 27) 1778.

29 Henry P Monaghan, 'Constitutional Fact Review' (1985) 85 Columbia Law Review 229, 235. The institution of jury trials, in which the fact-finding is done by a body composed of ordinary citizens, is partly based on this idea.

Table 4.2 Proportionality: Factual and Normative Elements (Theoretical Model)

Stage	Test	Nature of Inquiry
Legitimate Aim	Is the pursued policy objective legitimate?	Normative
Suitability	Does the measure further this objective?	Factual
Necessity	Is there a less restrictive but equally effective alternative measure?	Factual
Balancing	Do the benefits outweigh the costs?	Normative

may arise'.[30] The occurrence or non-occurrence of certain factual events has no implications for how a legal provision is to be interpreted.

To what extent does the distinction between law and fact help with allocating the tasks connected with justification and proportionality review? I will focus on proportionality here as it illustrates the main difficulties in this regard. In the Sunday trading cases, the ECJ stated that proportionality is a 'question of fact' and, as such, falls into the responsibility of national courts.[31] One can think of this proposition as the 'question of fact'-thesis: proportionality is about facts and facts only. Let us put it to the test.

The four-stage model that is common in national and international debates on proportionality can serve us as the point of departure; call this the 'theoretical model' (Table 4.2).[32] According to it, state action must fulfil four requirements to be proportionate: it must seek to attain a legitimate policy objective (*legitimate aim*); it must constitute an appropriate means to achieve this objective (*suitability*); there must be no less restrictive, equally effective alternative measure (*necessity*); finally, the costs for the right-bearer must not outweigh the policy benefits (*proportionality stricto sensu* or *balancing*).[33]

Already in this theoretical version, proportionality poses difficulties for the 'question of fact'-thesis. To be sure, proportionality analysis does contain factual elements. This notably concerns the suitability and necessity stages. In order to determine whether a measure is capable of contributing towards a policy aim, a court

[30] Casey, Camara, and Wright (n 28).

[31] *Torfaen Borough Council* (n 10), para 16; see also *Stoke-on-Trent* (n 11), paras 12–14.

[32] Robert Alexy, *A Theory of Constitutional Rights* (Oxford University Press 2002); Alec Stone Sweet and Jud Matthews, 'Proportionality and the Global Model of Balancing' (2008) 47 Columbia Journal of Transnational Law 72; Matthias Klatt and Moritz Meister, *The Constitutional Structure of Proportionality* (Oxford University Press 2012); Mattias Kumm, 'The Idea of Socratic Contestation and the Right to Justification: The Point of Rights-Based Proportionality Review' (2010) 4 Law and Ethics of Human Rights 140.

[33] Some scholars of EU law prefer to bracket the legitimate aim test and think of it as a preliminary inquiry (three-stage proportionality), while others question the ECJ's commitment to balancing or claim that the Court tends to engage in it in the context of necessity (two-stage proportionality). As shall become apparent, the problems for the allocation of judicial competences remain the same, regardless of which account one subscribes to.

Table 4.3 Proportionality: Factual and Normative Elements (ECJ Model)

Stage	Test	Nature of Inquiry
Legitimate Aim	Is the pursued policy objective legitimate?	Normative
	Is there a risk for the protected interest?	Factual
Suitability	Does the measure further the policy objective?	Factual
	Does it further the objective in a consistent and systematic manner?	Factual/Normative
Necessity	Is there a less restrictive but equally effective alternative measure?	Factual
Balancing	Do the benefits outweigh the costs?	Normative

has to examine the former's effects on the latter. Similarly, assessing the necessity of state action requires analysing which types of regulation work and which ones do not. Both are real-world phenomena, susceptible to empirical observation. This, however, cannot be said of the two other proportionality limbs. Whether a certain policy objective is legitimate is not a factual issue; it cannot be determined empirically. It constitutes a value judgment based on constitutional principles, moral considerations, and the like. The same goes for balancing. Whether the burden imposed on an individual is acceptable in light of the benefits for the polity (or other individuals) is primarily a normative decision.[34] It requires us to define which interests we seek to protect, to what extent, and with which priority, as well as how to reconcile competing interests in case of conflict. Proportionality, even in its theoretical form, is not about facts only. It involves a combination of factual and non-factual assessments.[35]

The 'question of fact'-thesis becomes even harder to sustain once we look at the proportionality test actually applied by the Court of Justice (Table 4.3).[36] Over the years, the Court has developed its own, distinct version of proportionality review, adding two further requirements to the four-prong structure; call this the 'practical' or 'ECJ model'.[37] Although these requirements have been formally made to fit

[34] I say primarily because balancing also requires a certain amount of factual information, notably as to the effects of a measure on the right holder as well as the policy benefits it generates.

[35] See also Mattias Kumm, 'Alexy's Theory of Constitutional Rights and the Problem of Judicial Review' in Matthias Klatt (ed), *Institutionalized Reason: The Jurisprudence of Robert Alexy* (Oxford University Press 2012); Moshe Cohen-Eliya and Iddo Porat, 'Proportionality and the Culture of Justification' (2011) 59 American Journal of Comparative Law 463, 471–72.

[36] The ECJ uses different formulas when applying the principle of proportionality and does not always engage in an examination of every limb of the test. The following provides an overview of all the requirements that have been accepted as parts of proportionality review.

[37] Stone Sweet and Matthews anticipate variations of such kind and suggest potential reasons (n 32) 162 et seq.

within the four established proportionality stages, they represent novel elements in substance. The most significant addendum is that Member State acts must be 'consistent and systematic' in their pursuit of the given policy objective.[38] Despite being presented by the Court as an innate, second part of the suitability stage, it is a novelty in proportionality review. Traditional proportionality analysis is not concerned with consistency or coherence.[39] In its original form, the suitability test merely requires that a measure contributes to the achievement of a policy objective to some degree. The second addendum is that Member States must show that there is a real risk for the protected interest. When a national law is intended to fight clandestine betting, illegal betting must be an actual problem in the Member State.[40] When it wants to reduce student numbers to protect the financial equilibrium of the higher education system, this equilibrium must actually be at risk.[41] The Court addresses this requirement within the legitimate aim stage, yet it differs from what the latter normally requires, namely simply that a given policy objective is acceptable.

Of these two new requirements only one is predominantly factual: the 'is there a risk?'-test. The question as to whether a danger for the protected interest exists can be investigated empirically. Yet, note that even here a normative judgment is necessary to decide how much risk a society is willing to accept in the first place. The consistency and systematicity test has a factual as well as a non-factual component. It requires both an assessment of the practice of national authorities (factual element) and an evaluative judgment as to whether that practice is coherent all things considered (normative element). The latter cannot simply be determined through empirical means.[42]

We see that the 'question of fact'-thesis is an oversimplification. Proportionality analysis, in both its theoretical and practical form, consists of a mix of factual and non-factual assessments. The Luxembourg judges, one should mention, are not the only ones to err when it comes to the nature of proportionality. Nor are they the only ones to struggle with the law/fact-distinction.[43] Courts around the world

[38] Case C-243/01 *Gambelli* [2003] ECLI:EU:C:2003:597, para 67; Case C-169/07 *Hartlauer* [2009] ECLI:EU:C:2009:141, para 55; Case C-137/09 *Josemans* [2010] ECLI:EU:C:2010:774, para 70; Case C-333/14 *Scotch Whisky Association* [2015] ECLI:EU:C:2015:845, para 37.

[39] Kai Möller, *The Global Model of Constitutional Rights* (Oxford University Press 2012) 125; Klatt and Meister (n 32) 8.

[40] Case C-258/08 *Ladbrokes* [2010] ECLI:EU:C:2010:308, para 26.

[41] Case C-147/03 *Commission v Austria (Higher Education)* [2005] ECLI:EU:C:2005:427, paras 64–65; Case C-73/08 *Bressol* [2010] ECLI:EU:C:2010:181, paras 50–51.

[42] The gambling case law illustrates this neatly. Take, for example, *Markus Stoß* (n 4) which raised the following issue: does a Member State pursue the aim of curbing gambling addiction consistently if it, on the one hand, creates a public monopoly on sports betting and thereby limits the opportunities to gamble but, on the other hand, advertises other games of chance, creates online casino games, and allows private companies to operate facilities for selected games of chance?

[43] The US Supreme Court called the distinction between law and fact 'vexing', see *Pullman-Standard v Swint* 456 US 273 (1982). American scholarship has, likewise, been critical of its usefulness for delineating judicial competences: see Monaghan (n 29); George C Christie, 'Judicial Review of

present proportionality as a factual and technical enquiry, a strategy employed to downplay the far-reaching review powers the test generates.[44] Parts of the literature also believe proportionality to be of a purely factual nature; some authors even consider this to be one of its central virtues.[45] Proportionality, however, is not a mere question of fact. It involves factual as well as normative judgments.

Debunking the 'question of fact'-thesis is easier than deciding which consequences to draw from it. One possibility would be to abandon the law/fact-distinction altogether. In this case, we would have to find other criteria to delineate the responsibilities between the EU and Member State courts. The alternative would be to follow it rigidly. Factual assessments would be the domain of national courts, while normative decisions would be for the ECJ. The suitability and necessity stages as well as the 'is there a risk?'-test would be dealt with at the national level. Balancing and the review of the Member States' policy objectives would be done in Luxembourg. There is reason to doubt the appeal of such a solution. Not only would proportionality, a review technique whose allure lies in its broad scope and easy structure,[46] be artificially broken up, but there would be serious consequences for free movement adjudication. The ECJ would be categorically barred from making any factual judgment, even if it had a just as good or even better understanding of the circumstances at stake. Also, *only* facts could be decided at the national level. Letting Member State courts make normative judgments would become impossible. Deciding between the first and the second option will require a more careful consideration of the underlying concerns, something which will be attempted at a later point. For now, suffice it to say that the law/fact-distinction fails to make sense of the nature of proportionality analysis. As a result, it is of little use when it comes to identifying the respective competences of EU and Member State courts.

B. Interpretation and Application

The second conceptual pair governing the division of judicial powers in the EU is interpretation and application. The ECJ is meant to interpret European law, while

Findings of Facts' (1992) 87 Northwestern University Law Review 14; Allen and Pardo (n 27); Elizabeth Thornburg, 'Law, Facts, and Power' (2009) 114 Penn State Law Review 1.

[44] Kumm, 'Alexy's Theory of Constitutional Rights and the Problem of Judicial Review' (n 35) 203; Bradley W Miller, 'Proportionality's Blind Spot: "Neutrality" and Political Philosophy' in Grant Huscroft, Bradley W Miller, and Grégoire CN Webber (eds), *Proportionality and the Rule of Law: Rights, Justification, Reasoning* (2014) 377.

[45] David Beatty, for instance, has argued that proportionality 'transforms questions that in moral philosophy are questions of value into questions of fact', see *The Ultimate Rule of Law* (Oxford University Press 2004) 170.

[46] See Chapter 5 II A.

national judges are supposed to apply it to the facts of the case. Both Treaties and case law are silent on what exactly these tasks entail. Commonly, however, interpretation is considered to amount to explaining something, rendering it intelligible. In the legal world, this something are rules, principles, and precedents.[47] Applying, by contrast, means to carry out an existing interpretation to a specific factual setting. The connection with law and fact is plain. Whereas interpretation requires a reflective act as to the content of legal norms (what do they allow or prohibit?), application requires an analysis of whether the facts of the dispute touch on this content (does the concrete situation fall within the scope of allowed or prohibited behaviour?).

The purpose of the interpretation/application-distinction is to limit the powers of different courts with respect to each other. This limitation works in two directions. On the one hand, the applying court is supposed to not meddle with the interpretation of the law. On the other, the interpreting court is supposed to not encroach upon its application. While the former has rarely, if ever, been perceived to constitute a danger in EU law, the latter has been a longstanding source of concern.[48] For the Court of Justice, this entails an important commitment: when it comes to judicial review of Member State acts, it must leave national courts a genuine role to play. There is agreement in the literature that this commitment is violated when the Court conclusively decides whether a national measure is justified and proportionate, without giving the referring judge any review power.[49] To think of these cases as instances of mere interpretation would be, as one author put it, 'disingenuous formalism'.[50] The national court has, to cite another scholar, 'little to do other than "execute" the ECJ's judgment'.[51] If the idea of application is to have any meaning at all, it must certainly entail more than that. It requires that national courts, at the bare minimum, have *some* responsibility when it comes to reviewing the justification and proportionality of Member State action.

[47] As to the reasons why the meaning of legal rules might not be clear and interpretation will be needed in the first place, see Robert Alexy, *A Theory of Legal Argumentation* (Clarendon Press 1989).

[48] G Federico Mancini, 'The Making of a Constitution for Europe' (1989) 26 Common Market Law Review 595, 604 et seq; see also Koen Lenaerts, 'The Court's Outer and Inner Selves: Exploring the External and Internal Legitimacy of the European Court of Justice' in Maurice Adams and others (eds), *Judging Europe's Judges* (Hart 2013) 14.

[49] Gareth Davies, 'Abstractness and Concreteness in the Preliminary Reference Procedure' in Niamh Nic Shuibhne (ed), *Regulating the Internal Market* (Edward Elgar 2006) 216; Catherine Barnard, 'Derogations, Justifications and The Four Freedoms: Is State Interest Really Protected?' in Catherine Barnard and Okeoghene Odudu (eds), *The Outer Limits of European Union Law* (Hart 2009) 295–96.

[50] Jeffrey C Cohen, 'The European Preliminary Reference and U.S. Supreme Court Review of State Court Judgments: A Study in Comparative Judicial Federalism' (1996) 44 American Journal of Comparative Law 421, 430–31.

[51] Paul Craig, *EU Administrative Law* (3rd edn, Oxford University Press 2018) 691. Similarly, the ever eloquent Federico Mancini (n 48) 606: 'having paid this lip service to the language of the Treaty and having clarified the meaning of the relevant Community measure, the Court usually went on to indicate to what extent a certain type of national legislation can be regarded as compatible with that measure. The national judge is thus led hand in hand as far as the door; crossing the threshold is his job, but now *a job no harder than child's play*.'

Do interpretation and application allow us to clearly allocate the tasks between the ECJ and national courts? The answer is no. The distinction suffers from a theoretical problem, which creates an ambiguity as to the separation of functions in practice.

The theoretical problem first. The distinction between interpretation and application is based on the assumption that the two are binary categories: a court can either interpret or apply the law—it cannot do both. This binarity is, of course, what makes the distinction operational to begin with. Only if there is a clear difference between the two categories can they serve as a means to allocate judicial competences. Theoretically, however, this is inaccurate. Interpretation and application are not binary concepts. They are the extreme poles of a sliding scale.[52] To be sure, there can be scenarios of pure interpretation or application. Clarifying the law without making any reference to the dispute's factual aspects amounts to the former. Deciding on the outcome of a case based on a rule the meaning of which was fully articulated by another court (or unequivocally laid down by the legislature) amounts to the latter. However, numerous in-between scenarios are equally possible. Interpretation is usually done in light of an actual dispute and therefore concerns specific factual circumstances. The interpreting court can, in different ways and to different degrees, choose to tailor its interpretation to this factual setting. It can say: 'The law requires A. Whether A has been complied with is for you, the applying court, to decide, but please take into account that event B has occurred, factual question C is relevant, concern D must be taken into consideration, etc.' We can imagine a continuum ranging from minimal to dense instructions. The less detailed the response, the closer we are to the interpretation pole. The more detailed it is, the further we move towards application. Through the lens of the interpretation/application-distinction, this continuum generates ambivalence. Whose responsibility are these intermediate scenarios: the interpreting or the applying court's?

Adjudicative practice neatly illustrates this theoretical conundrum. As was explained in Chapter 1, the guidance which the Court of Justice provides in free movement cases varies. The ECJ can restrict itself to stating that the Member State act under scrutiny must be proportionate and let the national judge decide freely (option 1: *fully decentralized judicial review*[53]). Alternatively, it can state that the

[52] The same, I should add, holds true for law and fact. An assessment of the law can incorporate factual elements to different degrees. Rather than being 'mutually exclusive kinds of questions', '[m]atters of law grow downward into roots of fact, and matters of fact reach upward, without a break, into matters of law', see Leon Green, *Judge and Jury* (Vernon Law Book 1930) 270. In US scholarship, it has been well accepted since the beginning of the twentieth century that 'mixed questions of law and fact' exist, see Frederick Green, 'Mixed Questions of Law and Fact' (1901) 15 Harvard Law Review 271 and JL Clark, 'A Mixed Question of Law and Fact' (1909) 18 Yale Law Journal 404.

[53] The *adoption* technique is not mentioned to simplify the argument. As it amounts to a decision freely made by the national judge, which is later adopted by the Court of Justice, it essentially corresponds to the full decentralization scenario. Both are instances of pure interpretation: the ECJ does not engage in fact-finding, leaving this task completely to the referring court.

act must be proportionate, let the national judge decide, but tell them that certain considerations have to be taken into account (option 2a: *decentralization with guidelines*) or that, upon a cursory inspection of the facts, the measure appears or does not appear to comply with proportionality (option 2b: *tendency*). Finally, the Court can state that the act must be proportionate, make all relevant factual assessments, and articulate a conclusive outcome (option 3: *centralized judicial review*). Only option 1 constitutes a case of pure interpretation. The Court merely stipulates the abstract legal requirement without enquiring into any of the factual aspects of the national legislation. Option 3 is a clear instance of application. The ECJ makes a definite judgment on the justification and proportionality of the Member State act; there is nothing left for the national judge to do but 'execute' this finding. Options 2a and 2b lie in-between. As both include factual elements, they go beyond pure interpretation. At the same time, they leave the national judge an actual role in proportionality review, which means that the ECJ does not, at least not completely, apply free movement law.

The Court of Justice's behaviour can, thus, amount to interpretation or application. Likewise, however, it can fall right in-between. This flexibility has been called 'of paramount importance for the proper functioning of the preliminary reference procedure'.[54] Yet, it creates a problem for the interpretation/application-distinction. The difficulty does not lie in the fact that the ECJ sometimes exercises judicial review in a way in which it, in principle, should not (option 3). That the Court comprehensively decides on the proportionality of Member State acts, and thereby effectively applies EU free movement law, does not call the very distinction between interpretation and application into question. It just demonstrates that the latter is violated in some cases. The true difficulty stems from the existence of in-between scenarios: whose responsibility are they? Can the ECJ provide more than interpretation as long as it does not fully apply the law? Or is any guidance going beyond mere interpretation forbidden as it contains elements of application? The interpretation/application-distinction cannot answer this question.

Note that the problem does not go away even if we opt for the former, more benevolent reading, according to which it is permissible to interpret the law without fully applying it.[55] Assuming that pure interpretation (option 1), interpretation with guidelines (option 2a), and interpretation with a tendency (option

[54] Lenaerts (n 48) 42.

[55] If we opted for a narrow reading of interpretation, any element of application would be forbidden. This would not only rule out that the ECJ decides conclusively on the justification and proportionality of a Member State act (option 3), but also that it makes use of any of the intermediate options (2a and 2b). The above-praised flexibility would disappear. More importantly, as the Court of Justice would be prevented from addressing any factual issues, its role would be essentially limited to reminding national courts that Member State laws must be justified and proportionate—the actual review of the proportionality of the measure would always be left with the referring court. Given the central role which proportionality has acquired within free movement adjudication, this would mean that the ECJ is, to a large extent, precluded from defining the content of free movement law.

2b) are all acceptable ways in which the Court can behave, we are left in the dark as to which option is warranted in which case. There are lightyears between the Court just saying 'the Member State act should be proportionate' and furnishing the referring judge with detailed instructions as to how to make that decision, accompanied by a prima facie assessment of the facts at hand. Yet, all these scenarios would fall under the same broad category of interpretation. Relying on interpretation and application does not enable us to decide which degree of guidance is warranted.

C. No 'Clear' Separation of Functions

The separation of functions between EU and Member State courts in free movement law is not as 'clear' as the ECJ suggests. Just as in EU law more generally, law/fact and interpretation/application are meant to delineate judicial competences here. Yet, both distinctions are ill-suited for this task. Distinguishing between law and fact is too simplistic. It fails to capture the nature of the justification and proportionality test, which requires judges to engage in both factual and normative judgments. Distinguishing between interpreting and applying is, by contrast, too stiff. It feigns binarity where, in fact, there is a continuum.

Many of the problems with the two distinctions stem from the fact that they were never intended for judicial review tools as complex as proportionality analysis. They come from a time when EU law was simpler, the era of *Van Gend & Loos* and *Costa/ENEL*. Back then, the Court of Justice could just clarify the meaning of a Treaty provision and leave it to the national court to verify whether the facts of the dispute complied with this meaning.[56] The rise of justification and proportionality analysis has rendered the work of judges much more complex. It brought an array of new questions into the courtroom, factual and normative, which can be determined by both the ECJ and national courts. To rely on the distinction between law and fact or interpretation and application in this context is impractical.

The Court of Justice appears to be aware of this and has started to break free from its doctrinal straitjacket. It has introduced three auxiliary criteria that are meant to help with determining which court should decide: the lack of sufficient information; the ability to assess the relevant question; and the need to provide guidance for the referring judge. These add-ons might not fit into the established categories of law/fact and interpretation/application, but they create the possibility for the Court of Justice to act in a more targeted way. It can ask national judges for help on matters it actually needs help with and provide guidance where guidance is needed.

[56] Although the ECJ was criticized already then for overstepping the line between interpretation and application, see Mancini (n 48).

II. Practice

Dividing judicial competences in free movement law is already challenging in theory. The distinctions between law/fact and interpretation/application, established in the Treaties and relied on by the ECJ, make it difficult to tell which judiciary, European or national, is responsible for what when it comes to reviewing the justification and proportionality of Member State action. A separate question, of course, is what the division of labour looks like in reality. There is a general feeling in the literature that the Court of Justice tends to overstep the boundary of interpretation and engage in factual assessments, thereby usurping the powers of the national judiciary.[57] To what extent transgressions of this sort occur is the object of varying estimates. More conservative authors claim that the Court does 'not always' respect the intended separation of functions,[58] others hold this to be the case 'often',[59] and still others suggest that 'more than two-thirds' of ECJ rulings might be affected.[60] Despite the popularity of such claims, broader systematic work on this issue is missing.[61] Consequently, we are left without a reliable understanding of one of the most fundamental questions regarding judicial review in EU law: what is the separation of powers between EU and Member State courts? Who decides on what, and to what extent?

In what follows, these questions will be investigated by drawing on the data from the case law survey. The focus will be on all preliminary reference rulings in the sample—that is, excluding infringement proceedings, given that national courts play no role in them—, with each ECJ judgment split into the different Member State acts under review (182 cases). As in the previous chapter, I will begin by providing some descriptive statistics about the degree to which the Court of Justice defers to national judges in the aforementioned scenarios. In a second step, it will be investigated to what extent these factors as well as some additional variables have a statistically significant effect on the decentralization of judicial review.

[57] Hjalte Rasmussen, *On Law and Policy in the European Court of Justice* (Nijhoff 1986) 447; Cohen (n 50) 430; Gareth Davies, 'Activism Relocated: The Self-Restraint of the European Court of Justice in Its National Context' (2011) 18 European Journal of Public Policy 76, 79.

[58] Craig (n 51) 691.

[59] Davies, 'Abstractness and Concreteness in the Preliminary Reference Procedure' (n 49) 216.

[60] Hjalte Rasmussen, 'Remedying the Crumbling EC Judicial System' (2000) 37 Common Market Law Review 1071, referring to a study conducted by Joseph Weiler in the 1980s.

[61] But see Hans-W Micklitz, *The Politics of Judicial Co-operation in the EU* (Cambridge University Press 2004); Takis Tridimas, 'Constitutional Review of Member State Action: The Virtues and Vices of an Incomplete Jurisdiction' (2011) 9 International Journal of Constitutional Law 737; Daniel Sarmiento, 'Half a Case at a Time: Dealing with Judicial Minimalism at the European Court of Justice' in Monica Claes and others (eds), *Constitutional Conversations in Europe* (Intersentia 2013) 13.

A. Patterns of Deference

1. Interpretation/Application

It is clear how much guidance the ECJ ought to provide: it is meant to interpret EU law and leave its application to the referring judge. How much guidance the Court provides in practice is far less obvious. Recently, this question sparked some controversy in an exchange between Koen Lenaerts and Joseph Weiler. In an edited volume dedicated to the legitimacy of the Court of Justice, Lenaerts addressed the separation of functions between the EU and the Member State judiciaries.[62] Although acknowledging that the Court's guidance can vary from case to case, he chose the *Bressol* judgment to illustrate how the European judges interact with their national counterparts.[63] In *Bressol*, the Belgian Constitutional Court had asked the ECJ whether national restrictions on access to medical training were compatible with the free movement of EU citizens. The ECJ left it for the Belgian judges to decide whether the national laws were proportionate but provided a list of instructions as to how this assessment should be made; it opted, in other words, for the guidelines approach. Weiler's riposte to Lenaerts was brief. It consisted in giving a counterexample: *Baumbast*.[64] Here, the Court of Justice chose to exercise centralized judicial review, providing a conclusive decision on the proportionality of a national law that denied non-nationals the right of residence if their health insurance did not cover emergency treatment. Weiler ends his critique by asking: 'Which is the more typical case: *Bressol* or *Baumbast*?' We may pose this question more broadly: how much guidance does the ECJ give national courts? To what extent does it respect the distinction between interpretation and application?

Chapter 2 revealed that the Court of Justice has, over time, come to defer increasingly often to national courts, with recent years showing deference rates as high as 40 per cent. Considering the limited role Member State judges played in the early days of free movement law, this number is remarkable. Nonetheless, it should not detract from the fact that decentralized judicial review has, overall, been the exception rather than the rule. In 135 out of 182 decisions from the sample the ECJ either centrally decides on the justification and proportionality of Member State acts or dispenses with examining the issue altogether (Table 4.4).[65] This means that in almost three out of four free movement cases the Court opts against decentralizing judicial review. Hence, Weiler's doubts as to the ubiquity of the *Bressol* method are well-founded. That the ECJ lets national courts review Member State laws autonomously is, at least looking at the past four decades, not typical. In the

[62] Lenaerts (n 48) 13.

[63] *Bressol* (n 41).

[64] Case C-413/99 *Baumbast* [2002] ECLI:EU:C:2002:493.

[65] For national courts, the latter option—the ECJ chooses to not engage in justification/proportionality review and finds a violation (or no violation) of EU law—has the same consequence: the Court of Justice conclusively decides the case, leaving the national judge without any review responsibility.

Table 4.4 Prevalence of Different Types of Decentralized Judicial Review

Type of DJR	Cases	Remarks
Full	6	
Adoption	6	in 2 cases combined with guidelines; in 1 case with guidelines and tendency
Tendency	4	in 3 cases combined with guidelines; in 1 with guidelines and adoption
Guidelines	38	in 6 cases combined with other types (see above)
None	135	= centralized judicial review
Total	182	

majority of cases, it conclusively determines whether a national measure was justified and proportionate.

However, Lenaerts is right in a different sense. Among the various types of decentralized judicial review, the guidelines approach is the Court of Justice's favourite. If, but only if, the ECJ chooses to decentralize review tasks, the most common way to do so is by furnishing the referring judge with instructions about which assessments to make, which points to take into consideration, or which evidence to demand from the parties. This technique is used 38 times. The guidelines laid down by the Court of Justice vary as to their level of detail. Some are relatively short and general, like in *Orfanopoulos*, where the referring court was only asked to check whether the public administration struck a fair balance between public policy and the right to family life.[66] Others are dense, such as in *Ottica New Line*, where the ECJ provided a detailed list of points for the national judge when deciding whether the local authorization requirements for opticians' shops were proportionate.[67] At times, the Court's guidelines can be so comprehensive that the difference with a centralized decision becomes microscopic.[68]

Other approaches are considerably less prominent in the case law. In 4 judgments the ECJ provides a prima facie assessment for the national court (*tendency*). In all of them it appears alongside guidelines: the Court sets out which conditions have to be fulfilled for the measure to be proportionate and, in addition, state that this 'would appear' or 'would not appear' to be the case.[69] The *adoption* approach, where the ECJ takes over the assessment submitted by the national court in its reference, is almost as rare (6 cases). Finally, on 6 occasions the Court of Justice

[66] Cases C-482/01 and 493/01 *Orfanopoulos* [2004] ECLI:EU:C:2004:262, para 95.

[67] *Ottica New Line* (n 8), paras 50–56.

[68] For one particularly striking example, see Cases C-369/96 and 376/96 *Arblade* [1999] ECLI:EU:C:1999:575.

[69] See Case C-212/11 *Jyske Bank Gibraltar* [2013] ECLI:EU:C:2013:270, para 83; *Arblade* (n 68), para 47.

defers the decision on justification and proportionality to the national judge *tout court*, without influencing or restricting the latter's judgment in any way (*full decentralization*).

The results show the limited practical relevance of the interpretation/application-distinction for the interaction between the ECJ and national courts. As explained earlier, the conceptual difference between the two is not so clear as is frequently assumed. Interpretation can, at least if understood broadly, encompass a wide range of review behaviour, from general statements such as 'this Member State act must be proportionate' to more context and fact-sensitive guidance. One scenario, however, was clearly ruled out: the ECJ conclusively deciding whether a Member State act is justified and proportionate. Judicial review of this sort amounts to application, a task reserved for the national judiciary. Yet, the above findings indicate that the Court of Justice, in around three-quarters of all preliminary references, settles the question of justification and proportionality centrally. It, thus, not only interprets but fully applies EU free movement law.

When the Court of Justice brings national judges on board in the review process, it likes to retain some decision-making power. In cases entailing a decentralization of judicial review there is a strong preference for intermediate models, notably the guidelines approach. That the ECJ grants the referring judge full discretion is, by contrast, extremely rare—it happens in only 3.75 per cent of cases. This, of course, is at odds with a strict reading of interpretation, according to which the Court must refrain from making any factual assessment at all and limit itself to setting out the law. Instances of such pure interpretation are the absolute exception.

2. Law/Fact I: Which Questions Do National Courts Get to Decide On?

While the ECJ is meant to settle questions of law, Member State courts are supposed to determine questions of fact. The analysis as to whether the idea of fact-finding adequately describes the role of the national judiciary will be divided into two parts. This section will give an overview of which types of decisions the ECJ decentralizes to national courts. The next one will address the specific issue of proportionality analysis.

Let me begin with an unsurprising observation. The decisions which the ECJ defers to national courts are partly of a factual nature. Some concern simple findings regarding the relevant national law and practice, such as questions on how certain domestic rules are interpreted[70] or how they are implemented by the local administrative authorities.[71] Others are more complex and concern what one

[70] Case C-33/97 *Colim* [1999] ECLI:EU:C:1999:274, para 42; Case C-60/03 *Wolff and Müller* [2004] ECLI:EU:C:2004:610, para 38.

[71] Case C-95/01 *Greenham and Abel* [2004] ECLI:EU:C:2004:71, para 49; *Mickelsson and Roos* (n 22), para 40.

could, borrowing from Hjalte Rasmussen,[72] call 'socio-economic findings': which legislative solutions are effective,[73] how local consumers behave,[74] and which economic consequences result from a regulatory choice.[75] The level of difficulty can vary greatly here. On one side of the spectrum, we find cases like *CMC Melkunie* in which the referring judge is only meant to establish how many days it usually takes a Dutch consumer to drink a bottle of milk once they purchase it in the supermarket.[76] On the other, there are decisions like *Campus Oil* in which the ECJ defers a series of complex and delicate assessments to the national court: what is the minimum supply of oil necessary for running Ireland's essential public services? Which quantity would ensure that the state refinery operates at a production level that prepares it for the event of a geopolitical crisis? And how much oil would be needed so that Ireland can fulfil the obligations from the long-term contracts it has concluded?[77]

The role of national judges does not stop at fact-finding, though. Member State courts are given a variety of decision-making tasks by the ECJ which, importantly, include normative judgments as well. In some cases, the decentralization of normative decisions happens relatively openly. This is notably the case when the ECJ hands over the balancing test or the entire proportionality assessment to the referring court.[78] Other times, the delegation of normative judgments occurs in a more disguised manner, when the ECJ defers decisions which it presents as factual but which are normative in substance. *Collins* is one example.[79] The Court of Justice stated that Member States could impose conditions for paying job seekers' allowance to foreigners but that the referring court ought to review whether these did not go beyond what was necessary to establish that a 'genuine link' existed between the person and the domestic employment market. Despite its factual tone, the national judge's task here was a deeply normative one, with considerations of social justice inevitably playing a role in the decision.

This overview testifies, once more, to the powerful role national courts have acquired in free movement adjudication. The notion of 'questions of fact' may create the impression that the influence of the national judiciary is restricted to determining issues of detail or minor importance. Nothing could be further from the

[72] Rasmussen, *On Law and Policy in the European Court of Justice* (n 57) 428.

[73] Case C-577/11 *DKV Belgium* [2013] ECLI:EU:C:2013:146, para 47; *Jyske Bank Gibraltar* (n 69), paras 70 and 85.

[74] Case C-383/97 *Van der Laan* [1999] ECLI:EU:C:1999:64, para 33; Case C-478/07 *Budějovický Budvar* [2009] ECLI:EU:C:2011:605.

[75] Case C-350/07 *Kattner Stahlbau* [2009] ECLI:EU:C:2009:127.

[76] Case 97/83 *CMC Melkunie* [1984] ECLI:EU:C:1984:212, para 19.

[77] Case 72/83 *Campus Oil* [1984] ECLI:EU:C:1984:256, paras 47–48. For further examples, see Cases C-197/11 and 203/11 *Libert* [2013] ECLI:EU:C:2013:288, paras 67–68; *Kattner Stahlbau* (n 75), paras 90–91; Case C-327/12 *SOA Nazionale Costruttori* [2013] ECLI:EU:C:2013:827, paras 65–68.

[78] Case C-309/02 *Radlberger Getränkegesellschaft* [2004] ECLI:EU:C:2004:799, paras 81–82; Case C-379/87 *Groener* [1989] ECLI:EU:C:1989:599, para 21.

[79] Case C-138/02 *Collins* [2004] ECLI:EU:C:2013:860.

truth. In addition to deferring to Member State courts on more mundane matters such as the interpretation of national legal rules, the ECJ lets domestic judges make autonomous value judgments and assessments on various socio-economic problems.

The term is misleading in another way. It makes it sound as though the ECJ reaches out to national judges for all types of factual questions. In truth, the Court's practice of decentralizing review decisions is concentrated on a much narrower class of queries. National courts are asked to inquire into national law, administrative practice, and socio-economic or cultural particularities. Their knowledge of or ability to obtain information on local matters appears to be the driving force behind the practice of decentralized judicial review. It is, thus, not the general factual expertise of national judges which the ECJ relies on, but their local expertise.

3. Law/Fact II: Who Is in Charge of Proportionality Review?

A separate note is warranted on proportionality, undoubtedly the most important 'question of fact' in free movement law. In *Torfaen Borough Council*, the ECJ held that it falls to national courts to examine whether Member State acts are proportionate.[80] Consequently, the Court of Justice is in principle meant to refrain from exercising proportionality scrutiny on its own, thus bypassing the national judiciary. It should be mentioned that a similar conclusion equally follows from the distinction between interpretation and application. Although, as explained, the two are not fixed, mutually exclusive categories, application requires that national courts have some role during proportionality review. This, at the bare minimum, rules out that the ECJ decides on the proportionality of a Member State act without involving them at all.

Therefore, in theory, every judgment in which the Court of Justice relies on proportionality should include a decentralizing of review responsibilities in one form or another. To what extent is this principle respected in practice? In the sample, proportionality is applied in 91 cases. Within this group one finds decentralized judicial review—in any of the four variants—in 41 decisions (45.05 per cent). Deference to national courts is much less common in non-proportionality cases, that is, in judgments in which the ECJ resorts to other, more general justification tests (6 decisions, or 6.59 per cent).[81] The results suggest the Court of Justice is much more likely to defer to Member State judges when applying proportionality analysis. This makes sense in light of the findings of the previous section. Examining proportionality requires a great deal of knowledge about the legal and

[80] *Torfaen Borough Council* (n 10), para 16. But see, in a similar vein, already Case 251/78 *Denkavit Futtermittel* [1979] ECLI:EU:C:1979:211, Opinion of AG Warner, 3404–05.

[81] See, for instance, Case 34/79 *Henn and Darby* [1979] ECLI:EU:C:1979:295, para 15 or Case C-348/96 *Calfa* [1999] ECLI:EU:C:1999:6, paras 21 et seq.

factual circumstances in a given Member State, knowledge which the Court of Justice will not always possess.

The meaning of these findings for the *Torfaen* principle, however, only becomes clear once we turn the numbers upside down. In 50 out of 91 proportionality cases the ECJ exercises centralized judicial review (54.95 per cent). In other words: more than half of the time, it acts in violation of *Torfaen*, according no role to national courts when it comes to proportionality review, a scenario we had discarded in theory. Note that this figure only captures decisions in which national judges are not involved in the review process at all. It rises even further if one includes cases in which the Court defers the decision on some elements of proportionality but decides itself on others, that is, any scenario except fully decentralized judicial review (93.41 per cent). Such partial review activity may be compatible with a wide reading of interpretation, as it does not amount to full application. Yet, it is at odds with the law/fact-distinction, under which proportionality completely belongs with the referring court.

4. Information and the 'Better Placed'-Principle

It was mentioned that, in more recent case law, the ECJ has started to hint at the relevance of factors other than law/fact and interpretation/application for the separation of functions between the EU and the national judiciaries. In *A-Punkt Schmuckhandels*, it stated that it could not review a Member State act as it lacked a sufficient understanding of the domestic context.[82] In *Gourmet*, it ruled that it was for the referring court to exercise proportionality review as the latter was in a 'better position' to carry out the necessary factual judgments.[83] (The 'all the necessary guidance'-doctrine will be omitted here due to its imprecise content.[84]) This suggests that information and decision-making ability have come to matter for the division of judicial competences in EU law. Does the case law survey confirm this?

It is impossible to measure the role and effects of information as systematically as that of other factors. Judgments of the ECJ usually do not allow us to tell whether the European judges did or did not have sufficient knowledge of the factual circumstances at stake. The reasons for this are twofold. First, we have no access to the orders of reference and the submissions of the actors involved in the proceedings (the parties, the Commission, and the Member States), which constitute the Court of Justice's main sources of information.[85] Second, this problem is aggravated by the fact that the ECJ only rarely addresses the issue of information. In the entire

[82] *A-Punkt Schmuckhandels* (n 16), para 25.

[83] *Gourmet International* (n 18), para 33.

[84] The ECJ has not laid down in which scenarios it deems guidance to be necessary (and how much of it), making a systematic analysis impossible.

[85] This has changed to some extent with the opening of the ECJ's archives to the public. All documents produced or received by the Court which have been selected to be permanently retained and date from more than 30 years ago are transferred to the Historical Archives of the European Union in Florence.

sample, it explicitly admits to lacking the necessary knowledge to exercise proportionality review just in one case; in *Läärä*, it complains about the 'absence of detailed information concerning the practical effect which the legislation has'.[86] For the rest, we are left with circumstantial evidence.

Nonetheless, it is apparent that the ECJ struggles with some of the questions brought before it due to a lack of knowledge and, as a result, will defer the decision to national courts. This often concerns the content of national law. One can sense such problems in *Wencel*, where the Court provides long explanations as to the potential implications of Regulation 1408/71 on Polish law but finishes by querying: 'if such a rule exists in the Polish legal system'.[87] In *Konle*, the Court of Justice appears to be confused about the temporal effects of judgments of the Austrian Constitutional Court, a matter which it ask the referring judge to determine.[88] Sometimes, the ECJ's knowledge gaps concern other factual circumstances. In the aforementioned *Ottica New Line*, it seems to feel under-informed about administrative practice in Sicily and therefore hands the decision on whether the local pharmacy regulation is consistent over to the referring court.[89] In *Rouffeteau*, it is unsure as to whether the submission of the French government on the widespread use of unauthorized phones is true, leaving it to the national court to establish the statement's accuracy.[90]

Although the findings remain unsystematic, they suggest that information and decision-making competence do affect the ECJ's readiness to defer to the Member State judiciaries. It bears adding that it is likely to be counterproductive that the Court of Justice is not more outspoken about this connection. Justification and proportionality review require a wide range of information without which the Court will find it difficult to decide or, even worse, decide based on an incorrect understanding of the factual context. Emphasizing more strongly that national courts will receive an incomplete decision on proportionality, or none at all, as long as they do not furnish the ECJ with sufficient information on the domestic setting—that is, not only an interpretation of the relevant national law, but an explanation of its socio-economic effects, possible local sensitivities in the area, the political significance of the dispute, and so on—would incentivize Member State courts to submit better references.[91] By the same token, it might contribute to improving the quality of the ECJ's judgments.

86 Case C-124/97 *Läärä* [1999] ECLI:EU:C:1999:435, para 26.
87 Case C-589/10 *Wencel* [2013] ECLI:EU:C:2013:303, para 63.
88 *Konle* (n 8), paras 26–30.
89 *Ottica New Line* (n 8), paras 50 and 56.
90 Case C-314/93 *Rouffeteau* [1994] ECLI:EU:C:1994:284, paras 9–10.
91 The ECJ has recently made an effort in this direction by issuing the Recommendations to national courts and tribunals in relation to the initiation of preliminary ruling proceedings [2012] OJ C338/1, in which it clarifies what information it expects national courts to provide when submitting a reference. These recommendations, however, do not include socio-economic facts. Therefore, they seem to be of limited use as a remedy for the informational problems of the Court in relation to justification and proportionality review.

5. Other Factors: Judicial Hierarchy, Length of EU Membership, and Formation of the ECJ

Given that the aforementioned factors capture the phenomenon of decentralized judicial review only poorly, three further variables that may influence the Court's practice were examined. The first is the referring court's *rank in the national judicial hierarchy*. Much ink has been spilled over the different roles which higher and lower national courts have played in the history of European integration.[92] Lower courts were, from the beginning, relatively eager to refer questions to the ECJ and implement its judgments, while domestic high courts were not only reluctant to apply doctrines such as direct effect and supremacy but to even use the preliminary reference mechanism in the first place. One may therefore wonder whether the ECJ, too, treats national courts differently depending on their rank in the judicial hierarchy. Given the special role which supreme and constitutional courts play in the domestic legal orders,[93] as well as their experience with constitutional review and interpretation, the Court of Justice may see them as privileged interlocutors and defer to them more willingly. A look at the data casts doubt on this hypothesis. If we divide the sample into preliminary references submitted by national high courts—including supreme and, where they exist, constitutional courts[94]—and lower courts, the differences in terms of deference rates are small. The ECJ decentralizes judicial review in 19.64 per cent of cases when the referring court is a high court and in 28.57 per cent of cases when it is not. Interestingly, the results indicate a lower deference rate for the former than for the latter, suggesting that supreme and constitutional court judges are not treated in a preferential manner.

[92] Joseph HH Weiler, 'The Transformation of Europe' (1991) 100 Yale Law Journal 2403, 2426; Alter, *Establishing the Supremacy of European Law* (n 1); Stone Sweet and Brunell (n 2).

[93] Jan Komárek, 'National Constitutional Courts in the European Constitutional Democracy' (2014) 12 International Journal of Constitutional Law 525.

[94] All courts whose decisions could, as a matter of national law, not be appealed were considered to be supreme. For the Member States from which preliminary questions were referred to the ECJ in the sample, this gave the following list of supreme and constitutional courts: Austria: Oberster Gerichtshof, Verwaltungsgerichtshof, Verfassungsgerichtshof; Belgium: Cour de Cassation/Hof van Cassatie, Conseil d'État/Raad van State, Cour Constitutionelle/Grondwettelijk Hof; Czech Republic: Ústavní soud, Nejvyšší správní soud, Nejvyšší soud; Germany: Bundesgerichtshof, Bundesfinanzgericht, Bundesarbeitsgericht, Bundessozialgericht, Bundesverwaltungsgericht, Bundesverfassungsgericht; Denmark: Højesteret; Spain: Tribunal Supremo and Tribunal Constitucional; Estonia: Riigikohus; France: Cour de Cassation, Conseil d'État, Conseil Constitutionnel; Finland: Korkein Oikeus and Korkein Hallinto-Oikeus; Greece: Areios Pagos and Simvoúlio tis Epikratías; Hungary: Legfelsőbb Bíróság Magyarország and Magyarország Alkotmánybírósága; Italy: Corte Suprema di Cassazione and Corte Costituzionale; Ireland: Supreme Court of Ireland/Cúirt Uachtarach na hÉireann; Luxembourg: Cour Supérieure de Justice, Cour Administrative, Cour Constitutionnelle; Netherlands: Raad van State, Centrale Raad van Beroep, College van beroep voor het bedrijfsleven, Hoge Raad; Portugal: Supremo Tribunal de Justiça, Supremo Tribunal Administrativo, Tribunal de Contas, Tribunal Constitucional; Poland: Sąd Najwyższy, Naczelny Sąd Administracyjny, Trybunał Konstytucyjny; Sweden: Högsta domstolen, Högsta förvaltningsdomstolen (until 2011: Regeringsrätten); UK: Supreme Court (until 2009, House of Lords).

A second factor that could matter for decentralized judicial review is the *length of EU membership* of the state where the preliminary reference has originated. The longer a country is part of the European Union, the greater the familiarity of its courts with EU law. This could make judges from older Member States more trustworthy review partners in the eyes of the ECJ which, in turn, might translate into higher deference rates.[95] The results of the case law study do not support this thesis either. If we divide the preliminary references in the sample into three groups—those coming from the founding Member States (accession 1957), 'middle phase' members (accession between 1973 and 1986), and the most recent additions to the Union (accession post-1995)—, the variation in deference rates is small. Somewhat surprisingly, the rates for courts from the newest EU countries (31.82 per cent) are higher than those from older Member States ('middle phase': 30.77 per cent; founding members: 23.88 per cent). This suggests that longer EU membership does not result in greater deference.

The *formation of the ECJ* could be a final factor influencing deference to national courts. In the beginning, the Court of Justice decided every case sitting in full court. As its caseload grew, this approach became untenable and was replaced with a chamber system. The practice emerged to assign the most difficult and important cases to the Grand Chamber (or, in exceptional circumstances, the Full Court), and leave the less ground-breaking ones for chambers of three or five judges.[96] Against this background, the choice of formation might affect the Court of Justice's willingness to defer to national judges. It could be lower in cases decided in larger chambers due to their complexity or significance for EU law and, *vice versa*, higher for those allocated to smaller ones.[97] The data, again, suggest otherwise. If we divide the cases into those decided in 'small' (three judges), 'regular' (five judges), and 'large' chambers (seven judges or more),[98] there is more variation compared with the previous two variables. But the results show that the ECJ defers to national courts more frequently when deciding in larger formations. The deference rates for judgments rendered by small chambers are lower (13.33 per cent) than those for regular (30 per cent) and large chambers (26.39 per cent). Difficult and important matters of EU law do not appear to be decided in a more centralized fashion than ordinary problems.

[95] It has been shown that the familiarity of national courts with EU law works in the other direction, positively affecting the number of preliminary references which they submit, see Lars Hornuf and Stefan Voigt, 'Analyzing Preliminary References as the Powerbase of the European Court of Justice' (2015) 39 European Journal of Law and Economics 287.

[96] See Art 11 of the Rules of Procedure and Art 16 of the Statute of the Court of Justice.

[97] Sarmiento, 'Half a Case at a Time' (n 61) 28. Carrubba, Gabel, and Hankla found that chamber size affects the outcome of infringement proceedings, but not preliminary reference rulings; see 'Judicial Behavior under Political Constraints: Evidence from the European Court of Justice' (2008) 102 American Political Science Review 435, 445.

[98] This categorization ensures a degree of consistency across time. The number of ECJ judges has increased over the years, but decisions rendered by 7 or more judges have always been those of the Grand Chamber or Full Court, while chamber decisions have been rendered by 3 or 5 judges.

B. Effects on Deference

Do any of these variables have a statistically significant effect on decentralized judicial review? Do they influence the ECJ's interaction with national courts? To find out, a logistic regression was conducted. Decentralized judicial review was coded in a dichotomous way, leaving aside the different types of decentralization (0 = no, 1 = yes).[99] Most of the previously discussed factors were included in the analysis as independent variables, with two exceptions. Interpretation/application could not be considered because it is, as explained, not truly independent of the phenomenon of decentralized judicial review: when the ECJ limits itself to interpreting EU law (be it in the broader or narrower sense), it always decentralizes at least some review responsibilities to the referring court; when it fully applies the free movement rules, this excludes the possibility that judicial review is decentralized. The question of sufficient information was not examined given the lack of reliable data. For the law/fact-distinction, the analysis concentrates on whether proportionality analysis was applied (0 = no, 1 = yes).[100] To get as full a picture of the Court's practice as possible, the variables from the margin of appreciation analysis and the year of the judgment were also considered. The results are reported in Table 4.5.

From the ten independent variables that were tested, only proportionality shows a statistically significant effect on decentralized judicial review. In line with the earlier descriptive findings which indicated higher deference rates in cases applying proportionality analysis, the effect is positive. This means that the ECJ is more likely to defer to national courts in proportionality than in non-proportionality cases, a phenomenon which may have to do with the extensive amount of information about the domestic setting which is required for applying the test.

None of the other variables prove statistically significant at the 5 per cent level. This goes for the court-specific variables such as the referring court's rank in the domestic judicial hierarchy, the length of EU membership of the country in which the preliminary reference originates, and the formation of the ECJ. It also holds true for all variables from the margin of appreciation catalogue: the applicable free movement right; the policy field of the dispute;[101] the level of EU harmonization; the degree of discrimination; and the relevance of fundamental rights matters. Interestingly, we find three variables with a statistically weaker relationship with decentralized judicial review (significant at 10 per cent level). This concerns public policy, which has a positive effect (meaning that the ECJ is more likely to defer to national judges if a case falls into this area), and tax law, which has a negative one.

[99] Any of the four types of decentralized judicial review (full decentralization, adoption, tendency, and guidelines) were coded as 1. As in Chapter 3, this was done because the number of observations would have otherwise been too low for some variables, making regression analysis difficult.

[100] Dividing ECJ rulings more generally into those raising 'questions of fact' and those turning on 'questions of law' would, in most cases, be impossible because each free movement dispute typically involves assessments of both factual and non-factual nature.

[101] The high standard error for road safety is due to the lack of positive outcomes of the dependent variable.

Table 4.5 Logistic Regression: Effects of Variables on Decentralized Judicial Review

Independent Variable	Coefficient (Standard Error)
Proportionality	3.226***
	(0.952)
Supreme or Constitutional Court	–0.965
	(0.675)
Length EU Membership	
Accession 1973–1986	–0.182
	(0.819)
Accession post-1995	0.125
	(0.831)
Formation ECJ	
Regular Chamber	1.527
	(0.973)
Large Chamber	1.639
	(1.011)
Policy Field	
Public Health	-1.365
	(0.859)
Games of Chance	-1.332
	(1.089)
Public Policy and Morality	3.156†
	(1.678)
Road Safety	-17.364
	(40,192)
Consumer Protection	–0.954
	(1.031)
Professional Qualifications	2.025
	(1.516)
Social Policy	0.933
	(1.227)
Intellectual Property	1.824
	(1.242)
Tax Law	–2.140†
	(1.108)
Level of EU Harmonization	
Medium	–0.551
	(0.661)
High	–0.688
	(1.008)

Continued

Table 4.5 *Continued*

Independent Variable	Coefficient (Standard Error)
Free Movement Right	
Goods	1.686
	(1.081)
Workers	−2.047
	(1.586)
Establishment	−0.103
	(1.169)
Services	1.091
	(0.979)
Capital	1.309
	(1.167)
Fundamental Rights	0.545
	(2.046)
Discrimination	
Indirect	0.211
	(0.655)
Direct	0.270
	(1.019)
Year	0.306†
	(0.184)
Constant	−6.685***
	(2.076)
Chi-Square	70.681
R^2	0.507
N	167

*** $p < 0.001$, ** $p < 0.01$, * $p < 0.05$, † $p < 0.1$

Notes:

1. Dependent variable is decentralized judicial review (0 = no decentralization, 1 = decentralization).
2. Base categories are: not applied (proportionality); reference from lower court (supreme or constitutional court); founding Member State (length of EU membership); decision by three-judge chamber (formation of the ECJ); others (policy fields); no harmonization (EU harmonization); multiple (free movement rights); not applied (fundamental rights); no discrimination (discrimination).
3. Cases with missing values ($n = 15$) were excluded from the analysis.

Likewise, the year of the ruling has a positive impact on decentralized judicial review, suggesting that the ECJ has become more deferential over the years.

This means that the only strong indication of whether the Court of Justice will defer to national courts that we have is whether a case involves proportionality analysis. One may not find this overly concerning. The regression analysis tested factors most of which were never said to matter, at least not by the Court, and concluded that none of them does. The practice of decentralizing judicial review proves much less targeted than that of the margin of appreciation. The involvement of national courts cuts through both different free movement rights and policy fields. It does not depend on the referring court's rank in the national judicial hierarchy, the length of EU membership of its country of origin, or the formation of the ECJ when deciding a case. It is not influenced by the level of harmonization or the application of fundamental rights either.

Yet, overall, a problematic picture emerges. Both the distinctions between law/fact and interpretation/application largely fail to capture the Court of Justice's interaction with the national judiciary. Information seems to play a role, but one which cannot be confirmed systematically. As a consequence, it is hard to tell in which types of cases the ECJ will defer to national courts and in which ones it will decide itself. From a perspective of judicial competences, this, of course, is troubling: who decides on what in free movement law remains, to a large extent, a mystery.

III. Conclusion

The power of Member State courts has grown immensely over the past four decades. More and more, the Court of Justice delegates decision-making tasks to the national judiciary instead of, as it used to, exercising free movement review in a centralized fashion. The increase in the importance of national courts is, on the one hand, quantitative. As Chapter 2 showed, the number of cases which involve deference to national judges has considerably gone up since the mid-1970s. On the other hand, and perhaps more importantly, it is qualitative. The matters which Member State courts are entrusted with include various, often complex factual assessments and value judgments with, at times, significant political ramifications.

As a result of this, EU free movement law is being increasingly shaped at the national level. Member State courts are given the power to decide what forms of regulation are effective, how to reconcile economic freedom with social policy concerns, and which laws are compatible with the free movement rules. The result is a departure from the model of 'monopolistic interpretation', under which the Court of Justice assumes the competence to centrally determine all questions relating to the internal market, and a step towards what has been dubbed 'interpretive pluralism': domestic—possibly diverging—readings of what free movement law means are accepted, even encouraged.[102] In this way, national judges contribute to forging the substance of European law.

[102] Gareth Davies, 'Does the Court of Justice own the Treaties? Interpretative Pluralism as a Solution to Over-Constitutionalisation' (2018) 24 European Law Journal 358.

The growing involvement of national courts is, one should add, not an isolated development limited to free movement jurisprudence. Similar tendencies can be observed in other areas of EU law. Can homosexual men be excluded from donating blood due to worries about HIV transmission?[103] Can a company dismiss a Muslim employee because she refuses to remove her headscarf at work?[104] Does a municipality's air quality action plan adequately take into account the interests of residents and motorists?[105] The Court of Justice has gone over to delegate such decisions to Member State judges.

The traditional distinctions that are meant to capture the division of functions in the EU—law/fact and interpretation/application—fail to do justice to the national courts' new role. The idea that the ECJ strictly limits itself to interpreting European law, which national judges then apply to the facts of a case, misses two essential traits of contemporary free movement adjudication. For one thing, due to the rise of justification and proportionality analysis, judicial review nowadays always requires courts to engage in both factual and normative assessments. It would, consequently, be artificial to differentiate rigidly between law and fact. For another, EU and Member State courts can decide different questions to different degrees, depending on their capacity and competence. To demand that review behaviour falls into either interpretation or application is, in this light, outdated.

The two distinctions are impractical in another more fundamental way. They do not allow the ECJ to seek the help of national courts where it needs it most. The Court of Justice decentralizes decisions concerning questions that require knowledge of national or regional characteristics (legal, political, and socio-economic), knowledge it will frequently lack itself. It is therefore not facts, and sometimes not only facts, that the ECJ needs its national counterparts for; it is their local expertise. The possibility of profiting from this expertise is one major benefit arising from the preliminary reference system. Only recently has the Court of Justice begun to emphasize this more openly by saying that it cannot decide certain issues due to the lack of sufficient information or because national courts are 'better placed' to assess the national setting. Although just sporadically referred to in the case law, these considerations seem more sensible as a means to delineate the respective roles of the European and national judiciary.

[103] Case C-528/13 *Léger* [2015] ECLI:EU:C:2015:288.

[104] *Achbita* (n 21); Case C-188/15 *Bougnaoui* [2017] ECLI:EU:C:2017:204.

[105] Case C-237/07 *Janecek* [2008] ECLI:EU:C:2008:447.

5
Proportionality and Its Discontents

Throughout this book we have seen many examples of the European Court of Justice (ECJ) not using the full force of judicial review and deferring to national institutions. Such restraint can occasionally be observed when the Court applies general justification tests, that is, examines whether Member State action is justified without resorting to a formalized structure. Yet, it appears much more commonly in cases involving proportionality analysis. The Court of Justice routinely defers to national authorities on matters such as the consistency of domestic legislation, the effectiveness of alternative measures, or the proper balance between free movement and competing policy objectives.

That the ECJ passes on the opportunity to exercise full proportionality scrutiny with such regularity poses a conundrum. Over the past two decades, proportionality has been the object of extensive research at the national, European, and international level.[1] Fascinated by its rapid spread across the world, scholars have studied the principle's content, the reasons for its dissemination, and the implications for constitutional adjudication. Although some disagreement remains—is proportionality at odds with representative democracy because it gives courts too much power?[2] Does it fail to provide sufficient guidance on complex moral problems?[3] Does it stand in the way of social change?[4]—this endeavour has yielded

[1] For a small selection, see Robert Alexy, *A Theory of Constitutional Rights* (Oxford University Press 2002); David M Beatty, *The Ultimate Rule of Law* (Oxford University Press 2004); Mattias Kumm, 'The Idea of Socratic Contestation and the Right to Justification: The Point of Rights-Based Proportionality Review' (2010) 4 Law and Ethics of Human Rights 140; Alec Stone Sweet and Jud Matthews, 'Proportionality and the Global Model of Balancing' (2008) 47 Columbia Journal of Transnational Law 72; Aharon Barak, *Proportionality: Constitutional Rights and Their Limitations* (Cambridge University Press 2012); Matthias Klatt and Moritz Meister, *The Constitutional Structure of Proportionality* (Oxford University Press 2012); Moshe Cohen-Eliya and Iddo Porat, *Proportionality and Constitutional Culture* (Cambridge University Press 2013).

[2] Mattias Kumm, 'Alexy's Theory of Constitutional Rights and the Problem of Judicial Review' in Matthias Klatt (ed), *Institutionalized Reason: The Jurisprudence of Robert Alexy* (Oxford University Press 2012); Robert Alexy, 'Formal Principles: Some Replies to Critics' (2014) 12 International Journal of Constitutional Law 511; Stephen Gardbaum, 'Proportionality and Democratic Constitutionalism' in Grant Huscroft, Bradley W Miller, and Grégoire CN Webber (eds), *Proportionality and the Rule of Law: Rights, Justification, Reasoning* (Cambridge University Press 2014) 259.

[3] Francisco Urbina, 'Balancing as Reasoning and the Problems of Legally Unaided Adjudication: A Reply to Kai Möller' (2014) 12 International Journal of Constitutional Law 214; Kai Möller, '"Balancing as Reasoning" and the Problems of Legally Unaided Adjudication: A Rejoinder to Francisco Urbina' (2014) 12 International Journal of Constitutional Law 222.

[4] Vanessa MacDonnell, 'The Reductionism of Global Models of Constitutional Rights' (2018) 12 Law & Ethics of Human Rights 73; Kai Möller, 'Stability and Change under the Global Model of Constitutional Rights: A Reply to Vanessa MacDonnell' (2018) 12 Law & Ethics of Human Rights 103.

Europe's Passive Virtues. Jan Zglinski, Oxford University Press (2020). © Oxford University Press.
DOI: 10.1093/oso/9780198844792.001.0001

consensus on a number of points. One of them is that the principle brings great advantages for judges. Proportionality provides a clear argumentation framework, comes with far-reaching review powers, and is a useful tool for resolving constitutional conflicts. In this light, the way in which it is employed by the ECJ in free movement cases might seem puzzling. Why do the European judges so frequently choose to apply deferential versions of the test? What explains their reluctance to exercise comprehensive proportionality review?

This chapter attempts to show that the Court of Justice's behaviour is neither irrational nor surprising. It is the sensible reaction to dealing with a tool for judicial review that carries the potential of overburdening judges. Existing literature has largely concentrated on the benefits of proportionality analysis, not on its costs. Yet, the four-stage test creates duties which can, under certain circumstances, be hard to fulfil. Courts will react to this pressure by resorting to deference techniques. The main thesis advanced in this chapter is that proportionality needs deference. The more widely courts apply proportionality, the more frequently they will be forced to opt for deferential forms of proportionality scrutiny.

In order to make my case, I will offer four arguments: historical, theoretical, comparative, and empirical. Each will look at the matter from a different angle. A historical analysis will trace the development of proportionality in the ECJ's case law and uncover parallels with the emergence of the margin of appreciation and decentralized judicial review. An enquiry into the nature of proportionality will explain the far-reaching obligations which the principle generates. A look at the US Supreme Court's standards of review jurisprudence will show why proportionality needs to be coupled with deference doctrines. Finally, an empirical analysis of free movement case law will reveal that the ECJ's application of proportionality has become increasingly deferential over time.

I. A Short History of Proportionality and Deference

Proportionality is a centrepiece in every history of EU law. It is part of the tale of how the ECJ, by gradually widening its review powers over Member State law, assumed a leading role in the integration process. Joseph Weiler is among the scholars who have told this tale. In 'The Constitution of the Market Place', he describes the evolution of the jurisprudence on the free movement of goods, outlining the Court of Justice's doctrinal and constitutional choices from the mid-1960s to the beginning of the 1980s.[5] The Court's activity in these early years—Weiler calls this the

[5] Joseph HH Weiler, 'The Constitution of the Common Market Place: Text and Context in the Evolution of the Free Movement of Goods' in Paul Craig and Gráinne de Búrca (eds), *The Evolution of EU Law* (1st edn, Oxford University Press 1999) 349. This is the first part of the essay; the rest covers the developments in the case law until the mid-1990s.

first and second generation of free movement case law—is presented as a process of broadening and intensifying of judicial review. It culminates with the adoption of proportionality analysis in *Cassis de Dijon*, a ruling which had the effect of 'deepening the enmeshment of the Court in the evaluation and sanctioning of Member State social policies in conflict with free movement, and this in ever more delicate areas'.[6]

This narrative, emphasizing a 'deepening' of review powers, is widely shared among scholars of European law.[7] It selects *Dassonville* and *Cassis* as the emblematic cases which represent how the Court of Justice acted during the first decade-and-a-half of free movement adjudication. Yet, in doing so, it disregards another important development that occurred during the same period: the emergence of doctrinal tools that allow the ECJ to restrict its involvement in national affairs. Against this background, I want to attempt a re-reading of the early years of free movement case law, that is, the Court's jurisprudence until the beginning of the 1980s. I will start by recalling the (better known[8]) history of proportionality and sketch out how it entered free movement law, a process which began outside the four freedoms and took approximately two decades, before then laying out the (less familiar) history of deference.

A. Establishing Proportionality

Proportionality vocabulary features in the ECJ's case law already in the 1950s. The initial measures subjected to proportionality scrutiny are administrative and regulatory acts of the High Authority, the predecessor of the Commission. They include decisions establishing fixed prices in the coal and steel sector,[9] fines imposed on companies in violations of these,[10] and penalties for failing to submit invoices connected with equalization schemes.[11] Proportionality here has a limited function and is minimally developed in content. The Court uses it to examine whether the High Authority's measures are not entirely 'out of proportion'[12] or the sanctions

[6] ibid 367.

[7] See Eric L White, 'In Search of the Limits of Article 30 of the EEC Treaty' (1989) 26 Common Market Law Review 235; Josephine Steiner, 'Drawing the Line: Uses and Abuses of Article 30 EEC' (1992) 29 Common Market Law Review 749; Miguel Poiares Maduro, *We the Court* (Hart 1998); Thomas Horsley, 'Unearthing Buried Treasures: Art. 34 TFEU and the Exclusionary Rules' (2012) 37 European Law Review 734.

[8] Takis Tridimas provides an authoritative account in *The General Principles of EU Law* (2nd edn, Oxford University Press 2006) 141. See also Clemens Kaupa, *The Pluralist Character of the European Economic Constitution* (Hart 2016) 174.

[9] Case 8/55 *Fédération Charbonnière de Belgique* [1956] ECLI:EU:C:1956:11, 299.

[10] Case 1/59 *Macchiorlati Dalmas* [1959] ECLI:EU:C:1959:29, 205.

[11] Cases 2 to 10/63 *Società Industriale Acciaierie San Michele* [1963] ECLI:EU:C:1963:59.

[12] ibid 345.

imposed are evidently excessive. The signature subdivision into separate stages is still missing.

This early usage continues through the 1960s. In the meantime, there is much lobbying to give proportionality a more important role in European law. Three actors are central to this process. Private parties start to invoke proportionality in proceedings before the Court of Justice as a means of challenging the legality of unwanted European and domestic measures.[13] Member State courts, predominantly from Germany, submit preliminary references which explicitly problematize the proportionality of EEC acts.[14] Finally, some Advocates Generals address the question of proportionality in their opinions and feed the ECJ with information as to how the test is applied by national courts.[15] In *Internationale Handelsgesellschaft* (1970), the Court of Justice eventually yields to this joint effort and, examining the validity of an EEC regulation of export licences for cereals, engages in proportionality analysis more properly speaking.[16] It investigates whether the objectives of the licensing system 'could have been attained by methods of intervention having less serious consequences' for the applicants, concluding that the measure was 'necessary and appropriate'.[17] The test laid down in *Internationale Handelsgesellschaft* turns into a cornerstone of the Court of Justice's fundamental rights jurisprudence.[18]

From thereon, the principle slowly makes its way into free movement law. Some free movement decisions in the mid-1970s already resemble proportionality scrutiny to a significant extent. *Sacchi* forbids, drawing on Directive 70/50, Member State acts whose 'restrictive effects are out of proportion to their purpose'.[19] *Van Binsbergen* holds that residence requirements for advocates are compatible with the freedom to provide services if they are 'objectively justified by the need to ensure the observance of professional rules of conduct', a line of reasoning repeated in *Thieffry* in relation to the right to establishment.[20] *Dassonville* allows national measures protecting the authenticity of designations of origin only as long as they

[13] Case 14/61 *Koninklijke Nederlandsche Hoogovens en Staalfabrieken* [1962] ECLI:EU:C:1962:28, 258; Cases 56 and 58/64 *Établissements Consten* [1966] ECLI:EU:C:1966:41, 314; Cases 5, 7, and 13 to 24/66 *Kampffmeyer* [1967] ECLI:EU:C:1967:31; Case 73/69 *Oehlmann* [1970] ECLI:EU:C:1970:59, para 4.

[14] See, for example, Case 11/70 *Internationale Handelsgesellschaft* [1970] ECLI:EU:C:1970:114.

[15] Advocate General Roehmer stands out in this respect. From the very beginning, he reasoned on the basis of proportionality, called it a 'principle' of European law, and cited examples of proportionality review from German doctrine and jurisprudence: see Case 31/59 *Acciaieria e Tubificio di Brescia* [1960] ECLI:EU:C:1960:3, Opinion of AG Roemer, 88 et seq; Cases 106 and 107/63 *Getreide-Import Gesellschaft* [1965] ECLI:EU:C:1965:65, 428; Case 73/69 *Oehlmann* [1970] ECLI:EU:C:1970:42, Opinion of AG Roemer, 481 et seq.

[16] *Internationale Handelsgesellschaft* (n 14).

[17] ibid, para 24.

[18] Case 4/73 *Nold* [1974] ECLI:EU:C:1974:51; Case 44/79 *Hauer* [1979] ECLI:EU:C:1979:290.

[19] Case 155/73 *Sacchi* [1974] ECLI:EU:C:1974:40, para 8.

[20] Case 33/74 *Van Binsbergen* [1974] ECLI:EU:C:1974:131, para 14; Case 71/76 *Thieffry* [1977] ECLI:EU:C:1977:65, para 15.

are 'reasonable'.[21] *De Peijper* establishes that public health regulation is not justified under Article 36 TFEU in cases in which human health could be 'as effectively protected by measures which do not restrict intra-Community trade so much'.[22]

The breakthrough comes with *Cassis de Dijon*. After affirming that minimum alcohol content requirements impede the free movement of goods, the ECJ examines whether these are, as purported by the German government, justified for reasons of consumer protection, public health, and commercial fairness. Although the Court does not call the test it sets out proportionality—instead stating that national measures have to be 'necessary in order to satisfy mandatory requirements'[23]—, the review it engages in amounts to proportionality analysis in substance. The Court examines the policy aims of the domestic regulation, assesses whether the latter is suitable to attain these aims, and inspects its necessity. Due to the frequent reliance on the ruling by private litigants and the Commission in the aftermath of *Cassis*, the use of proportionality skyrockets. The 'mandatory requirements'-test quickly becomes the dominant technique for reviewing Member State restrictions on the free movement of goods and, a little later, for free movement law in general.

This process—from the European Coal and Steel Community, to *Internationale Handelsgesellschaft*, to *Cassis de Dijon*—leads to an intensification of judicial review at the European level. By embracing proportionality analysis, the Court of Justice acquires the power to decide on a growing range of questions relating to Member State and EU acts, and starts to pronounce itself on the legitimacy of policy objectives, the effectiveness of laws, and the acceptable costs of regulation. In parallel, however, another development unfolds which pulls in the opposite direction. The ECJ creates doctrines enabling it to limit its scrutiny: the margin of appreciation and decentralized judicial review.

B. Establishing Deference

Just as with proportionality, margin of appreciation type arguments can be traced to the very beginning of the Court of Justice's activity. The first document published by the Court, the 1954 Opinion of Advocate General Lagrange in *Commission v France*, already discusses the 'power of appreciation' (*pouvoir d'appréciation*) of the High Authority.[24] The doctrine is initially used in three case groups. It is applied to review decisions setting maximum prices for the sale of coal and steel.[25] It appears

[21] Case 8/74 *Dassonville* [1974] ECLI:EU:C:1974:82, para 6.

[22] Case 104/75 *De Peijper* [1976] ECLI:EU:C:1976:67, para 17.

[23] Case 120/78 *Rewe-Zentral AG v Bundesmonopolverwaltung für Branntwein ('Cassis de Dijon')* [1979] ECLI:EU:C:1979:42, para 8.

[24] Case 1/54 *Commission v France* [1954] ECLI:EU:C:1954:4, Opinion of AG Lagrange, 23 and 31.

[25] Case 6/54 *Netherlands v High Authority* [1955] ECLI:EU:C:1955:1, Opinion of AG Roemer, 133; Case 8/55 *Fédération Charbonnière de Belgique* [1956] ECLI:EU:C:1956:11, Opinion of AG Lagrange.

in disputes about staff selection and disciplinary proceedings against Community officials.[26] Finally, it is employed in cases against regulatory measures concerning common agricultural policy,[27] transport,[28] and currency exchange rates.[29]

In relation to Member State acts, the margin of appreciation has a slower start. Its first usage is negative and concerns the issue of direct effect. In *Van Gend & Loos*, the Court of Justice declares that European rules, in order to have direct effect, must be self-executing which, in turn, requires Member States *not* to have a margin of appreciation.[30] After the decision, national judges submit a number of references with the aim of determining the direct effect of various primary and secondary law provisions.

This limited role changes as a result of two judgments which introduce the doctrine to free movement law. The first is the 1974 case of *Van Duyn*.[31] The Court of Justice articulates the existence of a national margin of appreciation in relation to public policy, making the doctrine a critical part of the judgment. *Van Duyn* touches a nerve. The *dictum* that public policy may 'vary from one country to another and from one period to another' resonates with national governments and appears in a series of proceedings on the free movement of workers shortly after.[32] In *Henn and Darby* (1979), the Court adopts the doctrine for the free movement of goods, letting each Member State determine the requirements of public morality 'in accordance with its own scale of values and in the form selected by it'.[33]

The second impetus comes from *De Peijper* (1976).[34] While examining the justification of legislation restricting the importation and sale of pharmaceutical products, the Court of Justice states that:

> Health and the life of humans rank first among the property or interests protected by Article 36 and it is for the Member States, within the limits imposed by the Treaty, to decide what degree of protection they intend to assure and in particular how strict the checks to be carried out are to be.[35]

[26] Case 1/56 *Bourgaux* [1956] ECLI:EU:C:1956:15, Opinion of AG Roemer, 308; Cases 94 and 96/63 *Bernusset* [1964] ECLI:EU:C:1964:41, 610; Case 10/64 *Jullien* [1965] ECLI:EU:C:1965:16, 7; Case 13/69 *Van Eick* [1970] ECLI:EU:C:1970:5, para 24; Case 46/69 *Reinarz* [1970] ECLI:EU:C:1970:39, para 11.

[27] Case 5/67 *Beus* [1968] ECLI:EU:C:1968:13; Case 57/72 *Westzucker* [1973] ECLI:EU:C:1973:30; Case 136/77 *Racke* [1978] ECLI:EU:C:1978:114.

[28] Case 1/69 *Italy v Commission* [1969] ECLI:EU:C:1969:34.

[29] Case 29/77 *Roquette Frères* [1977] ECLI:EU:C:1977:164.

[30] Case 27/67 *Firma Fink-Frucht* [1968] ECLI:EU:C:1968:22; Case 13/68 *Salgoil* [1968] ECLI:EU:C:1968:54.

[31] Case 41/74 *Van Duyn* [1974] ECLI:EU:C:1974:133.

[32] Case 67/74 *Bonsignore* [1975] ECLI:EU:C:1975:34; Case 36/75 *Rutili* [1975] ECLI:EU:C:1975:137; Case 30/77 *Bouchereau* [1977] ECLI:EU:C:1977:172; Cases 115 and 116/81 *Adoui* [1982] ECLI:EU:C:1982:183.

[33] Case 34/79 *Henn and Darby* [1979] ECLI:EU:C:1979:295, para 44.

[34] *De Peijper* (n 22).

[35] ibid, para 15.

This formula, whereby Member States are free to set the level of protection in public health, generates a discrete strand of margin of appreciation case law. It permits the Court to apply the doctrine beyond the realm of thick value judgments to decisions with technical or scientific aspects.[36]

In the meantime, the ECJ begins to work on a second deference route: Member State courts. With the rise of free movement litigation, it commences with passing substantive review tasks onto the national judiciary.[37] In *Rewe Zentralfinanz* (1975), it leaves the decision as to whether phytosanitary checks of imported apples are necessary to protect public health, and therefore justified under Article 36 TFEU, in the hands of the national judge.[38] One year later, it does the same in *De Peijper*, deferring—against the explicit advice of Advocate General Mayras—the assessment as to whether the national law is unnecessarily restrictive to the referring tribunal.[39] In *Donckerwolcke* (1976), the ECJ lets the national judge decide whether a French rule demanding certificates of origin for imported goods requires importers to declare more than they may 'reasonably be expected to know' and whether it imposes disproportionate penalties.[40]

That questions relating to the justification and proportionality of Member State acts belong with national courts is, around the time of *Cassis de Dijon*, already well-established case law. In his opinion in *Denkavit* (1979), Advocate General Warner even considers it to belong to the 'basic principles' of free movement law. After explaining that the 'test of validity' under Article 34 TFEU is whether national laws are necessary for attaining a given policy objective, he goes on to say that:

> where the validity of measures taken by a Member State ... is challenged before a court or tribunal of that Member State, it is for that court or tribunal to apply the test in the light of all the facts of the case, including the details of the legislation applicable in that State and the conditions prevailing there as a result of that legislation. On a reference under [Article 267 TFEU], this Court cannot, without exceeding its jurisdiction, go much further than to restate the test; at most it can indicate to the national court or tribunal factors that it should or should not take into account in applying the test.[41]

[36] See Case 53/80 *Kaasfabriek Eyssen* [1981] ECLI:EU:C:1981:35, 415 et seq; Case 132/80 *United Foods* [1981] ECLI:EU:C:1981:87, para 12; Case 272/80 *Biologische Producten* [1981] ECLI:EU:C:1981:312, para 12.

[37] See the discussion in Case 67/74 *Bonsignore* [1975] ECLI:EU:C:1975:22, Opinion of AG Mayras, 316; Case 104/75 *De Peijper* [1976] ECLI:EU:C:1976:43, Opinion of AG Mayras, 643; Case 251/78 *Denkavit Futtermittel* [1979] ECLI:EU:C:1979:211, Opinion of AG Warner, 3405.

[38] Case 4/75 *Rewe Zentralfinanz* [1975] ECLI:EU:C:1975:98, para 42.

[39] *De Peijper* (n 22), para 32.

[40] Case 41/76 *Donckerwolcke* [1976] ECLI:EU:C:1976:182, para 42.

[41] *Denkavit Futtermittel*, Opinion of AG Warner (n 37), 3404–05; see also Case 53/80 *Kaasfabriek Eyssen* [1981] ECLI:EU:C:1980:272, Opinion of AG Warner, 430 (pointing out some inconsistencies in the case law).

The ECJ follows Warner's suggestion in *Denkavit* and hands down the decision on the compatibility of the national law at stake with Article 36 TFEU to the domestic judge.[42]

C. A Parallel Evolution

Thus, by the end of the 1970s, the Court of Justice had established both proportionality and deference. Their emergence was not just parallel but, to an important extent, interdependent. Many of the early proportionality cases address the margin of appreciation of the High Authority or Commission.[43] The Advocate Generals' opinions in landmark cases on the Member States' margin of appreciation, such as *De Peijper* and *Henn and Darby*, constitute pioneering usages of proportionality analysis in free movement law.[44] Applying the 'mandatory requirements'-test from *Cassis de Dijon* becomes the first major task assigned to national courts.

By developing its jurisprudence in both directions—towards intensifying and limiting European judicial oversight—the ECJ created a spectrum of judicial review approaches in this period. Searching forms of proportionality scrutiny surfaced alongside more deferential variants. On the one side, the Court paved the way for strict proportionality scrutiny of Member State laws in rulings such as *Cassis*. On the other, it lay the foundations for more lenient proportionality review in decisions like *Van Duyn, Henn and Darby*, and *De Peijper*.

The early days of free movement adjudication were, consequently, more complex than commonly assumed. The Court of Justice was not only preoccupied with deepening its enmeshment in Member State policies. It equally made a visible effort to develop mechanisms that would allow it to reduce this enmeshment. The traditional portrayal of the evolution of free movement law misses the latter dimension. This, of course, is not to say that it is incorrect—the Court certainly did create far-reaching review powers over national laws. Nor is it to say that it wrongly singles out cases like *Dassonville* and *Cassis*—these judgments did leave an immense mark on the jurisprudence of the time and subsequent decades. Yet, told like this, the story is incomplete. Underneath the loud roars of activism were discernible sounds of restraint. Why were deference doctrines integrated into proportionality analysis by the ECJ right from the start? The answer requires us to delve into the question as to what the proportionality analysis enables and, by the same token, what it obliges judges to do.

[42] Case 251/78 *Denkavit Futtermittel* [1979] ECLI:EU:C:1979:252, paras 24 and 28.

[43] *Fédération Charbonnière de Belgique* (n 9), 300; *Koninklijke Nederlandsche Hoogovens en Staalfabrieken* (n 13), para 3.

[44] *De Peijper* (n 22), 648 et seq; Case 34/79 *Henn and Darby* [1979] ECLI:EU:C:1979:246, Opinion of AG Warner, 3830 et seq.

II. A Blessing and a Curse

Perhaps the most remarkable thing about proportionality is its success. Within less than four decades from its first modern usage by the German Federal Constitutional Court,[45] the principle has been adopted not only by domestic judiciaries on all continents but also by most important international courts.[46] In the literature, this expansion is read as a sign of proportionality's appeal to judges. Scholars have identified the reason for this in certain properties of the test: its comprehensiveness, structure, and legal nature.[47] Proportionality allows courts to do things they would otherwise be unable to do, through a method they would otherwise not have at their disposal.

A. Proportionality as a Blessing

1. Comprehensiveness

The allure of proportionality has centrally to do with its broad scope. Proportionality is, as one author has remarked, the 'most far-reaching ground for review, the most potent weapon in the arsenal of a public law judge'.[48] Compared with other judicial review techniques, it substantially widens the range of questions which courts can investigate. This does not mean that other tests yield less consequential outcomes. Yet, they do not allow judges to pronounce themselves on a panorama of issues nearly as wide as with proportionality.

Consider 'rule-like' tests against which proportionality is often contrasted. Legal norms can be divided into rules and standards.[49] Rules are clear and precise norms which make it possible to determine whether a given action is permissible in advance of a court judgment. Standards involve open-ended criteria and typically rely on a balancing of interests. Discrimination tests, to name one example familiar to free movement lawyers, are rules in this sense.[50] They involve an examination of whether two groups are treated differently despite showing no significant differences (or treated alike despite being different). The same goes for typological tests

[45] BVerfGE 7, 377 *Pharmacies Judgment* (1958).

[46] Barak (n 1) provides an overview of proportionality's history of migration at 182.

[47] Cohen-Eliya and Porat offer a slightly different account in 'Proportionality and the Culture of Justification' (2011) 59 American Journal of Comparative Law 463.

[48] Tridimas (n 8) 140.

[49] See Alexy, *A Theory of Constitutional Rights* (n 1); more recently, also Elke Cloots, *National Identity in EU Law* (Oxford University Press 2015) 198 et seq.

[50] In some early free movement cases, the Court of Justice did not make use yet of the two-part structure characterizing later judgments (first, examination of scope of application/restriction and, second, justification) but engaged in a single-step enquiry: if a national law was discriminatory, it was held incompatible with EU law; if it was not discriminatory, it was upheld. See, for example, Case 167/73 *Commission v France (Maritime Employment)* [1974] ECLI:EU:C:1974:35 and Case 182/83 *Fearon* [1984] ECLI:EU:C:1984:335.

which allow or prohibit specific forms of action, such as the 'selling arrangements' from *Keck*, or the 'essence of rights' tests sometimes used in human rights cases, which permit restrictions on a right as long as its core is not touched upon.[51] When a court invalidates a state measure because it violates rules of this sort, the implications can be profound. States will have to amend their legislation, change their regulatory approach, and include concerns in their decision-making that they had hitherto neglected. Yet, what judges can do when applying such tests is, formally speaking, relatively limited. They can examine whether two groups are treated differently although they show no significant differences, if a law falls into the prohibited class of action, or whether the essence of the right is violated. It is plain that their decision is likely to be motivated by considerations beyond this formal test such as: what are the economic consequences of my decision? What were the policy reasons behind the adoption of the law? Will society be better off if it is upheld? Yet, these will typically remain unarticulated.

Proportionality analysis radically changes this. It permits judges to address all of the above issues and, what is more, to do so head-on. Courts can examine whether the reasons behind adopting a piece of legislation are acceptable, the law works as intended, alternatives would have worked equally well, and legislating was worth it all things considered. This brings a new scope and quality to the judges' task. It allows them to engage with many or, more precisely, most important aspects of state action,[52] which is why the test is frequently referred to as 'full scrutiny' or, in French law, 'contrôle maximum'.[53] The corollary of this, of course, is power.[54] Proportionality gives judges a say on a variety of empirical and normative questions, resulting in an important increase in influence for the judiciary.

2. Structure

Proportionality comes in a form—the four stages, prongs, or limbs—that is practical for both courts and their audience. Modern constitutional adjudication is marked by judges deciding on many issues they traditionally did not have to deal with, such as matters of policy making and moral and socio-economic assessments. In spite of the complexity of this duty, constitutional rights tend to be the most

[51] The ECJ sometimes refers to the 'essence' or 'very substance' of rights in fundamental rights cases (even if this is often followed by, or embedded in, proportionality analysis), see Case 5/88 *Wachauf* [1989] ECLI:EU:C:1989:321, para 18 and Cases C-293/12 and 594/12 *Digital Rights Ireland* [2014] ECLI:EU:C:2014:238, paras 38 et seq. Essence of rights tests are more widely applied in the European Convention on Human Rights context and some domestic jurisdictions, such as India and Germany.

[52] But see Mattias Kumm, 'Political Liberalism and the Structure of Rights: On the Place and Limits of the Proportionality Requirement' in George Pavlakos and Stanley Poulson (eds), *Law, Rights and Discourse: the Legal Philosophy of Robert Alexy* (Hart 2007).

[53] French administrative law distinguishes between three standards of review: *contrôle restraint, contrôle entier* (or 'normale'), and *contrôle maximum*.

[54] Cohen-Eliya and Porat, 'Proportionality and the Culture of Justification' (n 47) 473 et seq.

indeterminate parts of a legal system. As a result, courts find themselves facing a difficult task without much guidance. They need to work without 'many of the constraining features that otherwise characterize legal reasoning', such as a clear wording, the legislative context, or the law maker's intent behind a provision.[55] Proportionality comes in handy in this respect. It creates a structure where there would otherwise be none. By setting out a four-step legal test, it turns the judges' work into something which they are more accustomed to: '[i]nstead of having to dispute contested questions of political philosophy', they can 'focus on a discrete set of technically worded inquiries'.[56]

At the same time, proportionality analysis has proven practical for resolving the sorts of conflicts that arise in pluralist societies. Laws often affect a variety of competing interests at once. Proportionality permits courts not only to identify these interests, but to also assess their relevance and relative weight. This ensures a well-rounded decision which, to the greatest extent possible, does justice to the concerns of all affected. Likewise, it allows judges to express their respect for the conflicting positions. As Alec Stone Sweet and Jud Matthews explain: '[in] situations where the judges cannot avoid declaring a winner, they can at least make a series of ritual bows to the losing party'.[57] Proportionality analysis facilitates these bows by enabling courts to acknowledge all interests that are at stake. Even if ultimately not affecting the outcome of the case, the element of bowing is crucial. It makes it easier for the losing party to accept their defeat.

3. Legal Nature

Proportionality comes with a final benefit: it is a legal test. This may sound trivial at first—in reality, it is anything but. Proportionality analysis brings assessments into the courtroom which, in substance, correspond to the political assessments the legislative and executive branches make, if in a less formal way, when adopting a measure in the first place.[58] They, too, must deliberate on which policy aims to protect, which regulatory solution is effective, and whether regulating is worth it all things considered. By allowing courts to re-evaluate these decisions, proportionality aligns their work with that of legislatures and executives to an important degree.[59]

[55] Kumm, 'The Idea of Socratic Contestation and the Right to Justification' (n 1) 150.

[56] Bradley W Miller, 'Proportionality's Blind Spot: "Neutrality" and Political Philosophy' in Grant Huscroft, Bradley W Miller, and Grégoire CN Webber (eds), *Proportionality and the Rule of Law: Rights, Justification, Reasoning* (2014) 379. See also Kai Möller, *The Global Model of Constitutional Rights* (Oxford University Press 2012) 179.

[57] Stone Sweet and Matthews (n 1) 89. In a similar vein, Steve Weatherill calls proportionality 'a type of politeness': see 'Justification, Proportionality and Consumer Protection' in Panos Koutrakos, Niamh Nic Shuibhne, and Phil Syrpis (eds), *Exceptions from EU Free Movement Law: Derogation, Justification and Proportionality* (Hart 2016) 248.

[58] Kumm, 'Alexy's Theory of Constitutional Rights and the Problem of Judicial Review' (n 2) 203.

[59] It is for this reason that the principle of proportionality caused considerable resistance in some European countries. British lawyers were at the forefront of this proportionality scepticism. In an opinion which eventually gave rise to the ECJ's judgment in *Stoke-on-Trent*, Justice (later Lord)

Now, judges do not feel comfortable in openly making political decisions. It is a central element of their self-understanding, and an expectation of the legal order towards them, that they engage in law not politics.[60] The US Supreme Court called political issues as off limits from as early as *Marbury v Madison*, where it stated that 'questions, in their nature political ... can never be made in this court'.[61] The European Court of Human Rights (ECtHR), when first applying proportionality analysis, felt the need to emphasize that it did not 'assume the role of the competent national authorities' to decide which regulatory measures were appropriate; its task was only to assess 'the conformity of the measures with the requirements of the Convention'.[62] The UK Supreme Court, most recently, reminded its audience that 'courts cannot decide political questions'.[63] Judges avoid presenting their decisions as going beyond the boundaries of law at all costs. This is an important way of defending the legitimacy of what they do.

Proportionality allows them to circumvent this problem by turning a deeply political inquiry into a legal test. In the words of Mattias Kumm:

> Perhaps the secret of the success of rights-based proportionality review is directly connected to its technocratic camouflage (a multi-prong legalistic sounding test) and its embeddedness in legal institutions that work together to obscure its true nature.[64]

In court rulings across the world, proportionality is portrayed as a mechanical, objective and altogether unremarkable review tool. This is a feature of its technocratic and legalistic 'camouflage'. Despite containing moral and empirical judgments normally reserved for the political process, proportionality permits courts to present their activity as purely legal. This conversion from politics to law is crucial. It allows judges to act in their comfort zone.

Hoffman famously warned: 'It is not my function to carry out the balancing exercise to form my own view on whether the legislative objective could be achieved by other means. These questions involved compromises between competing interests which in a democratic society must be resolved by the legislator.' See *Stoke-on-Trent City Council v B & Q* [1990] 3 Common Market Law Reports 31 (English High Court, Chancery Division), para 47.

[60] The distrust towards courts as political actors has a long pedigree and was perhaps most famously articulated by Montesquieu who wanted judges to be a mere 'mouthpiece of the law' (*bouche de la loi*). See also Bogdan Iancu, 'Law/Politics Distinctions: The Elusive Reference Points' in Bogdan Iancu (ed), *The Law/Politics Distinction in Contemporary Public Law Adjudication* (Eleven International 2009).

[61] *Marbury v Madison* 5 US 137 (1803).

[62] *Case 'Relating to Certain Aspects of the Laws on the Use of Languages in Education in Belgium' v Belgium* (1968) 1 EHRR 252, 32. In his dissent, Judge Wold warned that balancing carried the Strasbourg Court 'into the very middle of the internal political questions of each Member State, which it has never been the intention that the Court should deal with.'

[63] Even if also stating that 'the fact that a legal dispute concerns the conduct of politicians, or arises from a matter of political controversy, has never been sufficient reason for the courts to refuse to consider it', see *R (Miller) v Prime Minister* [2019] UKSC 41, para 32.

[64] Kumm, 'The Idea of Socratic Contestation and the Right to Justification' (n 1) 174.

B. Proportionality as a Curse

Embracing proportionality as a tool for judicial review, thus, brings definite advantages for courts. It gives them far-reaching decision-making powers, furnishes them with a useful analytical structure, and even makes their activity look like law. Yet, proportionality also has some less welcome side effects which can turn the duty of judicial review into a burden. Ironically, this has to do with the same characteristics that make the principle appealing to begin with.

The broad scope or comprehensiveness of proportionality gives courts the opportunity to subject state action to a full 'check-up', that is, to examine a variety of factual and normative questions relating to the justification of the given measure or, more precisely, most factual and normative questions that matter. There is a flipside to this power. Courts applying proportionality not only *can* make these assessments—they *must*. For judges, this means having to assess complex empirical problems, make delicate value judgments, and draw difficult compromises between rights and policy interests on a regular basis. Resolving issues of this sort on occasion would be challenging. Proportionality normalizes their appearance on the judicial docket.

The four-prong structure generates additional pressure. For litigants, it makes it easy to put forward, with a bit of ingenuity, any sound argument against the regulatory measure they want to invalidate. For public authorities, it makes it easy to defend the legality of their action by invoking policy reasons in support of their action. From the perspective of pluralism, this is valuable as it permits taking on board the concerns of everyone affected. For the court in charge, however, it means having to engage with all of these concerns and assessing their plausibility, significance, and implications.

Finally, due to its legal nature, proportionality is a relatively uncontroversial tool for judicial review. Yet, for the same reason, it is an unyielding principle. Courts cannot deviate from the four-prong structure whenever convenient. Every time the conditions for applying proportionality are fulfilled, the test must, in principle, be applied in its entirety.[65] For courts, this means having to check whether state action complies with each of the four proportionality requirements (and making the related factual and normative judgments).

Two potential problems follow from this. The first one is judicial overload. Courts will struggle to deal with all the questions proportionality puts before them. The second risk, perhaps more serious, is that of judicial overreach. Courts will, because of proportionality analysis, find subject matters on their agenda they may lack the legitimacy to settle.

[65] Note, however, that the ECJ sometimes omits the balancing stage when exercising proportionality review, but will address it explicitly if this point is raised by the parties or is otherwise relevant: see Paul Craig, *EU Administrative Law* (3rd edn, Oxford University Press 2018) 644.

A structural development outside of proportionality further magnifies the burden. Just like the ECJ, courts across the world increasingly split constitutional review into two stages: first, the question of whether the scope of a right has been interfered with and, second, whether this interference can be justified. One can think of the former as an entrance gate to the latter. Only if state action restricts a right will a court proceed into justification review. As proportionality analysis forms part of the second stage, one could consider a simple way to prevent the just-described problems. Courts could close the entrance gate a little or, to put it in legal terms, narrow down the scope of rights. The duty to exercise proportionality scrutiny would, then, at least be confined to a more limited set of cases and scenarios. Alas, the trend across the world is a different one. Courts tend to widen the scope of rights they protect by interpreting constitutional rights broadly or creating new rights in addition to existing ones. Kai Möller considers this phenomenon to be so pronounced that it forms part of the new 'global model of constitutional rights'.[66]

Combining proportionality analysis with a broad definition of rights produces a tricky mixture. Having to remake, due to proportionality, most salient factual and normative assessments connected with some state action is one thing. Having to do this for most, potentially all state action is something quite different. For courts, this is a responsibility which can be hard to fulfil.

Deference provides a solution to this issue or, at least, helps to alleviate the pressure. It allows courts who have opted for the 'global model of constitutional rights' to make their Herculean task manageable. It gives them the chance to hand down certain socio-economic assessments to the legislature and complex technical decisions to agencies. It allows them to refrain from settling some constitutional conflicts and pass the responsibility of deciding them onto the political branches. Inserting elements of deference into proportionality, thus, mitigates the dangers of overload and overreach.[67]

[66] Möller, *The Global Model of Constitutional Rights* (n 56).

[67] Curiously enough, there is no universal support for this proposition in proportionality scholarship. Some of the leading names in the field reject the idea of courts granting other institutions deference altogether. Aharon Barak, for instance, is of the opinion that exercising proportionality review is, quite simply, 'the judge's kingdom'. Courts can show deference to the legislative branch in the sense of respect (treating the latter's decisions 'with all seriousness and caution'), not however in the sense of 'submission' (accepting that the legislature is more legitimate or competent to make certain judgments), see *Proportionality* (n 1) 396 et seq. Other scholars acknowledge that deference ought to play a role in proportionality review but discuss the matter only peripherally. In the original version of Robert Alexy's seminal *A Theory of Constitutional Rights* (n 1) deference was no more than a marginal theme and has received greater attention just recently, see the postscript to the English translation as well as Alexy, 'Formal Principles' (n 2).

C. Doing Too Much Too Often

The above theoretical reflections make it easy to understand the dilemma in which the ECJ finds itself. The Court quickly adopted proportionality analysis as a tool for judicial review, a choice that came with a number of benefits. Proportionality enabled the Court to examine Member State laws in extraordinary depth. The European judges could lay down what consumer protection was required, which types of measures adequately safeguarded public health, and how free movement was to be reconciled with policy objectives such as national security, intellectual property, or commercial fairness.

As was explained in Chapter 1, during the same period, the Court also dramatically widened the scope of free movement law. Initially, this just affected the free movement of goods. The rulings in *Dassonville* and *Cassis de Dijon* went beyond more limited, discrimination-oriented understandings of free movement and paved the way for reviewing a broad range of Member State acts. Step-by-step, this approach was transposed to all four freedoms. As a result, not only the number of areas to decide on has grown for the Court, but the amount of litigation against national laws has increased. Tools aimed at limiting the excesses of this development, such as *Keck*,[68] had, as we shall see below, only modest salutary effects.

The consequences of these doctrinal choices are twofold. By adopting proportionality, the ECJ obliged itself to scrutinize Member State regulation in a comprehensive manner. By broadening the scope of free movement law, it committed to exercising judicial review in a wide array of fields. If one combines the two, the problem quickly becomes clear: a test raising challenging questions (proportionality analysis) is applied in a high number of cases and areas (wide scope of application). Put simply, the Court of Justice has to do too much too often.

Deference doctrines such as the margin of appreciation and decentralized judicial review provide a remedy in this situation. They allow the Court to regulate its activity and scale down, where necessary, its involvement in judicial review. Despite carrying different legal consequences—more lenient scrutiny (margin of appreciation) as opposed to full scrutiny which is just exercised by Member State courts (decentralized judicial review)—, the effect of both doctrines on the ECJ's activity is similar: they allow the European judges to limit their far-reaching review obligations. The question arises as to why one needs such ancillary doctrines to accomplish this variation. The answer lies in the design of proportionality analysis. A look at the jurisprudence of the US Supreme Court will explain the problem.

68 Case C-267/91 *Keck and Mithouard* [1993] ECLI:EU:C:1993:905.

III. Resolving the Paradox: Proportionality and Standards of Review

A. Standards of Review in US Constitutional Law

The US Supreme Court is a notorious outlier when it comes to proportionality review. Unlike most supreme and constitutional courts around the globe, it has so far (almost) entirely resisted the charms of the principle.[69] One may therefore wonder why we should compare the ECJ with the Supreme Court at all. The reason is a threefold similarity. Both courts occupy comparable positions within their legal order, perform comparable tasks, and have comparable set-ups. As the highest courts of the land, they have the duty to exercise generalist constitutional review, while having limited resources for this task. As a result of this, both also face similar problems regarding caseload, competence, and legitimacy.

How does the US Supreme Court manage its duty of constitutional review? The Court has developed three tests of different intensity for constitutional challenges to legislative and regulatory acts: rational basis review, heightened scrutiny, and strict scrutiny.[70] These are, in American parlance, the so-called 'standards of review'. The first, least demanding standard is rational basis review. It merely requires state action to be 'rationally related' to a 'legitimate' government interest.[71] More searching is heightened or intermediate scrutiny, which stipulates that measures be 'substantially related' to the achievement of 'important governmental objectives'.[72] At the top of the scale we find strict scrutiny. Legislation subjected to this standard will only pass if it seeks to attain a 'compelling state interest' and is 'narrowly tailored' to do so,[73] a requirement which includes the least-restrictive-measure test.[74]

Rational basis review is the Supreme Court's default mode of scrutiny. Most cases involving a constitutional challenge to a statute are decided using this lenient standard. This includes, inter alia, the broad category of economic regulation[75] and legislation that differentiates on grounds of age[76] and disability.[77] More intense review is reserved for specific scenarios. Heightened scrutiny has been accepted

[69] In his dissent in *District of Columbia v Heller* 554 US 570 (2008), Justice Breyer advocated the use of proportionality analysis and linked the principle to previous Supreme Court rulings. For balancing more broadly, see T Alexander Aleinikoff, 'Constitutional Law in the Age of Balancing' (1987) 96 Yale Law Journal 943.

[70] This includes executive orders. The standards of review are not employed in cases concerning non-regulatory acts. Here, however, a number of other procedural and justiciability barriers can apply, such as the political question doctrine; see n 96 to 98.

[71] *United States v Carolene Products* 304 US 144 (1938).

[72] *Craig v Boren* 429 US 190 (1976).

[73] *United States v Korematsu* 323 US 214 (1944).

[74] *Thomas v Review Bd, Ind Empl Sec Div* 450 US 707 (1981).

[75] *United States v Carolene Products* (n 71).

[76] *Massachusetts Board of Retirement v Murgia* 427 US 307 (1976).

[77] *City of Cleburne v Cleburne Living Center, Inc* 473 US 432 (1985).

for classifications based on gender[78] and illegitimacy[79] as well as content-neutral regulations of speech.[80] Strict scrutiny is only triggered in narrow circumstances. This includes acts infringing on fundamental rights[81] or targeting 'suspect classes', such as insular and discrete minorities that have been historically discriminated against.[82] Classifications based on race[83] and nationality[84] fall into this category.

Which standard of review applies is of key importance. Legendary are the words of Gerald Gunther who called strict scrutiny 'strict in theory and fatal in fact'.[85] More recently, Kenji Yoshino quipped that, although the notion of standards of review suggests 'an examination rather than a result', 'looks can kill'.[86] Empirical evidence points, albeit less drastically than submitted by Gunther and Yoshino, to clear differences in survival rates between the three standards. Whereas state action reviewed under the rational basis test is upheld in over 90 per cent of cases, the corresponding rate for strict scrutiny lies under 30 per cent.[87] Parties will therefore push to get their case decided under the most intense (if their aim is to invalidate the state action) or the most lenient test (if their aim is to uphold it). The recent *Windsor* litigation illustrates how central the issue remains.[88] In a rare move, the Obama Administration decided against defending the Defense of Marriage Act (DOMA), a law which denied same-sex couples federal marriage benefits. Politically, this was a powerful sign of support for the LGBT community. Legally, it was translated into an argument from standards of review. The Administration advocated that—contrary to previous case law on discrimination on grounds of sexual orientation—not rational basis review but heightened scrutiny should be applied. In the end, DOMA was invalidated.

Reality is, of course, not always as clear-cut as theory. At times, the US Supreme Court engages in a more searching scrutiny than the applicable standard of review

[78] *Craig v Boren* (n 72).

[79] *Clark v Jeter* 486 US 456 (1988).

[80] *Grayned v Rockford* 408 US 104 (1972); *Chicago Police Department v Mosley* 408 US 92 (1972).

[81] *National Association for the Advancement of Colored People v Alabama* 357 US 449 (1958) (freedom of association); *Sherbert v Verner* 374 US 398 (1963) (religious freedom); *Roe v Wade* 410 US 113 (1973) (abortion rights).

[82] See footnote four of *United States v Carolene Products* (n 71).

[83] *United States v Korematsu* (n 73). Despite the application of strict scrutiny, the executive order that allowed the military to force Japanese-Americans into internment camps was upheld by the Supreme Court.

[84] *Graham v Richardson* 403 US 365 (1971); *Nyquist v Mauclet* 432 US 1 (1977).

[85] Gerald Gunther, 'The Supreme Court, 1971 Term—Foreword: In Search of Evolving Doctrine on a Changing Court: A Model for a Newer Equal Protection' (1972) 86 Harvard Law Review 1, 8.

[86] Kenji Yoshino, 'The New Equal Protection' (2011) 124 Harvard Law Review 747, 756.

[87] Robert C Farrell studied the US Supreme Court's application of rational basis review over a 25-year period and found that from a total of 110 cases only 10 were successful, see 'Successful Rational Basis Claims in the Supreme Court from the 1971 Term through *Romer v. Evans*' (1999) 32 Indiana Law Review 357. Adam Winkler's analysis of strict scrutiny cases in the US federal judiciary shows that between 1990 and 2003 state action was invalidated in 322 out of 459 decisions: see 'Fatal in Theory and Strict in Fact: An Empirical Analysis of Strict Scrutiny in the Federal Courts' (2006) 59 Vanderbilt Law Review 793.

[88] *United States v Windsor* 570 US 744 (2013).

would warrant.[89] At other times, it does not make clear which review standard applies at all.[90] Nonetheless, the three-tiered model has proven to be an effective means for the Supreme Court to regulate its involvement in constitutional affairs. It enables the Court to be more interventionist in some areas and more restrained in others. Economic regulation is subjected to rational basis review because, as is commonly argued, the legislature is better at dealing with socio-economic problems. Laws directed at vulnerable minorities are, by contrast, subjected to strict scrutiny given the risk of discrimination by the majority population. By the same token, the standards of review model allows the Supreme Court to regulate its workload and incentivize the bringing of certain kinds of cases (and not others). Subjecting a type of dispute to rational basis review discourages litigation in a given field as the Court signals that the prospects of winning are low; the opposite message is sent out when strict scrutiny is adopted.[91] This influences not only the total caseload but also the composition of the Court's docket.

It is worthwhile mentioning that the US Supreme Court has, in addition to the standards of review, a number of other mechanisms serving similar purposes at its disposal. The first is the *certiorari* system. Legislative reforms in the first half of the twentieth century eliminated, for the most part, the right to appeal to the Supreme Court and granted the Court broad discretion as to which cases to accept onto its docket through a writ of *certiorari*.[92] This enables the Supreme Court justices to limit their workload—typically, only 70 to 100 cases *per annum* are granted plenary review with oral arguments[93]—and concentrate on the problems they consider most pressing, such as providing guidance on new important legal questions or settling disagreements between lower-instance courts ('circuit splits').[94] In addition, the Court has developed a series of justiciability doctrines, often called 'avoidance techniques',[95] which allow the Court to refrain from ruling

89 Gayle Lynn Pettinga, 'Rational Basis With Bite: Intermediate Scrutiny by Any Other Name' (1987) 62 Indiana Law Journal 779; Jeremy B Smith, 'The Flaws of Rational Basis with Bite: Why the Supreme Court Should Acknowledge its Application of Heightened Scrutiny to Classifications Based on Sexual Orientation' (2005) 73 Fordham Law Review 2769; Robert C Farrell, 'The Two Versions of Rational-Basis Review and Same-Sex Relationships' (2011) 86 Washington Law Review 281.

90 The *Windsor* ruling is a case in point. Although the Supreme Court was widely perceived to engage in what resembled heightened scrutiny in substance, it left the question of which standard of review applied open.

91 Neil Komesar, *Imperfect Alternatives* (University of Chicago Press 1997) 147; Andrew Coan, *Rationing the Constitution: How Judicial Capacity Shapes Supreme Court Decision-Making* (Harvard University Press 2019) 3.

92 The use of the writ of *certiorari* was first introduced by the Judiciary Act of 1891 but substantially widened by the Judiciary Act of 1925. The right to appeal state court decisions has, more recently, been further curtailed by the Supreme Court Case Selections Act of 1988.

93 Lee Epstein and others, *The Supreme Court Compendium: Data, Decisions, and Developments* (6th edn, CQ Press 2015) ch 2.

94 Rule 10 of the Rules of the US Supreme Court establishes that a 'petition for a writ of *certiorari* will be granted only for compelling reasons'.

95 Gerald Gunther, 'The Subtle Vices of the "Passive Virtues"—A Comment on Principle and Expediency in Judicial Review' (1964) 64 Columbia Law Review 1, 9.

on certain substantive constitutional issues. Among these is the political question doctrine, through which the Court can dismiss cases involving matters of political nature and, thus, avoid becoming entangled in some controversial topics, such as the termination of international treaties[96] or decisions on impeachment proceedings.[97] Further examples include doctrines such as ripeness, mootness, vagueness, standing, and sovereign immunity.[98] Although not concerning the intensity of judicial review, but rather jurisdiction, they fulfil a similar function by enabling the Supreme Court to decide when to get involved and when not.

B. Flexibility Despite Uniformity

How does the Court of Justice's doctrinal tool-box fare in comparison? The most striking difference is that it is much simpler. In a nutshell: (almost) everything is proportionality.[99] The ECJ has never explicitly adopted different standards of review. From an American perspective, this will seem baffling. In EU law there is, on the surface, no doctrinal difference between cases on economic regulation[100] and fundamental rights,[101] or classifications based on age[102] and nationality.[103] The Court of Justice applies proportionality in all of these scenarios. Considering that, from the three standards of review, it is strict scrutiny that structurally resembles proportionality the most—it essentially amounts to proportionality minus balancing—, this is quite a surprise. The US Supreme Court has used strict scrutiny only 12 times between 1990 and 2003.[104] It would give an American constitutional lawyer cold sweat to hear that it is not unusual for the ECJ to apply proportionality in free movement disputes twice as often within a single year. If one adds to the balance that the Court has neither the luxury of direct docket control through the *certiorari* system nor tools such as the political question doctrine, its reliance on proportionality analysis appears even more astonishing. For a task comparable to that of the US Supreme Court, the ECJ uses just one test which, to make things worse, is of extensive scope.

[96] *Goldwater v Carter* 444 US 996 (1979).

[97] *Nixon v United States* 506 US 224 (1993).

[98] For a more detailed overview of the manifold 'avoidance techniques', see Alexander M Bickel, *The Least Dangerous Branch: The Supreme Court at the Bar of Politics* (Bobbs-Merrill 1962) ch 4.

[99] For some exceptions, see n 112.

[100] Case 382/87 *Buet* [1989] ECLI:EU:C:1989:198; Case C-442/02 *CaixaBank France* [2004] ECLI:EU:C:2004:586; Case C-169/07 *Hartlauer* [2009] ECLI:EU:C:2009:141.

[101] *Internationale Handelsgesellschaft* (n 14); Case C-112/00 *Schmidberger* [2003] ECLI:EU:C:2003:333; Case C-438/05 *Viking Line* [2007] ECLI:EU:C:2007:772.

[102] Case C-144/04 *Mangold* [2005] ECLI:EU:C:2005:709; Case C-555/07 *Kücükdeveci* [2010] ECLI:EU:C:2010:21.

[103] Case C-302/97 *Konle* [1999] ECLI:EU:C:1999:271; Cases C-482/01 and 493/01 *Orfanopoulos* [2004] ECLI:EU:C:2004:262.

[104] Winkler (n 87) 796.

This lack of explicit standards of review in EU law, however, is not the Court of Justice's fault. It is the result of the principle it applies. Proportionality analysis does not, at least without additional doctrinal efforts, allow for different levels of scrutiny. The problem is simple but fundamental. Proportionality is a single uniform test which requires four things: that state action pursues a legitimate purpose; that it furthers this purpose; that there are no less restrictive measures which would be just as effective; and that the benefits of achieving the policy objective do not outweigh the costs for the right-bearer. Whenever proportionality analysis is applied, all of these requirements have to be fulfilled. The logic behind this completely differs from the standards of review model, where different types of cases are governed by different sets of conditions. Under proportionality, all cases are in principle treated equally. Every state action must comply with the same set of conditions.

The claim that proportionality scrutiny is uniform, and hostile to the idea of variation, will strike many scholars of EU law as odd. It is common knowledge that the ECJ sometimes applies stricter and at other times more lenient versions of proportionality analysis; that the way its intensity of review ranges from a 'light touch' to a 'hard look' approach, from 'marginal review' to 'strict' or 'searching' scrutiny.[105] This seems to pose a paradox. How does the Court of Justice manage to apply the same test in different ways?

The answer, at this point, will seem obvious. Complementing proportionality with deference doctrines allows the ECJ to square the circle: it creates variation where there is, in principle, none. The three approaches developed by the Court in relation to the margin of appreciation—no, partial, and full—create a veritable system of standards of review (Figure 5.1). When granting national authorities no margin of appreciation, the Court of Justice's scrutiny is the strictest, and its

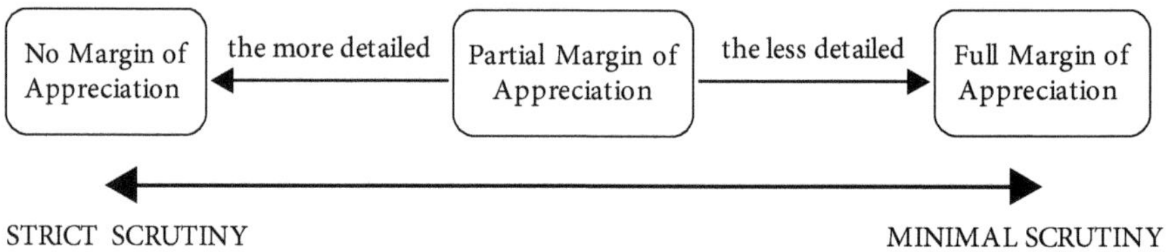

Figure 5.1 Proportionality: Standards of Review

[105] See Craig (n 65) 682; Janneke Gerards, 'Pluralism, Deference and the Margin of Appreciation Doctrine' (2011) 17 European Law Journal 80; Norbert Reich, 'How Proportionate is the Proportionality Principle?' in Hans Micklitz and Bruno de Witte (eds), *The European Court of Justice and the Autonomy of the Member States* (Intersentia 2012); Floris de Witte, 'Sex, Drugs & EU Law: The Recognition of Moral and Ethical Diversity in EU Law' (2013) 50 Common Market Law Review 1545, 1566; Dimitrios Doukas, 'Morality, Free Movement and Judicial Restraint at the European Court of Justice' in Panos Koutrakos, Niamh Nic Schuibhne, and Phil Syrpis (eds), *Exceptions from EU Free Movement Law: Derogation, Justification and Proportionality* (Hart 2016).

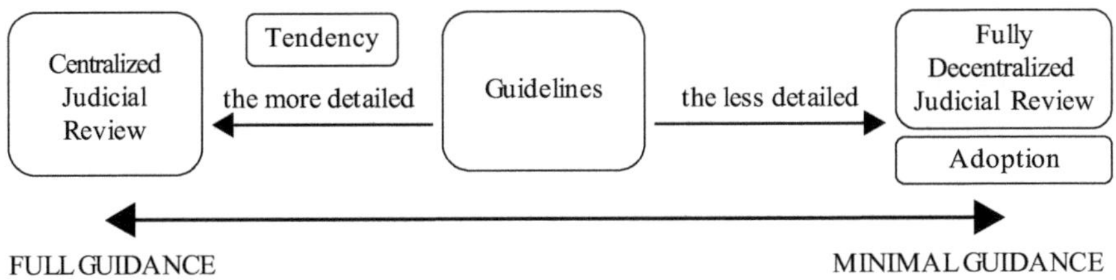

Figure 5.2 Proportionality: Standards of Guidance

involvement the highest. The Court closely examines the policy choices made by the Member State. Less intense scrutiny follows from the partial margin of appreciation. The ECJ does not settle the regulatory question but limits itself to setting out instructions for the national rule-maker. (The more detailed these instructions, the stricter the Court's intensity of review, and *vice versa*.) The most lenient scrutiny occurs in cases in which a full margin of appreciation is granted. The Court completely defers a regulatory decision to the national authority, without reviewing its merits.

Despite not affecting the intensity of scrutiny to which national laws are subjected, decentralized judicial review generates similar flexibility by varying the ECJ's involvement in the review process (Figure 5.2); instead of standards of review, it is more appropriate to speak of standards of guidance in this context.[106] Centralized proportionality review constitutes the highest level of guidance, with the Court being most intensely involved in the review process as it fulfils the task of judicial review entirely on its own. A decentralization of judicial review tasks alongside guidelines or a tendency requires less activity on its part. The Court hands the final decision on proportionality over to the referring judge, merely stipulating how this decision should be made or hinting at what it deems to be the right outcome. The lowest degree of guidance can be found in cases in which the ECJ fully decentralizes proportionality analysis, without giving any instructions, or adopts the referring court's assessment. In this scenario, the responsibility for judicial review lies completely with the national judge.

We see that although the jurisprudence of the US Supreme Court and the ECJ could not be more different on the surface, the behaviour of both courts resembles each other in substance. The Court of Justice may not use the term standards of review, nor has it expressly set out different tests for different case groups. It exercises judicial review through a single test: proportionality analysis. Nonetheless, within this test, the Court has created different approaches by resorting to the margin of

[106] In US law, the term 'standard of review' is also used for the type of scrutiny which an appellate court will exercise when reviewing a decision of a lower-instance court. Given the lack of an appellate system in the EU (between national courts and the ECJ), European scholarship speaks of 'guidance' instead: see Pedro Cruz Villalón, '"All the Guidance", *ERT* and *Wachauf*' in Miguel Poiares Maduro and Loïc Azoulai (eds), *The Past and Future of EU Law* (Hart 2010).

appreciation and decentralized judicial review. These doctrines allow the Court to modify the way in which it exercises proportionality scrutiny, either by lowering the intensity with which it applies the test or by passing elements of it over to national judges. In this way, through the back door, deference doctrines introduce variation into the four-prong test.

IV. The Evolution of Proportionality Review in Free Movement Law

The foregoing sections show that, for various reasons, it is hard to imagine proportionality without deference. There is a final piece of evidence, of empirical nature, I want to present in support of this proposition. There has been a change in how proportionality is used in free movement jurisprudence, a change which suggests that the Court of Justice increasingly struggles with applying a full, non-deferential version of the test. The case law survey underpinning Chapters 2 to 4 will provide the necessary data to illustrate this.[107]

A. More Proportionality, More Deference

To understand the evolution of proportionality review in free movement adjudication it is useful to begin with how frequently the test is applied by the Court of Justice, and how this frequency has developed over time. The growth curve is impressive (Figure 5.3). We see a steep increase in absolute as well as in relative numbers. Still absent from the case law as a tool for judicial review of Member State laws in 1974, the principle was applied four times in 1979, the year of the *Cassis de Dijon* ruling, representing one quarter of all free movement cases at that point.[108] This figure, after a little dip in the 1990s, went up to 28 by 2004, almost three quarters of the ECJ's judgments in this area (71.79 per cent). In 2009 and 2013, it was around 64 per cent and 56 per cent respectively.

The findings show that free movement adjudication has, to a large extent, become proportionality adjudication. It is no exaggeration to say that, in EU free movement law, what is legal and what is not is nowadays largely decided by the

[107] As in Chapter 2, every judgment is counted as one observation, however including all free movement cases decided in the sample years (247 in total).

[108] This includes all cases in which the ECJ said that it applied proportionality review and addressed, policy aims aside, at least one further stage of the principle. In some older decisions, it was difficult to establish whether this was the case because the Court did not set out clearly the test which it applied. These judgments were coded as proportionality cases only when the reasoning strongly resembled the proportionality structure (including decisions applying the 'mandatory requirements' test). Rulings whose reasoning could, *ex post facto*, simply be translated into a proportionality-style examination were not accepted.

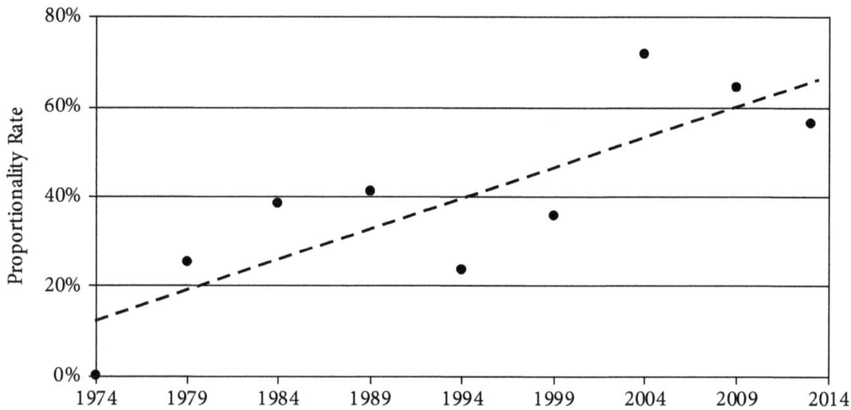

Figure 5.3 Proportionality Review in Free Movement Cases, 1974–2013

Notes: Percentage of proportionality cases in all free movement cases (infringement proceedings and preliminary references). Trendline serves interpretative purposes only and does not make predictive claims about in-between years.

question 'what is proportionate?'[109] Against this background, the claim that proportionality overburdens the European Court seems to be already refuted. To the contrary, the above numbers appear to further demonstrate how attractive the principle is. Proportionality does not only have the tendency to spread across different legal orders.[110] Even within the same jurisdiction, once the principle enters the system, courts are more and more eager to resort to it for the purpose of judicial review.[111] There appears to be, just as scholarship theorized, something distinctly appealing about proportionality, indeed.[112]

[109] Gareth Davies, 'Abstractness and Concreteness in the Preliminary Reference Procedure' in Niamh Nic Shuibhne (ed), *Regulating the Internal Market* (Edward Elgar 2006) 218; similarly, Barend van Leeuwen, 'Rethinking the Structure of Free Movement Law: the Centralisation of Proportionality in the Internal Market' (2017) 10 European Journal of Legal Studies 235; Jukka Snell, 'General Principles in Free Movement Law: Applicability and Application' in Katja Ziegler, Päivi Neuvonen, and Violeta Moreno-Lax (eds), *Research Handbook on General Principles of EU Law* (Edward Elgar forthcoming).

[110] Barak (n 1) 182; Cohen-Eliya and Porat (n 47) 472; Möller, *The Global Model of Constitutional Rights* (n 56).

[111] This contradicts claims that proportionality analysis is a judicial review tool for 'young' legal systems, which is replaced by rule-like doctrines at more mature stages of development. For a discussion of this argument, put forward most prominently by Frederick Schauer, see Cohen-Eliya and Porat (n 47) 467 et seq.

[112] Note, however, that in a non-negligible share of cases the ECJ does not engage in proportionality review. This is not limited to the early years—one would expect it to take some time for proportionality to 'settle in' and penetrate all areas of free movement law—but includes current decisions as well. A number of case groups appear to be largely immune to the principle's allures, notably decisions on IP rights, social security, tax law, public procurement, and professional qualifications. Here, the Court has developed alternatives to proportionality scrutiny, typically applying provisions from EU secondary legislation or other tests that are better suited for solving the problems that arise in the given field. For instance, in cases on IP rights, its jurisprudence draws on the principle of territoriality, objective

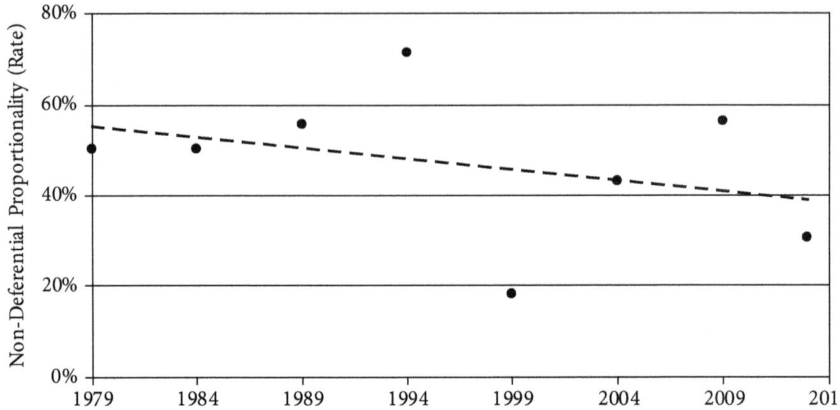

Figure 5.4 Non-Deferential Proportionality Review in Free Movement Cases, 1979–2013

Notes: Percentage of proportionality cases in which the ECJ exercises non-deferential scrutiny, ie does not grant national authorities a margin of appreciation or defers to national courts (infringement proceedings and preliminary references). Trendline serves interpretative purposes only and does not make predictive claims about in-between years.

However, the increase in the application of proportionality analysis in the ECJ's case law is just one part of the story. It has gone hand in hand with another development: a decrease in full or non-deferential proportionality review, something which was called the *Cassis* approach earlier. If we distinguish between deferential and non-deferential forms of proportionality scrutiny, a very different picture emerges (Figure 5.4). The Court of Justice may be applying proportionality much more frequently than it used to. Yet, it is also less likely to engage in a strict and comprehensive review of the proportionality of Member State action. In 1979, the Court exercised full proportionality review in every other case. This ratio went up continuously until 1994, where it peaked at 71.43 per cent. (The turn towards more searching proportionality scrutiny which we see in the data during this period is in line with standard accounts in free movement literature of the ECJ taking a more activist stance in the years between *Cassis de Dijon* and *Keck*.) From thereon, the share of non-deferential proportionality review fell, and quite considerably so. In 1999, the Court of Justice settled only 18.18 per cent of proportionality cases without deferring to national authorities. This figure has increased slightly since and reached 30.43 per cent in 2013.

differences between products, essence of exclusive rights, etc. Cases on tax law are governed by the direct link doctrine, the principle of unjustified benefits, and examinations of risks for the coherence of the national tax systems.

The data are less neatly aligned than in previous graphs. Especially the strong drop between the years 1994 and 1999—no statistical outliers, despite marking the highest and lowest point in the data set—is striking. One can only speculate about the reasons for this, especially as the in-between years are missing, but the abrupt decline might be connected to the Court's reorientation in *Keck* (decided in 1993) or constitute a reaction to the constitutional changes in the Maastricht Treaty (adopted in 1992).

Nonetheless, we see a tangible difference in the intensity of proportionality review before and after the mid-1990s. The mean rate of non-deferential proportionality review for the last four years in the sample (1999 to 2013: 36.87 per cent) is noticeably lower than the average for the first four years (1979 to 1994: 56.75 per cent). These numbers suggest that worries, commonly expressed in the EU law literature, whereby the Court of Justice is constantly increasing the intensity of proportionality scrutiny, making it ever harder for national authorities to satisfy the test, are unfounded.[113] In fact, the more the ECJ applies proportionality analysis, the more it opts for deferential forms of the test. It is far less common now for the Court of Justice to engage in *Cassis*-style scrutiny than when *Cassis* was first decided. In over two-thirds of cases, the Court exercises deferential proportionality review instead.

Note that this development affects all elements of proportionality. Usually, the balancing stage is considered to be the principle's most problematic component as it is said to put courts in the shoes of legislators.[114] The case law analysis shows that the ECJ indeed sometimes defers to national authorities on questions relating to balancing (9 cases). Yet, the Court equally does so on questions from every other proportionality stage. Balancing does not even appear to be the most challenging task for the European judges. The proportionality limb which most frequently attracts deferential scrutiny is the necessity stage (24 cases). It is followed by the assessment of whether a real risk exists for the policy objective advanced as a justificatory ground by the national government, which has come to be part of the legitimate aim stage (11 cases).[115] This is understandable given that both limbs involve complex factual enquiries and, at times, make difficult evaluative judgments necessary. The remaining proportionality stages prompt deferential scrutiny less frequently. The ECJ defers assessments of whether Member State acts pursue a policy goal in a consistent and systematic manner in 7 cases and concerning their suitability more in general 3 times.

[113] Catherine Barnard, 'Derogations, Justifications and The Four Freedoms: Is State Interest Really Protected?' in Catherine Barnard and Okeoghene Odudu (eds), *The Outer Limits of European Union Law* (Hart 2009); Dorte Sindbjerg Martinsen, 'Judicial Policy-Making and Europeanization: The Proportionality of National Control and Administrative Discretion' (2011) 18 Journal of European Public Policy 944; Jotte Mulder, *Social Legitimacy in the Internal Market* (Hart 2018).

[114] See Lord Hoffman's opinion in *Stoke-on-Trent* (n 59).

[115] See Chapter 4 I A.

B. The Ineffectiveness of Alternative Filters

The Court of Justice's increasing reliance on deferential forms of proportionality review makes sense given the lack of alternatives. As was explained, it is essential for courts charged with the task of judicial review to be able to regulate their activity. That the ECJ does this predominantly by lowering the intensity with which it conducts proportionality analysis is due to the ineffectiveness of filters at earlier points in the review process: the restriction/scope of application and admissibility stages. This is not to say that the ECJ has not created filters at these stages. They have just not been overly successful at reducing the Court of Justice's docket.

1. Scope of Free Movement Rights

It is an obvious point, but important nonetheless, that not all cases brought before the ECJ fall within the scope of the free movement provisions and never have. From the beginning, the ECJ excluded certain types of national laws and disputes from free movement scrutiny, such as instances of reverse discrimination, purely internal situations, or cases in which the applicant did not meet the criteria of a 'worker' or an activity did not qualify as a 'service'. Yet, it was only when free movement litigation exploded after *Dassonville* and *Cassis de Dijon* that the Court made more visible efforts to set some doctrinal boundaries. Thomas Horsley has helpfully named these 'exclusionary rules' as they remove from the scope of free movement law national measures that would, applying the *Dassonville* formula or equivalents thereof, otherwise constitute restrictions on freedom of movement and trigger justification and proportionality review.[116]

The most prominent exclusionary rule was established in *Keck and Mithouard*. With rare frankness, the Court announced that it felt compelled to re-examine its position on the scope of Article 34 TFEU 'in view of the increasing tendency of traders to invoke [the provision] as a means of challenging any rules whose effect is to limit their commercial freedom'.[117] To counteract this trend, it decided to exclude non-discriminatory 'selling arrangements' from the reach of the free movement of goods. *Keck* was perceived to be a signal and a turning point. It was expected to limit the interference of EU law into national regulatory autonomy and, by the same token, provide some much-needed relief for the ECJ in terms of workload. But *Keck* was not the only attempt in this direction. In a less emphatic way, the Court introduced *de minimis* and remoteness doctrines into its case law. Having initially refused to exempt national measures from judicial review that affect freedom of movement only slightly or indirectly,[118] the Court began to rethink

[116] Horsley (n 7).

[117] *Keck and Mithouard* (n 68), para 14.

[118] Cases 177 and 178/82 *Van de Haar* [1984] ECLI:EU:C:1984:144; Case 16/83 *Prantl* [1984] ECLI:EU:C:1984:101, para 20; Case 270/83 *Commission v France (Shareholders' Tax Credits)* [1986] ECLI:EU:C:1986:37, para 21; Case C-49/89 *Corsica Ferries* [1989] ECLI:EU:C:1989:649, para 8.

this stance in the early 1990s. In *Krantz*, it stated that Member State acts would not be caught by Article 34 TFEU if they had 'too uncertain and indirect' effects on trade,[119] a formula reiterated in judgments such as *Peralta*,[120] *TK-Heimdienst*,[121] and, in a slightly varied version, *Burmanjer*.[122] The same idea later appeared in the case law on the other freedoms of movement.[123]

There is, hence, no lack of filters in relation to the scope of free movement law. The problem is that none of these have been particularly effective as means for dismissing cases brought before the ECJ. The sample shows only 3 successful applications of *Keck*.[124] In a handful of cases the Court, in addition, makes use of *de minimis* rules.[125] Finally, some disputes are held to fall outside the scope of application because they concern a purely internal situation, the national law is not discriminatory, or other criteria are not met. Yet, in the grand scheme of things, these cases are exceptions. From the 247 judgments analysed, the ECJ finds that a measure falls outside the scope of free movement law altogether, that is, for all the freedoms invoked, just on 30 occasions.[126] This amounts to a mere 12.15 per cent.

What is more, despite the considerable increase in workload over the years, the Court's use of this option has remained surprisingly limited (Figure 5.5). The share of cases disposed of at the scope of application stage has—with the exception of 1984 (23.81 per cent), a statistical outlier—stayed at a constantly low level, close to the mean rate. Recent years even show a slight downward trend.[127] In 2004, Member State acts were found to fall outside the scope of free movement rights in 10.26 per cent of cases. In 2009, the rate was just 7.69 per cent.

Four factors seem to be responsible for this development. First, *Keck* had only limited success in reducing the scope of the Court's activity. Not only was the doctrine never transposed to the free movement of persons, services, and capital, even in the free movement of goods case law its role has been modest due to the Court's

[119] Case C-69/88 *Krantz* [1990] ECLI:EU:C:1990:97, para 11.

[120] Case C-379/92 *Peralta* [1994] ECLI:EU:C:1994:296, para 24.

[121] Case C-254/98 *TK-Heimdienst* [2000] ECLI:EU:C:2000:12, para 30.

[122] Case C-20/03 *Burmanjer* [2005] ECLI:EU:C:2005:307, para 31 ('too insignificant and uncertain').

[123] Case C-418/93 *Semeraro Casa Uno* [1996] ECLI:EU:C:1996:242, para 32 (establishment); Case C-190/98 *Graf* [2000] ECLI:EU:C:2000:49, para 25 (workers); Case C-256/06 *Jäger* [2008] ECLI:EU:C:2008:20, paras 29 and 33 (capital); Case C-211/08 *Commission v Spain (Hospital Care)* [2010] ECLI:EU:C:2010:340, para 72 (services).

[124] Cases C-401 and 402/92 *Tankstation 't Heukske* [1994] ECLI:EU:C:1994:220; Cases C-69 and 258/93 *Punto Casa* [1994] ECLI:EU:C:1994:226; Case C-71/02 *Karner* [2004] ECLI:EU:C:2004:181.

[125] Case C-412/97 *ED* [1999] ECLI:EU:C:1999:324, para 11; Case C-44/98 *BASF* [1999] ECLI:EU:C:1999:440, para 11; Case 202/82 *Commission v France (Durum Pasta)* [1984] ECLI:EU:C:1984:67, para 5; Case C-186/12 *Impacto Azul* [2013] ECLI:EU:C:2013:412, para 36. However, there is no evidence for the claim that remoteness tests are increasingly gaining relevance in the Court's case law; cf Niamh Nic Shuibhne, *The Coherence of EU Free Movement Law* (Oxford University Press 2013) ch 5.

[126] There are a few further cases in which the Court finds that a dispute does not fall into the scope of one out of multiple free movement rights invoked, yet these cases do not lead to a genuine reduction of the Court's workload. One applicable free movement right is sufficient to trigger a full justification and proportionality review of the given Member State act.

[127] If we remove the two statistical outliers (1974 and 1984), the rate is falling slightly.

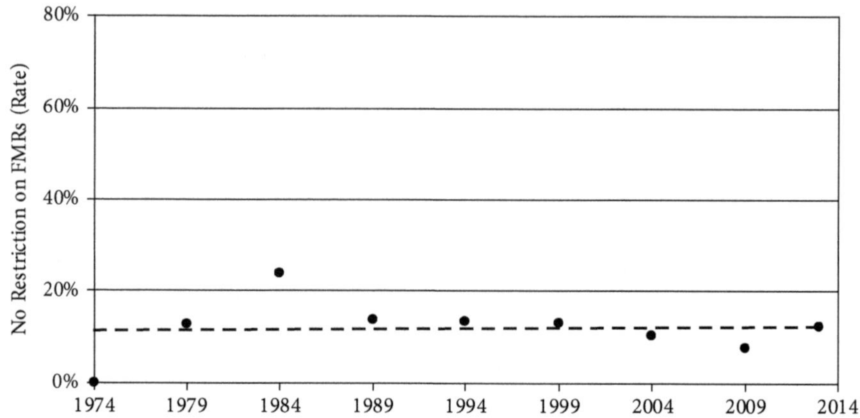

Figure 5.5 Cases Falling Outside the Scope of Free Movement Law, 1974–2013
Notes: Percentage of cases in which a national measure is found to fall outside the scope of free movement law (infringement proceedings and preliminary references). Trendline serves interpretative purposes only and does not make predictive claims about in-between years.

lax handling of the criterion of indirect discrimination.[128] (*Keck* might have, however, contributed to bringing down the number of Article 34 TFEU cases, which have decreased over the past two decades, suggesting that litigants and national courts have received the ECJ's message that it is no longer willing to review any Member State law affecting trade.) Second, the *de minimis* rules have not been too effective either. Partly, this is due to the lack of a clear statement from the ECJ—despite the occasional nudges from its Advocates General in this direction[129]—that it will not review minimal obstacles to free movement.[130] Partly, it is also because the Court, at times, actively sabotages its own efforts. Recent decisions like *Salzburger Landeskliniken* emphasize that restrictions on any of the four freedoms, 'however minor', are prohibited.[131] Third, over the past decades, the Court of Justice has affirmed its jurisdiction over every new regulatory field it was presented with. Having had the chance to opt out from judicial review of national measures in areas like gambling, health care, and tax law, it chose to apply the free movement

[128] The existing empirical analyses of the use of the *Keck* doctrine vary in tone but essentially paint the same picture. Horsley counts 14 successful applications overall (n 7) 744. Spaventa highlights that this number goes down to just 2 cases if one excludes the initial phase until 1997, see 'Leaving Keck Behind? The Free Movement of Goods after the Rulings in Commission v Italy and Mickelsson and Roos' (2009) 34 European Law Review 914, 920.

[129] See, for instance, Case C-222/07 *Unión de Televisiones Comerciales Asociadas (UTECA)* [2009] ECLI:EU:C:2008:468, Opinion of AG Kokott, para 53 and Case C-110/05 *Commission v Italy (Italian Trailers)* [2009] ECLI:EU:C:2006:646, Opinion of AG Bot, para 117.

[130] Case C-379/98 *PreussenElektra* [2001] ECLI:EU:C:2000:585, Opinion of AG Jacobs, para 204.

[131] Case C-514/12 *Zentralbetriebsrat der Gemeinnützigen Salzburger Landeskliniken* [2013] ECLI:EU:C:2013:799, para 34. Similarly, see Case C-9/02 *De Lasteyrie du Saillant* [2004] ECLI:EU:C:2004:138, para 43; Case C-67/97 *Bluhme* [1998] ECLI:EU:C:1998:584.

rules to all of them.[132] Finally, it has even expanded the reach of free movement law, establishing a broad market access test across the four freedoms.[133]

2. Inadmissibility Rulings

Declaring a dispute inadmissible is a very efficient means of docket control.[134] It allows a court to dismiss a case without having to enter into the examination of the merits. The US Supreme Court frequently denies its jurisdiction, either by not granting a writ of *certiorari* or by resorting to one of the aforementioned 'avoidance techniques'. The ECJ was, in the beginning, notoriously reluctant to exercise this option, a strategy motivated by the desire to create a docket to start with. It was not before 1978 that the European Court declared the first preliminary reference inadmissible.[135] Subsequent decades brought about a more frequent use of this route as the Court laid down several scenarios under which requests from national courts or proceedings brought by the Commission would be dismissed. This includes artificial disputes,[136] hypothetical problems,[137] questions unrelated to EU law,[138] and references failing to provide sufficient information on the relevant factual and legislative context.[139]

How effective have these filters been for reducing the Court's activity? If we search the sample years for cases which were held inadmissible, fully or even partly, we find only 7 decisions.[140] One may wonder why this number is so low. One reason is certainly doctrinal. The inadmissibility conditions which the ECJ has laid down are narrow. Their scope comes nowhere near the practically unlimited discretion that comes with the *certiorari* system or even more confined tools like the political question doctrine. The Court of Justice cannot deny its jurisdiction because a case is factually complex, politically sensitive, or because it is simply not sufficiently important from the perspective of EU law. The other reason is attitudinal. It has been a deliberate choice on the part of the European judges to make restrained use of inadmissibility rulings. Although this appears to have changed more recently—with

[132] Case C-275/92 *Schindler* [1994] ECLI:EU:C:1994:119; Case C-158/96 *Kohll* [1998] ECLI:EU:C:1998:171 and Case C-120/95 *Decker* [1998] ECLI:EU:C:1998:167; Case C-279/93 *Schumacker* [1995] ECLI:EU:C:1995:31.

[133] Alina Tryfonidou, 'Further Steps on the Road to Convergence Among the Market Freedoms' (2010) 35 European Law Review 36; Snell (n 109).

[134] I do not distinguish in the following between the concepts of jurisdiction and admissibility as both lead to the same outcome: the Court dismisses a case without examining its substance: see Nils Wahl and Luca Prete, 'The Gatekeepers of Article 267 TFEU: On Jurisdiction and Admissibility of References for Preliminary Rulings' (2018) 55 Common Market Law Review 511.

[135] Case 93/78 *Matheus* [1978] ECLI:EU:C:1978:206.

[136] Case 104/79 *Foglia* [1980] ECLI:EU:C:1980:73, paras 10–11.

[137] Case 126/80 *Salonia* [1981] ECLI:EU:C:1981:136, para 6; Case C-186/90 *Durighello* [1991] ECLI:EU:C:1991:453, para 9; Case C-62/93 *BP Soupergaz* [1995] ECLI:EU:C:1995:223, para 10.

[138] Case C-269/89 *Bonfait* [1990] ECLI:EU:C:1990:399, para 8; Case C-424/97 *Haim* [2000] ECLI:EU:C:2000:357, paras 55–56.

[139] Cases C-320/90, 321/90 and 322/90 *Telemarsicabruzzo* [1993] ECLI:EU:C:1993:26.

[140] This includes all judgments as well as orders rendered in preliminary references and infringement proceedings in the sample years .

an increasing number of references being held inadmissible[141]—it remains, looking at the past four decades, a discernible trait of the Court's approach.

These figures hint at the pressure the ECJ finds itself under. The use of proportionality analysis has significantly grown. The principle has come to be applied in the vast majority of free movement cases. In addition, the scope of free movement law is as wide as ever. Despite the signals in cases like *Keck* and *Krantz*, there has been no palpable limitation of the reach of the four freedoms, with the Court even expanding their material scope. Finally, the admissibility stage has had little bite. The number of cases dismissed on procedural grounds has, despite some recent changes, been negligible overall.

Against this background, it is clear why deference doctrines such as the margin of appreciation and decentralized judicial review are vital for the Court of Justice. Given the failure to stipulate meaningful limits at the scope of application and admissibility stages, the ECJ has to find alternative ways to reduce its activity. The obligation to make the empirical and normative assessments that are part of proportionality review is, as case numbers grow, something which the Court is increasingly less capable of doing and, in some scenarios, will be wary of doing for reasons of legitimacy. Lowering the intensity of judicial review by means of deference provides a partial remedy to this problem.

V. Conclusion: A Global Phenomenon

Is the importance of proportionality analysis in free movement law likely to diminish? Nothing points in this direction. The constantly growing reliance on proportionality and its expansion into ever more areas of EU law make it unthinkable that the ECJ will cease to apply the principle.[142] Yet, modifications to full proportionality review *à la Cassis de Dijon* through doctrines such as the margin of appreciation and decentralized judicial review have become increasingly common. This flexibility is indispensable for the Court of Justice's functioning.

The findings of this chapter suggest that there is a connection between the rise of proportionality and that of deference. The more proportionality analysis becomes the dominant technique for judicial review of Member State acts, the more exceptions or deviations from full proportionality review become necessary. At some point, these exceptions are likely to turn into the rule. The data from recent years indicate that this point may have already come, with deferential forms of proportionality review having overtaken non-deferential approaches.

[141] Tommaso Pavone and R Daniel Kelemen, 'The Evolving Judicial Politics of European Integration: The European Court of Justice and National Courts Revisited' (2019) 25 European Law Journal 1, 18; see also Wahl and Prete (n 134) 543.

[142] cf Cloots (n 49) 234.

There is reason to believe that the developments which have taken place in the ECJ's case law are not an EU anomaly. Rather, they are symptomatic of more universal problems that arise in present-day judicial review across the world. Over the past couple of decades, many national and international courts have adopted proportionality analysis or judicial review tools of comparable scope. Human rights bodies such as the ECtHR, the Inter-American Court of Human Rights (IACHR), and the UN Human Rights Council (UN HRC) all make use of proportionality or variations of it.[143] The least-restrictive-means test, a first cousin of proportionality, has become a staple element of the jurisprudence of the World Trade Organization (WTO) Appellate Body.[144] Investment arbitration tribunals apply the 'fair and equitable treatment' test, essentially a balancing exercise, and have recently even started to openly rely on proportionality.[145]

While expanding their review powers in this manner—this is what adopting proportionality analysis means—, all of the aforementioned courts have gradually embraced deference doctrines.[146] The ECtHR, IACHR, and UN HRC expressly refer to the domestic authorities' margin of appreciation in their judgments.[147] So do investment tribunals.[148] WTO law grants Member States the freedom to set their level of protection, a mechanism akin to the margin of appreciation.[149] In all these legal orders, the move towards proportionality has been flanked by deference techniques. This chapter shows why. The choice to use comprehensive tools for judicial review, especially when paired with a wide jurisdiction and a broad understanding of rights, means that these courts face the same dilemma as the ECJ. They are forced to assess complex factual and normative questions on a regular basis. Yet, this is a task which courts will sometimes feel they lack the competence or legitimacy to exercise. Adopting doctrines of deference is, in this light, a basic necessity.

143 *Case 'Relating to Certain Aspects of the Laws on the Use of Languages in Education in Belgium' v Belgium* (n 62) (ECtHR); *Herrera-Ulloa v Costa Rica* [2004] IACHR 3 (Inter-American Court of Human Rights); *Ballantyne v Canada* CCPR/C/47/D/359/1989 (UN Human Rights Council), para 11.4.

144 *Korea Beef* WT/DS161/AB/R (WTO Appellate Body), paras 157 et seq.

145 *TECMED* Case ARB (AF)/00/2 (International Centre for Settlement of Investment Disputes), para 122. For a discussion of the emergence of proportionality reasoning in international investment law, see Alec Stone Sweet, 'Investor-State Arbitration: Proportionality's New Frontier' (2010) 4 Law & Ethics of Human Rights 47.

146 See Andrew Legg, *The Margin of Appreciation in International Human Rights Law* (Oxford University Press 2012); Caroline Henckels, *Proportionality and Deference in Investor-State Arbitration: Balancing Investment Protection and Regulatory Autonomy* (Cambridge University Press 2015); Julian Arato, 'The Margin of Appreciation in International Investment Law' (2014) 53 Virginia Journal of International Law 545; Donald H Regan, 'The Meaning of "Necessary" in GATT Article XX and GATS Article XIV: The Myth of Cost–Benefit Balancing' (2007) 6 World Trade Review 347.

147 *Handyside v UK* (1976) 1 EHRR 737, para 48; Opinion OC-4/84 *Proposed Amendments to the Naturalization Provisions of the Constitution of Costa Rica* Series A No 4 (Inter-American Court of Human Rights); *Raihman v Latvia* CCPR/C/100/D/1621/2007 (UN Human Rights Council).

148 *Continental Casualty v Argentina* Case ARB/03/9 (International Centre for Settlement of Investment Disputes).

149 *Asbestos* WT/DS135/AB/R (WTO Appellate Body).

6
Discovering Passive Virtues

Deference has, as the foregoing chapters reveal, become a defining feature of the European Court of Justice's (ECJ) free movement jurisprudence. By means of the margin of appreciation doctrine, the Court increasingly grants national legislatures the freedom to settle certain regulatory issues autonomously. Through decentralized judicial review, it outsources ever more review responsibilities to Member State courts. The previous chapters have investigated the conceptual nature of these doctrines, examined the circumstances in which they are applied, and shed light on their implications for principles like proportionality analysis. One question, however, still remains open: is all of this a good development? Is it constitutionally justified, perhaps even desirable, that the ECJ defers to national authorities? Or are we, to the contrary, witnessing a problematic trend?

That the Court of Justice's practice should be applauded is anything but evident. Judicial deference has attracted harsh criticism from human rights scholars. It is said to lead to moral and cultural relativism.[1] The margin of appreciation was branded a 'Trojan horse'[2] which 'jeopardizes'[3] the rights and freedoms guaranteed by the European Convention on Human Rights. Eyal Benvenisti warned that, if 'applied liberally', the doctrine can 'undermine seriously the promise of international enforcement of human rights'.[4] TRS Allan went so far as to suggest that deference amounts to an 'abdication of the judicial role'.[5]

This chapter will try to defend the use of deference in free movement law. This will be a constitutional defence, that is, one rooted in the EU's constitutional principles, which draws on insights from comparative institutional analysis. The argument will build on the findings gathered throughout this book. This notably includes the realization that the context in which the ECJ operates has changed over the past decades. EU law in general and free movement law in particular have matured, while compliance at the national level has improved. The European

[1] James A Sweeney, 'Margins of Appreciation: Cultural Relativity and the European Court of Human Rights in the Post-Cold War Era' (2005) 54 International and Comparative Law Quarterly 459.

[2] Ignacio de la Rasilla del Moral, 'The Increasingly Marginal Appreciation of the Margin-of-Appreciation Doctrine' (2006) 7 German Law Journal 611.

[3] Cora S Feingold, 'The Margin of Appreciation and the European Convention on Human Rights' (1977–1978) 53 Notre Dame Lawyer 90, 95.

[4] Eyal Benvenisti, 'Margin of Appreciation, Consensus, and Universal Standards' (1999) 31 International Law and Politics 843, 844.

[5] TRS Allan, 'Human Rights and Judicial Review: A Critique of "Due Deference"' (2006) 65 Cambridge Law Journal 671, 680.

Europe's Passive Virtues. Jan Zglinski, Oxford University Press (2020). © Oxford University Press.
DOI: 10.1093/oso/9780198844792.001.0001

political process is no longer dysfunctional and yields internal market legislation. The Court of Justice's workload has, at the same time, dramatically grown.

This chapter will begin by explaining why the question of deference matters normatively. I will argue that the choice of review standard affects which institution ends up deciding: the ECJ, the national legislature, or the national judiciary. I will go on to show that allocating responsibilities between the three is difficult due to the constitutional developments that have taken place. The EU has come to embrace a number of constitutional aspirations that cannot all be fulfilled, aspirations which the margin of appreciation and decentralized judicial review are trapped between. I will propose a way out of this dilemma based on two considerations: representation and expertise. When deciding on the intensity with which Member State action is reviewed as well as on who should exercise this review, we should aim at ensuring that decision-making is, on the one hand, sensitive to the interests of all affected and, on the other, lies in the hands of actors who are well informed about the subject matter at stake. Representation and expertise give us reason to believe that deferring to national institutions is, at times, the best option for the ECJ. The final part of the chapter will examine to what extent the Court complies with these desiderata.

I. Why Does the Standard of Review Matter?

Free movement scholars have long worried about Member State action being subjected to exceedingly far-reaching scrutiny by the Court of Justice. Traditionally, these worries manifest themselves in pleas for narrowing down the scope of application of the free movement provisions.[6] The broader the net of the four freedoms is cast, the greater the range of national laws that are potentially called into question, thereby affecting the extent of national decision-making autonomy. *Whether* and *where* the Court of Justice exercises free movement review thus constitutes a constitutional concern. That the same should be true of *how* the Court performs this function may be less obvious. Why does the standard of review in free movement cases matter from a normative perspective? What difference does it make if the ECJ engages in strict, *Cassis*-style review of Member State action or, instead, chooses to exercise deferential scrutiny *à la Schindler* or *Familiapress*? Three ideas can help with understanding the issue: plurality, disagreement, and decision-making ability.

[6] Guliano Marenco, 'Pour une Interprétation Traditionnelle de la Notion de Mésure d'Effet Equivalent à une Restriction Quantitative' (1984) 20 Cahiers de Droit Européen 291; Eric L White, 'In Search of the Limits of Article 30 of the EEC Treaty' (1989) 26 Common Market Law Review 235; Eleanor Spaventa, 'Leaving Keck Behind? The Free Movement of Goods after the Rulings in Commission v Italy and Mickelsson and Roos' (2009) 34 European Law Review 914; Gareth Davies, 'Understanding Market Access: Exploring the Economic Rationality of Different Conceptions of Free Movement Law' (2010) 11 German Law Journal 671; Thomas Horsley, 'Unearthing Buried Treasures: Art. 34 TFEU and the Exclusionary Rules' (2012) 37 European Law Review 734.

A. Plurality

The idea of plurality, one might equally say parity, pervades American constitutional thinking to such an extent that it is hardly ever spelled out anymore.[7] In a constitutional order, multiple institutional actors co-exist, all of which are in principle capable of determining what the constitution means and requires. This ability is, of course, clear when it comes to the judiciary. It is the traditional role of courts, especially those of supreme and constitutional rank, to define what liberty, equality, or free speech entail, to what extent they can be limited, and on what grounds. The crux of the argument from plurality is that other institutions, including non-judicial actors, can make these judgments, too.[8] Transposed into the European context, plurality implies that there is more than one institution that can determine what state action is justified and proportionate or, more precisely, institutions other than the ECJ. It is here that the standard of review becomes relevant: it affects who ends up deciding.

Chapter 1 already explained in brief terms the connection between doctrine (which review standard?) and institutions (which actor decides?). When engaging in substantive or centralized judicial review, that is, the *Cassis de Dijon* model, the ECJ examines all questions relating to the justification and proportionality of Member State action. Do consumers read labels? Are creditors of companies without minimum capital requirements sufficiently protected? What is an acceptable balance between free movement and free speech? The *Cassis* approach entails that the Court reassesses the regulatory judgments made at the national level and, thus, defines the content of free movement law.

When the ECJ, by contrast, opts for deferential forms of review, it hands this power over to national authorities to varying degrees. This may be more apparent when it comes to Member State courts. In cases of decentralized judicial review, it is the referring court that will ultimately decide which regulatory behaviour is acceptable and which is not. It will determine whether particular policy objectives are legitimate, the legislation adopted to achieve them is effective, and the burden on free movement is tolerable. The same shift happens, in essence, when the ECJ grants domestic political actors a margin of appreciation. As explained in the previous chapter, legislatures and executives engage, if in a less formal way, in justification and proportionality analysis, too. They consider which policy goals to pursue, how to best achieve them, and whether the degree of regulatory intervention is

[7] The first chapter of Alexander Bickel's *The Least Dangerous Branch: The Supreme Court at the Bar of Politics* (Bobbs-Merrill 1962) is commonly taken as its starting point, but predecessors can be found as early as in the Realist movement.

[8] Commenting on the opinion of Justice Marshall in *Marbury v Madison*, Bickel writes that 'Marshall knew... that a statute's repugnancy to the Constitution is in most instances not self-evident; it is, rather, an issue of policy that someone must decide. The problem is who: the courts, the legislature itself, the President, perhaps juries for purposes of criminal trials, or ultimately and finally the people through the electoral process?' (at 3).

excessive. When the Court grants Member States a margin of appreciation, it does not subject this primary assessment to a second look. This gives national legislatures the freedom to regulate with limited or no substantial external control.

Thus, depending on which review standard is applied, different actors are involved in the shaping of the internal market to different extents. The choice between centrally exercised substantive review, the margin of appreciation, and decentralized judicial review can therefore be translated into a choice between the Court of Justice, national legislatures or executives, and national courts.[9] The lesson from plurality is that, at least in principle, each of these actors can decide what free movement law means, how it is to be reconciled with conflicting policy concerns, and which restrictions count as proportionate.

B. Disagreement

Plurality gains special force when combined with a second idea: disagreement. The argument from disagreement was introduced into the debate on judicial review by Jeremy Waldron.[10] It holds, in a nutshell, that different people may hold differing opinions on what constitutional rights entail. Their disagreement need not be due to biases, egoisms, or misunderstandings of the moral implications of their position. It will often be 'reasonable' or 'good faith' disagreement, that is, the genuine and plausible conviction that a certain right should mean X and not Y.

Disagreement illustrates the consequences of plurality. It suggests that different institutional actors are likely to answer the same question in different ways. For our purposes, it is not necessary to argue that everything constitutional, or every problem relating to free movement law, will be the object of disagreement. It is sufficient to accept that a substantial share of issues brought before the ECJ will be disagreed on. The case law discussed in earlier chapters provides us with numerous examples. Are the activities of Scientology socially harmful? Should there be a minimum wage? What is the appropriate length of TV advertisements? There is no obvious answer to any of these questions, even if the problem is approached in good faith. Against this background, who decides is crucial as it influences the outcome. The Court of Justice may not consider Scientology as great a threat as the

[9] A further institutional actor involved in the shaping of the internal market and free movement law is the European legislative process. However, it is not, or at least not directly, affected by the degree of deference which the ECJ grants national authorities. The standard of scrutiny applied to EU legislation has, traditionally, been very deferential, even if, more recently, the Court appears to engage in more searching review in certain scenarios, see Eirik Bjorge and Jan Zglinski, 'The Principle of Proportionality in EU Law and Its Domestic Application: *Ni tout à fait le même, ni tout à fait un autre*' in Katja Ziegler, Päivi Neuvonen, and Violeta Moreno-Lax (eds), *Research Handbook on General Principles of EU Law* (Edward Elgar forthcoming).

[10] Jeremy Waldron, *Law and Disagreement* (Oxford University Press 1999); Jeremy Waldron, 'The Core of the Case Against Judicial Review' (2006) 115 Yale Law Journal 1346.

British government does; it may not be convinced of the benefits of minimum wage to the same degree that the Belgian judiciary is; and it may differ in its view of how long TV breaks should last from the German parliament. This can be due to a different mindset, preferences, or sensitivities on the matter.

Note that proportionality does not provide a fix for the problems connected with disagreement. In a scenario in which we disagree as to what a constitutional right should mean, or to what extent restrictions on it are justified, it simply subdivides and structures our debate.[11] This, of course, is helpful as it allows us to put our finger on the exact points of contention. Yet, it does not solve the disagreement. The given question is only broken down into four smaller ones, none of them necessarily less controversial than the bigger problem. Take, for instance, the issue of rent control, a topic which has received political attention in many corners of the EU recently (as well as in urban areas across the world). It will be useful to turn the general question of whether there should be limits on what landlords can charge their tenants, and what these limits should be, into more specific ones such as: should the state intervene in the formation of rental prices? Is rent control an effective tool for creating affordable housing? To what extent will it deter investments in the housing market? And how far can we restrict the property rights of landlords for the sake of the greater social good? Subdividing our debate in this way certainly facilitates the decision-making process as it lays bare what exactly it is that we have to make up our mind about. From the perspective of disagreement, however, nothing is won. We are likely to disagree on all of these smaller issues as well. Therefore, whoever is in charge of applying proportionality will eventually decide how they are answered.[12]

C. Institutional Strengths and Weaknesses

Variation in decision-making ability is the final reason why it matters who decides. Different institutions are good at making different types of decisions. A central bank is likely to make sound prognoses when it comes to inflation rates, but will be ill-suited to assess the risks of a new influenza virus. A first-instance criminal court will expediently carry out a theft trial, but struggle with determining the socio-economic consequences of austerity measures. When allocating the authority to decide, it is crucial that we take these relative strengths

[11] cf. Mattias Kumm, 'The Idea of Socratic Contestation and the Right to Justification: The Point of Rights-Based Proportionality Review' (2010) 4 Law and Ethics of Human Rights 140, 170 (who argues that proportionality allows courts to ascertain whether a disagreement is, in fact, reasonable).

[12] This is not to say that courts, when examining whether state action is proportionate, must inevitably engage in 'correctness review', see Kai Möller, *The Global Model of Constitutional Rights* (Oxford University Press 2012) 177. Even under the more lenient 'reasonableness' standard, it will be the court in charge that, at the end of the day, polices the boundaries of what counts as reasonable.

and weaknesses into account or, in other words, that we engage in comparative institutional analysis.

The origins of comparative institutional analysis lie in economic theory, but Neil Komesar has demonstrated the relevance of considering institutional questions for law and adjudication.[13] The actors involved in the creation and application of law vary in size, competence, and their ability to capture certain interests.[14] These features affect how much they can do and, more importantly, how well they will do it. The size of an institution determines how many decisions it can make. The experience and training in a given field has an impact on its ability to assess complex subject matters. The way in which it operates (eg formal or informal procedure, low or high access costs) determines which persons or groups of persons will participate in the decision-making process, which has consequences for the question of whose concerns will be taken into consideration.

A comparison of the political and judicial branches illustrates these differences. The political process is a relatively large institution, as reflected by the number of legislators, agencies, and experts, with specialized competence in many areas.[15] It has, due to mechanisms like periodic elections, direct and constant exposure to public opinion. This, for one, increases its ability to handle complex regulatory problems. For another, it makes it easier to capture and incorporate the interests present among the members of a polity while, however, also creating the risk that some of them are over- or under-represented.[16] The judiciary is, to the contrary, a much smaller actor, notably in terms of human resources.[17] As a result, it can 'produce' less, as evidenced by the limited number of judgments a court can render.[18] Yet, at the same time, it is, due to the independence of judges, also less open to the biases to which the political process is prone.[19]

Although developed for the domestic context, the basic insights of comparative institutional analysis apply to the actors involved in EU free movement law. Some of them will be better at understanding and handling a particular issue, others worse. On another topic, their roles may reverse. At this point, it is not important that we fully grasp each actor's strengths and weaknesses. For now, I would just like to make the more modest point that, when it comes to decision-making

[13] Neil Komesar, *Imperfect Alternatives* (University of Chicago Press 1997); Neil Komesar, *Law's Limits* (Cambridge University Press 2001).

[14] For a detailed exposition of the relevant strengths and weaknesses of different institutional actors, see Komesar, *Imperfect Alternatives* (n 13) chs 3–5 (discussing the political, market, and adjudicative process).

[15] ibid 53 et seq.

[16] Komesar identifies two potential problems: minoritarian bias (special-interest legislation) and majoritarian bias (discrimination of political and social minorities); see Komesar, *Law's Limits* (n 13) 60. These can result from the costs of participation and the distribution of the (potential) benefits.

[17] ibid 35 et seq.

[18] See Andrew Coan, *Rationing the Constitution: How Judicial Capacity Shapes Supreme Court Decision-Making* (Harvard University Press 2019).

[19] Komesar, *Imperfect Alternatives* (n 13) 124 et seq.

ability, there are likely to be *some* differences between the ECJ, national legislatures and executives, and national judiciaries. Given its nature as a generalist court, the Court of Justice will occasionally struggle with comprehending certain technical issues, which specialized agencies have longstanding experience with. Given its nature as a supranational institution, it will at times not understand the factual circumstances in a Member State, a task with which national judges will have fewer difficulties. Given its nature as an EU organ, it is likely to be more sensitive to the European dimension of regulatory decisions than a domestic parliament. Against this background, every time we decide between the ECJ, national legislatures, and national courts—or between centralized substantive review, the margin of appreciation, and decentralized judicial review—, our choice affects the outcome and quality of the final decision.

Note that the foregoing does not provide a normative argument in favour of deference yet. Nor does it tell us in which scenarios the Court of Justice should defer to Member State authorities. This will require setting out the constitutional mandate of the ECJ as well as the respective roles of national legislatures and courts. To do that, we must take a closer look at the constitutional materials of the EU.

II. Three Constitutional Tensions

With the ECJ, national legislatures, and national courts, we do not only have different institutional actors, we have very different types of actors. One dividing line runs between courts and legislatures. These are, at the same time, European and national institutions. Finally, there is, in the form of the ECJ, one 'high' or quasi-constitutional court and numerous 'lower' domestic courts. To assess whether and when the application of doctrines such as the margin of appreciation and decentralized judicial review is constitutionally warranted, we must therefore simultaneously enter three debates that are usually held separately: first, what is the appropriate role of the judiciary vis-à-vis the legislative and executive branches? Second, what is the appropriate role of the EU vis-à-vis the Member States? Third, what is the appropriate division of labour between the ECJ and national courts?

By their very nature, these are difficult questions. What further complicates things is that the EU has, in relation to them, embraced different constitutional goals and ambitions that conflict with one another. Some were inherent to the European project from the start. Most, however, are the result of developments that have taken place since the adoption of the Maastricht Treaty. Put simply, we want to achieve things that cannot be achieved together and harbour constitutional desires that cannot be fulfilled at the same time. The resulting tensions directly affect how we expect the Court of Justice to behave and complicate the normative appraisal of deference.

A. Democratic Governance *v* Judicial Review

The phenomenon of constitutionalism has made parliaments the centres of gravity in legal orders across the globe. At the same time, and more subtly, it has turned courts into a powerful institutional actor.[20] Supreme and, where they exist, constitutional courts review and invalidate acts of legislatures. Normatively, this creates a legitimacy problem famously called the 'counter-majoritarian difficulty': should a handful of unelected judges be allowed to overturn decisions of a democratic majority and, if so, under which circumstances?[21] This conundrum has kept American constitutional scholars busy for the better part of the twentieth century.[22] Supporters of judicial review have stressed that courts are necessary to guard constitutional principles,[23] protect minorities from discrimination,[24] or prevent interest groups from hijacking the political process.[25] Opponents have highlighted the pitfalls of having courts decide on behalf of, or against, a democratically elected body that is equally committed to realizing the constitution.[26]

What is at the root of this debate is a conflict between two constitutional aspirations: democratic (or majoritarian) governance and judicial control.[27] On the one hand, we want 'we the people' to be in charge and decide freely on matters of policy. At the same time, we want courts to monitor their decisions. EU constitutional law has, like most legal orders around the world, come to embrace these aspirations as well. This might be more evident for the former of the two. From the very beginning, the European Treaties established a Court of Justice and created procedures to ensure that both the Union's institutions and the Member States complied with the provisions of the Treaties. The Court quickly became an important actor and has remained so until today. Partly as a result of its success, the EU judiciary was expanded and two further courts were created, the General Court and the (now defunct) Civil Service Tribunal.

Democratic concerns were less present in the beginning of the European project. As its competences and regulatory impact grew, the EU was increasingly criticized for its democratic deficit.[28] This led to gradual changes in the Union's

[20] Alec Stone Sweet, *Governing With Judges* (Oxford University Press 2000).

[21] Bickel (n 7).

[22] Barry Friedmann, 'The Birth of an Academic Obsession: The History of the Countermajoritarian Difficulty, Part Five' (2002) 112 Yale Law Journal 153.

[23] Bickel (n 7); Ronald Dworkin, *Law's Empire* (Hart 1998).

[24] John Hart Ely, *Democracy and Distrust* (Harvard University Press 1980).

[25] Komesar, *Imperfect Alternatives* (n 13).

[26] Waldron, 'The Core of the Case Against Judicial Review' (n 10); Mark Tushnet, *Weak Courts, Strong Rights* (Princeton University Press 2008).

[27] This could equally be called the tension between democratic governance and (judicially-enforced) rights protection.

[28] Giandomenico Majone, 'Europe's "Democratic Deficit": The Question of Standards' (1998) 4 European Law Journal 5; Andrew Moravcsik, 'In Defence of the "Democratic Deficit": Reassessing Legitimacy in the European Union' (2002) 40 Journal of Common Market Studies 603; Christophe Crombez, 'The Democratic Deficit in the European Union: Much Ado about Nothing?' (2003) 4

institutional architecture. The most visible sign of this is the evolution of the European Parliament which, within thirty years, progressed from being a mere advisory body to a co-decision-maker. Other changes concern the legislative process, such as the shift from unanimity to qualified majority voting (which ensures that Member States cannot block the decision-making process against a European majority) and the introduction of the comitology mechanism. Constitutional language reflects this evolution, too. The Maastricht Treaty first mentioned the 'attachment to democracy', referring not only to the EU but also to its Member States. Subsequent treaty amendments led to a proliferation of such vocabulary. Post-Lisbon, the TEU is filled with references to democracy, grants it the status of a foundational value (Article 2), and dedicates an entire Title to the 'Provisions on Democratic Principles'. Promoting democracy at the European and national level has, at least formally, become a serious goal of the Union.[29]

That EU constitutional law has, in this way, come to pursue democratic governance as well as judicial review affects our normative expectations as to how the Court of Justice—and, by association, national courts—should behave in relation to Member State legislation. Yet, it does so in two opposing ways, reflecting both strands of the evolution. Recent scholarship illustrates this neatly. On the one hand, judicial review of domestic legislation is still considered a welcome, even indispensable feature of European law. Authors present it as a means to fight discriminatory practices;[30] highlight that it promotes regulatory efficiency and ensures competitiveness;[31] and point out that it is essential for protecting fundamental rights and minority groups.[32] On the other hand, judicial review is increasingly perceived as problematic. Free movement jurisprudence in areas like social policy, higher education, and health care is criticized for being exceedingly interventionist.[33] The ECJ is said to lack not just the democratic legitimacy to overturn Member State policies in these domains but the ability to understand, as a court,

European Union Politics 101; Andreas Føllesdal and Simon Hix, 'Why There is a Democratic Deficit in the EU: A Response to Majone and Moravcsik' (2006) 44 Journal of Common Market Studies 533.

29 The realities of European democracy are quite another matter; for some of the persisting problems, see Joseph HH Weiler, 'The Political and Legal Culture of European Integration: An Exploratory Essay' (2011) 9 International Journal of Constitutional Law 678, 679 et seq.

30 Miguel Poiares Maduro, *We the Court* (Hart 1998).

31 Spaventa 'Leaving Keck Behind?' (n 6); Aurelien Portuese, 'Principle of Proportionality as Principle of Economic Efficiency' (2013) 19 European Law Journal 612.

32 Andrew Williams, *EU Human Rights Policies: A Study in Irony* (Oxford University Press 2004).

33 Peter Hilpold, 'Hochschulzugang und Unionsbürgerschaft: Das Urteil des EuGH vom 7. 7. 2005 in der Rechtssache C-147/03, Kommission gegen Österreich' (2005) 16 Europäische Zeitschrift für Wirtschaftsrecht 647; Christian Joerges and Florian Rödl, 'Informal Politics, Formalised Law and the Social Deficit of European Integration: Reflections after the Judgments of the ECJ in *Viking* and *Laval*' (2009) 15 European Law Journal 1; Fritz W Scharpf, 'Legitimacy in the Multilevel European Polity' (2009) 1 European Political Science Review 173; Jotte Mulder, *Social Legitimacy in the Internal Market* (Hart 2018).

the communitarian and non-quantitative considerations that are at stake.[34] As different as they may be, both positions find support in the constitutional principles of the EU. We want national legislative processes to be subjected to thorough control by the ECJ and national courts while, likewise, trying to respect their decisions and democratic credentials. The tension thus created is one between democratic rule and judicial review, or between courts and legislatures.

B. Centralization *v* Decentralization

A second tension concerns the scope of the European project or, to put it differently, the question of federalism. The post-Maastricht era has brought about a simultaneous growth of both centripetal and centrifugal forces in EU law. Call this the conflict between centralization and decentralization. On the one hand, we want a more powerful and active Union. On the other, we want a more significant role for the Member States. Two developments manifest this tension.

The first concerns legislative competences. The powers of the EU have been continuously extended over the past two and a half decades. Its current competence catalogue covers a wide array of policy fields, ranging from traditional responsibilities such as agriculture, transport, and external commercial policy, to areas like education, energy, and environmental protection. What is more, exercising these powers has become easier due to the replacing of unanimity with majority voting at the Council. The result has been an important increase in European legislation. The EU can do more and it seems, by and large, willing to make use of this potential.

In parallel, however, the Treaties have begun to increasingly emphasize the legislative competences of the Member States. The principles of conferral, subsidiarity, and proportionality (Article 5 TEU) all signal that law making is, in principle, the prerogative of national—and, to some extent, local[35]—authorities, which should only be deprived of this power when EU action is indispensable. An 'Early Warning Mechanism' has been introduced as a political safeguard, allowing national parliaments to voice their opposition to EU measures violating the principle of subsidiarity.[36] The red lines laid down in competence norms such as Articles 79(5) TFEU (immigration), 153(4) TFEU (social policy), 168(7) TFEU

[34] Gareth Davies, for instance, argues that 'communitarian reasons are subtle, non-quantitative, subjective, unprovable—the very essence of the kind of judgments that politicians make and *courts rightly shy away from*' (emphasis added): see 'The Price of Letting Courts Value Solidarity: The Judicial Role in Liberalizing Welfare' in Malcolm Ross and Yuri Borgmann-Prebil (eds), *Promoting Solidarity in the European Union* (OUP 2010) 114:

[35] The principle of subsidiarity states that 'the Union shall act only if and in so far as the objectives of the proposed action cannot be sufficiently achieved by the Member States, either at central level or at *regional and local level*' (emphasis added) (Art 5(3) TEU).

[36] Protocol 2 to the Lisbon Treaty on the application of the principles of subsidiarity and proportionality.

(public health), and 194(2) TFEU (energy) reflect similar concerns by removing, in areas that have been Europeanized, decisions on certain salient policy questions from the Union's reach.[37]

The expansion of EU competences is, of course, not logically incompatible with the setting of limits on how to exercise them. One might even say that such a far-reaching widening of powers must almost necessarily prompt a more detailed specification of boundaries. Nonetheless, both developments pull in two different directions: while the former signals a desire for 'more Europe', the latter stresses the importance of national decision-making.

One finds the same tension in relation to value judgments. Step by step—and the pace has increased since Maastricht—the EU has embraced a broad range of values which take it radically beyond its initial, almost exclusively economic focus.[38] Article 2 TEU, a product of the Lisbon Treaty, is the most visible manifestation of this process. It contains a list of thirteen values said to be foundational to both the Union and its Member States. Among them, we find liberal classics such as freedom, equality, and minority protection alongside more recent constitutional concerns like dignity, pluralism, and solidarity. But there is more. Articles 8 to 12 TFEU commit the EU to promoting gender equality, combating discrimination, and protecting the environment. Further, the Union has adopted its own Charter of Fundamental Rights, now a binding element of primary law, and has pledged to promote the European Social Charter and the Charter of the Fundamental Social Rights of Workers (Article 151 TFEU).[39] Accomplishing the internal market, the former heartland of the European project, still remains a constitutional objective. Yet, it has become only one among many. The ECJ has long recognized this transformation. In *Viking* and *Laval*, it made clear that the Union has 'not only an economic but also a social purpose'.[40] Elsewhere, it has underlined the EU's responsibility for furthering equality between men and women, fighting age discrimination, and protecting human dignity.[41] The result is a 'thickening' of the European normative sphere and a centralization of values. The EU can, and is increasingly expected to, be active with regard to normative questions.

[37] These are only the most recently introduced red lines. Similar provisions existed in previous Treaty versions, for example Arts 72 and 276 TFEU (law and order and internal security), Art 345 TFEU (private ownership), and Art 346(1)(b) (production of arms and war material).

[38] The Treaty of Rome already contained a few rules on non-economic matters, such as social policy.

[39] The new Art 3(3) TEU also proclaims that the EU is, or shall strive to be, a 'social market economy'.

[40] Case C-341/05 *Laval* [2007] ECLI:EU:C:2007:809, para 105; Case C-438/05 *Viking Line* [2007] ECLI:EU:C:2007:772, para 79; also, more recently, Case C-201/15 *AGET Iraklis* [2016] ECLI:EU:C:2016:972, para 76. Note that this line of reasoning has its roots in decisions like Case 43/75 *Defrenne (No 2)* [1976] ECLI:EU:C:1976:56, where the Court emphasized that 'the Community ... is not merely an economic union, but is at the same time intended, by common action, to ensure social progress and seek the constant improvement of the living and working conditions of their peoples' (para 10).

[41] Case C-36/02 *Omega Spielhallen* [2004] ECLI:EU:C:2004:614, para 34; Case C-555/07 *Kücükdeveci* [2010] ECLI:EU:C:2010:21, paras 20–22; Case C-236/09 *Test-Achats* [2011] ECLI:EU:C:2011:100, para 19.

At the same time, there has been a growing emphasis on the importance of national values and cultural differences. Article 4(2) TEU stipulates that the national identities of Member States shall be respected. This includes territorial integrity, law and order, and national security but, on the reading of the ECJ, also matters such as language policy,[42] questions of federalism,[43] and fundamental political and ethical choices.[44] Article 22 of the Charter of Fundamental Rights states that the Union shall honour cultural, religious, and linguistic diversity. Similarly, Article 167(1) TFEU charges the EU with contributing to the 'flowering of the cultures of the Member States' and demands that 'national and regional diversity' be respected. All of this suggests that it is the Member States, not the Union, which are meant to play the decisive role when it comes to value choices.

The European project, hence, displays contradictory traits. A constantly stronger EU increasingly accentuates national powers and particularities. This quandary shows in the normative expectations which scholars hold towards the ECJ. Parts of the literature claim that the Court should actively promote European values by being a guardian of social welfare,[45] protector of racial and ethnic minorities,[46] and a guarantor of justice.[47] Others advocate that the Court of Justice should show greater self-restraint, respect the moral and ethical choices made by the Member States,[48] and stay out of topics which are 'primarily a matter for national consideration'.[49] Again, we seem to want both. We expect the ECJ to enforce the growing set of EU objectives and defend them against violations at the national level. Likewise, we do not want the Court to interfere in Member State affairs too strongly and

[42] Case C-391/09 *Runevič-Vardyn and Wardyn* [2011] ECLI:EU:C:2011:291, para 86; Case C-202/11 *Las* [2013] ECLI:EU:C:2013:239, para 26.

[43] Case C-156/13 *Digibet* [2014] ECLI:EU:C:2014:1756, para 34 (division of Germany into *Länder*).

[44] Case C-208/09 *Sayn-Wittgenstein* [2010] ECLI:EU:C:2010:806, para 83; Case C-438/14 *Bogendorff von Wolffersdorff* [2016] ECLI:EU:C:2016:401, para 73 (both abolition of nobility); Case C-673/16 *Coman* [2018] ECLI:EU:C:2018:385 (same-sex marriage).

[45] Miguel Poiares Maduro, 'Europe's Social Self: "The Sickness Unto Death"' in Jo Shaw (ed), *Social Law and Policy in an Evolving European Union* (Hart 2000) 325; Loïc Azoulai, 'The Court of Justice and the Social Market Economy: The Emergence of an Ideal and the Conditions for Its Realisation' (2008) 45 Common Market Law Review 1335; Anne Davies, 'One Step Forward, Two Steps Back? The *Viking* and *Laval* Cases in the ECJ' (2008) 37 Industrial Law Journal 126; Claire Kilpatrick, 'Internal Market Architecture and the Accommodation of Labour Rights: As Good as it Gets?' EUI Working Paper LAW 2011/04.

[46] Williams (n 32); Mathias Möschel, 'Race Discrimination and Access to the European Court of Justice: *Belov*' (2013) 50 Common Market Law Review 1433.

[47] Dimitry Kochenov, Gráinne de Búrca, and Andrew Williams (eds), *Europe's Justice Deficit?* (Hart 2015); Floris de Witte, *Justice in the EU: The Emergence of Transnational Solidarity* (Oxford University Press 2015).

[48] Niamh Nic Shuibhne, 'Margins of Appreciation: National Values, Fundamental Rights and EC Free Movement Law' (2009) 34 European Law Review 230; Floris de Witte, 'Sex, Drugs & EU Law: The Recognition of Moral and Ethical Diversity in EU Law' (2013) 50 Common Market Law Review 1545.

[49] Jan H Jans, 'Proportionality Revisited' (2000) 27 Legal Issues of Economic Integration 239, 263; Gráinne de Búrca, 'The Principle of Proportionality and Its Application in EU Law' (1994) 14 Yearbook of European Law 105, 112; Janneke Gerards, 'Pluralism, Deference and the Margin of Appreciation Doctrine' (2011) 17 European Law Journal 80, 85.

defer to domestic decisions. It is the old chestnut of unity and diversity, just that we want more unity and more diversity at the same time.

C. Uniformity of EU Law *v* National Application

A third tension concerns the relationship between, on the one hand, the unity of EU law and the uniformity of its application and, on the other, the role of national courts with regard to judicial review. It results not so much from changes in the EU's constitutional rules—the main provision being Article 267 TFEU, which has remained largely the same since the Treaty of Rome[50]—but from the Court of Justice's reading of them. Two perspectives have developed over time.

The uniform interpretation and application of European rules across all Member States has been called a 'fundamental requirement of the [Union] legal order'.[51] Legal fragmentation has always been perceived of as a risk in the EU and preventing it constitutes one of the Court of Justice's priorities. The preliminary reference mechanism plays a central function in this respect. Opinion 2/13 puts it in the following terms:

> In order to ensure that the specific characteristics and the autonomy of [the EU] legal order are preserved, the Treaties have established a judicial system intended to ensure consistency and uniformity in the interpretation of EU law ... In particular, the judicial system as thus conceived has as its keystone the preliminary ruling procedure provided for in Article 267 TFEU, which, by setting up a dialogue between one court and another, specifically between the Court of Justice and the courts and tribunals of the Member States, has the object of securing uniform interpretation of EU law, thereby serving to ensure its consistency, its full effect and its autonomy as well as, ultimately, the particular nature of the law established by the Treaties.[52]

National courts are meant to submit questions relating to EU law through the Article 267 procedure so that the ECJ can lay down an answer which is valid for the whole of the Union. It is this desire to ensure consistency and uniformity that has led the Court to forbid national judges to invalidate secondary legislation in *Foto-Frost*: '[d]ivergences between courts in the Member States as to the validity of [Union] acts would be liable to place in jeopardy the very unity of the [Union] legal order'.[53] It is the same desire that made the Court emphasize the duty to refer

[50] The only modification to Art 267 TFEU has been the addition of the fourth paragraph, which states the ECJ shall act with minimum delay if a preliminary reference concerns a case with regard to a person in custody.

[51] Cases C-143/88 and 92/89 *Zuckerfabrik Süderdithmarschen* [1991] ECLI:EU:C:1991:65, para 26.

[52] Opinion 2/13 *Accession of the EU to the ECHR* [2014] EU:C:2014:2454, para 176.

[53] Case 314/85 *Foto-Frost* [1987] ECLI:EU:C:1987:452, para 15.

of domestic last-instance courts in *Köbler* and, more recently, sanctioned breaches in *Da Silva e Brito* and *Commission v France*.[54] (It is this very rationale that also explains the Court's reluctance to let other actors, such as the European Court of Human Rights and investment arbitration tribunals, interpret, apply, or evaluate EU rules.[55])

The vision articulated in rulings like *Foto-Frost* and *Köbler* puts the ECJ in the driver's seat when it comes to judicial review. It is the only body which can truly secure the unity and uniformity of EU law. The more the Court of Justice does itself, the lower the risk of fragmentation. National courts are, from this perspective, a risk factor: granting them autonomous review powers creates the possibility of diverging positions across the Member States. The more that is left for national judges to decide, the higher the chances that EU law disintegrates, or at least so the worry goes.

Yet, at the same time, Member State courts are supposed to occupy an important place in the EU's judicial architecture. The new Article 19(1) TEU hints at this when stating that Member States shall provide remedies to ensure effective legal protection in areas covered by Union law. The ECJ, as was explained in Chapter 4, highlighted the relevance of the national judiciary from the very start. In *Van Gend & Loos* and *Costa/ENEL*, it emphasized that the preliminary reference system established in Article 267 TFEU allocated the tasks of fact-finding and application to national judges, tasks which the Court would not encroach upon.[56] More recently, it stated that national courts should exercise judicial review when they are 'better placed' to assess the factual and legal circumstances of a dispute.[57] Likewise, it has warmed up to the idea that national judges can, in some scenarios, apply national standards of protection of fundamental rights.[58]

Again, both perspectives are not necessarily incompatible with each other. One can have a system in which the ECJ provides strong guidance on EU law *and* national courts play a meaningful role. Nonetheless, the ultimate orientation of the two differs. Whereas the former pulls towards accepting wider review tasks for the Court of Justice, the latter pulls towards decentralizing these to the Member State judiciary.

Perhaps nowhere is this tension as visible as in the case law on proportionality. On the one hand, proportionality review is, as a 'question of fact', said to be the prerogative of national judges.[59] The Court of Justice is not supposed to examine

[54] Case C-224/01 *Köbler* [2003] ECLI:EU:C:2003:513; Case C-160/14 *Da Silva e Brito* [2015] ECLI:EU:C:2015:565; Case C-416/17 *Commission v France (Duty to Refer)* [2018] ECLI:EU:C:2018:811.

[55] Opinion 2/13 (n 52); Case C-284/16 *Achmea* [2018] ECLI:EU:C:2018:158.

[56] Case 26/62 *Van Gend & Loos* [1963] ECLI:EU:C:1963:1, para 11; Case 6/64 *Costa v ENEL* [1964] ECLI:EU:C:1964:66, 593.

[57] Case C-405/98 *Gourmet International* [2001] ECLI:EU:C:2001:135; *Bogendorff von Wolffersdorff* (n 44).

[58] Case C-42/17 *MAS* [2017] ECLI:EU:C:2017:936.

[59] Case C-145/88 *Torfaen Borough Council* [1989] ECLI:EU:C:1989:593, para 16.

whether national measures are proportionate and should let domestic courts decide. At the same time, the ECJ is expected to provide 'all the necessary guidance', a duty directly connected with its role as guarantor of the unity of EU law.[60] It is meant to clarify what exactly the free movement rules require and where their limits lie. A lack of uniformity in how they are applied—and this is the unavoidable consequence of allowing Member State courts to exercise proportionality review autonomously—is problematic in this light. The result is a catch-22 situation. We want a system which is marked by a high level of uniformity but is, to an important extent, administered decentrally by a multitude of Member State courts. Alas, you cannot have your cake and eat it, too.

III. Active and Passive Virtues

The constitutional developments within the EU put us in an uncomfortable position. They create desires and expectations that cannot be satisfied together. On the one hand, we want democratic governance; on the other, a system of strong judicial review. We want a politically 'thicker' and more powerful Union as well as a greater role for the Member States. Finally, we want EU law to be applied uniformly but, likewise, national courts to play a central role when it comes to judicial review. It is time to pause at this point for a first conclusion. When defining the appropriate role of free movement law vis-à-vis national legal orders, and that of the ECJ vis-à-vis Member State institutions, we will always have to make trade-offs between these objectives. The more we will emphasize some, the more we will restrict others.

The more important value of the foregoing analysis, however, lies elsewhere. Almost in passing, it has yielded a *general* constitutional defence of deference. The margin of appreciation doctrine is in line with the EU's aim of promoting democracy and decentralization; where applied, it gives domestic political branches the freedom to settle certain regulatory issues without European judicial intrusion. The decentralizing of review responsibilities to Member State courts ensures a meaningful function for Europe's 'lower' judiciary. I emphasize the word 'general' because the fact that both doctrines are compatible with some of the EU's constitutional goals does not, of course, mean that their application will always be warranted. Giving Member States *carte blanche* on all questions of policy-making does not sit well with the idea of judicial review and risks facilitating violations of European values. The need to guarantee an appropriate level of uniformity of EU law will make it unacceptable that national judges decide freely on the legality of Member State action all the time.

[60] Case C-142/05 *Mickelsson and Roos* [2009] ECLI:EU:C:2009:336, para 41.

The challenge, against this background, is to define when the ECJ should defer to national authorities and when it should not. The basis for our considerations must be that the Court of Justice does not operate in a vacuum. There are other institutions whose role is constitutionally protected and which, therefore, must be taken seriously. We will, in this light, want the Court to step in where it offers an added value due to its nature as a judicial body, a European institution, or the 'supreme court of the land'. At the same time, we will insist on restraint where other actors are better placed to decide. Our task, in other words, is to set out the Court's active and passive virtues.

In what follows I will suggest that two considerations should guide this endeavour: representation and expertise. When deciding on the intensity with which national laws are subjected to free movement review and who exercises this review, we should aim to put in charge the actor who is most likely to ensure an adequate consideration of all members of the polity (*representation*) and, at the same time, best suited to understand and deal with the factual questions relevant for the decision (*expertise*). It is not my intention to claim that this is the only way to solve the dilemmas described above—other possibilities exist, some of which will be discussed below. Nonetheless, I want to suggest that the proposal is attractive as it respects the EU's constitutional principles while taking seriously the tenets of comparative institutional analysis.[61]

Before I flesh out my argument in greater detail, a brief disclaimer is necessary. The aims of representation and expertise will conflict at times. A national legislature may be expedient with regard to public health matters but blatantly discriminate against foreign businesses. A Member State court may understand local mores but not be the legitimate authority to make fundamental ethical choices. Representation and expertise will not provide automatic answers here. Yet, they furnish us with a set of considerations we can draw on when deciding who should decide. Accepting selectivity is crucial in this respect. Free movement scholars often seek to find a single solution that would work for the entire case law of the Court of Justice. There is no such holy grail. Judicial review in free movement law has become too complex a task for cross-cutting solutions. Different settings create different problems which particular institutions are more or less legitimate and better or worse equipped to solve. We will want the Court to be active in some situations and deferential in others. The overall picture may become more complicated, but it also stands the chance of being normatively more satisfying.

[61] In the following, I will be drawing on the work of Neil Komesar (n 13), notably regarding the differences between the adjudicative and political processes as well as the relevance of representation/participation for constitutional decision-making. Komesar's scholarship expands on the themes and insights of Ely's *Democracy and Distrust* (n 24) and has found its way into the literature on EU free movement law through Maduro, *We the Court* (n 30); see, more recently, also Johanna Croon-Gestefeld, *Reconceptualising European Equality Law: A Comparative Institutional Analysis* (Hart 2017).

A. Representation

It is a basic premise of egalitarian democratic systems that everyone should have a voice in every decision taken, not only those forming part of the current political majority.[62] This does not mean that the position of minorities—ideological, ethnic, or social—must always prevail. Yet, it requires that the latter's concerns are adequately taken into consideration. When the political process fails to ensure such representation, it does not do what it is meant to do. This can, under certain conditions, give us reason to let courts correct, or at the least review, its outcomes.

The case for focusing on representation in constitutional adjudication has been made before. So has the case for making it a principle of free movement law, in the particular form I will call 'European representation'. My central aim here will not be to restate this claim. It will be to show that, despite retaining some validity, it does not align with the constitutional foundations of the EU anymore. In exclusively focusing on the concerns of non-nationals, it is both too wide and too narrow. It is too wide in failing to provide Member States sufficient space for meaningful self-determination. It is too narrow in focusing on non-nationals as a protected class. In doing so, it is incapable of fulfilling more recent normative commitments of the Union, such as social justice, gender equality, and minority protection. At times, it may even obstruct their achievement.

1. Of Europeans

Making sense of representation requires answering the question: who is to be represented? If we have traditionally defined majorities and minorities within nation-states, the European project forces us to re-draw this line. In the words of Miguel Maduro:

> [We] can no longer allow Member States to take decisions from a purely national perspective. State regulation is now almost always regulation of the common market as well. Within the framework of the European Economic Constitution, Member States should take all interests affected into account when regulating the common market. This includes out-of-State interests. Member States should be able to make different policy judgments. What we should not permit is that they ignore out-of-State interests in making those judgments.[63]

[62] Although this claim is most closely associated with Ely, it is equally reflected in the work of many other constitutional thinkers, including his critics: see Laurence H Tribe, 'The Puzzling Persistence of Process-Based Constitutional Theories' (1980) 89 Yale Law Journal 1063, 1070 et seq; Bruce Ackerman, 'Beyond *Carolene Products*' (1985) 98 Harvard Law Review 713; Waldron, 'The Core of the Case Against Judicial Review' (n 10), 1361 et seq.

[63] Maduro, *We the Court* (n 30) 171.

Given that domestic regulatory decisions produce effects beyond the boundaries of the Member State in which they are taken, they should consider the interests of non-nationals as much as those of nationals. Some authors have called this 'deliberative supranationalism',[64] others the 'argument from transnational effects';[65] I shall refer to it as the 'representation of Europeans' or, in short, 'European representation' as its crux lies in the widening of who ought to be represented. Not just the citizens of the Member State but all Europeans become our point of reference.

As non-nationals lack the power to vote and will often be unable to voice their concerns in the political processes of other Member States in alternative ways, they are prone to be disadvantaged. It is the Court of Justice's role to step in when their interests are under-represented. Different tools can help with detecting such representational problems. One of them is what, in American terminology, would be called 'suspect classifications'. If a Member State law differentiates between nationals and non-nationals when imposing a burden or granting benefits, there is a risk that the concerns of the former have not been treated as seriously as those of the latter. Another proxy is the difference between interests that benefit nationals only (eg promoting local consumer habits or imposing geographical limits on production) and those common to all Europeans (eg protecting the environment or ensuring road safety).[66] Where cross-national interests are pursued, one can presume that non-nationals have been 'virtually' represented through the nationals of the Member State. Where purely national interests are embraced, there is a risk that out-of-state concerns have been disregarded.

The idea of European representation takes free movement law beyond traditional, narrower anti-protectionist approaches, while also allowing us to define a constitutional mandate for the ECJ which is both limited and reflective of its institutional strengths. The Court of Justice's task is not to assume universal authority over what is efficient and inefficient, reasonable and unreasonable by controlling all Member State restrictions on economic activity, or to exercise 'economic due process'. The Court is meant to intervene only—that is, to exercise strict

[64] Christian Joerges and Jürgen Neyer, 'From Intergovernmental Bargaining to Deliberative Political Processes: The Constitutionalisation of Comitology' (1997) 3 European Law Journal, 273, 294–95: 'A supranational constitutional charter ... does not need to represent a new "state". Nor does supranationalism require that democracies concede a right to vote to non-nationals. What it does require is that the interests and concerns of non-nationals should be considered even within the national polity. In this sense, supranationalism does convey political rights and not just economic freedoms to Community citizens.'

[65] Alexander Somek, 'The Argument from Transnational Effects I: Representing Outsiders Through Freedom of Movement' (2010) 16 European Law Journal 315; De Witte, 'Sex, Drugs & EU Law' (n 48).

[66] Maduro, *We the Court* (n 30), 173–74. For criticisms of this distinction, see Donald H Regan, 'Judicial Review of Member-State Regulation of Trade within a Federal or Quasi-Federal System: Protectionism and Proportionality, *Da Capo*' (2001) 99 Michigan Law Review 1853 (who claims that there will be an adequate representation of all non-national interests where there is an adequate representation of all national interests) and Robert Schütze, 'Judicial Majoritarianism Revisited: "We, the Other Court"?' (2018) 43 European Law Review 269, 276 (who highlights practical difficulties in distinguishing between national and cross-national interests).

scrutiny[67]—when European interests are not adequately considered in national decision-making. This is in line with the primacy of democratic governance and the respect for national regulatory autonomy. Likewise, it permits the ECJ to make good use of its structural advantages. The Court is detached from the game of national politics, which makes it less likely to suffer from the same biases that created the disregard for out-of-state concerns in the first place, and is, as a European institution, more sensitive to the Europe-wide implications of local decisions.

The intellectual pedigree of this model lies in John Hart Ely's *Democracy and Distrust*.[68] Instead of trying to protect substantive values, courts should, Ely argued, clear the 'channels of political change' and ensure that decisions take into consideration the interests of all groups of society. The reliance on a process-oriented theory in the European setting—recently, it appears to have gained traction in other areas of international economic law as well[69]—may strike some as odd. Ely's main concern was that the principle of 'one person, one vote' was not enough to ensure that domestic racial and social minorities had a genuine say in the political process as their interests could simply be disregarded by the majority.[70] In the EU, this principle does not even exist to begin with. The most basic form of procedural legitimacy, casting a vote, is not open to foreigners, even if they are likely to be affected by national legislation.[71] As a consequence, representation does not act as a corrective device for participation problems here, as it does, to a large extent, in the US setting, but as a substitute for the otherwise complete lack of possibilities to influence decision-making.

This is important for two reasons. For one, it shows that it would be misleading to think about European representation in terms of the dichotomy between process and substantive values, a distinction so fiercely debated in the American literature (yet, eventually shown to be somewhat elusive[72]). European representation

[67] The original motivation behind projects like *We the Court* was to define jurisdictional boundaries, that is, determine when the ECJ should apply the free movement rules at all. Yet, as explained in Chapter 1, the jurisprudence on the four freedoms has developed in a different direction: towards a broad scope of rights and, consequently, a focus on justification and proportionality. The ideas articulated by scholars like Maduro can, however, be used in the current setting for the question of intensity of review given that what is at stake is ultimately similar: the question as to who decides. This is not to say that narrowing down the scope of free movement law would no longer be a sensible idea, see Chapter 5 II and IV.

[68] Ely (n 24).

[69] Benedikt Pirker, 'Democracy and Distrust in International Law' in Lukasz Gruszczynski and Wouter Werner (eds), *Deference in International Courts and Tribunals: Standard of Review and Margin of Appreciation* (Oxford University Press 2014); Regan (n 66).

[70] See, perhaps most clearly, Ely (n 24) 135: 'the duty of representation requires more than a voice and a vote. No matter how open the [political] process, those with most of the votes are in a position to vote themselves advantages at the expense of the others, or otherwise to refuse to take their interests into account. "One person, one vote", under these circumstances, makes a travesty of the equality principle.' Ely does, however, recognize that persons lacking the right to vote will face similar difficulties in making their concerns heard, see 83 (for out-of-staters) and 161 (for non-US citizens).

[71] Art 20(2)(b) TFEU, which gives EU citizens the right to vote in local elections, does not change this as the vast majority of regulatory measures are adopted at the national or, in Member States with a federal structure, state level.

[72] See Tribe (n 62).

is more than a purely process-oriented argument. It is best understood as an attempt to use process-related assumptions to achieve a substantive value. This value is traditionally said to lie in efficiency;[73] it also, however, constitutes a commitment to equality.[74] Second, and relatedly, it relativizes democratic criticisms which frequently centre around the point that virtual representation (via the ECJ) is not as 'good' as real representation (as archetypically embodied in national parliaments).[75] The idea of representation reinforcement through courts is certainly no substitute for ordinary democratic processes. Yet, for non-nationals, the latter route is, quite simply, not an option. The choice here is not between virtual and real representation—it is between virtual and no representation.

For the ECJ, some 'active' duties follow from this. When the interests of non-nationals risk being under-represented in national decision-making, the Court should step in and engage in substantive judicial review. This does not mean that the domestic legislation will automatically be incompatible with free movement law. Even open forms of discrimination may be found legal if they are justified all things considered. The important point is that we have, in the form of the ECJ, a European institution which reassesses the reasonableness of the given regulation. *Josemans* is a good recent example.[76] The city of Maastricht restricted access to coffee shops, which sell marijuana, solely to residents of the municipality. The intention behind the measure was to fight the growing drug tourism from neighbouring countries and the public nuisance that came with it. The Court of Justice, focusing on the effects of the measure for the sale of beverages and food,[77] recognized that the residence requirement operated 'mainly to the detriment of nationals of other Member States'.[78] It therefore chose to give the measure a close look and engaged in full proportionality review. Examining the roots and extent of drug tourism, the general principles of the Netherlands' policy on soft drugs, and the effectiveness of alternative regulatory attempts, it concluded that the restriction was justified.[79] Excluding non-residents was deemed acceptable because the latter were the prime cause of the problem. At the same time, it was crucial that the Court critically examined whether the measure was justified as it posed the risk of unduly disadvantaging non-nationals.[80]

[73] Maduro, *We the Court* (n 30) 152–53.

[74] See Croon-Gestefeld (n 61) 72.

[75] This argument is explored in greatest detail in Alexander Somek's 'The Argument from Transnational Effects It' (n 65) and 'The Argument from Transnational Effects II: Establishing Transnational Democracy' (2010) 16 European Law Journal 375. See also Schütze (n 66), 276.

[76] Case C-137/09 *Josemans* [2010] ECLI:EU:C:2010:774.

[77] The Court ruled that coffee shop owners could not rely on the free movement provisions to challenge the general prohibition of selling marijuana in the Netherlands, given that drugs are illegal in all Member States (even if soft drugs are tolerated in some of them); ibid, para 42.

[78] *Josemans* (n 76), para 59.

[79] ibid, paras 60–84.

[80] It is an entirely different question whether the ECJ (and the municipality of Maastricht) got it right in substance, with claims having surfaced that the city's policy has, in fact, been counter-productive in reducing public nuisance by incentivizing street sales of drugs.

However, besides these active virtues, European representation has an equally important passive dimension. The flipside of asking the ECJ to be attentive to situations in which foreigners are inadequately represented is demanding that it should let go of Member State action which poses no or little risk for them. This notably applies to national measures that show no signs of disregard for out-of-state interests, especially if they restrict economic freedom only minimally. Take a case like *Schmidberger*. The blocking of one highway for the sake of an environmental protest, without discriminatory intent or effects and for a short period only, is something the Court of Justice should not have to deal with in great detail.[81] No disregard for out-of-state interests was visible, which is why the question as to how to strike a balance between free movement and free speech could be safely handed over to the national authorities.[82] The same goes for decisions such as *Mickelsson and Roos* and *Commission v Italy (Trailers)*. The rules that were challenged in these cases, even if seriously restricting the sale of motorboats and trailers, in no way placed non-national concerns below national ones.

That the ECJ does not exercise substantive review in these scenarios is a question of legitimacy. There is no reason to believe that it is better equipped to make all the socio-economic judgments that underlie national regulatory measures. Yet, more than ever, greater restraint is also indispensable for securing the Court's own functioning. As was explained in Chapter 2, due to the significant growth of its caseload and review responsibilities, the Court of Justice is approaching, or perhaps has already reached, full capacity. It is, therefore, forced to limit its activity more effectively by focusing on the most serious problems occurring in the internal market. Setting out detailed judge-made rules on topics ranging from consumer protection, to intellectual property, to food production as in the days of *Dassonville* and *Cassis* is, against this background, no longer a viable option. It is also no longer necessary: in the EU political process, the Court of Justice has a partner it can rely on when it comes to internal market governance.

2. Of Nationals

a) *The Case for Thinking Nationally*

The representation of non-nationals should guide free movement adjudication and influence the decision as to how intensely Member State acts are reviewed. Yet, representation so understood is only one building block of a normatively attractive vision for the role of the Court of Justice and EU free movement law. It needs complementing with a second element: the representation of nationals. Let me explain.

[81] Case C-112/00 *Schmidberger* [2003] ECLI:EU:C:2003:333, paras 81 et seq.

[82] Compare this with the factually similar *Spanish Strawberries* case, where French farmers purposefully targeted foreign products, a scenario which rightly triggered strict scrutiny; Case C-265/95 *Commission v France (Spanish Strawberries)* [1997] ECLI:EU:C:1997:595.

I want to begin with a descriptive observation. The idea of representing all Europeans fails to account for some of the best-known margin of appreciation cases. Take, by means of illustration, *Sayn-Wittgenstein*.[83] An Austrian luxury real estate agent with business in Germany was adopted by a local *Fürst* and, in accordance with German law, changed her name to 'Princess von Sayn-Wittgenstein'. After initially recording the applicant's new name in the register of civil status, the Austrian authorities realized their mistake and removed the designation 'Princess von'. Austria had, upon becoming a republic in the aftermath of World War I, abolished the institution of nobility and prohibited the carrying of nobility titles.[84] The ECJ acknowledged that the discrepancy between the German and Austrian surnames was likely to inconvenience the applicant and that the prohibition, therefore, constituted a restriction on her freedom of movement.[85] However, when reviewing the proportionality of the rule, which had constitutional status domestically, the Court stressed that:

> [I]t must be accepted that, in the context of Austrian constitutional history, the Law on the abolition of the nobility, as an element of national identity, may be taken into consideration when a balance is struck between legitimate interests and the right of free movement of persons recognised under European Union law.[86]

This, importantly, meant that it was not required for the law to:

> correspond to a conception shared by all Member States as regards the precise way in which the fundamental right or legitimate interest in question is to be protected.[87]

The Court of Justice granted Austria a margin of appreciation and upheld the prohibition. Yet, if we think through the lens of European representation, both the deferential approach and the reasoning behind it are puzzling. The beliefs of Austrians most certainly did not align here with those of the Brits, Belgians, or Spanish, who embrace monarchy and nobility. The prohibition of nobility seems to be a distinctly (albeit not uniquely) Austrian decision, a collective national judgment on the meaning of equality. In its decision, the Court of Justice did not retreat from full proportionality review because Austria had demonstrated an adequate representation of all Europeans. (Nor did it do so simply because the applicant was Austrian

[83] *Sayn-Wittgenstein* (n 44). Note that the case turns on the free movement of EU citizens (Art 21(1) TFEU) but can, given the structural similarities of the ECJ's case law in this area with that on the four freedoms, serve as an illustration.

[84] Germany, too, had abolished nobility in 1919 but had taken a more permissive approach in relation to designations of nobility, which can be carried as part of a person's surname.

[85] *Sayn-Wittgenstein* (n 44), paras 66–67.

[86] ibid, para 83.

[87] ibid, para 91.

and no out-of-state interests were at stake.[88]) Quite the opposite: it stepped back because what was at stake was a *national* issue, decided on the basis of *national* beliefs, which formed part of a *national* identity.

We have come across many similar cases in the course of this book. In *Van Duyn*, the Court was confronted with the particularly critical position of the British government on religious sects. *Henn and Darby* turned on the United Kingdom's comparatively restrictive pornography laws. *Omega* dealt with the peculiar understanding and constitutional status of human dignity in Germany. All these disputes were defined by national particularities; not pan-European, but markedly local views on public policy and morality. Yet, in all of them, the Court granted the Member States a margin of appreciation although—sometimes because—their choice differed from the rest of the EU. If protecting non-national interests were the exclusive focus of free movement law, none of these cases should have been decided the way they were.[89] Their point is not commonality, it is diversity. They are based on the idea that values may 'vary from one country to another' and that regulatory and ideological choices need not correspond to a 'conception shared by all Member States'.

These descriptive inaccuracies point us to a normative problem. It may not be enough to ask whether non-national concerns are under-represented in domestic decisions. We have to address another question first: when should non-national concerns be represented at all? 'Always' is the answer advocates of European representation have given. In their view, every time non-nationals are put at a disadvantage, the Court of Justice should step in and double-check the substance of the Member State measure (even if it may eventually be justified). There is no scenario in which excluding the concerns of non-nationals from consideration, or lowering the weight which they are given in the decision-making process, would be desirable. Remember: 'What we should not permit is that [Member States] ignore out-of-State interests'. This is an account based on unity. We think in a pan-European way all the time.

Yet, the European project has changed, or perhaps it has just been forced to articulate itself more clearly. We do not want all national decision-making to be constrained by EU law. There must be sufficient room for national and local self-determination. This, for one thing, requires that Member States have meaningful

[88] The ECJ emphasizes that it is the exercise of free movement and the 'importation' of the German naming practice that gives rise to the inconvenience for the applicant. It is instructive to compare the Court's approach here with the factually similar Case C-148/02 *Garcia Avello* [2003] ECLI:EU:C:2003:539. A Belgian-Spanish couple residing in Belgium wanted to give their children, who had dual nationality but had never lived outside Belgium, a surname in accordance with Spanish law (consisting of two family names, paternal and maternal). Belgian law made this impossible, leading to a situation akin to *Sayn-Wittgenstein*, where the applicants had diverging surnames in the two countries. Yet, in *Garcia Avello*, the Court did not grant Belgium a margin of appreciation and exercised strict proportionality review instead, ultimately quashing the legislation.

[89] This is not to say that the relevant national laws would have been struck down but that they should have been, if European representation mattered, subjected to strict scrutiny.

decision-making powers. They should be able, as is often poetically said, to determine their own faith. Likewise, however, it affects how this self-determination is to take place. Member States must have the possibility to act based on the concerns of their nationals and prioritize the latter's views and preferences.

This is perhaps easiest explained with the aid of national identity. It was mentioned that, since Maastricht, the European Treaties grant constitutional protection to the identity of the Member States.[90] Forming and maintaining a national identity has to do with decision-making authority. Member States must be able to decide on the fundamental features of their political and constitutional structure. At the same time, however, it requires that they can restrict their focus on their own citizens. There is no way to express a distinctly national identity if a polity is permanently forced to consider the interests and concerns of other Europeans; it would become a European identity, just articulated by the French, Germans, or Poles. To do so, Member States must be granted the right to think nationally. This is what I mean by 'representation of nationals': the focus on national concerns only.

We see the similarity between the ideas of European and national representation. The key, to use a distinction sometimes made in the literature, is not the difference between 'communitarian' (national) and 'individualistic' (European).[91] Both European and national representation are communitarian in the sense that they aim at considering the concerns all members of the polity. They vary in size. In the former case, the reference point is the big polity (ie all Europeans); in the latter, the small polity (ie all nationals or locals). The EU constitutional order protects both perspectives.

What does this mean for the standard of review in free movement cases? Where we seek to protect the representation of national interests, the ECJ should not subject Member State action to substantive proportionality review and opt for more deferential forms of scrutiny. This is not, as is sometimes claimed, because the logic of proportionality analysis is 'not pluralist', that is, disregards by design national

[90] Note that this is something quite extraordinary. As Cloots points out, 'no other treaty or constitution exists that contains a provision commanding the central polity to respect the national identity of its constituent entities', see *National Identity in EU Law* (Oxford University Press 2015) 85. For the problematic status of arguments from state identity in US constitutional law, see Heather K Gerken, 'Foreword: Federalism All the Way Down' (2010) 124 Harvard Law Review 6, 16; Vicki C Jackson, 'Federalism and the Uses and Limits of Law: *Printz* and Principle?' (1998) 111 Harvard Law Review 2180, 2220; Ernest A Young, 'The Volk of New Jersey? State Identity, Distinctiveness, and Political Culture in the American Federal System' Duke Law School Public Law & Legal Theory Series No 2015-11.

[91] Somek speaks of the 'individualistic fallacy' of EU free movement law, something which he contrasts with the communitarian nature of national decision-making, see 'The Argument from Transnational Effects II' (n 75) 386 et seq; similarly also de Witte, 'Sex, Drugs & EU Law' (n 48) 1552. Although it is certainly true that the EU does not have mechanisms comparable to domestic deliberative processes, the idea of 'European representation', or what Somek refers to as the 'argument from transnational effects', is communitarian at its basis: it is premised on the existence of a bond between all Europeans.

values and conceptions of policy objectives.[92] Proportionality, even in the form of strict proportionality review, does allow the Court to take into consideration national preferences, beliefs, and decisions. It can, to go back to the example of *Sayn-Wittgenstein*, be applied in a way that acknowledges the Austrian conception of equality ('the institution of nobility violates equality'), checks how this conception can be achieved, and examines whether the solution chosen is an excessive intrusion into the life of citizens. The crux is that there is no reason to believe that entrusting the ECJ with this task is a good idea. This is, as we shall see in greater detail below, partly due to questions of information. As a European institution, the Court is distant from the domestic setting; national authorities are likely to have a better understanding of the cultural, social, and political aspects underlying the issue. Equally important, however, are the lessons from disagreement. The Court of Justice has a different perspective, a distinctly European one, which is not embedded in the local value matrix. This perspective will come to the fore during proportionality analysis. Although there is no reason to believe that the European judges will always do a bad job at reflecting the concerns of the national polity, they are likely to do a worse job than national authorities. What was identified as a comparative advantage when it comes to the representation of non-nationals—the European mindset—amounts to an important deficit when it comes to the representation of nationals.

If the ECJ is not an adequate decision-maker, then who is? Would national representation be enhanced by handing decision-making powers to any Member State institution, be it political or judicial? One should be wary of this tempting but simplistic way of thinking. Consider the Sunday trading saga. When the issue of domestic Sunday trading bans was first referred to the Luxembourg Court, it famously chose to defer the decision on the right balance between free movement and social policy to the national judiciary.[93] Many considered this initial approach, later corrected,[94] to be problematic. They lamented that it led to contradictory positions among the British judiciary, the result of which was a period of regulatory uncertainty in the UK—the ECJ should have settled the issue. The idea of national representation suggests that this strategy was problematic for a different reason. Although the Court's intuition about lacking the legitimacy to decide a matter of such high socio-economic importance was certainly correct,[95] the choice to defer this decision to the national judiciary was more dubious. Is a decision made by three judges in Cwmbran more reflective of the concerns of all Brits than one

[92] De Witte, 'Sex, Drugs & EU Law' (n 48) 1569. For a similar criticism, see Mulder (n 33) 85 (arguing that strict proportionality scrutiny is 'unable to take account of the potential systemic effects of certain policy choices in the Member States').

[93] *Torfaen Borough Council* (n 59).

[94] Case C-169/91 *Stoke-on-Trent* [1992] ECLI:EU:C:1992:519.

[95] A further justification for granting deference in the Sunday trading cases is that the legislation did not put the interest of nationals over those of non-nationals.

rendered by the ECJ? Is it more legitimate? To ensure a representative depiction of national concerns, the British political process would have certainly been the better choice.[96] Due to their accountability to, and institutionalized contact with, the domestic populace, legislatures are more likely to guarantee the representation of its views and interests.

b) The Place for Thinking Nationally

If the EU is constitutionally committed both to thinking European and to thinking nationally, the crucial question becomes when to give priority to the former and when to the latter. The parallel emergence of centralizing and decentralizing tendencies makes this increasingly difficult to answer. As wrong as it would be to shield every Member State act from the duty to consider European interests, as important it is that national concerns are given greater weight in some decisions.

The division of competences between the EU and the Member States can serve as one important reference point in this respect.[97] Different policy areas have been Europeanized to different extents. The TFEU distinguishes between three types of Union competences: exclusive, shared, and supporting or supplementary.[98] Not explicitly mentioned, but equally important, are the exclusive competences of the Member States, which follow *ex contrario* from the principle of conferral. Although the degree to which a domain falls within the scope of the EU's legislative competences has no implications for whether free movement rights apply—the negative reach of free movement law is wider than its positive reach[99]—it gives an indication of the willingness to embrace the European perspective. The strong Europeanization of a field signals that thinking in purely domestic terms is no longer acceptable, while its remaining within the remit of the Member States suggests a greater legitimacy for thinking nationally. In this light, it appears warranted to subject cases in areas falling into the exclusive competence of the Member States (eg public order and policy) or in which the EU merely has a supporting function (eg health and culture) to more deferential scrutiny than those pertaining to

96 See Lord Hoffmann in 'The Influence of the European Principle of Proportionality upon UK Law' in Eveylin Ellis (ed), *Proportionality in the Laws of Europe* (Hart 1999) 113: 'What I have said so far should explain the dismay and incredulity shown by the English courts when asked by the ECJ in *Torfaen Borough Council v. B & Q plc* to apply the principle of proportionality in the Sunday trading cases. If ever there was a case in which it should have been obvious to the ECJ that the question was one for decision by the democratically elected organs of state, this was it ... It was in my view quite wrong to try to allocate that decisionmaking power to the judiciary of the Member State rather than its legislature. And this was in effect what the Court of Justice recognised in its subsequent decision in *Stoke on Trent City Council v. B & Q plc*.'

97 Floris de Witte, 'The Constitutional Quality of the Free Movement Provisions: Looking for Context in the Case Law on Article 56 TFEU' (2017) 42 European Law Review 313.

98 Arts 3 to 6 TFEU. Prior to Lisbon, these categories were not explicitly set out in the European Treaties, even if they were widely recognized in EU legal scholarship and, to an important extent, in the ECJ's jurisprudence.

99 Loïc Azoulai, 'The "Retained Powers" Formula in the Case Law of the European Court of Justice: EU Law as Total Law?' (2011) 4 European Journal of Legal Studies 192.

domains in which a shared competence exists (eg consumer protection, environment, and intellectual property).

Another relevant consideration is the salience of the regulatory question at stake. *Sub silencio*, a distinction has emerged in EU law literature between what can be called 'ordinary' and 'fundamental' matters. Few scholars dispute the need for European representation with regard to ordinary economic regulation, at least not anymore.[100] When Member States introduce technical standards for products, define professional qualifications, or set out requirements for the provision of services, we expect them to consider out-of-state interests. A growing number of voices, however, insist on giving national authorities a greater degree of deference when it comes to decisions on certain salient policy questions[101] or, to borrow a term from Jeremy Waldron, 'watershed' issues, that is, major political choices with significant ramifications for the polity.[102]

What justifies deferring to the Member States on such watershed issues? One way of seeing this is as a simple trade-off. Given that we cannot always have European and national representation, preference should be given to the former when EU interests are most seriously affected and to the latter when issues arise that are central to the national level. The stronger argument, however, lies elsewhere. It comes from recognizing that Member States—and the forum for autonomy and self-determination which they provide[103]—are an essential component of the EU, and that deciding on watershed issues is an indispensable mark of a state. It is, of course, difficult to draw a bright line as to which issues count as sufficiently important in this sense. Formal indicators, such as the status of a norm within the legal hierarchy (constitutional or statutory), but also informal indicators, such as how deeply a polity feels about a given question, may play a role. What is clear, however, is that this goes beyond, as the wording of Article 4(2) TEU suggests, questions concerning the political structure and territorial organization of a Member State. It also goes beyond, as has been proposed in the literature on the supremacy of EU law, 'clear and precise' domestic constitutional norms.[104] Not everything constitutional is a watershed issue[105] but, equally importantly, not all watershed issues are constitutional. A society is essentially defined or, more precisely, defines itself by its position on questions such as euthanasia, gambling, sex work, and surrogacy, none of which typically have constitutional rank. To take away a State's decision-making

[100] But see Somek (nn 65 and 75).

[101] De Witte, 'Sex, Drugs & EU Law' (n 48); Tor-Inge Harbo, 'Introducing Procedural Proportionality Review in European Law' (2017) 30 Leiden Journal of International Law 25; Davies, 'The Price of Letting Courts Value Solidarity' (n 34).

[102] Waldron, 'The Core of the Case Against Judicial Review' (n 10) 1367.

[103] Cloots (n 90) 93; De Witte, 'Sex, Drugs & EU Law' (n 48) 1551.

[104] Mattias Kumm, 'The Jurisprudence of Constitutional Conflict: Constitutional Supremacy in Europe before and after the Constitutional Treaty' (2005) 11 European Law Journal 262, 296 et seq.

[105] See, in relation to Art 4(2) TEU, Armin von Bogdandy and Stephan Schill, 'Overcoming Absolute Privacy: The Respect for National Identity under the Lisbon Treaty' (2011) 48 Common Market Law Review 1417, 1430.

powers on these questions means not just to rob it off its 'eros',[106] it means to rob it off its *raison d'être*.[107]

Although it can, at times, be difficult to determine which issues pass this threshold, I want to avoid two misunderstandings. The first concerns fundamental rights. It has become common to think of cases involving fundamental rights as salient and sensitive by default.[108] This argument has its roots in the rulings of several national constitutional courts which have insisted that EU law respect certain basic features of Member State constitutions, to which the protection of fundamental rights is typically considered to belong.[109] It is, to some extent, also echoed in the ECJ's case law, as decisions like *Schmidberger* illustrate. Yet, there is nothing to justify the suggestion that all cases touching on fundamental rights count as watershed issues in the above sense. In fact, such a claim is even potentially dangerous as it can lead to removing a wide class of Member State action from judicial control. As Mattias Kumm highlighted, fundamental rights have long ceased to be about 'things fundamental' only; they are increasingly also about 'things mundane'.[110] The Court of Justice's jurisprudence illustrates this all too well. Whereas disputes on human dignity[111] and language policies[112] may be qualified as sensitive and important, decisions about rules on the advertising of insolvency stock[113] or the disclosure of accounting documents[114] surely cannot. The mere fact that a dispute raises fundamental rights problems does not automatically make it a watershed issue. This may, in fact, even be a fairly poor proxy.

The second question concerns a more intricate matter: should *all* morally, culturally, and politically salient judgments follow the logic of national representation and, thus, be subjected to deferential treatment? Floris de Witte has offered

[106] Joseph HH Weiler, *The Constitution of Europe* (Cambridge University Press 1999) 324.

[107] The much-criticized *Lisbon* judgment of the German Federal Constitutional Court (FCC), which insists on 'sufficient space' for the Member States for 'the political formation of the economic, cultural and social living conditions', is therefore certainly right in this sense, at least regarding the general direction of the argument, see BVerfGE 123, 267. The FCC considers this space to require the freedom to decide on issues such as citizenship, the use of force (military and civil), deprivation of liberty under criminal law, language, family and education, freedom of speech, press, and association, as well as freedom of religion and thought.

[108] Weiler, *The Constitution of Europe* (n 106) 102; Paul Craig, *EU Administrative Law* (3rd edn, Oxford University Press 2018) 684; Gerards (n 49) 88; Francisco Javier Mena Parras, 'Libertés de circulation et conceptions particulières de droits fondamentaux: quelle conciliation à travers la marge nationale d'appréciation et le respect de l'identité constitutionnelle?' in Nicolas Levrat and Samantha Besson (eds), *(Dés)ordres juridiques européens / European Legal (Dis)orders* (LGDJ. 2012) 154.

[109] See Case 183/1973 *Frontini* (Italian Constitutional Court); BVerfGE 37, 271 *Solange I* (German Federal Constitutional Court); Declaration 1/2004 (Spanish Constitutional Court); Pl ÚS 29/09 *Lisbon Treaty II* (Czech Constitutional Court); Case K 32/09 *Lisbon Judgment* (Polish Constitutional Tribunal).

[110] Mattias Kumm, '*Internationale Handelsgesellschaft, Nold* and the New Human Rights Paradigm' in Miguel Poiares Maduro and Loïc Azoulai (eds), *The Past and Future of EU Law* (Hart 2010).

[111] *Omega Spielhallen* (n 41).

[112] *Las* (n 42).

[113] Case C-71/02 *Karner* [2004] ECLI:EU:C:2004:181.

[114] Case C-418/11 *Texdata Software* [2013] ECLI:EU:C:2013:588.

a powerful argument in this direction. He advocates against the creation of a 'monolithic European morality' as the EU, unlike its Member States, does not have the institutional mechanisms and political space that would allow its citizens to express themselves on moral and ethical questions.[115] European control over domestic choices in this area should, therefore, be limited to a coherence check. The constitutional developments that have taken place make such a blanket exclusion hard to justify. Although the EU is incapable of mimicking the deliberative processes at the national level, it can and does make value judgments itself. Sometimes this happens in judicial decisions, more frequently however in legislative acts.[116] Through its regulations and directives, the EU tells us that killing seals is wrong, smoking is bad, protecting the environment is important, and so on. In this way, it creates a limited yet palpable European morality. This should not come as a surprise—we have made it part of its mission statement. The Union is meant to protect human dignity, social welfare, tolerance, and the many other values set out in the Treaties. The consequence is as simple as it is brutal: Member States have lost their absolute monopoly on value judgments. As the EU becomes a 'community of values', the idea of shielding every moral and ethical decision made at the national level from European scrutiny becomes untenable; 'the respect for "national" constitutional identities will find its boundaries in the "European" constitutional identity', however defined.[117] This means that for some morally, culturally, or politically salient matters, we will not permit Member States to deviate from our common European expectations, especially the most important ones. The past years have delivered some examples in relation to ethnic discrimination (the deportation of Roma from France), the rule of law (the constitutional crises in Hungary and Poland), and equality (recognition of same-sex marriages).[118] In the future, this list is likely to expand.

[115] De Witte, 'Sex, Drugs & EU Law' (n 48) 1561.

[116] See Bruno de Witte, 'A Competence to Protect: The Pursuit of Non-Market Aims through Internal Market Regulation' in Philip Syrpis (ed), *The Judiciary, the Legislature and the EU Internal Market* (Cambridge University Press 2012).

[117] Francois-Xavier Millet, 'The Respect for National Constitutional Identity in the European Legal Space: An Approach to Federalism as Constitutionalism' in Loic Azoulai (ed), *The Question of Competence in the European Union* (Oxford University Press 2014) 264. For the risks attached with giving Member States *carte blanche* in relation to matters they claim to belong to their national identity, see Federico Fabbrini and András Sajó, 'The Dangers of Constitutional Identity' (2019) 25 European Law Journal 1.

[118] While the deportation of the Roma only led to protests of the EU Commission, the reforms in Hungary and Poland triggered formal infringement actions and, in the latter case, the first Art 7 TEU procedure: see Case C-286/12 *Commission v Hungary (Judicial Reforms)* [2012] ECLI:EU:C:2012:687; C-619/18 *Commission v Poland (Supreme Court Reforms)* [2019] ECLI:EU:C:2019:615; Case C-192/18 *Commission v Poland (Retirement Age of Judges and Prosecutors)* [2019] ECLI:EU:C:2019:924. The ruling in *Coman* (n 44) on the free movement of EU citizens demonstrates that in situations in which national and European moralities clash compromise solutions can be possible: EU law will accept the domestic choice to not legalize same-sex marriage while insisting on the recognition of same-sex marriages concluded in other Member States.

3. Of Others

The EU's development towards becoming a 'community of values' has a further implication for free movement law (and European law more in general): it puts the concerns of groups beyond the national/non-national divide on the agenda. The commitment to promoting values such as pluralism, tolerance, and social welfare makes it necessary to consider the fate of ethnic minorities, religious diasporas, and those living in poverty. This renders thinking exclusively, or even predominantly, in terms of nationality inadequate. Focusing on non-nationals as the sole 'suspect class' no longer reflects the current state and ambition of EU law.[119]

For the Court of Justice, this means that protecting European representation is not enough anymore; in fact, it can even be harmful at times. Some social groups will be just as under-represented across Europe as they are in individual Member States. Taking all Europeans, or what I had called the 'big polity', as the reference point will not only fail to help them, it can even magnify existing problems with making their concerns heard. Think about Muslims, the Roma, or the LGBT community, who constitute minorities with limited political influence in every Member State; or women, who, despite being the numerical majority, continue to be under-represented in political processes across the continent. In order to promote the manifold values adopted by the EU, non-nationals will have to cease to be our sole 'suspect class'.[120] The normative matrix of the Court of Justice will have to become more complex.

Much of the work in this area will happen outside the courtroom, and much of the adjudicative work will take place outside free movement law. The EU has, especially since being given an express competence on anti-discrimination in the Treaty of Amsterdam (Article 19 TFEU), adopted a number of legislative measures prohibiting discrimination on grounds such as gender, race, religion, disability, and age.[121] Litigants have discovered these as a potential route for fighting

[119] Another way of putting this is to recognize that the classes of 'nationals' and 'non-nationals', which we often think of as homogeneous, are in fact internally diverse. The interests of German business owners will often diverge from those of German strawberry pickers, the concerns of Polish banks will not necessarily align with those of Polish high-school teachers; similarly, see Mark Dawson and Floris de Witte, 'From Balance to Conflict: A New Constitution for the EU' (2016) 22 European Law Journal, 204, 210 and 218.

[120] For a similar argument in the US context, see Ackerman (n 62).

[121] Directive 2000/43 implementing the principle of equal treatment between persons irrespective of racial or ethnic origin [2000] OJ L180/22; Directive 2000/78 establishing a general framework for equal treatment in employment and occupation; Directive 2004/113 implementing the principle of equal treatment between men and women in the access to and supply of goods and services [2004] OJ L373/37; Directive 2006/54 on the implementation of the principle of equal opportunities and equal treatment of men and women in matters of employment and occupation [2006] OJ L204/23. In the field of gender equality, the EU has been active since the 1970s: see notably Directive 75/117 on the approximation of the laws of the Member States relating to the application of the principle of equal pay for men and women [1975] OJ L45/19 and Directive 76/207 on the implementation of the principle of equal treatment for men and women as regards access to employment, vocational training and promotion, and working conditions [1976] OJ L39/40.

discriminatory practices and effecting broader change, even if cases are clustered in certain areas.[122]

But free movement jurisprudence may equally contribute to, and profit from, a broadening of the EU's normative perspective. Scholars like Charlotte O'Brien have demonstrated that judgments on the four freedoms often have significant ramifications for wealth, class, and gender.[123] They can disparately affect the most vulnerable types of migrants, namely those working in low-paid jobs, lacking sufficient financial resources, or not displaying sufficient 'reproductive restraint'. Paying greater attention to the concerns of these social groups through adjusting standards of review will better align free movement law with the wider constitutional developments of the EU.[124]

B. Expertise

Representation should, in the different ways outlined above, be a factor that guides the way in which Court of Justice exercises judicial review—yet, it is not everything. Decisions relating to free movement law and the internal market are not just meant to protect the concerns of the various affected social groups. They are equally supposed to be well informed, marked by an understanding of the relevant factual context, and made by institutions which are capable of handling the problem. Call this the concern for expertise.

Expertise permeates many of the constitutional developments and debates that were discussed earlier. Virtually all scholars who have grappled with the issue of judicial review factor in what courts are good at, what they know about, and what other institutional actors are better equipped to deal with.[125] EU constitutional

[122] See n 153 to n 156.

[123] Charlotte O'Brien, 'Civis Capitalist Sum: Class as the New Guiding Principle of EU Free Movement Rights' (2016) 53 Common Market Law Review 937. See also Samantha Currie, 'Pregnancy-Related Employment Breaks: The Gender Dynamics of Free Movement Law and Curtailed Citizenship: *Jessy Saint Prix*' (2016) 53 Common Market Law Review 543; similarly, in the context of citizenship, Michael Dougan, 'The Constitutional Dimension to the Case Law on Union Citizenship' (2006) 31 European Law Review 613, 622.

[124] Note that this need not necessarily mean intensifying judicial scrutiny. In some situations, doing less can mean doing more. Scholars have, for instance, pointed out the dangers of exceedingly strict scrutiny of domestic social policies in light of the lack of equivalent EU mechanisms in this area: see Fritz W Scharpf, 'The European Social Model: Coping with the Challenges of Diversity' (2002) 40 Journal of Common Market Studies 645; Scharpf, 'Legitimacy in the Multilevel European Polity' (n 33); Mulder (n 33). A lower intensity of judicial scrutiny can, against this backdrop, be ultimately more beneficial for the groups affected.

[125] Although Komesar's work constitutes the most serious engagement with this issue, we find reflections on decision-making competence also in the writings of other constitutional theorists. Bickel thought it essential to search for a function for courts 'which is peculiarly suited to [their] capabilities', which he claimed was in principled reasoning, see Bickel (n 7) 24. Waldron addresses this issue, too, even if he comes to a different conclusion, arguing that legislators, not judges, are the better moral reasoners, see *Law and Disagreement* (n 10). Tushnet's argument against judicial review stands in the same tradition and rests on the proposition that legislatures are equally good as, if not better than judges at interpreting the Constitution, see *Taking Away the Constitution from the Courts* (Princeton University

law recognizes, through principles such as subsidiarity and proportionality, that the Union should not act where Member States are more competent and promise to better achieve an objective. Academic observers have advocated that the ECJ should show restraint where it lacks an understanding of a subject matter.[126] Even the Court itself has acknowledged that it will not decide certain matters which are factually complex[127] or on which it has insufficient information.[128] Against this background, it is important to consider questions of expertise when it comes to the intensity and locus of judicial scrutiny in free movement cases. Two types of expertise can become relevant: technical and local.

1. Technical

Technical expertise concerns information on and the capability to assess phenomena that require expert knowledge or special training. Do genetically modified crops pose a risk to human health? What are the macroeconomic consequences of cutting interests rates? How will global warming affect biodiversity? Expertise on these matters is 'universal', in the sense of not being primarily defined by a particular domestic context.

The problem of how to deal with questions of high technical or factual complexity is not specific to the ECJ. It affects courts around the world.[129] The lack of training and capacity puts the judiciary in a difficult position vis-à-vis the legislative and executive branches. Courts typically work with limited human resources on a diverse range of topics.[130] With every new proceeding, they have to acquire basic knowledge on the problems at stake. For this sort of information gathering the legislature has its committees, support staff, and consultants. The executive has specialized agencies with experience in different areas. Generalist courts like the ECJ have none of that.[131] Therefore, they are structurally disadvantaged

Press 1999). Even Ely, in many respects an outlier in American constitutional theory, does not manage without emphasizing that judges are good at reviewing 'process writ small' and 'writ large', see Ely (n 24) 102 (note, however, his slightly flippant remark that 'too much shouldn't be made of this').

[126] See, inter alia, Davies, 'The Price of Letting Courts Value Solidarity' (n 34); Ellen Vos, 'The European Court of Justice in the Face of Scientific Uncertainty and Complexity' in Mark Dawson, Bruno de Witte, and Elise Muir (eds), *Judicial Activism at the European Court of Justice* (Edward Elgar 2013); Eric Barbier de la Serre and Anne-Lise Sibony, 'Expert Evidence Before the EC Courts' (2008) 45 Common Market Law Review 941.

[127] Case 40/72 *Schroeder* [1973] ECLI:EU:C:1973:14; Case 29/77 *Roquette Frères* [1977] ECLI:EU:C:1977:164; Cases C-27/00 and 122/00 *Omega Air* [2002] ECLI:EU:C:2002:161.

[128] Case C-9/93 *IHT Internationale Heiztechnik* [1994] ECLI:EU:C:1994:261; *Gourmet International* (n 57); Case C-441/04 *A-Punkt Schmuckhandels* [2006] ECLI:EU:C:2006:141.

[129] Andrew Legg, *The Margin of Appreciation in International Human Rights Law* (Oxford University Press 2012) 148 et seq; Scott Brewer, 'Scientific Expert Testimony and Intellectual Due Process' (1998) 107 Yale Law Journal 1535; Joachim Schmidt-Salzer, *Der Beurteilungsspielraum der Verwaltungsbehörden: Zum Verhältnis zwischen Verwaltung und Verwaltungsgerichtsbarkeit* (Duncker & Humblot 1968).

[130] Komesar, *Law's Limits* (n 13) 35 et seq.

[131] The General Court has, as of 2019, six specialized chambers that deal exclusively with intellectual property matters.

when it comes to assessing technically difficult issues and have shown to handle them poorly.[132] When presented with empirical evidence, they frequently misunderstand its meaning. When facing factually complex issues, they risk making incorrect assessments. In the case of the Court of Justice, this problem is further magnified by the reluctance to gather expert evidence.[133]

Against this background, it appears warranted that the Court, as a rule, grants national authorities a degree of deference when it comes to decisions on technically challenging and factually complex issues. Note that, once again, it is crucial to distinguish between the different actors here. Whereas national legislatures and executives promise to bring advantages in terms of decision-making ability, the same does not hold true for national courts. As courts, they will struggle just as greatly with factually difficult assessments as the ECJ. Letting national judges evaluate what current medical and epidemiological research says about the transmission of HIV,[134] or determine which quantities of oil are necessary to run a state during a geopolitical crisis,[135] is unlikely to bring any improvement from a perspective of technical expertise. In this scenario, deference via the margin of appreciation doctrine is a more promising strategy.

This general proposition requires one clarification and two qualifications. The clarification first. In its margin of appreciation jurisprudence, the ECJ frequently states that the doctrine applies to entire regulatory areas, such as public policy, road safety, or national security. And, indeed, there are clear relative differences in terms of factual complexity between the domains in which free movement adjudication takes place. Public health regulation perhaps most regularly involves specialist knowledge regarding anatomy, epidemiology, pharmacology, and chemistry. Other areas, such as tax law or social security, tend to be less technically challenging. Yet, not every question falling into a technically complex field is automatically difficult and, as such, deserving of deference. Consider a case like *Ker-Optika*.[136] Hungary prohibited the online sale of contact lenses. When the legislation was challenged before the ECJ, one point of discussion was whether the measure could be justified on grounds of public health as it would prevent the wearing of ill-fitting contact lenses. The case fell into the domain of public health, which is why the Court signalled that national authorities, in principle, enjoyed a margin of appreciation.[137] In substance, however, it opted to exercise strict proportionality review,

[132] Vos (n 126); Niels Petersen, 'Avoiding the Common-Wisdom Fallacy: The Role of Social Sciences in Constitutional Adjudication' (2013) 11 International Journal of Constitutional Law 294, 307 et seq; David L Faigman, '"Normative Constitutional Fact-Finding": Exploring the Empirical Component of Constitutional Interpretation' (1991) 139 University of Pennsylvania Law Review 541; Rosemary J Erickson and Rita J Simon, *The Use of Social Science Data in Supreme Court Decisions* (University of Illinois Press 1998).

[133] Barbier de la Serre and Sibony (n 126).

[134] Case C-528/13 *Léger* [2015] ECLI:EU:C:2015:288.

[135] Case 72/83 *Campus Oil* [1984] ECLI:EU:C:1984:256.

[136] Case C-108/09 *Ker-Optika* [2010] ECLI:EU:C:2010:725.

[137] ibid, para 58.

a convincing decision. Whether inadequate contact lenses can cause eye problems may be a medical question, but one not overly difficult to grasp for non-experts. Exempting matters like these from full judicial review just because they touch on public health is unnecessary for reasons of expertise.

Let me come to the qualifications. First, it can at times be warranted for the ECJ to examine a problem even though it is factually complex. This is namely so where we find scientific or regulatory consensus on the subject matter at stake. Consensus means that a large number of actors with knowledge of and experience in a certain area reach the same conclusion. This overlap increases the likelihood of their judgment being correct for a simple reason: one, two, or three experts may err, but the probability will decrease (albeit not be entirely eliminated) if 20, 25, or 28 opinions converge.[138] In such situations, the Court of Justice can have greater confidence in making an accurate decision. In this light, it makes sense to grant domestic authorities a margin of appreciation only as long as scientific uncertainties exist.[139]

Second, it is important to keep in mind that technical expertise is only one part of the calculus. The ECJ cannot just decide on its review standard based on whether it is knowledgeable in a certain field or likely to get the empirics right. This is especially so where it is confronted with Member State acts that, although touching on factually complex issues, pose risks for representation, for instance by openly discriminating against non-nationals. The aims of having a high level of expertise and protecting European representation will collide in such a scenario. Granting a partial margin of appreciation can provide a trade-off: national authorities are left to make a regulatory decision but are given instructions as to how to make it, that is, which questions to consider, which evidence to gather, and which analyses to undertake. This approach ensures that factually difficult assessments are made by the national regulator, while the Court does not completely abdicate control over the decision-making. It also comes with positive effects for the quality of policy-making. By stipulating procedural requirements for the Member State authorities, the ECJ turns into an 'informational catalyst' and, thus, promotes good governance.[140]

One would be mistaken to think that all of this allows the European judges to dispense with improving their own technical expertise. The Court of Justice may limit its decision-making role in relation to factually complex matters, but it still needs a basic understanding of them. More and more scientific evidence, statistical analyses, and empirical data are invoked in proceedings before the ECJ.[141] Likewise, domestic and European policy-making is becoming increasingly evidence-based.

[138] A proposition also known as Condorcet's theorem.

[139] Case 174/82 *Sandoz* [1983] ECLI:EU:C:1983:213, para 16; Case C-192/01 *Commission v Denmark (Food Additives)* [2003] ECLI:EU:C:2003:492, para 42; Case C-387/99 *Commission v Germany (Vitamins)* [2004] ECLI:EU:C:2004:235, para 69.

[140] Vos (n 126).

[141] See Chapter 3 II A 7.

To make an informed decision in this new environment, the Court must understand the information it is presented with at least to a minimal extent, including how the data were gathered, what they mean, and where their limitations lie. The more pronounced the 'evidence-based turn' becomes, the more imperative it will be for the ECJ to acquire a working knowledge of social science methods.[142] At the same time, it is inevitable that the Court create more resources, the most important one being time. It takes a long time to process empirical research and even longer to determine its relevance for a particular legal problem. The current docket of the ECJ makes a regular consideration of such research impossible. Part of the reason why the US Supreme Court frequently engages with scientific studies lies in the fact that it has managed to limit its activity so effectively. The more the ECJ will want to decide on factually complex matters, the more vigorously it will have to reduce its workload. The trick may lie in doing less but in greater depth.

2. Local

If technical expertise is a general problem of all courts, the lack of local expertise, that is, the knowledge relating to a particular domestic setting, is something specifically connected with the supranational nature of the ECJ. How do consumers behave in a certain Member State? What is the national legislation on a given issue? Is a question politically or culturally sensitive domestically?

The Court of Justice is far away from the Member States, both geographically and in spirit. When it comes to understanding the factual, legal, and political aspects of domestic regulation, it therefore has a clear disadvantage compared with national authorities.[143] What may seem obvious and easy to a national judge and legislator, can at times be very hard for the ECJ. This can concern even basic information, such as what the law on a certain topic is or how the national supreme court interprets it. It only takes a poorly drafted reference, a less than fully prepared government representative, and a chamber of three at the Court in which no judge has knowledge of the relevant jurisdiction.

Procedural mechanisms such as the possibility for parties, Member States, and the Commission to submit observations[144] as well as the requirement for the referring judge to explain the factual and legal context of the dispute are supposed to fill this information gap.[145] Yet, they do not always succeed. This has to do, in parts, with the low quality of some preliminary references.[146] The Court of

[142] See Faigman (n 132) 851; Petersen (n 132) 318.

[143] Gerards (n 49), 85.

[144] Art 23 of the Statute of the Court of Justice.

[145] The ECJ can also request a clarification from the referring court (Art 101(1) Rules of Procedure), but this option is used only rarely.

[146] Gaps and inconsistencies in the Commission's submissions can also contribute to this. See the strongly worded Opinion of AG Mancini in Case 407/85 *3 Glocken* [1988] ECLI:EU:C:1988:197, 4249: 'It must be stated with regret that ... the Commission has been a poor *amicus curiae*. There are three suitable adjectives to describe its submissions: contradictory, inexact and incomplete.'

Justice has reacted to the problem by publishing recommendations in which it sets out what information national judges are expected to provide.[147] This includes a summary of the subject matter of the dispute, the applicable national law and case law, and a statement of the reasons which prompted the court to refer.[148] Not required, at least not explicitly, are observations on what were earlier called 'socio-economic facts', such as information about the policy aims pursued by the Member State, the effectiveness of the legislation at stake, and its socio-economic impact. The Court receives submissions on these questions only rarely, even though they are crucial for assessing the justification and proportionality of national measures.

Thus, deferring to Member State authorities is a wise strategy for the ECJ when the factual circumstances of a case are unclear, a field is marked by local particularities, or the information on the domestic setting is hard to gather. Although local expertise can be enhanced here through either deference route—both national legislatures and judiciaries have a greater knowledge of local matters—, it is decentralized judicial review that will often be a particularly attractive option for the ECJ.[149] Where Member State regulation must be judicially reviewed (due to the risks it poses for the internal market) but the Court has an inadequate understanding of the local context, national judges can act on its behalf. Such a delegation of review responsibilities has become, for the reasons explained in Chapter 2, an increasingly viable strategy with time. The fundamentals of free movement law have been laid down by the ECJ and, by and large, internalized at the national level. Moreover, domestic courts have proven to be trustworthy partners in protecting European interests, especially those choosing to participate in the preliminary reference procedure.

This 'outsourcing' of judicial review, it should be underlined, is not without costs. Free movement law risks not being applied uniformly across the Member States. The Court of Justice ceases to be the final arbiter of the internal market; the decision on the proportionality of a national regulation is out of its hands. The crucial point is that, overall, this still may be the normatively preferable solution. When the Court is uncertain about the functioning of a national press market, the scope of domestic food legislation, or the consumer behaviour in a given Member State, leaving the question for the referring judge—coupled with clear instructions as to what needs to be determined and how—means getting a more accurate assessment. The ECJ will struggle with obtaining the relevant information and may

[147] Recommendations to National Courts and Tribunals in Relation to the Initiation of Preliminary Ruling Proceedings [2012] OJ C338/01. The predecessor of these recommendations was the Information Note on References from National Courts for a Preliminary Ruling [2011] OJ C160/01.

[148] Recommendations to National Courts and Tribunals in Relation to the Initiation of Preliminary Ruling Proceedings [2012] OJ C338/01, para 22.

[149] But see Case C-110/05 *Commission v Italy (Italian Trailers)* [2009] ECLI:EU:C:2009:66, paras 83–85 (deference to the national legislature regarding the question as to which motor vehicle insurance schemes will work in a region of Italy which is notorious for traffic problems and car theft).

ultimately get it wrong, anyway.[150] In these situations, a poorly-informed decision by the Court will, all things considered, be worse than a decentralized decision by national judges.

IV. The European Court's Virtuousness

The claims made in the last section are ought statements. They lay down a role for the ECJ that is both reflective of the EU's constitutional principles and rooted in comparative institutional analysis. Chapters 2 to 5 provided an empirical analysis of the Court of Justice's free movement jurisprudence. The question that naturally arises against this background is: to what extent do *ought* and *is* overlap? Does the ECJ's case law align with the desiderata of representation and expertise?

I should begin by saying that one cannot simply superimpose the above normative matrix on the empirical findings. When examining the application of the margin of appreciation doctrine and decentralized judicial review, we were not looking for problems with representation or differences in expertise. We were testing the effects of the factors laid down in the Treaties or established in the ECJ's jurisprudence, such as consensus, discrimination, and EU harmonization, for the standard of review in free movement cases. Nonetheless, many of the variables are connected to the normative arguments put forward in this chapter. Their impact on the Court's behaviour, or the lack thereof, gives us an indication of the extent to which the ideas of representation and expertise are respected in free movement adjudication.

Let me begin with representation. As was explained, representation can become relevant in three different forms, the first being that of all Europeans. The argument from European representation posits that the ECJ should not review all national laws restricting economic freedom, but focus on cases in which out-of-state interests are disregarded. The empirical findings suggest that this principle guides the ECJ's activity. The Court does not respond to mere restrictions on commercial freedom, even where these are serious (monopolies, product bans, expulsions, etc). It is, by contrast, highly attentive to measures disadvantaging non-nationals, often denying the Member States a margin of appreciation if they discriminate against foreigners. This bifurcated approach—hands-on regarding discriminatory measures, hands-off regarding general restrictions on economic freedom—is in line with the idea of European representation. Only where out-of-state interests risk being disregarded is there a reason for the ECJ to subject the outcome of the

[150] Cases like *Henn and Darby* and *Conegate* are well-known examples. The ECJ's factual assessments, notably as to the alleged lack of a 'lawful trade' in pornography and rubber dolls, turned out to be largely inaccurate: see Malcolm A Jarvis, *The Application of EC Law by National Courts: The Free Movement of Goods* (Clarendon Press 1998) 236 et seq.

regulatory process to substantive review. Likewise, it demonstrates that there are no signs of the Court engaging in 'economic due process'.

The argument from national representation holds that deference to Member State authorities is warranted in scenarios where focusing on domestic concerns is justified. This, for one, includes domains which remain within the remit of Member State competence. The data provide support for a connection between the degree to which a policy field has been Europeanized and the intensity of scrutiny. Judicial review of laws in areas of exclusive national competence, such as public policy/morality and public security, or in which the EU merely has a supporting competence (notably public health) tends to be more deferential than that in fields falling within the shared competence of the Union and the Member States, such as consumer protection and intellectual property. The (few) cases on road safety can be seen as an exception in this context, with the Court of Justice showing a high degree of deference to national authorities despite the shared legislative competence in this domain.[151]

Second, it was argued that the Court should allow Member States to think nationally when matters of fundamental importance are at stake, notably as regards important moral and ethical choices. To what extent national authorities are granted deference in such cases is harder to determine based on the empirical results. Chapter 3 examined the role of political sensitivity and concluded that it had no tangible impact on the standard of review. However, the classification of entire policy fields into sensitive and non-sensitive areas goes beyond the idea of 'watershed' issues, which is a much narrower class of the most salient political choices only. One is therefore left with analysing individual decisions. The rulings in some of the well-known margin of appreciation cases, where the ECJ defers to national decisions on issues like human dignity, gambling, pornography, and religious sects, appear to suggest that free movement adjudication does comply with the idea of national representation, even if counterexamples exist.[152]

The ECJ's record regarding the third form of representation, that of social groups beyond the national/non-national divide, is the least clear. This has largely to do with the fact that many of these disputes are, as was explained, not free movement but anti-discrimination cases. The jurisprudence in this field, which is outside the scope of the study, appears to provide some clues that the Court of Justice is taking its new role seriously. This regards not just traditional focus areas of EU anti-discrimination law like gender[153] but also cases on age,[154] religion,[155] ethnicity, and

[151] Tax law is a special case for the reasons explained in Chapter 3 (n 34).

[152] See, for instance, *Las* (n 42) and Case C-379/87 *Groener* [1989] ECLI:EU:C:1989:599 (promotion of national language).

[153] *Defrenne (No 2)* (n 40); Case 170/84 *Bilka-Kaufhaus* [1986] ECLI:EU:C:1986:204; Case C-33/89 *Kowalska* [1990] ECLI:EU:C:1990:265; Case C-285/98 *Kreil* [2000] ECLI:EU:C:2000:2.

[154] Case C-144/04 *Mangold* [2005] ECLI:EU:C:2005:709; *Kücükdeveci* (n 41); Case C-544/11 *Petersen* [2013] ECLI:EU:C:2013:124; Case C-441/14 *Dansk Industri* [2016] ECLI:EU:C:2016:278.

[155] Case C-414/16 *Egenberger* [2018] ECLI:EU:C:2018:257; Case C-68/17 *IR v JQ* [2018] ECLI:EU:C:2018:696. But contrast with the deferential rulings in the two 'headscarf cases' (Case C-157/15

race.[156] In free movement law, there seems to be less cause for celebration. The few cases in the sample with more obvious implications for social minorities, such as disputes on laws promoting social housing[157] or strengthening the rights of low-paid workers,[158] do not seem to indicate a strong preoccupation of the European Court with the concerns of the affected groups.

Let me turn to technical expertise. I have claimed that, given its relative structural disadvantages, the ECJ is well-advised to defer to national authorities in cases involving factually complex problems. I have also argued that it is crucial to distinguish in this respect between national legislatures and executives (who are better equipped to deal with these issues) and national courts (who will struggle just like the ECJ). The findings from the case law study suggest that the Court of Justice's practice follows the former, more general proposition, but warrant some criticism when it comes to the latter. The analysis of the margin of appreciation case law showed that the Court tends to defer to national legislative and executive bodies in policy fields that raise factually complex questions, notably public health, as well as in cases of scientific uncertainties. Although, again, policy fields are only imperfect proxies for factual complexity (remember *Ker-Optika*), the results suggest that the Court of Justice is, indeed, aware of its lack of technical expertise. The problem, however, is that the Court appears to not distinguish sufficiently between the different national institutions. National courts are regularly given the responsibility to decide on factually complex matters.[159] Yet, courts remain courts, no matter if they are in Luxembourg, Florence, or Ljubljana. A national judge is likely to have just as serious difficulties with assessing issues of great factual complexity as the ECJ.

Finally, there is the issue of local expertise. In cases in which the Court of Justice fails to understand the details of a dispute or the domestic setting in which it takes place, it should defer the task of reviewing Member State action to the national judiciary. The results from the analysis in Chapter 4 demonstrated that the Court decentralizes judicial review more frequently in proportionality cases. This makes sense from the perspective of local expertise. Proportionality scrutiny requires a range of information on the domestic context which the Court of Justice will often lack. Similarly, the findings showed that the ECJ appears to seek the help of national courts when having insufficient information on the factual and legal circumstances of a dispute. Yet, the investigation also revealed that the way in which the Court approaches the issue is counterproductive. Although signalling the relevance of

Achbita [2017] ECLI:EU:C:2017:203 and Case C-188/15 *Bougnaoui* [2017] ECLI:EU:C:2017:204), which appear to be driven by the respect for the domestic choices on this controversial matter, thus following the idea of national representation.

156 Case C-54/07 *Firma Feryn* [2008] ECLI:EU:C:2008:397; Case C-83/14 *CHEZ* [2015] ECLI:EU:C:2015:480.

157 Cases C-197/11 and 203/11 *Libert* [2013] ECLI:EU:C:2013:288.

158 Case C-60/03 *Wolff and Müller* [2004] ECLI:EU:C:2004:610.

159 See Chapter 4 II B.

information and competence in rulings such as *Gourmet*, where it deferred the assessment of the proportionality of the national law to the referring court as it was in a 'better position' to carry out the analysis, pronouncements like these are scarce. That national judges are, in principle, better equipped to solve many of the contextual problems that arise in free movement cases—or that they, alternatively, need to submit as detailed information as possible on the domestic setting if they want to receive a comprehensive response from the ECJ—is not communicated clearly.

V. Conclusion

This chapter set out to evaluate the use of deference in free movement law. It explained that the decision as to whether the ECJ defers to Member State authorities, and where it does, is consequential as it determines who will decide to what extent: the Court itself, national legislatures/executives, or national courts. Each actor's normative perspective on and factual understanding of a particular subject matter is likely to vary. Therefore, both the outcome and the quality of a decision depend on whom we entrust it to.

Choosing the appropriate standard of review is a formidable challenge due to the conflicting constitutional ambitions espoused by the EU. Nonetheless, I have argued that it is possible to achieve the fundamental ideas to which European law is committed, while taking into account the institutional strengths and weaknesses of the actors involved, by relying on two considerations. The first one is representation. It stipulates that a decision should be placed in the hands of institutions that promise to take into account the concerns and interests of all affected. This will at times include all Europeans, at other times just the nationals of a Member State, and yet other times social groups beyond the national/non-national divide. The second consideration is expertise. It requires that a decision should be entrusted with the actor that promises to have the greatest knowledge of the relevant problem, or the highest chances of gathering it.

Representation and expertise suggest that there are often good reasons for the ECJ to defer to national authorities. When we want to ensure the representation of all Europeans, judicial intervention is unnecessary if out-of-state interests are not or only minimally affected. Where we aim at representing nationals, the relevant concerns are likely to be better protected by the national political process. As to expertise, a distinction must be made between technical and local matters. In cases where the Court of Justice fails to grasp the technical aspects of a regulatory problem, it should defer to the national legislature or limit itself to setting out the requirements for the decision-making process. Where it does not have a full understanding of the local aspects of a dispute, letting the national court decide will be the better alternative.

That the ECJ defers in these scenarios is, first of all, a question of legitimacy. It would be hard to square a universal reach of judicial review with the idea of democratic governance. The same, *mutatis mutandis*, follows from considerations of federalism. The interference of the EU in national matters is meant to be wide, but not unlimited. Second, it is warranted for reasons of decision-making quality. Unless there is reason to believe that the Court of Justice is the best-equipped institution to determine every economic and non-economic question arising in the internal market—unlikely, as I have attempted to show—, it seems questionable to let it substitute its view for that of national legislators and judges at all times. Finally, a more selective exercise of substantive review is a question of rationalization. As the case law study exposed, the Court of Justice has come to the limits of what it can do. Its workload and scope of activity have considerably increased. Therefore, the Court must, much more frequently than in its early days, choose which matters to look into in greater depth and which ones to entrust to other institutions. Consequently, we should expect it to concentrate on issues that are most significant from a European perspective.

This is not to say that there are always good reasons for the ECJ to reduce control. Some scenarios call for active virtues instead. This includes Member State acts that disregard concerns of non-nationals where European representation is warranted. Protecting out-of-state interests remains an important objective of free movement law. But others have emerged. The EU has ceased to be a purely economic endeavour, a change which must affect our expectations towards the Court of Justice. Exclusively protecting non-nationals is no longer sufficient at a point of time where gender equality, social justice, and minority rights are equally on the Union's agenda. This obliges the Court to be sensitive to the problems of women, ethnic minorities, and the economically underprivileged—in free movement law and beyond.

Conclusion

Four decades have passed since the Court of Justice rendered its *grands arrêts* in the *Dassonville* and *Cassis de Dijon* cases, setting in motion a process that would profoundly affect the European integration project. While the free movement provisions in the Treaties have, in essence, remained the same, free movement law has substantially changed in the meantime. This has, to an important extent, to do with the growth of internal market legislation, which has led to an increasing codification of the field. It is, likewise, the result of the ECJ's interpretation and reinterpretation of the four freedoms. Step by step, the Court has widened their scope of application, thus expanding their radius to an ever-wider range of Member State action, and has introduced new techniques for judicial review, the most significant of which is proportionality analysis. At the same time, and less prominently, the Court has begun to defer certain regulatory and legal decisions to national authorities. How, when, and why such deference occurs—and what this tells us about the European Court, free movement law, and the state of Union—has been the topic of this book.

Two forms of deference have emerged in EU free movement law: the margin of appreciation and decentralized judicial review. The margin of appreciation doctrine allows the Court of Justice to defer to national legislatures and executives on regulatory matters. Decentralized judicial review enables it to delegate assessments relating to the compatibility of national measures with the free movement rules to Member State courts. Both doctrines are structurally similar: they limit the extent to which the ECJ reviews the justification and proportionality of Member State action, entail a handing over of decision-making power to domestic institutions, and can be applied to varying degrees. Yet, they differ in one crucial aspect. Whereas deference through the margin of appreciation route lowers the intensity of judicial scrutiny in free movement cases, deference by means of decentralized judicial review merely affects the place of this scrutiny, i.e. whether it is conducted at the European or national level.

The empirical analysis of the ECJ's case law on free movement rights (1974–2013) revealed that deference is on the rise. While the Court deferred to national authorities only exceptionally in the early days of the single market project, it has now come to do so in almost half of its decisions. This suggests that the European judges display greater restraint and are gradually scaling down their involvement in free movement matters. The consequence of this development is that Member State institutions are more heavily involved in the making and shaping of the

Europe's Passive Virtues. Jan Zglinski, Oxford University Press (2020). © Oxford University Press.
DOI: 10.1093/oso/9780198844792.001.0001

internal market. Free movement law, thus, acquires a stronger national flavour. It is infused with domestic legislative preferences and articulated by national courts. This creates the potential for greater regulatory diversity and interpretive pluralism in the EU.

That the Court of Justice's approach to free movement adjudication has evolved should not surprise us. There have been profound changes in its operating context during the past four decades. The Union no longer constitutes a 'new legal order', as the *Van Gend en Loos* ruling famously proclaimed.[1] It has become an established and, for the most part, accepted entity which has substantially matured in legal terms, especially in the area of free movement law. Member States comply more willingly with EU rules and ECJ rulings, even if, in recent years, there have been some prominent examples of resistance. The European political process, a notoriously unreliable actor in the first phase of the integration project, has assumed co-responsibility for the governance of the internal market. In the same period, and partly as a result of the previous factors, the Court of Justice's workload has significantly grown, reaching levels that put a strain on its functioning.

The analysis showed that deference is 'a sometime thing': the ECJ defers to Member State authorities in certain scenarios, not in others.[2] It also exposed important discrepancies between theory and practice. Whereas the Court's statements on the margin of appreciation suggest that a complex web of factors determine whether or not the doctrine is applied, in fact only three variables turn out to influence its usage. A handful of policy fields increase the chances of national institutions being given a margin of appreciation (public health; games of chance; public policy/morality and security; road safety), while discriminatory action and a high level of EU harmonization decrease them. In the case of decentralized judicial review, the divergences are even more pronounced. The principles laid down in the Treaties and, at least formally, embraced by the ECJ—that the interpretation of European law is for the Court of Justice, while its application to the facts of the case is for the national judiciary—largely fail to capture its relationship with domestic courts. The sole exception is proportionality (a 'question of fact'), the decision on which is frequently delegated to Member State judges.

Is the European Court's deference to national authorities a virtue? I have argued that deference is justified, at times even warranted, for constitutional and institutional reasons. Given that national authorities are meant to play an important role in the EU constitutional order and have comparative advantages when it comes to making certain types of judgments, it is desirable that the ECJ defers to them in some scenarios. In others, more searching forms of scrutiny are in order. The

[1] Case 26/62 *Van Gend & Loos* [1963] ECLI:EU:C:1963:1.

[2] Fred Rodell, 'For Every Justice, Judicial Deference Is a Sometime Thing' (1962) *50 Georgetown Law Journal* 700. Note that Rodell is ultimately critical of the idea of deference and argues, in good realist tradition, that only a thorough examination of the political and social preferences of judges can explain their behaviour.

ideas of representation and expertise can help determine whether and which form of deference is appropriate. Where there is no risk of non-nationals being under-represented in domestic legislation, or their representation is not required, national authorities should be granted a margin of appreciation. Where the Court of Justice lacks the necessary expertise to decide a given matter, it is well-advised to defer to national law-makers (technical knowledge) or courts (local knowledge).

The ECJ's restraint in certain areas will set free capacities for greater activity in others. This could lead to a change of priorities within free movement law. Instead of concentrating on perfecting the internal market in goods, the Court of Justice may invest more energy into tackling problems connected with the free movement of persons, services, and capital—a development which, as the empirical findings suggest, appears to be underway already. (The interpretation of secondary legislation will, due to the expansion of EU harmonization, also bind more resources.) But it could also prompt a shift in attention towards other fields. Among these 'new terrains' might be anti-discrimination law, where we have seen an increase in judicial activity over the past decade-and-a-half,[3] as well as domains like data and environmental protection, in which the Court's involvement has recently intensified.[4]

Although the foregoing is a study of EU free movement law, the findings carry importance beyond the *plateau de Kirchberg*. The developments that can be observed in the ECJ's jurisprudence represent some common challenges which courts and tribunals around the world have come to face. Deference doctrines like the margin of appreciation have become global phenomena. They have turned into doctrinal cornerstones of areas ranging from human rights law, to investment arbitration, to international trade law. This spread is no coincidence. It has to do with the worldwide trend towards expanding the scope of rights and the breadth of judicial review—developments which resemble those we find in free movement law. The result is a widening and intensifying of judicial involvement which, in turn, leads to problems of workload, legitimacy, and competence. As a consequence, many national and international courts must increasingly make a choice as to where to intervene and where not, where to exercise more intense and where more lenient scrutiny. Therefore, just like the ECJ, they are driven towards adopting doctrines of judicial deference.

This book hopes to further illustrate the benefits of empirical methods to studying EU law and the Court of Justice. Systematic enquiries allow us to put intuitions about 'trends', 'patterns', and 'factors' to the test, examine—or expose—practices and developments and, thus, ultimately gain a better understanding of how European law operates. The value of such an approach has, perhaps, become

[3] This is, to a large extent, connected with the EU's legislative activity in this area since the Treaty of Amsterdam, see Chapter 6 (n 121).

[4] See, for instance, Cases C-293/12 and 594/12 *Digital Rights Ireland* [2014] ECLI:EU:C:2014:238; Case C-362/14 *Schrems* [2015] ECLI:EU:C:2015:650; Case C-237/07 *Janecek* [2008] ECLI:EU:C:2008:447; Case C-441/17 *Commission v Poland (Białowieża Forest)* [2018] ECLI:EU:C:2018:80.

most apparent during the analysis of the evolution of deference. Academic and non-academic commentators have claimed that the Court has continuously intensified its level of scrutiny in free movement cases, thus indulging in judicial activism and putting an undue burden on national autonomy. This is a sensitive critique in times when a Member State appears to be leaving the Union, partly, because of the broad interpretation of the free movement rules.[5] The empirical investigation showed that although there continue to be ECJ judgments that are marked by stricter forms of review, their overall share has been constantly dropping during the past decades; for every *Cassis*-style ruling there is now a judgment of the *Schindler* or *Familiapress* variety. There is, hence, no support for the suggestion that national interests are no longer protected in free movement law or that, even worse, the Court has gone 'rogue'. Developments like Brexit, aimed at 'taking back control' over law and adjudication,[6] come, somewhat ironically, at a point where the ECJ is more willing than ever to defer to domestic regulatory and judicial choices.

By the same token, the analysis hopes to contribute to advancing the understanding of judicial behaviour in the EU. Judicial decision-making is a complex phenomenon which, in part, can be explained based on rules, principles, and precedents but is, likewise, affected by a variety of other factors. This holds true for the ECJ as much as it does for other courts. The study has shown that the Court prioritizes certain problems and concerns in its case law, that it is more active in some fields and more deferential in others, and that it adjusts its behaviour to the given context and period. These choices are influenced by its reading of the Treaty provisions, the jurisprudential *acquis* in free movement law, and the constitutional principles of the EU. Yet, they are equally the result of variables such as capacity and competence, compliance and trust, as well as the availability of decision-making alternatives. To fully grasp the choices made by the Court of Justice it is crucial to look at the legal as well as the institutional, political, and socio-economic factors at stake.

Although the book provides a longitudinal analysis of the developments that have taken place in EU free movement law, it remains a snapshot, limited in time and validity. The internal market is a dynamic process.[7] It is, to an important degree, an open-ended project whose substance is shaped by various underlying

[5] David Cameron, 'Free Movement Needs to be Less Free' *Financial Times* (London, 26 November 2013).

[6] Taking back control over the adjudicative process has been an important objective of the advocates (and executors) of Brexit. Boris Johnson promised, before the 2016 referendum, that the UK would 'extricate itself from the EU's extraordinary and opaque system of legislation: the vast and growing corpus of law enacted (sic!) by a European Court of Justice from which there can be no appeal'. In a similar vein, Theresa May declared that: 'Leaving the European Union will mean that our laws will be made in Westminster, Edinburgh, Cardiff and Belfast. And those laws will be interpreted by judges not in Luxembourg, but in courts across this country.'

[7] Stephen Weatherill, *The Internal Market as a Legal Concept* (Oxford University Press 2017) 27.

constitutional, political, and economic forces. The erstwhile idea of 'completing' the internal market may have suggested a final destination, a state which, once reached, remains constant.[8] Yet, things can and—judging by the experience in other federal or composite markets, such as the U.S., Canada, and Australia—do change. Periods of greater centralization are followed by periods of greater decentralization. Phases of higher judicial involvement are followed by phases of deference to the political branches.[9]

Some of the trends identified in the present study are likely to continue and deepen. The maturing process of free movement law, for instance, will inevitably progress. The rights and obligations under the four freedoms will be further clarified, both in relation to existing regulatory problems as well as to those yet to arise. Likewise, the Court of Justice's caseload promises to remain at a high level in the future. This will increasingly force the European judges to decide how to best invest their resources and will render doctrinal tools for reducing judicial activity, including but not limited to deference, indispensable.

Others may undergo changes. The level of Member State compliance with EU law is likely to fluctuate; recent years have demonstrated how quickly shifts, even of significant magnitude, can occur. Similarly, future Treaty amendments may accentuate the need for 'more Europe' and expand the Union's competences or, to the contrary, protect national decision-making powers in certain areas. The EU legislature may take a more active role in internal market governance, thus further limiting the need for negative integration through the four freedoms, or decide to reduce the scope of its regulatory activity.[10] Free movement law will have to adapt to these changes, as it has adapted to them in the past. As a consequence, it may look considerably different in 40 years from now than it does today.

[8] Commission, White Paper on 'Completing the Internal Market' COM(85) 310 final. In a similar spirit, the Treaty of Rome envisaged that the common market would be 'established during a transitional period of twelve years' (Art 8(1)).

[9] The US provide, once again, a valuable lesson in this respect. The four-decade long *Lochner* era, during which the Supreme Court subjected economic regulation adopted at the state level to strict scrutiny, has been followed by a highly deferential approach (as of the late-1930s). Similarly, in relation to the Commerce Clause, the rulings in *United States v Lopez* 514 US 549 (1995) and *Printz v United States* 521 US 898 (1997) brought about a greater emphasis on states' rights after the Court had, for decades, embraced a more federal vision.

[10] See, inter alia, the Report of the Commission's Task Force on Subsidiarity, Proportionality and 'Doing Less More Efficiently' from 10 July 2018, available at < ec.europa.eu/commission/sites/beta-political/files/report-task-force-subsidiarity-proportionality-and-doing-less-more-efficiently_en.pdf >.

Bibliography

Ackerman B, 'Beyond *Carolene Products*' (1985) 98 Harvard Law Review 713

Adinolfi A, 'The Judicial Application of Community Law in Italy (1981–1997)' (1998) 35 Common Market Law Review 1313

Aleinikoff TA, 'Constitutional Law in the Age of Balancing' (1987) 96 Yale Law Journal 943

Alemanno A and Garde A, 'The Emergence of EU Lifestyle Risk Regulation: New Trends in Evidence, Proportionality and Judicial Review' in H-W Micklitz and T Tridimas (eds), *Risk and EU Law* (Edward Elgar 2015)

Alexy R, *A Theory of Legal Argumentation* (Clarendon Press 1989)

Alexy R, *A Theory of Constitutional Rights* (Oxford University Press 2002)

Alexy R, 'Formal Principles: Some Replies to Critics' (2014) 12 International Journal of Constitutional Law 511

Allan TRS, 'Human Rights and Judicial Review: A Critique of "Due Deference"' (2006) 65 Cambridge Law Journal 671

Allen RJ and Pardo MS, 'The Myth of the Law-Fact Distinction' (2003) 97 Northwestern University Law Review 1769

Alter KJ, *Establishing the Supremacy of European Law* (Oxford University Press 2001)

Alter KJ, *The European Court's Political Power* (Oxford University Press 2009)

Appelbaum PS, 'The Empirical Jurisprudence of the United States Supreme Court' (1987) 13 American Journal of Law & Medicine 335

Arai-Takahashi Y, *The Margin of Appreciation Doctrine and the Principle of Proportionality in the Jurisprudence of the ECHR* (Intersentia 2002)

Arato J, 'The Margin of Appreciation in International Investment Law' (2014) 53 Virginia Journal of International Law 545

Arnull A, 'What Shall We Do on Sunday?' (1991) 16 European Law Review 112

Arnull A, 'Judicial Activism and the Court of Justice: How Should Academics Respond?' Maastricht Faculty of Law Working Paper 2012/3

Azoulai L, 'The Court of Justice and the Social Market Economy: The Emergence of an Ideal and the Conditions for Its Realisation' (2008) 45 Common Market Law Review 1335

Azoulai L, 'The "Retained Powers" Formula in the Case Law of the European Court of Justice: EU Law as Total Law?' (2011) 4 European Journal of Legal Studies 192

Azoulai L, 'The European Court of Justice and the Duty to Respect Sensitive National Interests' in M Dawson, B de Witte, and E Muir (eds), *Judicial Activism at the European Court of Justice* (Edward Elgar 2013)

Barak A, *Proportionality: Constitutional Rights and Their Limitations* (Cambridge University Press 2012)

Barbier de la Serre E and Sibony A-L, 'Expert Evidence Before the EC Courts' (2008) 45 Common Market Law Review 941

Barents R, 'New Developments in Measures Having Equivalent Effect' (1981) 18 Common Market Law Review 271

Barnard C, 'Fitting the Remaining Pieces into the Goods and Persons Jigsaw?' (2001) 26 European Law Review 35

Barnard C, 'Derogations, Justifications and the Four Freedoms: Is State Interest Really Protected?' in C Barnard and O Odudu (eds), *The Outer Limits of European Union Law* (Hart 2009)

Barnard C, *The Substantive Law of the EU: The Four Freedoms* (5th edn, Oxford University Press 2016)

Barnard C, 'The Worker Protection Justification: Lessons from Consumer Law' in P Koutrakos, N Nic Shuibhne, and P Syrpis (eds), *Exceptions from EU Free Movement Law: Derogation, Justification and Proportionality* (Hart 2016)

Basedow J, 'The Judge's Role in European Integration' in H Micklitz and B de Witte (eds), *The European Court of Justice and the Autonomy of the Member States* (Intersentia 2012)

Beatty DM, *The Ultimate Rule of Law* (Oxford University Press 2004)

Benvenisti E, 'Margin of Appreciation, Consensus, and Universal Standards' (1999) 31 International Law and Politics 843

Bernitz U, 'Sweden and the European Union: On Sweden's Implementation and Application of European Law' (2001) 38 Common Market Law Review 903

Bickel AM, *The Least Dangerous Branch: The Supreme Court at the Bar of Politics* (Bobbs-Merrill 1962)

Bjorge E and Zglinski J, 'The Principle of Proportionality in EU Law and Its Domestic Application: *Ni tout à fait le même, ni tout à fait un autre*' in K Ziegler, P Neuvonen, and V Moreno-Lax (eds), *Research Handbook on General Principles of EU Law* (Edward Elgar forthcoming)

Blauberger M and others, 'ECJ Judges Read the Morning Papers: Explaining the Turnaround of European Citizenship Jurisprudence' (2018) 25 Journal of European Public Policy 1422

Boerger-De Smedt A, 'Negotiating the Foundations of European Law, 1950–1957: The Legal History of the Treaties of Paris and Rome' (2012) 21 Contemporary European History 339

Bogdandy A von and Schill S, 'Overcoming Absolute Privacy: The Respect for National Identity under the Lisbon Treaty' (2011) 48 Common Market Law Review 1417

Börzel T, 'Non-Compliance in the European Union: Pathology or Statistical Artefact?' (2001) 8 Journal of European Public Policy 803

Brewer S, 'Scientific Expert Testimony and Intellectual Due Process' (1998) 107 Yale Law Journal 1535

Broberg M and Fenger N, 'Variations in Member States' Preliminary References to the Court of Justice: Are Structural Factors (Part of) the Explanation?' (2013) 19 European Law Journal 488

De Búrca G, 'The Principle of Proportionality and Its Application in EU Law' (1994) 14 Yearbook of European Law 105

Cameron D, 'Free Movement Needs to be Less Free' *Financial Times* (London, 26 November 2013)

Cappelletti M, 'Judicial Review in Comparative Perspective' (1970) 58 California Law Review 1017

Carrubba CJ and Gabel MJ, *International Courts and the Performance of International Agreements: A General Theory with Evidence from the European Union* (Cambridge University Press 2015)

Carrubba CJ and Murrah L, 'Legal Integration and Use of the Preliminary Ruling Process in the European Union' (2005) 59 International Organization 399

Carrubba CJ, Gabel M, and Hankla C, 'Judicial Behavior under Political Constraints: Evidence from the European Court of Justice' (2008) 102 American Political Science Review 435

Casey K, Camara J, and Wright N, 'Standards of Appellate Review in the Federal Circuit: Substance and Semantics' (2002) 11 Federal Circuit Bar Journal 279

Chalmers D, 'The Application of Community Law in the United Kingdom, 1994–1998' (2000) 37 Common Market Law Review 83

Christie GC, 'Judicial Review of Findings of Facts' (1992) 87 Northwestern University Law Review 14

Clark JL, 'A Mixed Question of Law and Fact' (1909) 18 Yale Law Journal 404

Cloots E, *National Identity in EU Law* (Oxford University Press 2015)

Coan A, *Rationing the Constitution: How Judicial Capacity Shapes Supreme Court Decision-Making* (Harvard University Press 2019)

Cohen JC, 'The European Preliminary Reference and U.S. Supreme Court Review of State Court Judgments: A Study in Comparative Judicial Federalism' (1996) 44 American Journal of Comparative Law 421

Cohen-Eliya M and Porat I, 'Proportionality and the Culture of Justification' (2011) 59 American Journal of Comparative Law 463

Cohen-Eliya M and Porat I, *Proportionality and Constitutional Culture* (Cambridge University Press 2013)

Conant L, *Justice Contained: Law and Politics in the European Union* (Cornell University Press 2002)

Cohen-Eliya M and Porat I, 'Compliance and What EU Member States Make of It' in M Cremona (ed), *Compliance and the Enforcement of EU Law* (Oxford University Press 2012)

Coppel J and O'Neill A, 'The European Court of Justice: Taking Rights Seriously?' (1992) 29 Common Market Law Review 669

Craig P, *EU Administrative Law* (3rd edn, Oxford University Press 2018)

Craig P and de Búrca G, *EU Law* (6th edn, Oxford University Press 2015)

Crombez C, 'The Democratic Deficit in the European Union: Much Ado about Nothing?' (2003) 4 European Union Politics 101

Croon-Gestefeld J, *Reconceptualising European Equality Law: A Comparative Institutional Analysis* (Hart 2017)

Cruz Villalón PC, '"All the Guidance", *ERT* and *Wachauf*' in M P Maduro and L Azoulai (eds), *The Past and Future of EU Law* (Hart 2010)

Currie S, 'Pregnancy-Related Employment Breaks, the Gender Dynamics of Free movement Law and Curtailed Citizenship: *Jessy Saint Prix*' (2016) 53 Common Market Law Review 543

Davies A, 'One Step Forward, Two Steps Back? The *Viking* and *Laval* Cases in the ECJ' (2008) 37 Industrial Law Journal 126

Davies G, 'Abstractness and Concreteness in the Preliminary Reference Procedure' in N Nic Shuibhne (ed), *Regulating the Internal Market* (Edward Elgar 2006)

Davies G, 'The Price of Letting Courts Value Solidarity: The Judicial Role in Liberalizing Welfare' in M Ross and Y Borgmann-Prebil (eds), *Promoting Solidarity in the European Union* (OUP 2010)

Davies G, 'Understanding Market Access: Exploring the Economic Rationality of Different Conceptions of Free Movement Law' (2010) 11 German Law Journal 671

Davies G, 'Activism Relocated: The Self-Restraint of the European Court of Justice in Its National Context' (2011) 18 European Journal of Public Policy 76

Davies G, 'Free Movement, the Quality of Life and the Myth that the Court Balances Interests' in P Koutrakos, N Nic Shuibhne, and P Syrpis (eds), *Exceptions from EU Free Movement Law: Derogation, Justification and Proportionality* (Hart 2016)

Davies G, 'Does the Court of Justice own the Treaties? Interpretative Pluralism as a Solution to Over-Constitutionalisation' (2018) 24 European Law Journal 358
Dawson M and de Witte F, 'From Balance to Conflict: A New Constitution for the EU' (2016) 22 European Law Journal 204
Dehousse R, *The European Court of Justice: The Politics of Judicial Integration* (Macmillan 1998)
Dougan M, 'The Constitutional Dimension to the Case Law on Union Citizenship' (2006) 31 European Law Review 613
Dougan M, 'Legal Developments' (2010) 48 Journal of Common Market Studies 163
Doukas D, 'Morality, Free Movement and Judicial Restraint at the European Court of Justice' in P Koutrakos, N Nic Shuibhne, and P Syrpis (eds), *Exceptions from EU Free Movement Law: Derogation, Justification and Proportionality* (Hart 2016)
Dworkin R, *Law's Empire* (Hart 1998)
Edward D, 'The Exceptions to the Four Freedoms: The Historical Context' in P Koutrakos, N Nic Shuibhne, and P Syrpis (eds), *Exceptions from EU Free Movement Law: Derogation, Justification and Proportionality* (Hart 2016)
Ely JH, *Democracy and Distrust* (Harvard University Press 1980)
Enchelmaier S, 'Restrictions on the Use of Goods and Services' in M Andenas, T Bekkedal, and L Pantaleo (eds), *The Reach of Free Movement* (Springer 2017)
Epstein L and Segal JA, 'Measuring Issue Salience' (2000) 44 American Journal of Political Science 66
Epstein L and others, *The Supreme Court Compendium: Data, Decisions, and Developments* (6th edn, CQ Press 2015)
Erickson RJ and Simon RJ, *The Use of Social Science Data in Supreme Court Decisions* (University of Illinois Press 1998)
Fabbrini F and Sajó A, 'The Dangers of Constitutional Identity' (2019) 25 European Law Journal 1
Faigman DL, '"Normative Constitutional Fact-Finding": Exploring the Empirical Component of Constitutional Interpretation' (1991) 139 University of Pennsylvania Law Review 541
Falkner G and Treib O, 'Three Worlds of Compliance or Four: The EU-15 Compared to New Member States' (2008) 46 Journal of Common Market Studies 293
Farrell RC, 'Successful Rational Basis Claims in the Supreme Court from the 1971 Term through *Romer v Evans*' (1999) 32 Indiana Law Review 357
Farrell RC, 'The Two Versions of Rational-Basis Review and Same-Sex Relationships' (2011) 86 Washington Law Review 281
Feingold CS, 'The Margin of Appreciation and the European Convention on Human Rights' (1977–1978) 53 Notre Dame Lawyer 90
Finck M, *Subnational Authorities in EU Law* (Oxford University Press 2017)
Føllesdal A and Hix S, 'Why There is a Democratic Deficit in the EU: A Response to Majone and Moravcsik' (2006) 44 Journal of Common Market Studies 533
Friedmann B, 'The Birth of an Academic Obsession: The History of the Countermajoritarian Difficulty, Part Five' (2002) 112 Yale Law Journal 153
Gardbaum S, 'Proportionality and Democratic Constitutionalism' in G Huscroft, Bradley W Miller, and GCN Webber (eds), *Proportionality and the Rule of Law: Rights, Justification, Reasoning* (Cambridge University Press 2014)
Gerards J, 'Pluralism, Deference and the Margin of Appreciation Doctrine' (2011) 17 European Law Journal 80
Gerken HK, 'Foreword: Federalism All the Way Down' (2010) 124 Harvard Law Review 6

Gerken HK and Holtzblatt A, 'The Political Safeguards of Horizontal Federalism' (2014) 113 Michigan Law Review 57

Gormley LW, '"Actually or Potentially, Directly or Indirectly"?: Obstacles to the Free Movement of Goods' (1989) 9 Yearbook of European Law 197

Green F, 'Mixed Questions of Law and Fact' (1901) 15 Harvard Law Review 271

Green L, *Judge and Jury* (Vernon Law Book 1930)

Grimmel A, 'Judicial Interpretation or Judicial Activism? The Legacy of Rationalism in the Studies of the European Court of Justice' (2012) 18 European Law Journal 518

Gunther G, 'The Subtle Vices of the "Passive Virtues"—A Comment on Principle and Expediency in Judicial Review' (1964) 64 Columbia Law Review 1

Gunther G, 'The Supreme Court, 1971 Term—Foreword: In Search of Evolving Doctrine on a Changing Court: A Model for a Newer Equal Protection' (1972) 86 Harvard Law Review 1

Harbo T-I, 'The Function of the Proportionality Principle in EU Law' (2010) 16 European Law Journal 158

Harbo T-I, 'Introducing Procedural Proportionality Review in European Law' (2017) 30 Leiden Journal of International Law 25

Henckels C, *Proportionality and Deference in Investor-State Arbitration: Balancing Investment Protection and Regulatory Autonomy* (Cambridge University Press 2015)

Herzog R and Gerken L, 'Stoppt den Europäischen Gerichtshof' *Frankfurter Allgemeine Zeitung* (8 September 2008)

Hilpold P, 'Hochschulzugang und Unionsbürgerschaft: Das Urteil des EuGH vom 7 7 2005 in der Rechtssache C-147/03, Kommission gegen Österreich' (2005) 16 Europäische Zeitschrift für Wirtschaftsrecht 647

Hoffmann L, 'The Influence of the European Principle of Proportionality upon UK Law' in E Ellis (ed), *Proportionality in the Laws of Europe* (Hart 1999)

Hofmann A, 'Resistance against the Court of Justice of the European Union' (2018) 14 International Journal of Law in Context 258

Hornuf L and Voigt S, 'Analyzing Preliminary References as the Powerbase of the European Court of Justice' (2015) 39 European Journal of Law and Economics 287

Horsley T, 'Unearthing Buried Treasures: Art 34 TFEU and the Exclusionary Rules' (2012) 37 European Law Review 734

Hübner DC, 'The "National Decisions" Database (Dec.Nat): Introducing a Database on National Courts' Interactions with European Law' (2016) 17 European Union Politics 324

Iancu B, 'Law/Politics Distinctions: The Elusive Reference Points' in B Iancu (ed), *The Law/Politics Distinction in Contemporary Public Law Adjudication* (Eleven International 2009)

Jääskinen N, 'The Application of Community Law in Finland: 1995–1998' (1999) 36 Common Market Law Review 407

Jackson VC, 'Federalism and the Uses and Limits of Law: *Printz* and Principle?' (1998) 111 Harvard Law Review 2180

Jacqué JP and Weiler JHH, 'On the Road to European Union—A New Judicial Architecture: An Agenda for the Intergovernmental Conference' (1990) 27 Common Market Law Review 185

Jans JH, 'Proportionality Revisited' (2000) 27 Legal Issues of Economic Integration 239

Jarvis MA, *The Application of EC Law by National Courts: The Free Movement of Goods* (Clarendon Press 1998)

Jarvis MA, 'The Proportionality Test: Constructive Dialogue between the English and Scottish Courts' in P Koutrakos, N Nic Shuibhne, and P Syrpis (eds), *Exceptions from EU Free Movement Law: Derogation, Justification and Proportionality* (Hart 2016)

Joerges C and Neyer J, 'From Intergovernmental Bargaining to Deliberative Political Processes: The Constitutionalisation of Comitology' (1997) 3 European Law Journal 273

Joerges C and Rödl F, 'Informal Politics, Formalised Law and the Social Deficit of European Integration: Reflections after the Judgments of the ECJ in *Viking* and *Laval*' (2009) 15 European Law Journal 1

Kaupa C, *The Pluralist Character of the European Economic Constitution* (Hart 2016)

Keleman RD, *Eurolegalism: The Transformation of Law and Regulation in the European Union* (Harvard University Press 2011)

Keleman RD, 'Judicialisation, Democracy and European Integration' (2013) 49 Representation 295

Kilpatrick C, 'Internal Market Architecture and the Accommodation of Labour Rights: As Good as it Gets?' EUI Working Paper LAW 2011/04

Klatt M and Meister M, *The Constitutional Structure of Proportionality* (Oxford University Press 2012)

Klenk L, *Die Grenzen der Grundfreiheiten* (Mohr Siebeck 2019)

Kochenov D and others (eds), *Europe's Justice Deficit?* (Hart 2015)

Komárek J, 'In the Court(s) we Trust? On the Need for Hierarchy and Differentiation in the Preliminary Ruling Procedure' (2007) 32 European Law Review 467

Komárek J, 'Playing With Matches: The Czech Constitutional Court Declares a Judgment of the Court of Justice of the EU *Ultra Vires*' (2012) 8 European Constitutional Law Review 323

Komárek J, 'National Constitutional Courts in the European Constitutional Democracy' (2014) 12 International Journal of Constitutional Law 525

Komesar N, *Imperfect Alternatives* (University of Chicago Press 1997)

Komesar N, *Law's Limits* (Cambridge University Press 2001)

Korte J (ed), *Primus Inter Pares: The European Court and National Courts The Follow-up by National Courts of Preliminary Rulings ex Art 177 of the Treaty of Rome: A Report on the Situation in the Netherlands* (Nomos 1991)

Kratochvíl J, 'The Inflation of the Margin of Appreciation by the European Court of Human Rights' (2011) 29 Netherlands Quarterly of Human Rights 324

Krommendijk J, 'The Highest Dutch Courts and the Preliminary Ruling Procedure: Critically Obedient Interlocutors of the Court of Justice' (2019) 25 European Law Journal 1

Kumm M, 'The Jurisprudence of Constitutional Conflict: Constitutional Supremacy in Europe before and after the Constitutional Treaty' (2005) 11 European Law Journal 262

Kumm M, 'Political Liberalism and the Structure of Rights: On the Place and Limits of the Proportionality Requirement' in G Pavlakos and S Poulson (eds), *Law, Rights and Discourse: the Legal Philosophy of Robert Alexy* (Hart 2007)

Kumm M, 'The Idea of Socratic Contestation and the Right to Justification: The Point of Rights-Based Proportionality Review' (2010) 4 Law and Ethics of Human Rights 140

Kumm M, '*Internationale Handelsgesellschaft, Nold* and the New Human Rights Paradigm' in MP Maduro and L Azoulai (eds), *The Past and Future of EU Law* (Hart 2010)

Kumm M, 'Alexy's Theory of Constitutional Rights and the Problem of Judicial Review' in M Klatt (ed), *Institutionalized Reason: The Jurisprudence of Robert Alexy* (Oxford University Press 2012)

Łazowski A, 'Half Full and Half Empty Glass: The Application of EU Law in Poland' (2011) 48 Common Market Law Review 503

van Leeuwen B, 'Rethinking the Structure of Free Movement Law: The Centralisation of Proportionality in the Internal Market' (2017) 10 European Journal of Legal Studies 235

Legg A, *The Margin of Appreciation in International Human Rights Law* (Oxford University Press 2012)
Lenaerts K, 'The Court's Outer and Inner Selves: Exploring the External and Internal Legitimacy of the European Court of Justice' in M Adams and others (eds), *Judging Europe's Judges* (Hart 2013)
Letsas G, *A Theory of Interpretation of the European Convention of Human Rights* (OUP 2007)
Lianos I, 'Efficient Restrictions of Trade in the EU Law of the Internal Market: Trust, Distrust and the Nature of Economic Integration' CLES Research Paper 1/2010
MacDonnell V, 'The Reductionism of Global Models of Constitutional Rights' (2018) 12 Law & Ethics of Human Rights 73
Madsen MR, 'Rebalancing European Human Rights: Has the Brighton Declaration Engendered a New Deal on Human Rights in Europe?' (2018) 9 Journal of International Dispute Settlement 199
Madsen MR, Olsen HP, and Šadl U, 'Competing Supremacies and Clashing Institutional Rationalities: the Danish Supreme Court's Decision in the *Ajos* Case and the National Limits of Judicial Cooperation' (2017) 23 European Law Review 140
Maduro MP, '*Keck*: The End? The Beginning of the End? Or Just the End of the Beginning?' (1994) 1 Irish Journal of European Law 30
Maduro MP, *We the Court* (Hart 1998)
Maduro MP, 'Europe's Social Self: "The Sickness Unto Death"' in J Shaw (ed), *Social Law and Policy in an Evolving European Union* (Hart 2000)
Majone G, 'Europe's "Democratic Deficit": The Question of Standards' (1998) 4 European Law Journal 5
Mancini F and Keeling D, 'From *CILFIT* to *ERT*: the Constitutional Challenge facing the European Court' (1991) 11 Yearbook of European Law 1
Mancini GF, 'The Making of a Constitution for Europe' (1989) 26 Common Market Law Review 595
de la Mare T and Donnelly C, 'Preliminary References and EU Legal Integration: Evolution and Stasis' in P Craig and G de Búrca (eds), *The Evolution of EU Law* (Oxford University Press 2011)
Marenco G, 'Pour une Interprétation Traditionnelle de la Notion de Mésure d'Effet Equivalent à une Restriction Quantitative' (1984) 20 Cahiers de Droit Européen 291
Martinsen DS, 'Judicial Policy-Making and Europeanization: The Proportionality of National Control and Administrative Discretion' (2011) 18 Journal of European Public Policy 944
Mayer F, 'Rebels Without a Cause? A Critical Analysis of the German Constitutional Court's *OMT* Reference' (2014) 15 German Law Journal 111
Mayoral JA, 'In the CJEU Judges Trust: A New Approach in the Judicial Construction of Europe' (2017) 55 Journal of Common Market Studies 551
Mayoral JA, 'Judicial Empowerment Expanded: Political Determinants of National Courts' Cooperation with the CJEU' (2019) 25 European Law Journal 374
Micklitz H-W, *The Politics of Judicial Co-operation in the EU* (Cambridge University Press 2004)
Miller BW, 'Proportionality's Blind Spot: "Neutrality" and Political Philosophy' in G Huscroft, BW Miller, and GCN Webber (eds), *Proportionality and the Rule of Law: Rights, Justification, Reasoning* (Cambridge University Press 2014)
Millet F-X, 'The Respect for National Constitutional Identity in the European Legal Space: An Approach to Federalism as Constitutionalism' in L Azoulai (ed), *The Question of Competence in the European Union* (Oxford University Press 2014)

Möller K, *The Global Model of Constitutional Rights* (Oxford University Press 2012)
Möller K, '"Balancing as Reasoning" and the Problems of Legally Unaided Adjudication: A Rejoinder to Francisco Urbina' (2014) 12 International Journal of Constitutional Law 222
Möller K, 'Stability and Change under the Global Model of Constitutional Rights: A Reply to Vanessa MacDonnell' (2018) 12 Law & Ethics of Human Rights 103
Monaghan HP, 'Constitutional Fact Review' (1985) 85 Columbia Law Review 229
Moravcsik A, 'In Defence of the "Democratic Deficit": Reassessing Legitimacy in the European Union' (2002) 40 Journal of Common Market Studies 603
Möschel M, 'Race Discrimination and Access to the European Court of Justice: *Belov*' (2013) 50 Common Market Law Review 1433
Mulder J, *Social Legitimacy in the Internal Market* (Hart 2018)
Nicolaïdis K, 'Kir Forever? The Journey of a Political Scientist in the Landscape of Mutual Recognition' in MP Maduro and L Azoulai (eds), *The Past and Future of EU Law* (Hart 2010)
Nic Shuibhne N, 'Margins of Appreciation: National Values, Fundamental Rights and EC Free Movement Law' (2009) 34 European Law Review 230
Nic Shuibhne N, *The Coherence of EU Free Movement Law* (Oxford University Press 2013)
Nyikos SA, 'The Preliminary Reference Process: National Court Implementation, Changing Opportunity Structures and Litigant Desistment' (2003) 4 European Union Politics 397
O'Brien C, 'Civis Capitalist Sum: Class as the New Guiding Principle of EU Free Movement Rights' (2016) 53 Common Market Law Review 937
Panke D, 'The European Court of Justice as an Agent of Europeanization? Restoring Compliance with EU law' (2007) 14 Journal of European Public Policy 847
Paris D, 'Carrot and Stick: The Italian Constitutional Court's Preliminary Reference in the Case Taricco' (2017) 37 Questions of International Law 5
Parras FJM, 'Libertés de circulation et conceptions particulières de droits fondamentaux: quelle conciliation à travers la marge nationale d'appréciation et le respect de l'identité constitutionnelle?' in N Levrat and S Besson (eds), *(Dés)ordres juridiques européens / European Legal (Dis)orders* (LGDJ 2012)
Pavone T and Kelemen RD, 'The Evolving Judicial Politics of European Integration: The European Court of Justice and National Courts Revisited' (2019) 25 European Law Journal 1
Pelkmans J, 'The New Approach to Technical Harmonization and Standardization' (1987) 25 Journal of Common Market Studies 249
Petersen N, 'Avoiding the Common-Wisdom Fallacy: The Role of Social Sciences in Constitutional Adjudication' (2013) 11 International Journal of Constitutional Law 294
Petkova B, 'The Notion of Consensus as a Route to Democratic Adjudication?' (2011–2012) 14 Cambridge Yearbook of European Legal Studies 663
Pettinga GL, 'Rational Basis With Bite: Intermediate Scrutiny by Any Other Name' (1987) 62 Indiana Law Journal 779
Pirker B, 'Democracy and Distrust in International Law' in L Gruszczynski and W Werner (eds), *Deference in International Courts and Tribunals: Standard of Review and Margin of Appreciation* (Oxford University Press 2014)
Portuese A, 'Principle of Proportionality as Principle of Economic Efficiency' (2013) 19 European Law Journal 612
Posner R, 'The Rise and Fall of Judicial Self-Restraint' (2012) 100 California Law Review 519
Prechal S, 'Free Movement and Procedural Requirements: Proportionality Reconsidered' (2008) 35 Legal Issues of Economic Integration 201

Purnhagen KP and Herpen E, 'Can Bonus Packs Mislead Consumers? A Demonstration of How Behavioural Consumer Research Can Inform Unfair Commercial Practices Law on the Example of the ECJ's *Mars* Judgement' (2017) 40 Journal of Consumer Policy 217

de la Rasilla del Moral I, 'The Increasingly Marginal Appreciation of the Margin-of-Appreciation Doctrine' (2006) 7 German Law Journal 611

Rasmussen, H, *On Law and Policy in the European Court of Justice* (Nijhoff 1986)

Rasmussen, H, 'Remedying the Crumbling EC Judicial System' (2000) 37 Common Market Law Review 1071

Regan DH, 'Judicial Review of Member-State Regulation of Trade within a Federal or Quasi-Federal System: Protectionism and Proportionality, *Da Capo*' (2001) 99 Michigan Law Review 1853

Regan DH, 'The Meaning of "Necessary" in GATT Article XX and GATS Article XIV: The Myth of Cost–Benefit Balancing' (2007) 6 World Trade Review 347

Reich N, 'How Proportionate is the Proportionality Principle?' in H Micklitz and B de Witte (eds), *The European Court of Justice and the Autonomy of the Member States* (Intersentia 2012)

Rodell F, 'For Every Justice, Judicial Deference Is a Sometime Thing' (1962) 50 Georgetown Law Journal 700

Romeu FR, 'Law and Politics in the Application of EC Law: Spanish Courts and the ECJ 1986–2000' (2006) 43 Common Market Law Review 395

Rosas A, 'Foreword' in P Koutrakos, N Nic Shuibhne, and P Syrpis (eds), *Exceptions from EU Free Movement Law: Derogation, Justification and Proportionality* (Hart 2016)

Roth W-H, 'The European Court of Justice's Case Law on Freedom to Provide Services: Is *Keck* Relevant?' in M Andenas and W-H Roth (eds), *Services and Free Movement in EU Law* (Oxford University Press 2002)

Sarmiento D, 'Half a Case at a Time: Dealing with Judicial Minimalism at the European Court of Justice' in M Claes and others (eds), *Constitutional Conversations in Europe* (Intersentia 2013)

Sarmiento D, 'An Instruction Manual to Stop a Judicial Rebellion (Before It Is Too Late, of Course)' *Verfassungsblog* (2 February 2017)

Scharpf FW, 'The European Social Model: Coping with the Challenges of Diversity' (2002) 40 Journal of Common Market Studies 645

Scharpf FW, 'Legitimacy in the Multilevel European Polity' (2009) 1 European Political Science Review 173

Schmidt-Salzer J, *Der Beurteilungsspielraum der Verwaltungsbehörden: Zum Verhältnis zwischen Verwaltung und Verwaltungsgerichtsbarkeit* (Duncker & Humblot 1968)

Schütze R, *From International to Federal Market: The Changing Structure of European Law* (Oxford University Press 2017)

Schütze R, 'Judicial Majoritarianism Revisited: "We, the Other Court"?' (2018) 43 European Law Review 269

Schwarze J, *Die Befolgung von Vorabentscheidungen des Europäischen Gerichtshofs durch deutsche Gerichte: Ergebnisse einer rechtstatsächlichen Bestandsaufnahme* (Nomos 1988)

Segal JA, 'Judicial Behavior' in GA Caldeira, RD Kelemen, and KE Whittington (eds), *The Oxford Handbook of Law and Politics* (Oxford University Press 2008)

Smith JB, 'The Flaws of Rational Basis with Bite: Why the Supreme Court Should Acknowledge Its Application of Heightened Scrutiny to Classifications Based on Sexual Orientation' (2005) 73 Fordham Law Review 2769

Snell J, 'The Notion of Market Access: A Concept or a Slogan?' (2010) 47 Common Market Law Review 437

Snell J, '*Cassis* at 40' (2019) 44 European Law Review 445

Snell J, 'General Principles in Free Movement Law: Applicability and Application' in K Ziegler, P Neuvonen, and V Moreno-Lax (eds), *Research Handbook on General Principles of EU Law* (Edward Elgar forthcoming)

Somek A, 'The Argument from Transnational Effects I: Representing Outsiders Through Freedom of Movement' (2010) 16 European Law Journal 315

Somek A, 'The Argument from Transnational Effects II: Establishing Transnational Democracy' (2010) 16 European Law Journal 375

Spaventa E, 'From *Gebhard* to *Carpenter*: Toward a (Non-)Economic European Constitution' (2004) 41 Common Market Law Review 743

Spaventa E, 'Leaving Keck Behind? The Free Movement of Goods after the Rulings in Commission v Italy and Mickelsson and Roos' (2009) 34 European Law Review 914

Spaventa E, 'The Outer Limits of the Treaty Free Movement Provisions: Some Reflections on the Significance of *Keck*, Remoteness and *Deliège*' in C Barnard and O Odudu (eds), *The Outer Limits of European Union Law* (Hart 2009)

Spielmann D, 'Allowing the Right Margin: The European Court of Human Rights and the National Margin of Appreciation Doctrine: Waiver or Subsidiarity of European Review?' (2011–2012) 14 Cambridge Yearbook of European Legal Studies 381

Steiner J, 'Drawing the Line: Uses and Abuses of Article 30 EEC' (1992) 29 Common Market Law Review 749

Steiner J, 'A "Margin of Appreciation" in the Internal Market: Lessons from the European Court of Human Rights' (2007) 34 Legal Issues of Economic Integration 27

Stone Sweet A, *Governing With Judges* (Oxford University Press 2000)

Stone Sweet A, *The Judicial Construction of Europe* (Oxford University Press 2004)

Stone Sweet A, 'Investor-State Arbitration: Proportionality's New Frontier' (2010) 4 Law & Ethics of Human Rights 47

Stone Sweet A and Brunell TL, 'The European Court and the National Courts: a Statistical Analysis of Preliminary References, 1961–95' (1998) 5 Journal of European Public Policy 66

Stone Sweet A and Matthews J, 'Proportionality and the Global Model of Balancing' (2008) 47 Columbia Journal of Transnational Law 72

Sweeney JA, 'Margins of Appreciation: Cultural Relativity and the European Court of Human Rights in the Post-Cold War Era' (2005) 54 International and Comparative Law Quarterly 459

Sweeney JA, 'A "Margin of Appreciation" in the Internal Market: Lessons from the European Court of Human Rights' (2007) *34 Legal Issues of Economic Integration* 27, 39

Terpan F and Saurugger S, 'Assessing Judicial Activism of the CJEU the Case of the Court's Defence Procurement Rulings' (2018) 20 Journal of European Integration 1

Thornburg E, 'Law, Facts, and Power' (2009) 114 Penn State Law Review 1

Thym D, 'The Constitutional Dimension of Public Policy Justifications' in P Koutrakos, N Nic Shuibhne, and P Syrpis (eds), *Exceptions from EU Free Movement Law: Derogation, Justification and Proportionality* (Hart 2016)

Tribe LH, 'The Puzzling Persistence of Process-Based Constitutional Theories' (1980) 89 Yale Law Journal 1063

Tridimas T, 'The Court of Justice and Judicial Activism' (1996) 21 European Law Review 199

Tridimas T, *The General Principles of EU Law* (2nd edn, Oxford University Press 2006)

Tridimas T, 'Constitutional Review of Member State Action: The Virtues and Vices of an Incomplete Jurisdiction' (2011) 9 International Journal of Constitutional Law 737

Tripković B and Zglinski J, 'Contestation and Accommodation: Constitutional and Private Law Pluralism(s) in the EU' in L de Almeida and others (eds), *The Transformation of Economic Law: Essays in Honour of Hans-W Micklitz* (Hart 2019)

Tryfonidou A, 'Further Steps on the Road to Convergence Among the Market Freedoms' (2010) 35 European Law Review 36

Tushnet M, *Taking Away the Constitution from the Courts* (Princeton University Press 1999)

Tushnet M, *Weak Courts, Strong Rights* (Princeton University Press 2008)

Urbina F, 'Balancing as Reasoning and the Problems of Legally Unaided Adjudication: A Reply to Kai Möller' (2014) 12 International Journal of Constitutional Law 214

Usher JA, 'The Evolution of the Free Movement of Capital' (2008) 31 Fordham Journal of International Law 1533

Versluis E, 'Even Rules, Uneven Practices: Opening the "Black Box" of EU Law in Action' (2007) 30 West European Politics 50

Vos E, 'The European Court of Justice in the Face of Scientific Uncertainty and Complexity' in M Dawson, Bde Witte, and E Muir (eds), *Judicial Activism at the European Court of Justice* (Edward Elgar 2013)

de Vries SA, 'Balancing Fundamental Rights with Economic Freedoms According to the European Court of Justice' (2013) 9 Utrecht Law Review 169

Wahl N and Prete L, 'The Gatekeepers of Article 267 TFEU: On Jurisdiction and Admissibility of References for Preliminary Rulings' (2018) 55 Common Market Law Review 511

Waldron J, *Law and Disagreement* (Oxford University Press 1999)

Waldron J, 'The Core of the Case Against Judicial Review' (2006) 115 Yale Law Journal 1346

Weatherill S, 'After *Keck*: Some Thoughts on How to Clarify the Clarification' (1996) 33 Common Market Law Review 885

Weatherill S, 'Competence Creep and Competence Control' (2004) 23 Yearbook of European Law 1

Weatherill S, 'Who Is the "Average Consumer"?' in Stephen Weatherill and Ulf Bernitz (eds), *The Regulation of Unfair Commercial Practices under EC Directive 2005/29* (Hart 2007)

Weatherill S, 'The Limits of Legislative Harmonization Ten Years after *Tobacco Advertising*: How the Court's Case Law has Become a Drafting Guide' (2011) 12 German Law Journal 827

Weatherill S, 'Maximum versus Minimum Harmonization: Choosing between Unity and Diversity in the Search for the Soul of the Internal Market' in N Nic Shuibhne and L W Gormley (eds), *From Single Market to Economic Union: Essays in Memory of John A Usher* (Oxford University Press 2012)

Weatherill S, 'Justification, Proportionality and Consumer Protection' in P Koutrakos, N Nic Shuibhne, and P Syrpis (eds), *Exceptions from EU Free Movement Law: Derogation, Justification and Proportionality* (Hart 2016)

Weatherill S, *The Internal Market as a Legal Concept* (Oxford University Press 2017)

Weatherill S, 'The Beauty and the Beast: Is EU Internal Market Law "Over-Constitutionalised"?' (forthcoming)

Weatherill S, 'Did *Cassis de Dijon* Make a Difference?' in C Barnard, A Albors-Llorens, and B Leucht (eds), *Cassis de Dijon: 40 Years On* (Bloomsbury forthcoming)

Weiler JHH, 'The Transformation of Europe' (1991) 100 Yale Law Journal 2403

Weiler JHH, 'A Quiet Revolution: The European Court of Justice and Its Interlocutors' (1994) 26 Comparative Political Studies 510

Weiler JHH, *The Constitution of Europe* (Cambridge University Press 1999)

Weiler JHH, 'The Constitution of the Common Market Place: Text and Context in the Evolution of the Free Movement of Goods' in P Craig and G de Búrca (eds), *The Evolution of EU Law* (1st edn, Oxford University Press 1999)

Weiler JHH, 'The Political and Legal Culture of European Integration: An Exploratory Essay' (2011) 9 International Journal of Constitutional Law 678

White EL, 'In Search of the Limits of Article 30 of the EEC Treaty' (1989) 26 Common Market Law Review 235

Williams A, *EU Human Rights Policies: A Study in Irony* (Oxford University Press 2004)

Wind M, 'The Nordics, the EU and the Reluctance Towards Supranational Judicial Review' (2010) 48 Journal of Common Market Studies 1039

Winkler A, 'Fatal in Theory and Strict in Fact: An Empirical Analysis of Strict Scrutiny in the Federal Courts' (2006) 59 Vanderbilt Law Review 793

de Witte B, 'A Competence to Protect: The Pursuit of Non-Market Aims through Internal Market Regulation' in P Syrpis (ed), *The Judiciary, the Legislature and the EU Internal Market* (Cambridge University Press 2012)

de Witte F, 'Sex, Drugs & EU Law: The Recognition of Moral and Ethical Diversity in EU Law' (2013) 50 Common Market Law Review 1545

de Witte F, *Justice in the EU: The Emergence of Transnational Solidarity* (Oxford University Press 2015)

de Witte F, 'The Constitutional Quality of the Free Movement Provisions: Looking for Context in the Case Law on Article 56 TFEU' (2017) 42 European Law Review 313

Wyatt D, 'Article 30 EEC and Non-Discriminatory Trade Restrictions' (1981) European Law Review 185

Yoshino K, 'The New Equal Protection' (2011) 124 Harvard Law Review 747

Young EA, 'The Volk of New Jersey? State Identity, Distinctiveness, and Political Culture in the American Federal System' Duke Law School Public Law & Legal Theory Series No 2015-11

Yourow HC, *The Margin of Appreciation in the Dynamics of European Human Rights Jurisprudence* (Kluwer 1996)

Zglinski J, 'Doing Too Little or Too Much? Private Law Before the European Court of Human Rights' (2018) 37 Yearbook of European Law 98

Zglinski J, 'The Rise of Deference: The Margin of Appreciation and Decentralized Judicial Review in EU Free Movement Law' (2018) 55 Common Market Law Review 1341

Index

Note: *For the benefit of digital users, indexed terms that span two pages (e.g., 52–53) may, on occasion, appear on only one of those pages.*